Recovering Political Philosophy

Postmodernism's challenge to the possibility of a rational foundation for and guidance of our political lives has provoked a searching re-examination of the works of past political philosophers. The re-examination seeks to recover the ancient or classical grounding for civic reason and to clarify the strengths and weaknesses of modern philosophic rationalism. This series responds to this ferment by making available outstanding new scholarship in the history of political philosophy, scholarship that is inspired by the rediscovery of the diverse rhetorical strategies employed by political philosophers. The series features interpretive studies attentive to historical context and language, and to the ways in which censorship and didactic concern impelled prudent thinkers, in widely diverse cultural conditions, to employ manifold strategies of writing strategies that allowed them to aim at different audiences with various degrees of openness to unconventional thinking. Recovering Political Philosophy emphasizes the close reading of ancient, medieval, early modern and late modern works that illuminate the human condition by attempting to answer its deepest, enduring questions, and that have (in the modern periods) laid the foundations for contemporary political, social, and economic life. The editors encourage manuscripts from both established and emerging scholars who focus on the careful study of texts, either through analysis of a single work or through thematic study of a problem or question in a number of works.

More information about this series at
http://www.springer.com/series/14517

Walter Nicgorski

Cicero's Skepticism and His Recovery of Political Philosophy

Walter Nicgorski
University of Notre Dame
Notre Dame, Indiana, USA

Recovering Political Philosophy
ISBN 978-1-349-95437-7   ISBN 978-1-137-58413-7 (eBook)
DOI 10.1057/978-1-137-58413-7

© The Editor(s) (if applicable) and The Author(s) 2016
Softcover reprint of the hardcover 1st edition 2016
This work is subject to copyright. All rights are solely and exclusively licensed by the Publisher, whether the whole or part of the material is concerned, specifically the rights of translation, reprinting, reuse of illustrations, recitation, broadcasting, reproduction on microfilms or in any other physical way, and transmission or information storage and retrieval, electronic adaptation, computer software, or by similar or dissimilar methodology now known or hereafter developed.
The use of general descriptive names, registered names, trademarks, service marks, etc. in this publication does not imply, even in the absence of a specific statement, that such names are exempt from the relevant protective laws and regulations and therefore free for general use.
The publisher, the authors and the editors are safe to assume that the advice and information in this book are believed to be true and accurate at the date of publication. Neither the publisher nor the authors or the editors give a warranty, express or implied, with respect to the material contained herein or for any errors or omissions that may have been made.

Cover illustration: © David Gee 4 / Alamy Stock Photo

Printed on acid-free paper

This Palgrave Macmillan imprint is published by Springer Nature
The registered company is Nature America Inc. New York

To Elaine
Without Whose Sustaining Love and Patience
This Contribution to Recovering Cicero's Thought
Would Not Have Been Possible

Series Editors' Foreword

Palgrave's *Recovering Political Philosophy* series was founded with an eye to postmodernism's challenge to the possibility of a rational foundation for and guidance of our political lives. This invigorating challenge has provoked a searching reexamination of classic texts, not only of political philosophers, but of poets, artists, theologians, scientists, and other thinkers who may not be regarded conventionally as political theorists. The series publishes studies that endeavor to take up this reexamination and thereby help to recover the classical grounding for civic reason, as well as studies that clarify the strengths and the weaknesses of modern philosophic rationalism. The interpretative studies in the series are particularly attentive to historical context and language, and to the ways in which both censorial persecution and didactic concerns have impelled prudent thinkers, in widely diverse cultural conditions, to employ manifold strategies of writing—strategies that allowed them to aim at different audiences with various degrees of openness to unconventional thinking. The series offers close readings of ancient, medieval, early modern, and late modern works that illuminate the human condition by attempting to answer its deepest, enduring questions, and that have (in the modern periods) laid the foundations for contemporary political, social, and economic life.

We are delighted to offer Walter Nicgorski's much-anticipated *Cicero's Skepticism and His Recovery of Political Philosophy*. Nicgorski, who has done much over the past 30 years to renew interest in the political philosophy of Cicero, brings to the reading of Cicero's works a keen awareness of what the philosophic life entails. Because of this, he is able to think his way past contemporary assumptions about Cicero's alleged enslavement to the prejudices of his social class and about the political agenda that would stem from them. Nicgorski examines, first, Cicero's professed Academic skepticism and, second, how this functions vis-à-vis the foundations of his apparent Stoicism and his political thought more generally. What emerges is a work that articulates Cicero's philosophic stance. Cicero becomes not merely an historical source of information on Roman schools of philosophy but a lively and original thinker in his own right, one whose thought is characterized by a cogency, originality, and, above all, a consistency that has often been overlooked but that Cicero himself claimed for all of his work, philosophical and political. Nicgorski finds that consistency to be rooted in what he calls Cicero's "practical perspective," which, as he makes clear, entails an elevation of the life of great, philosophic statesmanship and a consequent shaping of civic and moral education toward that life. Such statesmanship will include a focus on the question of the good and happy life. Perhaps most importantly, it is an education aiming at what Nicgorski calls Socratic statesmanship, marked by "a genuine appreciation for inquiry as well as its limits and yet embracing the responsibilities of leadership in the public realm."

Prefatory Note

This author welcomes the use of endnotes to keep textual citations and scholarly background and disputes from interfering in any way with a continuous reading of the text and the interpretation there of Cicero's thinking. Sometimes, there are multiple citations to Cicero's writings in a single note for the purpose of sustaining the credibility of one or two sentences in the text proper. So it seemed best to be consistent and rarely allow citations to Cicero's texts outside of the endnotes. The basis of my judgments and the contour of various scholarly disputes regarding Cicero is, of course, to be found quite often in these notes. There, one hopes, the scholar and student will turn as further inquiries into Cicero develop.

Abbreviations of the works of Cicero overall follow the standard of *The Oxford Classical Dictionary*. The full titles and key to the abbreviations are found in the Index of Citations of Cicero at the back of this book. The two indices have allowed the almost total elimination of cross-referencing in the text as well as within the endnotes.

The translations into English from the works of Cicero and other classical authors are mine unless otherwise noted. The Latin texts of Cicero's writings used are usually those of the Loeb Classical Library. In both translating and in utilizing the original Latin texts, I have consulted, as seemed necessary, in available alternatives. The ordering of Cicero's correspondence is that adopted by D.R. Shackleton Bailey and the referencing of the letters is in accord with his numbering.

Marcus Tullius Cicero (106–43 B.C.): Chronology of Life and Writings

106 Birth in Arpinum
—82 Education in Arpinum and Rome
91—80 Writes *De Inventione*
82—Starts Legal Career
81—*Pro Quinctio*
80—*Pro Roscio Amerino*
79—77 Cicero Travels and Studies in Greece and Asia Minor
75—Elected Quaestor and Enters Senate
71—68 *Pro Caecina*
70—*Divinatio in Caecilium, In Verrem*
69—Takes Office as Aedile, *Pro Fonteio*
68—Extant Correspondence with Atticus Begins
77—66 *Pro Roscio Comoedo*
66—Takes Office as Praetor, *Pro lege Manilia, Pro Cluentio*
65—*Pro Cornelio*
63—His Consulship, Catalinarian Conspiracy, *De lege agraria, Pro Rabirio perduellionis reo, De Othone, In Catilinam, Pro Murena*
62—*Pro Sulla, Pro Archia*, Extant Correspondence with Family and Friends Begins
61—*In Clodium et Curionem*
60—*De Consulatu suo*
59—*Pro Flacco*, Extant Correspondence with Brother Quintus Begins
58-57—Exiled and then Recalled
57—*Post reditum in senatu, Post reditum ad populum, De domo sua*

56—*Pro Sestio, In Vatinium, Pro Caelio, De haruspicum responsis, De provinciis consularibus, Pro Balbo*
56–55—Writes *De Oratore*
55—*In Pisonem, De jure civili in artem redigendo*
54—*Pro Scauro, Pro Plancio, Pro Rabirio Postumo, De temporibus suis*
54–51—Composes *De Re Publica*
54–44—Composes *Partitiones oratoriae*
52—*Pro Milone*, Begins Working on *De Legibus*
51–50—Governor of Cilicia
49–48—With Pompey
47—Pardoned by Caesar
46—*Brutus, Paradoxa stoicorum, De optimo genere oratorum, Orator, Pro Marcello, Pro Ligario*
45—Tullia, His Daughter, Dies, *Consolatio, Hortensius, Academica, De Finibus, Tusculanae Disputationes, De natura deorum, De rege Deiotaro*
44—Assassination of Caesar, *De Divinatione, De Senectute, De Fato, De Amicitia, De Gloria Topica, De Officiis*
44–43—*Philippicae*, Correspondence with Brutus Entirely in the Year 43.
43—Cicero is Murdered.

Acknowledgments

This book is a result of my efforts over many years to think through different aspects and the overall nature of Cicero's moral and political philosophy. The process has been so extended that it is likely that I will overlook some students and professional colleagues who have contributed to my thinking and writing in ways that deserve acknowledgment here. What I do recall is kind receptions and much encouragement in England by Elizabeth Rawson, Alan Douglas, Malcolm Schofield, and Myles Burnyeat, and the presentation of my initial work on Cicero's *Academica* at Douglas's workshop at the University of Birmingham. Those conversations came during 1985–1986 while I was supported on a research fellowship from the National Endowment for the Humanities, which subsequently sponsored my offering of two summer seminars on Cicero's texts for secondary school teachers. Along the way, I received assistance for this book from the Earhart Foundation, the Bradley Foundation, and the American Council of Learned Societies. The University of Notre Dame, especially through its Institute of Scholarship in the Liberal Arts, has been a generous and constant source of support.

Many colleagues at Notre Dame and throughout the USA have read and helpfully responded to parts of this book and related work on Cicero which I have prepared over the years. Most notable for the constancy and depth of his engagement with my work and his great personal encouragement was my late colleague Frederick Crosson. Crosson was no skeptic about the significance of Cicero. Nor was his close friend Father Ernest Fortin, who read and encouraged my work on Cicero into the 1990s. The 2006 Symposium on Cicero's Practical Philosophy at Notre Dame brought together scholars from far and wide, some of whom (J. Jackson Barlow and David Fott) had worked closely with me in bringing new attention to Cicero within American political science. Those efforts in American political science were aided by Carey Nederman and Gary Glenn, who, at times, gave critical responses to my work. The Symposium at Notre Dame provided momentum for the completion of this book, and Carlos Lévy among its participants came to be a helpful reader of some of the material being prepared for this book. I am indebted for the idea and support of the Symposium to my colleagues at *The Review of Politics*, W. Dennis Moran and Catherine Zuckert, my successor as editor at *The Review*, and to my colleague Gretchen Reydams-Schils, chair of the Program of Liberal Studies, the undergraduate program in which I did most of my teaching over the years. Moran has kindly read some of my chapters, and Reydams-Schils provided the forum of Notre Dame's Workshop on Ancient Philosophy to discuss a portion of the text of this book.

During recent years, I have benefited very much from workshops of The Center for Thomas More Studies at the University of Dallas. The workshops in this time have often focused on writings of Cicero as resources for Thomas More's intellectual and moral development. The founding director of the Center, Gerard Wegemer, not only has long encouraged my writing on Cicero but also often gave me a platform for presenting ongoing work in the workshops.

Students in my graduate seminar on "Cicero and the Romans" have contributed, in their exchanges with me and their papers, in ways beyond simple measurement and adequate acknowledgment. The work of two of those, Xavier Marquez and James Fetter, led to jointly authored publications with each of them. Recently, Bobby McFadden has been an engaged and helpful reader of much of this book; much earlier, Andrew Dinan was a particularly resourceful research assistant. Veronica Roberts generously accepted the responsibility for preparing the list of references and, thus necessarily, scrutinizing the notes with care. My former colleague and now good friend, John Lyon, has been a very helpful critical reader of the final manuscript, and my daughter Ann Nicgorski, an ancient art historian with a subspecialty in the iconography of Cicero, has been a treasure of ideas now and in the past for capturing for covers and posters images for any presentation of Cicero and his thinking. Finally, of course, the interest in the manuscript and the encouragement to complete it from the editors of the series on Recovering Political Philosophy, Thomas Pangle and Timothy Burns, have been heartening and critical. I am grateful to all named above without holding any but myself responsible for the ways the book may fall short.

No chapter in this book has been previously published, but there are occasional sentences and sections that come quite directly, by paraphrase or replication, from my own previously published work. In all cases but two, the use of my own writing is controlled at my discretion. The credits for the two instances where permission has been granted are "Cicero, Citizenship and the Epicurean Temptation," pp. 3–28 in *Cultivating Citizens*, eds. D. Allman and M. Beaty, published by Lexington Books in 2002, and "Cicero's Distinctive Voice on Friendship: *De Amicitia* and *De Re Publica*," pp. 84–111 in *Friendship and Politics*, eds. J. von Heyking and R. Avramenko, published by the University of Notre Dame Press in 2008.

Contents

	Introduction	1
1	**Skepticism, Politics, and a Philosophical Foundation**	15
	Cicero's Skepticism	18
	Skepticism Versus Wisdom	20
	Skepticism in the Service of Wisdom	31
2	**The Critical and Rhetorical Modes of Philosophy**	59
	Socratic Method	61
	Socratic Irony and Socratic Skepticism	63
	The Socratic Way of Life	67
	The Mixed Modes of Cicero	70
	Perfecta Philosophia	73
3	**Duties and Virtue**	97
	The Right and the Useful	101
	Nature, Natural Law, and the Virtues	104
	The Norms of Utility	112
	The Primary Need: Statesmanship	114
	Assessing the Philosophical Schools	119

4	Political Philosophy and the Roman Republic	155
	The Loving Quarrel with Plato	158
	The Imagery of Contract and the Importance of Consent	168
	The Assertion and Implication of Equality	175
	The Nature of Genuine Progress	179
	Property: End or Means?	183
	Beyond the Roman Community	184
5	The Socratic Statesman	205
	The Requisites of Statesmanship	207
	Developing the Prudent Statesman	214
	Friendship's Role in Statesmanship	218
	The Troubled Path of Glory	223
	Virtue as True Glory	228

Epilogue	245
References	251
Index of Citations of Cicero	267
Index	277

Introduction

This book presents an understanding of Cicero's political philosophy. Its focus, then, is on his writings that speak most directly to the fundamental questions of moral and political philosophy, which his great Greek predecessors raised for consideration. Cicero, so often seriously and enthusiastically studied in the West, has, in certain ways, been rediscovered in the last two generations. The revival of scholarship on his writings and the new resources for studying the philosophical schools that he engaged provide rich assistance toward this fresh effort to understand his moral and political philosophy as a whole.

In the pages that follow, Cicero is seen to adopt a Socratic mode in critically appropriating Greek political philosophy to his Roman context. He is recovering political philosophy. While the focus here is on his political philosophy, an inquiry into it cannot be simply divorced from Cicero's overall philosophy, from such questions as "how one can know" and "what is the ultimate nature of things"; nor can it be divorced entirely from his own active life as an acclaimed orator and rhetorical theorist as well as a controversial but overall successful republican statesman. The understanding offered here is the fruit of attention to all dimensions of Cicero's writings and achievements, in an effort to make sense of Cicero's deepest and principled thinking about politics. The coherence and ground of that thinking reveals a Cicero who offers an inviting voice in a postmodernity widely characterized both by foundational doubts and by yearnings for defenses of democratic practices and commitments such as those to human rights.

The book's title draws attention to Cicero's skeptical allegiance: an identification with the school of philosophy known, already well before Cicero's time, as the New Academy. That allegiance often troubles those attracted by the many edifying Stoic formulations found in Cicero's ethics and politics. It also troubled Christians such as St. Augustine, otherwise attracted to Cicero and seeking at one time or another the synthesis of the truths of Christian faith with those philosophically developed by Plato or Aristotle. That Cicero professes skepticism along with his commitment to the recovery of Greek political philosophy and ennobling Stoic truths can be seen as a puzzle that feeds the view that Cicero is an eclectic in some fashion, even if not in the hasty and nearly mindless way as suggested by earlier detractors. The recovery of Cicero's political philosophy, so that it might be more widely appreciated, requires attention to the nature of his skepticism and to how he finds the assurance or moral certitude from which to critically assess and present anew the teachings of his Greek predecessors. The recovery offered in this book necessarily draws us into Cicero's own recovery in and for his time as well as for posterity.

Nearly three generations ago, a senior scholar in the study of politics in America, Charles Hyneman, surveyed the scholarship of American political scientists and lamented the scarcity of monographs on classic writers on politics. There have been, he wrote in 1959, "very few attempts to bring into one account the most important thought of a great writer on politics."[1] Even as Hyneman wrote, a veritable renaissance of political philosophy in American political science was in its early stages: a movement resulting in the following years in a plenitude of monographs, books, new editions, and translations of such classic writers as Plato, Machiavelli, Rousseau, Locke, Montesquieu, and "Publius." Cicero, however, remained a relatively untouched and quiet presence in the scholarly explorations of Western political thought through this period. Only in 1988 did Cicero's political thought receive book-length consideration by Neal Wood. More recently, there has been considerable attention to Cicero's political philosophy, if not in entire monographs, then clearly in important articles and collections. The most comprehensive of the recent monographic treatments, notably those of Jed Atkins, Jonathan Zarecki, and Raphael Woolf, show, each in its own way, the rich fruit of reading Cicero with care and taking him seriously as a political philosopher.[2]

The germinal ideas for this book were nourished upon reading John Laursen's 1992 book on the politics of skepticism. Laursen, there, called for a study of Cicero's political thought and action in the light of his

Academic skepticism. He observed that Cicero's importance "is hard to overestimate" in the long tradition of skepticism's relationship to the life of action and politics.[3] A few years later Jonathan Powell remarked on the likely contemporary appeal of that skepticism, "[M]odern readers, living as they do in an age which has largely abandoned the belief in an attainable absolute truth, may well now regard Cicero's Academic probabilism as a more realistic strategy than the rational certainties of the Stoic or the materialist certainties of the Epicurean."[4] Simply understanding Cicero's own integrity as a thinker, and thus being able to consider the ways in which his thought may be significant, independent of his immediate political agenda and social class, requires attention to the nature of his Academic skepticism and the way it functions with respect to the foundations of his moral and political thought and his apparent Stoicism.[5] Cicero's education in philosophy and his initial love of it spawning a lifetime of serious philosophical interests took place in the context of competing philosophical schools such as the Stoics and Epicureans. His writings have come to serve as one of the chief sources, if not the primary source, for our knowledge of those schools. Understanding the teachings and methods of these schools, the goal which has driven much scholarly work on Hellenistic philosophy over more than two generations, has necessarily brought this scholarship into regular engagement with Cicero's texts and illuminated the intellectual context in which he lived, learned, and wrote.

The present book takes its shape in part from certain large questions that came to the fore as I studied and taught the texts of Cicero through the last third of the twentieth century. I found myself asking what standards or principles of choice Cicero employed as he sorted through and chose among the teachings of the philosophical schools of his time: How did he follow or break with his self-acknowledged greatest teachers, Plato and Aristotle, and what principles or factors governed his appropriation or deviation? What determined the limits of his embrace of Stoicism? And what considerations shaped his specific fusion of Greek and Roman ways? These questions pointed at a desire to get at the ground of Cicero's thought and test his coherence. They showed, in other words, the necessity to come to terms with Cicero's skepticism. They are pursued in this book through and in tandem with the kind of staple topics of political theory that were given new life and sometimes sharper focus in the previously noted renaissance of political philosophy and of classical political philosophy in particular. Those topics include the relation of right and utility, natural law and the universal human community, the virtues and especially prudence, the model or best regime, the mixed constitution, popular consent and democratic government, rhetoric and statesmanship, leadership, education and *humanitas*, the progressive development of peoples, and—what is especially prominent in Cicero's moral and political thought—the tensions between theory and practice and between the philosophical life and the active political life. In sum, Cicero is found presenting a quite compelling approach to reconciling a questioning skepticism with a certain assurance concerning moral and political principles. He is a strong voice for the way of persuasion and rule of law over the rule of force,[6] and he defends republican principle and institutions with an awareness of democratic as well as oligarchic excess. A thinker and an example of enduring relevance, Cicero appears in a special way attuned to the needs of the human communities of the twenty-first century.

The method used in pursuing these large questions and topics is simply one of trying to get at Cicero's mind through a careful reading across his writings—a reading marked by special attention to the interpretation of certain key passages and dimensions of his practical philosophical writings.[7] Cicero, then, is not approached as a source for recovering what we can know of the various philosophical schools that were present in the Hellenistic period. He might of course function as such a source and, as already indicated, is a major source, there being relatively little other information on the teachings of the schools in his time and the preceding period. Julia Annas's warning that something is missed if Cicero is read as a mere source is on the mark, and E.M. Atkins discerned a welcome trend early in the 1990s, noting the general rejection of the view that Cicero is a mere transcriber, and the growing number of studies concentrating "on his own ideas and methods."[8]

This tendency is supported by an equally welcome view respecting what eclecticism might be and often is. In this vein, David Sedley has remarked that no one in the Hellenistic world, not even Cicero, is an eclectic, in the sense that they are free from essential allegiance to one or another of the philosophical schools.[9] John Dillon has played a leading role in showing the basis for a fresh perspective on eclecticism, commenting at one point, "[T]here is nothing at all wrong with being 'eclectic,' if that means simply that one is prepared to adopt a good formulation, or valid line of argument, from a rival school or individual and adjust one's philosophical position accordingly. In this sense, most of the great philosophers are eclectics, and eclecticism is a mark of acuteness and originality, as opposed to narrow-minded sectarianism."[10] A.A. Long's comment on Posidonius could well be taken as fitting Cicero. Long observed, "[A] critical synthesis of existing knowledge may be highly original and a most fruitful source of new discoveries."[11]

One aspect of Cicero that would be missed in treating his texts as mere sourcebooks is what Thomas Habinek called "the greatest virtue" of such Roman texts, namely, "their deep engagement with Roman culture," showing, in the case of Cicero, a distinctive Roman appropriation of Greek philosophy.[12] Presenting and exploring Cicero's distinctive "philosophical stance" is another way to speak of the object of this book.[13] In attempting to find the basis or principles of Cicero's eclecticism, this book formulates a position on the "profound unity" that Carlos Lévy suggested is there in Cicero's work.[14] Insofar as this goal is attained, Cicero becomes more than a source but indeed a very important voice in Hellenistic philosophy. Overall, there is much evidence that Cicero puts his own mark on the philosophical resources he employs, in an honest pursuit of wisdom. As John Glucker once observed, Cicero's mind is too lively and original for the work of slavish adaptation.[15] And there is enough evidence in Cicero's self-reflectiveness and his chosen philosophical heroes not to embrace approaches to him that generally doubt his integrity as a thinker by viewing his thought primarily through the prism of personal interest or class bias.

This book presents a finding of remarkable coherence and consistency in Cicero's philosophical writings rooted in, what I am calling, the practical perspective and a certain concept of utility.[16] On that basis, Cicero elevates the life of statesmanship to priority and shapes educational priorities for the potential statesman. The statesmanship that he commends is clearly a philosophical statesmanship, explicitly a Socratic statesmanship marked by a genuine appreciation for inquiry as well as its limits, and yet embracing the responsibilities of leadership in the public realm. It is also a concept of the statesman shaped, in part, from his own experience and intended to set future directions for himself and others.

The book details the presence and operation of the perspective of practice in Cicero's thought. Though Cicero often complained that the political turmoil of his lifetime drew him reluctantly away from study and philosophical inquiry, his thought about all significant matters is affected in important ways by his orientation toward action and ultimately political action of the highest sort. Cicero's approach is a way of knowing or understanding that grows out of political involvement and, among other things, turns back seeking to comprehend the basis for that initial involvement. This way of knowing through the practical perspective is an approach to thought, philosophy, and action informed by a principle of utility that is unavoidable for the rational person engaged in practice and enriched by the experience that comes from such practice. The perspective is, in important respects, pre-philosophical, involving human inclinations, needs, and an inherent sense of propriety and right that clearly anticipates later notions of conscience. The Ciceronic notion of utility is grounded in the needs of human nature, expressed in the terms of good and evil. That the distinction between good and evil, which Cicero regarded as the foundation of philosophy (*fundamentum philosophiae*), is integral to the principle of utility shows the basis for the importance of moral and political philosophy to Cicero.[17] These branches of philosophy, seeking knowledge of good and evil as their distinctive concern, take priority over others in Cicero's explicit curricular advice, and his own philosophical writings reflect this priority and emphasis.[18] Although inquiry into the foundation is the highest priority among the tasks of philosophy, choices and decisions must be made among contending moral and political philosophies, in other words, among contending teachings about good and evil. Those choices could only be made from a basis yet more fundamental than moral philosophy, that being, in the case of Cicero, from a horizon which I am calling the practical perspective.

The elevation of the questions of morals and politics—namely of the good and happy life—in Cicero is one important reminder that he stands in the tradition of the Hellenistic schools, which were dominated by the question of happiness,[19] and that he likely benefits from efforts of synthesis among schools by thinkers who preceded him. The elevation also reveals the self-confessed Socratic orientation to Cicero's thought, and, in fact, in this book Cicero emerges as quite thoroughly Socratic, from his practical perspective to his professed Academic skepticism. Even Cicero's seemingly un-Socratic prioritizing of statesmanship will be seen to be one of the results of his Socratic orientation.

When the perspective of practice is properly appreciated in Cicero's thought, his philosophical work can be seen as more coherent, consistent, profound, and even synthetically original than has generally been thought. Furthermore, though what is at issue in considering this hypothesis is its plausibility and correctness as a focal point for the interpretation of Cicero, there is entailed a philosophical claim that we can, perhaps, hear Cicero making. It is that this perspective of practice provides the orientation for a correct philosophical approach, that it is an advantaged and true perspective and therefore the basis for life-directing wisdom insofar as that can be attained.

This philosophical approach found in Cicero has the potential to contribute significantly to contemporary discussions about the relationship between practice and theory, discussions that bear on the very foundations of philosophy. Cicero, the professed student of Socrates, Plato, Aristotle, and Carneades, respected and sought to advance in Rome the then emerging Western tradition of philosophy. He could hardly be said to be a man sympathetic with the notion that one should seek to change rather than to understand the world. Though giving no such authority to practice, Cicero's approach to philosophy seems to offer us much in a definitively post-Cartesian period, when clear and certain knowledge from assured premises have been ever more undermined and we are more cognizant of what we know from practice and tradition. Cicero was clearly and persistently critical of the tendency of philosophical men to withdraw from the political arena and its responsibilities, and it can be incontestably inferred that he rejects as ill-founded any pretensions to settle those primary questions of metaphysics and theology as a condition and basis for applications to morals and politics. St. Augustine reports, indications of what we find throughout the writings of Cicero, that Cicero deeply respected a group of Roman public men who welcomed philosophy into their lives and their city and whom he accordingly called "consular philosophers," literally philosophers who had held or were ready for the highest office of the Roman Republic.[20]

Cicero as a philosopher seems to have been most appreciated in the Renaissance, for, like many who gave that period its distinctive character, he sought to bring into fruitful interrelationship the present human dimension, including the urgent questions and responsibilities it raises, and earlier significant achievements of human thought. Later, in what has been justly called the golden age of the American political tradition, thoughtful statesmen as different as Thomas Jefferson and John Adams were attracted to Cicero's philosophical writings.[21] This book is written as an aid to the current renewal of interest in Cicero as a thinker and with the hope that it contributes to Cicero's properly articulated voice being heard in a world concerned anew about the relationship between pressing issues and tasks in morals and politics, and philosophical inquiry that might reach to the deepest questions of the meaning of the whole and beyond.

Since reservations about Cicero as philosopher have now and then been implicated with his political actions in the struggles of the late Republic, the inquiry into the stature of Cicero as a thinker cannot be innocent of the history of that time. No one person, of course, could possibly hope to resolve various and long-standing historical controversies about that period.[22] Cicero's actions and motives in the politics of this period have been more exposed to scrutiny than those of any ancient statesman or philosopher. This is chiefly because of the self-revealing sources he himself provides.[23] The number and complexity of the historical controversies is not the only reason, or perhaps the chief reason, that many a student and admirer of Cicero's thought has not wished to get entangled in the problems of his life and politics.[24] It seems that in philosophical work, as in all achievements of human genius, the quality of the product of thought or artistic creation is not necessarily dependent on the author's personal character and his or her wisdom in life's course. Just as beautiful music is, at times, the work of a dissolute character whom one would hardly welcome in the family, so too good analysis and arguments have been made by outright scoundrels. Perhaps, however, the connection between laudable work in moral and political philosophy and personal character is closer than in the instance of other works of the mind. There is after all an ancient conviction that moral virtues are a condition for seeing well in the pursuit of practical wisdom. Not only certain of Cicero's critics but also Cicero himself preferred and chose to look at his life and writings as one fabric. Cicero would not have welcomed praise based on the separation of his style from his substance or the distinction between his philosophical writings and his political efforts.[25]

Cicero sought, then, a consistency and integrity in thought and action, which entailed his rhetorical and political abilities and successes along with his love of philosophy and philosophical models. On some occasions, he may have failed in resolve or in moral and/or political judgment, but we are able to know this because his struggles are laid quite openly before us, and they are not unreasonable or simply scandalous incidents to anyone who has had the experience of actual political engagement. His awareness and candor respecting rhetorical power is especially noteworthy for this widely esteemed orator. He knows that the rhetorical mode is an inevitable part of human life and is not merely a contender with or distraction from philosophy but is also a potential contributor to philosophy's power to attract and to inspire to appropriate action.

Such enthusiasts for Cicero as St. Jerome and Petrarch warned against the dangers of "sainting" him and of going even further and making him faultless. Cicero himself would caution us in the same way, for he was a genuine lover of truth and a man of practical experience, who was acutely aware of his own human weaknesses and of the impossible task of infallibility in judgments entailing the host of variables usually present in concrete political situations. Cicero was ever uncomfortable with the illusory character of the perfect Wiseman, the Stoic model of intellectual and moral perfection.

NOTES

1. Hyneman (1959: 53).
2. Wood (1988), J. Atkins (2013), J. Zarecki (2014), and Woolf (2015). In 1978, in an essay in *The Political Science Reviewer*, I had sought to bring to wider attention the neglect of Cicero and the reasons for it. That essay, "Cicero and the Rebirth of Political Philosophy," was republished as an Appendix in a 2012 collection of contemporary scholarship on Cicero. Nicgorski (2012).
3. Laursen (1992: 59).
4. Powell (1995: 23).
5. Though not treating Cicero explicitly, Lom (2001) has well explored how later skeptics found ways to limit their skepticism in order to come to terms with the need for a ground for living and action. Garsten has directly considered how Cicero fits his skepticism with his apparent Stoicism (2009: 148, *passim*). More recently Woolf shows how Cicero's skepticism impacts on his overall thinking including his approach to politics and morals (2015: 7, *passim*).
6. This phrasing comes in part from an especially eloquent appeal for the study of Cicero in our time, an appeal made by the prolific British classicist, T. P. Wiseman: "Cicero matters not just to classical scholars" but also more broadly because his political career "for all its failings and compromises stood for the rule of law against the rule of force…" and because he gifted us with "a literary corpus that effectively defined our civilization's concepts of *humanitas* and the liberal virtues" (1990: 648).
7. The concept of "practical philosophy" is adapted from Aristotelian studies and refers to moral and political philosophy, in other words, philosophy directed at answering the questions about how to live or order human life. Cicero's *De Re Publica, De Legibus, De Finibus,* and *De Officiis* are his chief writings of this kind. His rhetorical writings, especially *De Oratore*, are properly also considered to belong to practical philosophy. Giving serious attention to *Academica* becomes, of course, necessary to defend a possible moral basis for the practical philosophy.
8. Annas (1989: 155). Atkins, in a bibliographical note to Griffin and Atkins (1991: xlii–xliii). Earlier, in defending Cicero's philosophical work on the

topic of justice, she observed, "The days are over when Cicero could be treated as merely a faithful (if not always competent) transcriber of Greek sources" (1990: 284). Barnes opened another kind of inquiry not only by distancing himself from source-hunting in Cicero but also by distancing himself on this occasion from seeking to determine which views Cicero accepts from those he expresses (1997: 140).

9. Sedley (1989: 118–19).
10. Dillon (1988: 104). Earlier, Buckley had protested the application of "eclectic" in a disparaging sense to Cicero as an instance "of a recurring failure to understand a philosophy within the context of its own methodological structures and coordinates" (1970: 154). Donini, cites the pejorative meaning of the term as denoting "a combination of heterogeneous elements that is substantially uncritical and more or less deliberate" and adds an observation that has seemed, in the inquiry this present book represents, particularly applicable to Cicero: "The more penetrating the interpretation of individual authors once contemptuously defined as eclectic becomes, the more inadequate this sense of eclecticism appears" (1970: 31). A decade earlier, in commenting on Aristotelian and Antiochian influences on Cicero, Horsley, while conceding that eclecticism in philosophy could be an indication of "poverty of thought," speculates that it might rather be "an indication of a genuine and creative search for new combinations of ideas, for intellectual solutions to live issues of the day for which the answer of any particular doctrine from the traditional schools no longer seemed adequate" (1978: 50). See also, Ferrary (1974: 768). Other recent discussions of eclecticism that directly entail Cicero can be found in Tarrant, Barnes, and Griffin. Tarrant sympathetically understands Cicero's eclecticism against a tradition of such in the Academic school (1985: 4). Barnes picks up and develops a distinction between a syncretist and an eclectic, seeing Cicero as the latter and associating with the former what has often been understood as eclectic in the pejorative sense, though Barnes even offers some defense of his exemplar syncretist, Antiochus (1989: 79–81). Griffin defends eclecticism in the ancient world chiefly because it represented a tradition of taking doctrines chosen seriously as the basis for living (1989: 15, esp. n. 25).
11. Long (1986: 217). Posidonius (c. 155–c. 51–50) was a man of wide-ranging learning, who, at one point, took up writing a history of Rome and interacted with Cicero both in his school in Rhodes and later in Rome. Like Panaetius, Cicero's teacher in Athens at one point, he was a somewhat unorthodox Stoic.
12. Habinek wrote, "The characteristic feature and, I believe, greatest virtue of these texts [Roman writings such as Cicero's]—their deep engagement with Roman culture—is their greatest weakness as sourcebooks for earlier

or alien modes of thought" (1990: 185). Davies (1971) emphasizes Cicero's "overall" originality in creating an effective literary genre for philosophy in the Roman context.
13. Görler's phrase where he looks for this stance in a single work of Cicero (1997: 36). The views of other scholars who appreciated the distinctive synthesis and substance of Cicero's thought are noted in Nicgorski (2012: 252–53).
14. Lévy (1992: 584, also 94–95) for the seriousness and, hence, significance with which Lévy takes Cicero as philosopher. More recently Baraz (2012: 6) has drawn new attention to Cicero's own sense that his philosophical work is "a unified project."
15. Glucker (1978: 420 n. 68). This comment is in the context (407 ff.) of Glucker narrowly interpreting Cicero's apparently dismissive comment that some of his philosophical writings are but "copies" of the work of others. Cicero's comment is made in a May 45 letter to Atticus (*Att.* 294.3) There is some consideration of this comment in Nicgorski (2012: 252, 280 n. 14). Lest one make too much of this indication of respect for Cicero the thinker, Glucker's description on another occasion of Cicero's eclectic procedure tends in the direction of seeing Cicero as at least "light-headed" in the synthesis he forms: here Glucker writes that Cicero's eclecticism should be seen as less programmatic and more in the model "of the bee flitting from flower to flower and choosing according to its taste and mood at the time" (1988: 63).
16. Lom (2001: 95) has pointed out the importance of consistency and coherence to later skeptics.
17. *Div.* 2.2. Consider how Aristotle links the human capacity for discourse on utility with that concerning justice in the opening pages of his *Politics* (1253a6–18).
18. *Fin.* 2.51–52; *Off.* 1.5,19.
19. Clearly illustrated in Annas (1993) and Nussbaum (1994).
20. Grilli (1962: fr. 114 & n., p. 53). These philosophers seem to be exemplified in the type of man chosen for roles in Cicero's dialogues, such as Scipio Africanus Minor and Gaius Laelius. These were men marked by what Cicero called *humanitas*; they were "genuinely cultured" men. Before his philosophical writings were undertaken, Cicero wrote to his brother of the need for rulers and leaders who are characterized by their pursuit of *doctrinam, virtutem et humanitatem* (*Q. Fr.* 1. 29). See also, *Fam.* 20.12. A number of passages from the texts of Cicero bearing on *humanitas* as the defining quality of Cicero's *princeps* or statesman are discussed in Wegemer (2014: 31 ff.).
21. Evidence of Cicero's presence, though limited influence, in this period of American history can be found in Richard (1994) and Rahe (1994: esp.

65–66). Throughout his life, Jefferson was clearly an engaged reader of Cicero, who found more significant thought and material in his writings than in Plato's. Jefferson's favorite ancient philosopher was Epicurus, and he was critical of Cicero for his attacks on Epicurus and Epicureanism. Cicero's critique of Epicureanism is explored in Chaps. 1 and 3. John Adams's attraction to Cicero was more enthusiastic and unqualified than Jefferson's. In writing about constitutional forms, he remarked "As all the ages of the world have not produced a greater statesman and philosopher united than Cicero, his authority should have great weight" (1851: vol. 4, 295). On another occasion, Adams approved Cicero's advice to his son (*Off.* 1.22) that we are not born simply for ourselves (cited in Richard 1994: 63).

22. Two biographies of Cicero are especially recommended for a fuller inquiry into his life and its context: Rawson (1994) and Petersson (1920).
23. Cicero's letters are, of course, the primary of those self-revealing sources. The letters available to us have fittingly been described as of "a volume and quality not to be reached again before Augustine—or even, it has been suggested, Elizabethan England" (Leach 1981: 382), One commentator even observes, "[W]e know more about the day-to-day Cicero from his twenty-sixth year forward than we can claim to know about most of our contemporaries" (Micken 1970: xv). Habicht (1990: 49) reports that the prominent early nineteenth-century historian Barthold Georg Niebuhr, apparently with Cicero's experience in mind, "went so far as to condemn the practice of publishing letters 'which reveal the inmost of an extraordinary human being, since it is neither right nor just to expose a single soul naked while most others are not.'" Carcopino's highly speculative study (1951: I, 201; II, 561, n. 1) of the motivation behind the publication of Cicero's letters includes the following observations on the letters from French scholarship in the 1930s: L. Laurand, "Never was any man so cast down. He sighs, he weeps. He writes pitiable letters, which unfortunately for his reputation his correspondents carefully preserved. They have been delivered to posterity, for whom they were by no means intended." Henri Marrou, "if we think so ill of Cicero, it is because he has confided in us in his *Letters* and we know about him many things which we do not know about other men." Besides the letters, note must be made of the self-revealing and self-promotional side of Cicero's orations. There are also his highly self-conscious and self-disclosing prefaces (*prooemia*) as well as other such passages in his philosophical works. Then too his autobiography, beyond what is spread throughout his letters and other works, is quite explicit in his *Brutus* (304–24). How different, then, he is in this respect from Plato and Aristotle! It is rightly thought that Cicero's writings mark the entrance into Western thought of a new emphasis in self-awareness, developed to

the form of the intellectual and spiritual autobiography by St. Augustine on whom Cicero had such a profound impact. These rich materials on the self-understanding of Cicero provide the basis for the assurance in this book that Cicero perceived his writings and political actions as consistent efforts of his own struggle with the challenges and opportunities of his time. He does not appear to be hiding one self from another self.

24. Very interesting and very significant to me was Strauss's observation (1973: 127), after finding Cicero's political action on behalf of philosophy comparable to Plato's, that this political action has nothing in common with his actions against Catiline and for Pompey. Yet Strauss may be questioning this very separation of ordinary politics from the high politics of defending philosophy when he adds of the West's successful political action on behalf of philosophy, "One sometimes wonders whether it has been too successful."

25. Consider *Rep.* 2.1 where Cicero has Cato the Elder praised for the consistency between his speech and his life. Lévy (1992: 121 ff.) has emphasized the continuity between Cicero the public man and his philosophy. Griffin (1989: 34 f.) brings forward the interaction between Cicero's real life political dilemmas and his philosophical writings.

CHAPTER 1

Skepticism, Politics, and a Philosophical Foundation

...the foundation of philosophy has come to be seen in the supreme good and evil...all of philosophy is illuminated to the greatest degree by the recognition that virtue suffices for living happily. (Cicero, *Div.* 2.2)[1]

...be on your guard lest some wicked tribune of the people arraign you and press on you the charge of inconsistency for denying the possibility of certain knowledge and yet claiming to have some. (Cicero, *Ac.* 2.63; having in mind Cicero's role as an exposer of the Catilinarian conspiracy, Catulus speaks these words to him.)

Casual and even systematic doubt about the reliability of anything we might "know" is not peculiar to modernity.[2] Despite his practical inclinations and interests, Cicero, as a student and professed lover of philosophy, found himself compelled to consider such skepticism as part of the heritage of philosophical schools, which provided the context and basis for his own philosophical education. He encountered the skeptical outlook in various forms, actually citing on one occasion the legendary opening line of the atomist Metrodorus in his work *On Nature*. "None of us," wrote Metrodorus, "knows anything, not even whether we know anything or not."[3] Cicero reveals the priorities on the philosophical agenda of the time, if not all times, when he reports in *Academica Priora* that Antiochus claimed that the two most important matters in philosophy are the criterion of truth (*judicium veri*) and the supreme end of goods (*finis bonorum*). An influential teacher of Cicero, Antiochus (c. 130/20–68) broke in Cicero's lifetime from the skeptical school known as the New Academy. He is reported as having said that no one could be deemed wise who is ignorant of the principle of knowing and the end of desiring.[4]

Although Cicero appears overall to share these Antiochean priorities for philosophy, he elevates the latter of the two and places the very foundation of philosophy in attaining an understanding of the supreme good and evil (*fines bonorum et malorum*).[5] This seems to indicate that Cicero's work on the ends, *Finibus*, is central to his approach to philosophy. Cicero's brief but revealing statement on this foundation in *De Divinatione* is followed by another metaphor that describes virtue— that chief among goods—as the primary illuminator of all philosophy.[6] Cicero's claims, rather than being anomalous or out of character, accord with the persistent emphasis throughout this work on the priority of moral philosophy among the topics of philosophy.[7] Cicero appears, then, to agree with words he puts in the mouth of Piso in *Finibus*, that in philosophy, when you settle the chief or highest end, you settle everything.[8]

Cicero does not, however, neglect the view that it is important to consider the criterion of truth. His *Academica* was written to manifest this consideration and address this issue, and he positions this work in his philosophical corpus to indicate its foundational importance to anything else one might seek to do in philosophy. Cicero, in fact, does more than merely pay his respect to the lively debate in Hellenistic philosophy and among his very teachers about the criterion of truth and then pass on to the knowledge that provides a direct basis for moral and political life. Cicero unambiguously associates himself with that school—the New Academy—that is especially responsible for making epistemological questions vital and important in the contentions among the schools in Hellenistic philosophy.[9] According to Cicero's account, the New Academy, which came in a later post-Ciceronian time to be known as the school of Academic skepticism, was founded by Arcesilaus (315–240) around 273B.C. and notably developed under Carneades (214/13–129/28), a later head of the Academy.[10] Cicero appears to be well-informed on what these masters of the New Academy taught, and his writings are among the most important sources for information on these teachings. He studied directly with Philo of Larissa (160/59–c. 80), also a head of the New Academy. Philo, in fact, was leading the Academy when, in about 87, Antiochus caused the previously mentioned split resulting in the founding the Old Academy, yet another alleged restoration of the "true" Academic teaching that all these parties traced back to Plato and Socrates.[11] In fact, certain texts of Cicero suggest that the Academy of Carneades and Philo was all but abandoned under the attack of Antiochus and others and that Cicero saw himself as one seeking to revive it.[12]

Cicero was immersed, then, in the strain of the skeptical tradition belonging to Carneades and Philo—that of the New Academy. Another strain of skepticism, that of Pyrrho (c.360–c.270), developed out of the Academy in the generation following Plato's death and was revived in Cicero's lifetime by Aenesidemus.[13] Cicero may have the neo-Pyrrhonic tradition in mind when he refuses to take seriously a skepticism which he finds disabling because it undermines human responsibility by leaving man unable to know standards and goals of action.[14] More likely, such comments by Cicero were directed at Arcesilaus and those Academics who were perceived as failing even to allow a standard of "probable" truth to guide action as Carneades apparently did.[15] Woldemar Görler, reflecting on Cicero's break with Arcesilaus, properly yet perhaps with some understatement, concludes, "Cicero has no great devotion to the more radical type of Academic skepticism."[16] Thus, Cicero is sometimes said to be a moderate or mitigated skeptic. His skepticism can also be called Socratic skepticism.

The problem and challenge of understanding Cicero's philosophical foundations necessarily takes the form of understanding how Cicero thinks through his commitment to Academic skepticism in relationship to his other aspirations for philosophy, including his key conviction that fundamental to all philosophy is inquiry into the chief of human goods. Even in his lifetime, Cicero was apparently seen by some as inconsistent insofar as he professed allegiance to the skepticism of the Academy and yet sought to determine and teach moral duties.[17] Understandably then, there has been a tendency at times to resolve the tension by overlooking Cicero's commitment to the Academics, even at times to treat him simply as a Stoic.[18] Cicero's attraction at times to Stoic teachings may, however, in some way grow out of and be consistent with his underlying Academic commitment.[19]

Before proceeding to examine more closely the nature and limits of Cicero's skepticism, it should be noted that the Greek word *skepsis*, or any Latin cognate or derivative of the word, is not in Cicero's time in general use; nor is it used by Cicero to describe his position or that of the Academics, nor in fact is the word employed to describe that of the Pyrrhonists until the period of Cicero's life or shortly thereafter.[20] This word, which primarily and literally means "inquirer," comes in this later time to be applied to those who make doubt about the possibility of knowing a fundamental dimension of their philosophical teaching. Academics and Pyrrhonists are, then, skeptics as we have come to use the term in the history of Western philosophy.

CICERO'S SKEPTICISM

H.A.K. Hunt, in *The Humanism of Cicero*, follows Eduard Zeller in finding the history of the Academic school marked by an effort to find a criterion for choice and action. He adds, "It is natural for the Sceptic to become dissatisfied with pure scepticism and to seek some criterion at all costs."[21] The subsequent tradition of skepticism seems to support Hunt's observation. David Hume's thought provides, perhaps, the most widely known instance. He joins to his skepticism an effort to understand the instinct or mechanism of belief that allows him and all humans to act in the business of ordinary life.[22]

Deepening our understanding of Cicero's skepticism calls for attention to how he lives with his skepticism,[23] to what is his "criterion for choice and action," to how he responds, in other words, to that first of the two key questions of philosophy which Antiochus highlighted: the one concerning the criterion of truth. What, then, is Cicero's way of determining the reliability of any perception and any assertions so as to allow meaningful human communication and action? Given Cicero's commitment to political action and leadership, one expects that he would strongly seek to avoid the often alleged socially and politically disabling aspects of a pure or even a strong skepticism. And as already suggested, one is not disappointed in this expectation. Just as clearly as Cicero associates himself with the school of the New Academy and the skepticism of Carneades and Philo, so too he embraces the criterion that they apparently utilized and thus limits his skepticism.[24] As Cicero states in *Finibus*, his philosophical "affiliation" with the New Academy allows him to approve and accept those matters that seem probable (*ea quae probabilia videantur*).[25] The probable for Cicero is the likely true (*simile veri*).[26] At times, Cicero conjoins these expressions (*probabile et simile veri*) in describing his criterion as an Academic.[27] Insofar as Cicero and the Academics allow, if not encourage, the inquirer to approve and accept (*probare* or *adprobare* are the terms used) a perception or proposition that is *simile veri*, they provide the basis for a clear, if elemental, understanding of the concept "probable" as used in an epistemological sense: The probable is literally that which is able to be accepted (approved) as likely to be true.[28] Thus Cicero effectively accepts as true, not however as certain and beyond philosophical doubt, whatever is probable. In *Academica* and speaking through himself as *persona*, Cicero insists that action and life can proceed quite satisfactorily with "nothing to follow but probability" because so many significant actions like going on a voyage, sowing a crop, marrying a wife, and procreating children already and manifestly rest on probability.[29]

Closely related to this last statement is a conviction of Cicero that is evident on several occasions where he is found discussing the criterion of probability. This conviction entails a claim that is, for instance, present in the previously cited passage in *Fin.* 5.76; Cicero's criterion of probability is there imbedded in a rhetorical question, "For who is able to refuse acceptance of those matters that appear to him probable?" (*Quis enim potest ea quae probabilia videantur ei non probare?*). Probability determinations are, thus, seen as instinctual or automatic. They simply spring from the way we ordinarily live—one might say, from the way we are. Cicero has apparently translated into "*probabile*" the Greek term *pithanon* which Philo and Carneades had used to designate the criterion.[30] That term is customarily rendered in English as "credible," "convincing," or "persuasive." It is not clear why Cicero chose "*probabile*" rather than "*credibile*" which was available to him to represent this key concept of the New Academy.[31] What is noteworthy is that the probable for Cicero, like *pithanon* prior to him and belief as operative much later in Hume's thought, overtakes one in the course of the practice of ordinary life.[32] The limits of skepticism are found in ordinary practice, but the intervening hand of philosophical doubt is evident insofar as the criterion comes to be described as the probable, the convincing, or the believable rather than the known and the certain.

Cicero's uncertainty or doubt is applied universally, for he applies it or derives it, one might better say, from a very fundamental experience: that of uncertainty regarding the reliability of perceptions.[33] It was at this basic level of perception that Academic skepticism had first and primarily challenged both Stoic and Epicurean assurances.[34] Certain impressions, formed primarily from but not limited to sense perceptions, were for the Stoics instances of sure and primary knowledge. They constituted the Stoic criterion of truth and have been widely called in English translation, "cognitive impressions"; they were in the Greek, *katalēpta*, or what was "grasped," this being the graphic term used by Zeno the Stoic founder.[35] This concept of a mode of possession carries through in the Latin form of perception. In this literal sense of "*percipio*," of thoroughly capturing or taking within oneself what is beheld (*visum*) so that one certainly grasps the reality before him, Cicero holds that such perception is not attainable by humans in this earthly life.[36] Some appearances, however, so strike us as to give probable assurance of perception. Cicero's stand, then, on the necessary uncertainty of perception is, in effect, an act of comprehensive or universal doubt; it is a quite conscious application of what later might be called formal philosophical doubt.

Doubt and uncertainty at this fundamental point of sense perception mean, in effect, that there is no assured or certain vantage point from which one can set truth off against mere probability or apparent truth. Cicero is aware of and does not run from the consistent and, hence, thorough skeptic's charge that asserting that there is no such vantage point is itself an uncertain claim. Cicero's fundamental philosophical doubt, then, differs from Cartesian doubt, that professed uncertainty which modern philosophy generally understands as formal philosophical or methodological doubt, insofar as it is merely provisional.[37] Cartesian doubt is allegedly propaedeutic; it is to give way to certain knowledge. Ciceronian or Academic doubt undergirds all and persists throughout inquiry; it is seen as an inescapable and enduring foundation of genuine philosophical inquiry. In this view, the traditional nature of philosophy understood as leading to wisdom, a notion that Cicero appears to espouse, cannot literally be described as a passage from doubt to certainty, from opinion to knowledge. Since all is opinion (for this, as Moliere might say, is what we have been speaking all along and all we can speak), philosophy, if it is to make any sense at all, must be a passage from opinion-formulated problems and some conjectures regarding answers to more credible or worthy opinions.[38]

Skepticism Versus Wisdom

Cicero's fundamental and thus apparently "radical" skepticism itself gives rise to two problems that pose challenges to Cicero's cogency. These related problems concern the very nature of philosophical activity. First, without a vantage point of truth or secure knowledge, how can any opinion be seen as more credible or worthy to be held than another? What, in other words, could philosophy be if there is no real basis for the greater credibility of one opinion over another?[39] The second problem involves Cicero's criterion of probability and its automatic or instinctual operation. This seems to be the more fundamental of the two problems. If we cannot help but affirm the more probable, what role is there for philosophy in life?[40] These problems threaten either to leave philosophy helplessly caught in the circle of opinion and thereby denied of its noble aspiration to truth, or to make it essentially irrelevant to the great questions of human life.

Cicero is explicitly aware of some in his time and before who, like certain modern existentialists, would strive to accept life along with its apparently ineluctable condition that nature's norms for it and its very meaning are out of human reach. In *Academica Priora*, he has Lucullus characterize certain skeptics as responding to the charge that universal uncertainty threatens any kind of stable and decent life by protesting, "What then is it to us. Surely we are not to blame. Bring your charge against nature which has, as Democritus puts it, buried truth deeply in an abyss."[41] In *Academica Posteriora* and in his own *persona*, Cicero invokes the same phrase of Democritus, as he describes how necessarily "clouded" this world was for Socrates and most of his predecessors.[42] So inaccessible was truth for these predecessors that, quite understandably, opinion and custom was made king. Cicero, then, presents Arcesilaus, founder of the New Academy, as emerging out of this ancient tradition emphasizing the inaccessibility of truth.[43] Believing that nothing can truly be perceived or known, Arcesilaus cultivated argument against all opinions and argument on opposite sides of the same issue in order to facilitate the withholding of assent to any and all positions. Cicero knows, then, that strain of skepticism which does not so much fear a life set in uncertainty as seek to accept it and thus, quite intentionally, to deflate common aspirations to attain truth.[44]

Such radical skepticism has sometimes turned on philosophy itself, rendering its supporters disinclined to philosophy and disposed to throw themselves into life as one might into a good dinner party in order to find the natural and instinctual direction.[45] After viewing Cicero's fundamental and thorough-going skepticism, one might be tempted to conclude that this is precisely what Cicero did, and in so concluding we find some understanding of the apparent incongruity of this Academic and politician-orator who is often found speaking Stoic truths.

Cicero, however, never abandoned philosophy, nor did he, however influenced by the skeptical tradition, embrace a philosophy whose sole goal is to disarm dogmatism.[46] In fact, his last few years, when he made indubitably clear his affiliation with the New Academics and his commitment to renewing this strain of the Academy, marked his philosophical fluorescence, and his explicit love of and dedication to philosophy were then more manifest than ever. So Cicero either did not realize the consequences of the comprehensive skepticism he embraced, and thus was as mindlessly eclectic as some have thought, or there is a dimension of his thought, specifically concerning how he understood the relation of his skepticism to philosophy and to action, the moral and political life, that yet requires attention and understanding.

It is the latter alternative, which gives Cicero the provisional benefit of the doubt, which must at the least be explored. This is not merely a matter of a good procedural principle regarding how to approach the thought of a person so often respected in the course of Western history. There are also in this case strong indications that philosophy (inclusive of his Academic skepticism) as represented in Cicero's life-long philosophical interests and his philosophical writings was seen to have a direct bearing on, and thus make a difference for, the life of action. This has already been suggested by reference to Cicero's emphasis on moral philosophy and by earlier allusion to his evident traditional conception of philosophy represented, for example, in his understanding of philosophy as the pursuit of wisdom and in his comfortable association of his own work with the grand tradition of Socrates, Plato, and Aristotle. More significant to the issue at hand is Cicero's drawing from that tradition his persistent theme that philosophy can make people good, that she is the mother of virtue. *Quoniam philosophia vir bonus efficitur et fortis,* "for philosophy makes a man good and brave," Cicero writes in *Divinatione*.[47] In the *Tusculans*, he introduces philosophy as concerned with the art of right living (*recta vivendi via*) and later presents philosophy as a teacher of justice, temperance, and magnanimity.[48] Cicero describes his own philosophical work as but another form of his long service to the Roman Republic; this service is said specifically to entail the moral reform of the young.[49] Clearly, Cicero's expectations for philosophy are quite different from a view that would hold that she cannot break out of the cycle of opinion and attain any real wisdom on the matters that concern most human beings and that she is irrelevant to human action.[50]

One way of seeing the import that philosophy has for life according to Cicero is to notice not only these claims for the morally beneficent effect of philosophy but also his awareness that some philosophical teachings threaten moral responsibility. One is given pause in this inquiry into

Cicero's philosophical foundations when noticing that on one occasion he includes among the threatening schools even that qualified Academic skepticism with which he often identifies. This occurs in the *Legibus*, where Cicero's professed interest is in teaching *ratio recte vivendi*, the way of right living, through a speech (*oratio*) intended to strengthen republics, stabilize cities, and bring people to their reason.[51]

As the discussion of this rhetorical dialogue approaches that key question of the natural foundation of justice, Cicero observes that what he is here seeking to present is not consistent with the teachings of all philosophical schools. And it is significant that the aspects of the teachings that he then reviews are those of the schools concerning the chief good or ultimate happiness for human beings. Though the dialogue portrays him, at this point, speaking with his Epicurean friend Atticus, Cicero seems harsh with the school of Epicurus, making, however, one perplexing concession to the school's followers.[52] The Epicureans are abruptly dismissed because, tending to the self and bound to the body, they determine what is to be done on the basis of pleasure or pain.[53] With an ironical twist that recalls the garden in which Epicurus taught and the legendary Epicurean preference for retirement to a garden, Cicero orders them to keep their talk to their gardens and requests them to abstain for now (*paulisper*) from every bond of political community, no part of which do they understand nor have they ever wished to (*ab omni societate rei publicae, cujus partem nec norunt ullam neque umquam nosse voluerunt*). In the course of the long sentence in which Cicero both describes the Epicurean position and seeks to isolate the school, he remarks that this exile to their gardens and away from civil community is demanded—and here is the important concession—even if they speak the truth about the end of human action (*etiamsi vera dicunt*), for this is not the occasion to dispute such matters (*nihil enim opus est hoc loco litibus*).[54]

Cicero, then, follows the banning of the Epicureans with the silencing of the skeptical New Academy of Arcesilaus and Carneades, for this school, which is said to confuse all such matters as those under discussion, would bring too much destruction on what seemed so well constructed and elaborated here.[55] It is, perhaps, notable that Cicero ordered (*jubeamus*) Epicurean talk to be confined to their gardens while he strongly endeavors to persuade (*exoremus*) the New Academy to be silent. At the least, it is indubitably clear and explicit that the skeptical Academics are not banned from hearing the discourse at hand, for Cicero wishes to win them over (*quam quidem ego placare cupio, summovere non audeo*). And presumably, in the light of the text we have, the Academics are not excluded even for a time from the bonds, including benefits and responsibilities, of civil society. This is apparently so because of what has just been implicitly referred to, namely that the Academics are capable of being persuaded to positions like that expounded by Cicero in the *Legibus*. The Academics have not a settled view of the end of human action. They can possibly be won over to one or another position by an elaboration of the comparative practical import of the teachings of the competing philosophical schools. This is, after all, the Academy with which Cicero has most often and essentially identified.[56]

Can one, however, draw the conclusion from the *Legibus* that Cicero's mature philosophical position included some fear of the effects of Academic skepticism? If the customary date for the writing of the *Legibus* is placed in the 50s, in conjunction with *Re Publica* and the *De Oratore*, one might be tempted to think that this silencing of the New Academy, which has just been noted, is an indication that Cicero does not, at this point in his life, see himself as an Academic or at least not a very overt one.[57] Consequently, later, in those last few years of his life, that remarkably prolific time as a writer of philosophy and a time in which his loyalty to the New Academy is indubitable, Cicero might be thought to be no longer mindful or fearful that the approach of these Academics is harmful to a sound teaching on morals and public life, so necessary to the republic he is trying to save.[58]

There is, however, evidence from both the writings of the 50s and those of his last years that suggests that Cicero consistently worried about the implications of the approach of the New Academy whether or not he was explicitly associating with that school. The very passage under consideration in the *Legibus*, when contextually examined, cannot be read as a statement of Cicero having distanced himself or disaffiliated from the New Academy. Immediately before the lengthy discourse by Cicero, which begins by his banning the Epicureans and silencing the New Academy, Atticus is portrayed as, in effect, teasing Cicero about the loyal Stoicism that Cicero announced he is about to propound, telling him, "And what has happened in fact is that your freedom in discussion has been surrendered, or you are the kind of person who submits to the authority of others rather than following his own judgment in disputations."[59] Cicero responds at once, "Not always, Titus; but do consider the thrust of this specific discourse...." (*Non semper, Tite, sed iter hujus sermonis quod sit vides....*).[60] The discourse, Cicero then adds as he breaks into a portion of it considered above, is an *oratio* intended to strengthen republics, stabilize cities and bring people to their reason.[61] Cicero's prompt denial accords with his strong feelings throughout his writings about the unSocratic character of discourses emerging out of the dogmatic camps of the various philosophical schools. Cicero has written this teasing by Atticus into the *Legibus* to alert the reader to the character of what is happening in this work and that it is out of character (*Non semper, Tite*) with what seems to be most properly philosophical discourse. Presumably the best method for attaining the truth, the best philosophical approach, is not being utilized here. "Presumably" is here used advisedly, for perhaps proper philosophical discourse or the way of the Academy needs in some way the discourse of the *Legibus* and the horizon or perspective from which it arises. Perhaps this speech is grounded on a determination of what is most likely true.

A similar concern about the import of the teaching of the New Academy can be found in Cicero's initial version of *Academica*, written in his last years. This work constitutes his major statement on the New Academy and his own attachment to it. In contrast with the *Legibus* where Cicero as *persona* in the dialogue is found setting aside the Academic school but clearly not disaffiliating himself, here in the *Academica Priora* Cicero as *persona* defends skepticism against the charge that it is inconsistent with the reliable knowledge necessary for political action—action such as Cicero himself took in exposing the Catilinarian conspiracy.[62] Lucullus, a statesman whom Cicero clearly admires as indicated in his preface to this work, is cast in the role of making the case of Antiochus against skepticism, and he draws attention to the practical certainty on which moral life and political life depend. Sensing Cicero's attraction to the position of Lucullus, Catulus, a champion of skepticism in the dialogue like Cicero himself, pleads that Cicero not be intimidated away from his skeptical convictions merely on the basis of their apparent inconsistency with needed practical certainties.[63] When Lucullus completes his presentation, Cicero finds it learned, well-informed, and comprehensive, but not beyond rebuttal.[64]

In this exchange of the *Academica* that is so explicitly technical and refined (Lucullus was introduced as one who will speak of the more recondite matters—*reconditiora*—with which one does not win popular approval),[65] Cicero stands by his comprehensive skepticism. His defense includes the theme that common-sense reliance on ordinary perception and common knowledge is not really undermined by confessing that what one thinks to be true can never be more than what is most probable or believable. Cicero presents himself as a great opinion-holder, that is as one who settles into opinions regarding the important questions of life, in fact not being able to withhold a kind of assent to the seemingly evident truth.[66] Cicero asserts, in other words, the automatic or instinctive criterion of probability as ever at work, especially readily overcoming formal doubts on the reliability of sense perception. Cicero, clearly, is concerned that fundamental and thorough-going skepticism would be practically disabling and harmful were it not that we are carried right past these problems by the natural tendency to accept and to rely on the commonly evident. Furthermore, the close of *Academica* indicates a real lack of interest on Cicero's part in the basic epistemological question (issues that are *reconditiora*), which the book has been probing. Skepticism at the fundamental perceptual level may seem the truest and most consistent with Academic teaching, but it appears at this level to bear no fruit, though it can be argued, as it is here at the end of the *Academica*, that it does no harm to common knowledge and the assurances necessary for life. The meaning of the closing section, as is the case with other works of Cicero, notably the *Natura Deorum* and *Finibus*, seems intended to leave the reader with some uncertainties; its interpretation which follows is done with difficulty.

The extant *Academica Priora* is an account of the second of a two-day discussion; the first day's discussion was reported in a now lost book often named after the primary spokesman therein, Catulus (just as this second day's account is named after Lucullus). In that first day's discussion, Catulus apparently gave an exposition and defense of the skeptical tradition as represented by Carneades, followed by comparable statements of Hortensius on Antiochus's break with skepticism and of Cicero on Philo's skepticism.[67] The second day's account, namely *Lucullus* or the extant *Academica Priora*, contains the already mentioned Antiochean attack on skepticism by Lucullus, followed by Cicero's defense of skepticism.[68]

The problematic end of the dialogue develops in the following way. Cicero's response to Lucullus draws him into a discussion of logic according to the Stoics and Antiochus, and therein Cicero is seen again encountering the Stoic assurance on the possibility of true perception and knowledge. That assurance of truth defies ordinary experience, according to Cicero, and paradoxically raises theoretical or formal doubts about the validity of the arts which must, in the Stoic view, be built upon true knowledge. No such perfect and firm knowledge, however, is really necessary for the arts, as they are known in their ordinary practitioners, nor is it necessary for the judgments of jurors in the courtroom. For both spheres, as it appears for all the practical needs of life, the standard of probable truth is adequate. At this point, when Cicero has again returned to the theme that skepticism is consistent with life's need for meaningful choice and action, he signals the end of the dialogue. The time has come for him and Lucullus to sail to their respective destinations.

Cicero then indicates that there will be future philosophical discussions but not on the epistemological topic of the reliability of sense perception or on the self-entangling logical traps in which the Stoics get caught. Cicero would rather discuss the differences among the best of men "on goods and their contraries." This is a matter on which nature is said to be obscure, and Cicero raises expectations by announcing that philosophical error on this topic abounds, that there can be only one truth on the matter, and that positions of many noble schools of thought will have to be set aside. Cicero the author is clearly pointing ahead to the next work in his philosophical program, the *Finibus*, and probably also to the *Tusculans*. He was apparently already at work on *Finibus* as he worked on *Academica*.[69]

After Lucullus remarks to Cicero the speaker that he found the present discussion bearable because there will be frequent future occasions, especially at their Tusculan villas, to discuss what they wish, Cicero asks the other interlocutors, Catulus and Hortensius, what their thoughts are. Catulus is the defender of skepticism and the person in the dialogue who pressed Cicero to remain faithful to thorough-going skepticism after the powerful appeal of Lucullus, an appeal specifically highlighting the apparent problems for choice and action in a skeptical commitment. Catulus seems caught by surprise on being asked his view. *Egone?* "My opinion?" he mutters. Then he falls back (*revolor*) to the view of his father who claimed to have taken the position of Carneades himself. Here, the great difficulties in interpreting the end of this dialogue begin to be encountered, and the difficulty posed by Cicero's subtlety or inconclusiveness at such times is compounded in this instance by our not possessing the first book of the *Academica Priora*, in which Catulus apparently made his major statement on behalf of skepticism.[70] Without access to that initial statement, it seems impossible to determine whether the summary statement of the teaching of Carneades, which Catulus here at the end offers as his opinion (and his father's), represents a development or refinement of the skeptical position he extensively explicated earlier.

If the summary statement does represent such a refinement or development, Catulus could be taken as the spokesman chosen by Cicero the author for summing up the discussion. No one else among the interlocutors, all of whom speak in this last exchange, appears to speak about the substantial issues on which the discussion of the last two days, or at least the last day, turned. Furthermore, the opinion of his father, and presumably of Carneades, that Catulus embraces does appear essentially to be the position that Cicero the *persona* has taken in the dialogue, namely that though nothing can be certainly known or perceived, a wise man is not prevented from holding an opinion as long as he understands that this, concerning which he opines, cannot be fully understood and known.

The weight of the evidence, however, seems to point to another interpretation of the intended significance of this final statement by Catulus. It appears that set among the comments of the other interlocutors in the last paragraph, Catulus's statement, like the others there, is meant, above all, to convey the frustrations of Cicero with the discussion that has preceded and to point to a domain of inquiry and discussion where philosophy can show its fruit and merit. The hesitating *Egone?* by Catulus and "the falling back" to the view of his father suggest, possibly, that skepticism does inhibit choice, or more likely, that Catulus has not found himself able to sort through the pros and cons of this particular discussion and come to any real opinion of his own. Rather, he stays where he was, or takes his stand with tradition, his father. Then after his formulation of the view of Carneades, which seems quite an adequate statement of where Cicero himself is on the issues of the dialogue, Catulus paraphrases what he just said in a way that shows none of the nuance of Cicero's efforts earlier in the dialogue and plunges Catulus into the morass of quibbling and contradiction in which Antiochus and Lucullus thought the skeptical position must fall. What Catulus says is

> *quare épochēn illam omnium rerum comprobans illi alteri sententiae, nihil esse quod percipi possit, vehementer adsentior.*

> Therefore approving the teaching of *épochē*, the suspension of assent, with respect to all matters, I strongly assent to that further opinion that there is nothing that can be truly perceived.[71]

Where the nuance is notably lacking and the key contradiction looms is in the forceful words *vehementer adsentior*.[72] It is as if a raw act of will had substituted for a measured philosophical conclusion. It is a language that is inappropriate to an effort to accept the uncertainty of all judgments and yet give way to our natural tendency to approve what appears probable. It is a language insensitive to the charge of Antiochus and Lucullus that skeptics must be consistent, as was Arcesilaus, in their skepticism, and thus must apply it to the central propositions of their own school.[73] The strong language tends to confirm the suspicion that Catulus is "digging in"; he is, on this matter, acting like a dogmatic man of the schools. His "*vehementer*" makes him similar, in a way, to the Stoic or to Lucullus who is so strongly assured of *perceptio*, of our capacity for true and certain knowledge. As Catulus, the Academic spokesman, is Stoic-like in his firm dogmatism, so Lucullus, whom Cicero so admires, was initially introduced as approaching his task of presenting the Stoic-like teaching of Antiochus in the Academic spirit—that is, Lucullus spoke of this position as seeming truest (*verissima*) to him and specifically welcomed correction of his view in the ensuing exchange.[74] One might also, here, recall Cicero's repeated admiration for Antiochus in this work and elsewhere and his deep admiration for that eminent student of Antiochus, Varro, the designated Antiochean spokesman in *Academica Posteriora*.[75] Cicero is, it appears, not approaching the issue of the *Academica*, the criterion of truth, as one seeking to set up and blow down a straw man.[76] The issue challenges him and perhaps frustrates him.

In the final statement of Catulus, there is found not only the strong assurance that makes him similar to Lucullus but also his statement of skepticism that sharply polarizes their positions. So here, nearly at the end, Lucullus and Catulus stand clearly and strongly opposed. What of the others—the two others, who despite their association with and, in fact, speaking for the major positions opposed in the dialogue, Hortensius for Lucullus and Cicero for Catulus, are clearly cast more in the role of jurors in this dispute? Catulus does not have the last word. As he completes his statement with his *vehementer adsentior*, Cicero approves in a way that suggests more necessity or instinct than choice and enthusiasm. "I hear your opinion," though it is all my own translation he says, and am not much inclined to resist it (*nec eam admodum aspernor*). He then turns to Hortensius for his view, and the host laughingly proclaims *Tollendum*, "Be gone with it all!" "I'm with you," adds Cicero, "that's the real view of the Academy." Thereupon, Lucullus and Cicero depart to their ships and the dialogue ends. The apparent concern of Hortensius and Cicero the *persona* is to get on with the business of life; in the case of Cicero the author, it is to turn to a more necessary and more fruitful line of inquiry for philosophy. Serious questions are thus raised at the very end about the necessity and usefulness of the preceding dialogue.[77] *Academica Priora* provides evidence, then, of a kind of ambivalence about Academic skepticism, an ambivalence also found in the *Legibus* and an apparently consistent strain in Cicero's thought.

Before returning to indications in *Academica Priora* of more necessary and fruitful pursuits for philosophy and following these with Cicero toward and into the *Finibus*, we should recapitulate the problem and the steps that drew us to the *Academica*. Cicero was shown to be a comprehensive skeptic in that he denies the possibility of certain and absolutely reliable knowledge in all matters, even at the level of sense perception. Cicero sees himself avoiding the incapacity of choice and action frequently attributed to skepticism, by being a skeptic of the probabilistic sort within the New Academy.[78] Furthermore, he is one who claims that reliance on the probable is the natural and instinctive way with humans. If such a skepticism provides Cicero's philosophical foundation, one would be compelled to ask how such a foundation related to or supported the traditional conception of philosophy as growth in wisdom: a growth or development in which philosophy is a significant autonomous act for the discovery of truth and moral direction rather than a simply instinctive act. Cicero gives ample indications of his high expectations for philosophy, and he is aware, as indicated in the preceding interpretations of the *Legibus* and *Academica Priora*, that the work of the skeptical New Academy can pose a threat to the fruitfulness expected of philosophy. The *Academica Priora* makes clear that Cicero's defense of and enthusiasm for philosophy does not rest on the philosophical probing of the epistemological issues of perception and knowledge. Skepticism and probabilism do undergird for Cicero all human knowing and acting, but they do not provide the foundation of philosophy in the sense of being a source that allows philosophy to be fruitful and to show its great significance for human life. Academic skepticism is procedural, not substantive.

Why, then, has Cicero bothered at all to make a skeptical profession of faith, to affiliate with the New Academy, and to entangle himself with the issues probed in the *Academica*? If one follows Cicero's own description in *Divinatione* of his philosophical program, including the apparently highly accurate sequence in which he did his philosophical works, and if one bears in mind what one can know of his *Hortensius* from the extant fragments, the *Academica* is found between Cicero's moving and quite Platonic exhortation to philosophy in *Hortensius* and the *Finibus*, in which Cicero claims that the foundations of philosophy are explored and to which Cicero is so evidently anxious to move in the latter portion of the *Academica Priora*.[79] When it is also recalled that Cicero threw out the *Academica Priora* in favor of the reworking known to scholars as the *Academica Posteriora*, evidence appears to be accumulating that Cicero was not at all comfortable with what he set himself to do in the *Academica*.[80] Cicero, perhaps, asked himself the question raised just above: Why has he bothered to make a skeptical profession, to affiliate with the New Academy, and to entangle himself with these more recondite (*reconditiora*) epistemological issues?[81] The effort to understand Cicero's philosophical coherence requires keeping this question before us. The question, however, can be approached well only after exploring further, but provisionally, the direction for philosophy that Cicero explicitly regards as fundamental insofar as it is both necessary and fruitful for human life.

Skepticism in the Service of Wisdom

Cicero sets the foundation of philosophy in the inquiry into goods, especially the ultimate good, and their contraries. Within the *Academica Priora* itself, he claims that this inquiry constitutes important work for philosophy; on this topic, philosophy is called upon to assist in discovering which of contending views is the truest.[82] The *Officiis* and *Finibus* make clear that this inquiry into the ends is ineluctably relevant to each person's life because some conception of good or ultimate happiness functions as the standard or good in terms of which duties or principles of action are determined.[83] And so it is that this inquiry into the ends is both necessary and fruitful. This inquiry grows out of the firm ground—firm in a sea of uncertainty—that all humans seek happiness.[84] This universal inclination to happiness, above all, moves people to philosophize.[85] Among philosophy's possible directions, Cicero, as already noted, assigns clear priority to moral philosophy. In this, he sees himself following Socrates and shows his understanding of Socrates as one who redirected philosophy from the heavens to the homes and cities of mankind.[86] This emphasis on the moral dimension of human life is an important part of the practical perspective that informs Cicero's approach to philosophy.

To note Cicero's emphasis on moral philosophy does not take one very far into Cicero's practical perspective, nor consequently yield much insight into the coherence of his philosophical work. At the least, the following two questions stand unaddressed and call out for responses: (1) In what way can inquiry into the greatest good and the greatest evil, moral philosophy, be foundational for all philosophy? (2) How does the probability criterion of Cicero's professed skepticism operate in this foundational moral inquiry? In pursuing the latter question, one can find an approach to a response to the first question. The second question is really a call for a close examination of how Cicero makes philosophical judgments when he investigates the supreme good, as he does in the *Finibus*. This question is another form, then, of the question "how does this Academic skeptic come to embrace certain Stoic or Stoic-like moral teachings". To say that he judges them probably true is itself correct, but this response, one that Cicero himself provides, leaves unarticulated how such a judgment is made. If this is a sphere where philosophy is both necessary and fruitful—where philosophy can "show its colors"—then one must expect that this judgment consists not in some instinctive response to alleged probabilities but in a process where some effective, defensible criterion is utilized to determine what is probably true. What is being sought, then, in pursuing the second question is what might be called the effective criterion that operates behind the formal criterion of probability.[87] What makes a proposed supreme good more or less probably true?

How, then, does Cicero make his judgments in favor of one school or another in the *Finibus* and elsewhere, when he considers the various views on the supreme good and evil? Early in his major discourse in *Academica Priora*, Cicero speaks of his own way of determining the probably true as one wherein broad understandings, rather than minutely refined arguments, play a greater part (*rationes has latiore specie, non ad tenue elimatas*).[88] This confession is useful to keep in mind in looking for the effective criterion in his judgments about ultimate ends. That effective criterion is most evident when he is able to be most decisive,[89] and that is when he is rejecting the Epicurean view of pleasure or the absence of pain as man's greatest good. Cicero uses moral and political consequences as his effective criterion. He looks for the consistency of a philosophical teaching on happiness with human needs especially with those evident to the moral sensibility, with common notions of duty, citizenship, virtue, and friendship.[90] Although Cicero does weaken certain philosophical teachings with the conventional approach of finding logical inconsistencies in them, his critical argument as to the probable or seeming truth of one or another teaching of a school takes a consequentialist turn. This is not to say that his argument is crudely utilitarian or pragmatic, for the natural moral sensibility is integral to the standards or goods used to determine consequences as good or bad. More plausible than the suspicion of a crude utilitarianism in Cicero is the charge that he is begging the question, that this moral sensibility assumes certain goods and that these, very likely, import the standards and prejudices of a specific social and economic class into his philosophical work.[91] Only the elaboration in subsequent chapters of Cicero's effective criterion will show that although custom and tradition influence his judgment of moral and political consequences, that judgment is capable of transcending in some way and, thus, of correcting customary ways.[92]

The effective criterion is what is known through the perspective of practice. This perspective provides the basis for judgments about goods that are latent if not explicit in a reflective, experienced person of action. This is the consular perspective, the perspective of consular philosophy. Its judgments are derivative from human experience with significant moral choice, which necessarily is social and political experience.[93] And these judgments, or more specifically the perspective or ground from which they emerge, involve ingredients that include a reading of man's interior inclinations, a determination of his external needs and situation in the world of nature, and his inherent sense of propriety or right. A whole range of instinctive probabilistic determinations, involving sense perceptions and relationships between and among external and internal factors, are imbedded in this perspective and the judgments derived from it.[94] The search for the effective criterion in Cicero appears to direct us to the fundamental orientations of human nature and to the fact that we have lived before we begin to understand how we have lived.

Fundamental philosophy, the inquiry into the ends, is for Cicero a testing of the schools against the sense of goods and the hierarchy of goods evident to the perspective of practice. It is a bringing to the form of explicit judgments what is implicit in that perspective. This seems a particularly important moment to remember the elemental truth that all philosophical work and systems proceed from some givens or assumptions; Cicero proceeds, most notably, from goods, hence from the needs, of the human person in society, as evident to the perspective of practice and expressed in certain natural inclinations to that unarticulated but common end of human desire, happiness. To speak of the human person in society is, of course, already to have made a judgment, at the least implicit, on a primary human good. This understanding of fundamental philosophy illuminates what Cicero apparently means in holding that philosophy mothers virtue and can shore up failing virtue. Philosophy does this insofar as it makes clear (that is, probably so) the consistent and inconsistent consequences of fundamental and derivative choices for goods, known by natural inclination developed in practice—the practical perspective. Philosophy does the work of moral reform and development, which Cicero expects of it, by relying on a sense of good bred of the moral experience of persons or that of the society that has nurtured them.[95] Fundamental philosophy, as we find it in Cicero, always proceeds from some moral awareness. It cannot simply supply this. Philosophy takes it as a premise of its work.[96]

Now it is possible to identify more specifically what seems to be an unconventional aspect in Cicero's approach to philosophical foundations. Cicero appeals to prudence to resolve the differences among philosophical schools concerning the supreme good. For Cicero, prudence is what is being practiced when moral and political consequences are assessed against a sense of good intimated or known in some way. The traditional sphere for prudence is in the choice of actions with respect to the ultimate good, personally known in some way other than through prudence itself.[97] Cicero is not oblivious of prudence in this ordinary sense; he presents the *Officiis* as specifically treating this sphere and recognizes that principles and guidelines for action are dependent on the determination of the ultimate good.[98] Prudence itself, however, or her twin sister—she might be called macro-prudence—comes for Cicero to be involved in the determination of the ultimate good.[99] Again, this may give Cicero's approach the appearance of being circular; the ultimate good is determined through a choice that is dependent on the good known in other forms, concrete manifestations of goods but clearly yet undetermined as ultimate good. No reader of Plato could find simply outrageous the necessary implication here, that Cicero's inquiry into the ultimate good looks to discover what is already in some sense known.

That inquiry into the supreme good is nonetheless an examination rather than a process of easy or instinctive reliance on the given. In this most important of human concerns, though not exclusively in this, Cicero seeks to make a determination, to exercise choice, to form and hold an opinion. Even if Cicero's assessment of consequences is conducted more with "broad understandings, rather than minutely refined arguments," there occurs a real inspection or examination of likely consequences in the choice of one or another solution to the question of the ultimate good. In this, Cicero sees himself as and appears true to the New Academy, even as it was later described by

Sextus Empiricus. In seeking to distinguish the New Academy's "dogmatic" way from his own Pyrrhonian stance, Sextus wrote, "Furthermore, as regards the End (or aim of life) we differ from the New Academy; for whereas the men who profess to conform to its doctrine use probability as the guide of life, we live in an undogmatic way by following the laws, customs, and natural affections."[100] In other words, we "let go," we go with a tradition "that works." In another work, Sextus claimed that Carneades advocated the greatest care in judgments pertaining to happiness by urging, in this important matter, "tested" judgments.[101] Carneades, then, may have been more influential on Cicero than even commonly thought, for his focus on the question of happiness in this way (in the Socratic tradition as Carneades apparently thought) can be seen in Cicero's emphasis on the question of the supreme good and evil and on the practical perspective (the multifaceted test of experience) as the criterion of truth on this question.

Among the great questions one might inquire into and decide by means of the probability criterion, Cicero held that the issue of the ultimate good yields to a more probable or credible resolution than other matters. In the *Academica Priora*, as he announces his turn to the ideas of good and evil (*ad bonorum malorumque notionem*) and what will constitute a preview of the *Finibus*, Cicero diverts from this course to observe that it is possible to lose authority for what is evident by claims of certainty in matters where there really is not compelling evidence. At this point, he has most in mind certain assured Stoic postures with respect to cosmological propositions and divination.[102] Cicero's placement of this apparent diversion suggests an observation that finds support throughout his writings and that explains his making the inquiry into the ends foundational to all philosophy. This inquiry into the ends probes where philosophy can make its surest judgments.[103] These judgments have comparative surety or can be said to yield practical assurance because humans are oriented to their ultimate good, to what is genuinely satisfying.[104] Furthermore, this happiness is not simply presented as a formal abstract object or end. Humans are attuned to pleasure in its ordinary sense as well as to the attractiveness of the virtues.[105] These human orientations, then, play a part in determinations of what constitutes happiness, a question whose answer is given and clarified through reflection on experience with choice. In this way, as Cicero's own inquiry into the ends illustrates, reliable judgments can be made in the light of goods known through the practical perspective. Because Cicero understands the relative surety of the fruit of this inquiry, his understanding of the moral and political good is always found playing a critical part in his determination of what is likely true in the more speculative issues of philosophy and theology.[106] Since philosophy's most assured position is that possible in the inquiry into the ultimate good, this inquiry into "ends" not only provides the immediate basis for ethics, principles for action and for the determination of duty, but also provides, in a sense, the foundation of all philosophy.

Beneath this "foundation," however, is what allows a judgment concerning the supreme good. This is the effective criterion or the true foundation of philosophy for Cicero. Cicero's very commitment to the Academic school can be seen to be a derivative from the effective criterion or what is known through the practical perspective. In the light of the seeming truth of the Academic method, Cicero requires of himself a consistent commitment even to the level of sense perception, of prescinding from anything more than judgments of probability. Some of those judgments will be easy and instinctive, and if Cicero hesitates to dwell on them or to seek to complicate or trouble that automatic process, it is likely because he is aware both that something must be assumed and that there is more significant work for the critical, doubting approach of the Academic school.

In that revealing characterization of his various philosophical writings at the start of *Divinatione 2* (that same place where he claims that the *Finibus* is concerned with the foundation of philosophy), Cicero describes his intent in writing *Academica* to be the demonstration of that mode of philosophizing: *minime arrogans maximeque et constans et elegans,* "that way of philosophizing that is least arrogant and especially consistent and selective."[107] That it is "least arrogant" in affirming with certainty not only distinguishes it from other schools but also allows the possibility of it being an arrogant Academic. Catulus with his *vehementer adsentior* at the end of the *Academica Priora* is such an example. Though they are not entirely free from the risk of arrogant dogmatism, the Academics as a school do not embrace specific teachings about the supreme good or the nature of the universe and the gods. Their school, in Cicero's time, is founded chiefly around a method, for selection among the various teachings. As a follower of this Academic approach, Cicero has aptly been called "an eclectic of the most responsible kind."[108] In the matters most important for philosophy to consider, Cicero thought that selectivity based on experience and discussion had to be restored or strengthened in place of the straightforward dogmatism of the other philosophical schools. Clear and profound differences of opinion on many of the traditional topics of philosophy left Cicero uneasy with those who would speak with absolute assurance on such matters. Cicero appeared, then, to find it persuasive, both for the sake of consistency and because it seemed true, to follow and to seek to revive the Academic and Socratic traditions in denying certainty not only on ultimate and speculative concerns of philosophy but also, and in accord with the broader tradition of skepticism, at the very level of sense perception. The doubts, at this basic level, were not to have practical bearing in the way that some might expect; in other words, they were not to impair practical assurance based on the instinctive operation of the probability principle.[109] What doubting at this level did is to uphold the consistency of the Academic position and Cicero's philosophical position and, thereby, strengthen it for the critical work it was called on to do in the other spheres of philosophical inquiry. At one point in the *Tusculans*, Cicero writes in a manner of looking back from the fruits of philosophy manifest in that work to his having settled the matter of the highest good "insofar as such is able to be known by humankind" (*quoad possunt ab homine cognosci*).[110] The implication here is that the coming to terms with pervasive uncertainty and the limits of knowledge allows one to find the relative surety on the matter of the ends or the highest good. Catulus, in his *vehementer adsentior*, may well represent a fundamental limit to skepticism—as Socrates, knowing that he does not know—from which Cicero moves to the relative assurances or probabilities that allow life to proceed in a meaningful way.

For all his allegiance to the Academic school and the Socratic tradition, Cicero's philosophical writings do not show a consistent or even overall commitment to the dialectical or brief question–and-answer format that one might expect. Cicero's frequent and quite conscious use of a more rhetorical mode of philosophy will be found to be related to his consistent ambivalence about Academic skepticism. The task of philosophy is never simply and solely to doubt and to question. The following chapter considers the different tasks and modes of philosophy in Cicero's writings and prepares the way for an effort to understand the details of this philosophy as defense and commendation as well as inspection and testing of a moral tradition and the very elements of the effective criterion, of the natural sense of good developed in moral choice.

Notes

1. With respect to the phrase, *finibus bonorum et malorum* (in effect, the full title of *De Finibus*), I am persuaded that Wright's translation (1991: note 2, 14) as "supreme good and evil" is both accurate as to the sense of Cicero and useful in integrating Cicero's thought with Western moral discourse. For a definitional statements in Cicero on *finis* as *ultima* or *summa bonorum et malorum*, see *Fin*. 2.4–5; 3.26; *Ac*. 2.129. Citations in this book follow the tradition of treating the extant *Academica* as one work. In accord with this convention, what remains of Cicero's first effort (*Academica Priora*) to write the work will be cited, as is done in this note, as the second book of the *Academica* and what remains of his second effort (*Academica Posteriora*) will be cited as the first book.
2. Many scholars of modern skepticism appreciate the impact of various strains of ancient skepticism on their subject and specifically the role of ancient versions in skepticism's revival in the Renaissance. Most notable is the scholarship of Richard H. Popkin; note especially (1979) "Preface" and Chap. II. Laursen (1992) provides a lucid and accurate survey of ancient skepticism in the first chapter and many insights and a rich bibliography relevant to the relationship of ancient and modern forms of skepticism. Annas and Barnes (1985), in their first chapter, provide a basic introduction to ancient skepticism, marked by an awareness of its relationship to modern skepticism. Also, see Hookway (1990) and Lom (2001).
3. *Ac*. 2.73; also a similar statement from Arcesilaus at *Ac*. 1.45, where he claims that Socrates slipped into dogmatism while claiming that he knows that he does not know. Metrodorus of Chios was a Fourth Century pupil of Democritus and an apparent proponent of atomism. This crisp English rendering of the fragment is by Sedley (1983: 14). See Sedley's subsequent phrasing of the passage in a reflexive version of skepticism (1998: 86). When Cicero cites Metrodorus, he appears to have a more complete source for this fragment, for he also attributes to Metrodorus the denial "that we know at all whether anything exists or nothing exists." Burnyeat endeavors to explain how such fragments might relate to Metrodorus's atomism and are not to be considered as indicators of a skepticism as comprehensive and thoroughgoing as is known in our post-Cartesian time (1982: 1: 32 n. 42, 16).
4. *Ac*. 2.29. Cicero's report here is in the voice of the dramatic persona, Lucullus.
5. At *Tusc*. 3.6 he describes his writings on the criterion of truth (*Academica*) and on the ends (*De Finibus*) as concerned with the most important matters (*de maximis rebus*) in the realm of philosophy (*universa philosophia*). The claim about the foundation of philosophy occurs in the important preface to the second book of *Divinatione* (2.2) where Cicero describes his

philosophical corpus by enumerating and characterizing each of his works. Also, *Tusc.* 4.82.
6. *Div.* 2.2. In *Fin.* 4.14, Cicero writes of the supreme good as that which supports or binds together philosophy itself (*continet philosophiam*).
7. For example, *Fin.* 2.51–52; 3.6; *Off.* 1.5,19.
8. *Fin.* 5.15. Also, *Ac.* 2.132. Varro, according to Augustine (*The City of God* XIX.1), saw different positions on the chief good as defining the various philosophical schools in his time.
9. See especially *Off.* 2.7–8; *Nat. D.* 1.11 and *Div.* 2.1–2, where Cicero indicates his Academic commitment and explicitly directs the reader to the *Academica* for a fuller exposition. *Ac.* 1.43; 2.7 are particularly noteworthy confessions of his philosophical affiliation. His Academic loyalties appear clear in his earliest work, *Inv.* 2.9–10. See also, Tarrant (1985: 152 nn. 43 and 44).
10. That Cicero saw Arcesilaus as founder of the New Academy rather than a "Middle Academy" is affirmed by Long and Sedley (1987: 1.448). Lévy (1992: 1–2, 9 ff.) makes this same point in the course of reconstructing a history of the Academy that utilizes fully, as he insists such a history should, Cicero's texts. Sextus Empiricus (early third century A. D.) reports that Arcesilaus was the founder of the "Middle" Academy and Carneades of the "New" (1967: I. 220).
11. Besides criticizing skepticism for internal contradictions, Antiochus emphasized the positive teaching in Socrates and shared much of the teaching of the Stoic school. Sextus (1967: I.235) described Antiochus as having "transplanted the Stoa into the Academy" and as showing "that the Stoics' doctrines are present in Plato." Also, Long and Sedley (1987: 1.444, 449) and Tarrant (1985: Chap. 5 and *passim*). On the "break" by Antiochus and the subsequent leadership of the school by Antiochus, Barnes (1989: esp. 54 ff.) and Sedley's dissent from what Barnes does here (1998: 77 n. 70); also, Glucker (1978: 27 ff. and *passim*) and Dillon (1988:104–06).
12. *Nat. D.* 1.6, 11; *Ac.* 2.11. For background on the failing of this Academy and its subtle transformation, see Tarrant (1985: 3127 and *passim*).
13. On the Pyrrhonist revival led by Aenesidemus, see Long and Sedley (1987: 1.449, 468–88) and Barnes (1989: 93–94). Tarrant (1985: 140 n. 4) thinks that it is an exaggeration to claim that Aenesidemus revived Pyrrhonism. Knowledge of Pyrrho, attained largely through work on Sextus Empiricus, has brought certain scholars to see his position as that of authentic or "classical" skepticism. Michael Frede, for one, sets this skepticism off against "dogmatic" skepticism, which is characterized by its proponents allowing themselves to have opinions, including the opinion that one cannot know with certainty. Frede sees the revival of Pyrrhonism as "not so much a revival of Pyrrho's philosophy, but a revival of classical

Academic skepticism under the name of Pyrronism (sic), to distinguish it from the dogmatism which Aenesidemus and Sextus Empiricus associated with the later sceptical Academy" (1987b: 218, 1987a: 182–83). Sextus held that the Academics who denied the possibility of knowing failed to suspend judgment and were not properly skeptics. See Annas and Barnes (1985: 1, 15) and also Annas (1986: 12 f.). Long and Sedley, however, interpret Pyrrho as a "dogmatic," (1987: 1.446–47, 472); also, Laursen (1992: 38–39) and Nussbaum argues persuasively that the skepticism of Sextus does not escape "dogmatism" (1994: 300 ff.).

14. *Ac.* 2.32; *Off.* 2.7. Hume, in his *Enquiry* (1939: 685–86), remarks that "the great subverter of Pyrrhonism or excessive principles of scepticism is action, and employment, and the occupations of common life." Then he described Pyrrhonism as being "corrected by common sense and reflection" and turned into Academic skepticism. Brochard (1923: 245) speculates that in *Ac.* 2.32 Lucullus, the spokesman for the Antiochean position, who denounces radical skepticism as unworthy of attention, has revived Pyrrhonism in mind. This was drawn to my attention by Gisela Striker (1980: 64). Brochard's suggestion must be seriously entertained in the light of the fact that though Pyrrho is specifically named only once in the extant *Ac.* (2.130), he is frequently cited in the *Finibus*. Though these references (see for example *Fin.* 2.35,43; 4.49,60; 5.23; also, *De Or.* 3.62), just as *Ac.* 2.130, portray the Pyrrhonist school as having been overcome, their frequency may be taken as evidence of a concern with a neo-Pyrrhonism. See the discussion of these passages by Glucker (1978: 116–17, n. 64) and Long and Sedley (1997: 1.21–22). Noting the claims that the Pyrrhonist revival of Aenesidemus first occurred in the 40s, Sedley (1998: 89) more recently finds no evidence in Cicero's writing through 45 of an awareness of a Pyrrhonist revival.Cicero accepts the view, namely the *apraxia* argument, then current in traditional Stoic attacks on skepticism, that such skepticism is disabling to purposeful action, and it seems that judged from the standpoint of usable standards for action, Pyrrhonian skepticism and that of Arcesilaus are similarly inadequate. It is likely that there was a strong Roman concern with skepticism's potential to be practically disabling, and thus threatening to the Roman way of life. See Lucretius, *De Rerum Natura* iv. 500–12. There are doubts in evidence in recent scholarship on whether "classical skepticism," either in its Pyrrhonian or Academic form, can fairly be said to be inadequate, and it is conjectured that it might be better perceived as another way to come to terms with the ethical dimension of life. See Long and Sedley (1997: 1.450–60) and Frede (1987a: esp. 180). Annas (1986: 22, 27) not only claims that the *apraxia* argument was taken seriously in ancient times but takes it so herself.

SKEPTICISM, POLITICS, AND A PHILOSOPHICAL FOUNDATION 41

15. Though this formulation of the position of Carneades is Cicero's (see what follows in this chapter), note should be taken of the attention in recent scholarship to what Carneades's position actually was and, in effect, to whether Cicero got it right. The most favorable view the new scholarship takes of Cicero's interpretation of Carneades seems to be that it represents one side in a dispute among pupils of Carneades about whether Carneades held that a wise person would have opinions even if only assenting to them as probable (see Frede (1987b: 213); Hankinson (1997:181 n. 36). The prevalent view of recent scholarship is, in Frede's terms (1987b: 203 ff.), that Carneades is a "classical" skeptic unlike the "dogmatic" Philo; like Arcesilaus, Carneades is seen as exemplifying a "dialectical" approach to dogmatic positions such as those of the Stoics. This means that Carneades is seen not as an advocate of "the probable" or "credible" as a standard for action but as one pointing out to the Stoics on their own terms, that this is all that is left when one has shown that there is no absolute wisdom based on assured perceptions which the Stoics took as the desirable standard for action. Interpreting Cicero's Carneades as radically committed to the dialectical approach is Allen (1997: 217–56). For more on the recent reinterpretation of Carneades, see the subtle and thorough defense of this position and the entailed exploration of how Arcesilaus and Carneades might have met the *apraxia* objection in Bett (1989: 59–94). Also, Long and Sedley (1987: 1.448–49, 457–60); Sedley (1983: esp. 18). For the "dialectical strategy" with respect to the Stoic understanding of the end, see Long (1967: 73 ff.). Also Couissin's seminal 1929 essay (reprinted 1983); Burnyeat (1984: esp. 227–28, nn. 6 and 7). See Tarrant (1985: 9, 13–18, and *passim*) for a case that Cicero's understanding of Carneades is plausible and in accord with what one might find and expect in the period of the Fourth Academy. Similarly Barnes (1989: 73–78) exploring the struggle between Philo and Antiochus and the nature of their "dogmatism" indicates how they appeared to pull the Carneadian legacy in their direction; also, Hankinson (1997: 183 ff.) and Striker (1997: 257–76). Lévy's approach (1992: 32 ff.) to Carneades includes a review of various interpretations of Carneades and the emergence of the dialectical-strategy hypothesis. For a more traditional and very thorough interpretation of Carneades see Stough (1969: 50–64).
16. Görler (1997: 45–46).
17. *Off.* 2.7; *Ac.* 2.63, *passim*.
18. One form of this is to neglect the *Academica*, which Schmitt observes (1983: 227–30) occurred during the Middle Ages and Renaissance, periods of high respect for Cicero as a philosopher. A much more complete statement and analysis of this neglect is found in Schmitt's book. Though noting there that "Cicero's influence during the Middle Ages was enor-

mous... perhaps as great as that of Aristotle...", he concludes that between Augustine's *Contra Academicos* and the Sixteenth Century, there is little serious concern with the *Academica* (1972: 33, 137). Schmitt also draws attention to the efforts in that century to emphasize Cicero's apparent dogmatic Stoicism in writings as *Re Publica* and *Officiis* (99). For the tendency, among recent political theorists, to regard Cicero simply as a Stoic, see Nicgorski (1984: 560 and 2012: 274, 277). Laursen notes (1992: 59 n.105) the same tendency among political theorists but is mistaken in pointing to Holton's introductory essay (1972: 130–50) as an instance of a failure to recognize Cicero as a skeptic.

19. Frede (1987b: 217), describing the "dogmatic" skeptic of Cicero's time. observes that "once the skeptic takes the liberty to take positions, his positions, given the eclecticism of the time, tend to become more or less identical with those of the Stoics, except on the question of knowledge itself." That Frede is, here, making chiefly a historical claim rather than one of philosophical or logical necessity is evident in 1987, 176. In unpublished material in making this point, Frede discussed the confluence of the Academic and Stoic schools in the last quarter of the second century B.C. Long writes of this peace between the Academy and the Stoa as ending "the longest continuous philosophical controversy in pre-Christian Greek philosophy...The Academy, to a large extent and only temporarily, absorbed the main doctrines of the Stoics" (1980: 162, 173). Also, Glucker (1995: 135). Annas (1994: 335). Tarrant, who protests (1985: 4, 29 ff., 66) against trying to understand Cicero and his period in terms of the "the sceptic-dogmatist dichotomy," adds an important perspective in his thesis on the Fourth Academy concerning how Academic and Stoic positions came together. This is not to say that certain skeptics such as Aenesidemus regarded skepticism as at all reconcilable with taking Stoic positions; he described (Photius, *Library*, 169b ff. in Long and Sedley 1987: 1.468–70) such Academics as "Stoics fighting with Stoics."

20. Sedley (1983: 20, 22), Annas and Barnes (1985: 1), and Tarrant (1985: 22ff).

21. Hunt (1954: 3–4).

22. Hume (1962: 318), Laursen (1992: 70) and his later chapters on Hume; Hookway (1990: 88, 100 ff.); Annas (1988 :111–12), and Olshewsky (1991 :269–87). Perhaps Hume underestimates Stoic assurance when he otherwise wisely remarks that the "dispute between the Sceptics and Dogmatists is entirely verbal, or at least regards only the degrees of doubt and assurance . . ." Hume adds,No philosophical Dogmatist denies, that there are difficulties both with regard to the senses and to all science; and that these difficulties are in a regular, logical method, absolutely insolvable. No Sceptic denies, that we lie under an absolute necessity, notwithstanding

these difficulties, of thinking, and believing, and reasoning with regard to all kind of subjects, and even of frequently assenting with confidence and security (1927: 390 n. 1).
23. Burnyeat examines this question specifically within the ancient tradition of skepticism and largely exclusive of Cicero (1983: 117–148). He provides valuable background and insight on how especially Pyrrhonian skepticism and Arcesilaus sought to deal with this question as well as a convincing conclusion on the inherent difficulty if not impossibility of the "witholding of belief" sought by such skeptics. For a well-argued dissent from Burnyeat and for an insistence that Hume's psychological basis for belief is distinct from assent or an epistemological conviction, see Williams (1988: 552, 555–56, 561, 582–83). Olshewsky (1991: 276) is inclined to the same side. For the claim that ancient skepticism was directed against belief and that neither Hume nor Cicero are properly skeptics, see Annas and Barnes (1985: 6–9). On "belief" (*pistis*) terminology in the Academy from Carneades, see Tarrant (1985: 38–39). Also see Burnyeat (1984: 229–30, 242–43), Frede (1987a, 1987b: 205: 207 ff.), Bett (1989 :60, *passim*), Nussbaum (1994: 312), and Laursen (1992: Chap. 3) where he follows the initial difference on the question between Frede and Burnyeat through the scholarly literature.
24. There are only a couple of indications in Cicero's writings of his possible awareness of a philosophical difference between Carneades and Philo: *Ac.* 2.12,78. Such a difference is made much of in some recent scholarship on Hellenistic philosophy and concerns Philo's apparent advocacy of reliance on "the probable" and his consequent approval and assimilation of findings or "dogmata" like certain teachings of the Stoics. At *Ac.* 2.78. and then at *Ac.* 2.99 ff, there are indications that Cicero does not find such a difference a significant one. On Cicero's seemingly distinctive appropriation of Carneades and Philo, see Lévy (1992: 291 ff., 634–35, 48ff.)
25. *Fin.* 5.76; *Ac.* 2.7–8, 99; *Nat. D.* 1.12; *Tusc.* 1.17.
26. *Ac.* 2.128.
27. *Ac.* fr.19; also *Ac.* 2.32, where the conjoining is put in the mouth of Lucullus describing the Academic position. For an exploration of Cicero's and others' use of these terms and their Greek originals, see Glucker (1995: 115–43) and Lévy's important discussion (1992: 284–90). Note Garsten's treatment (2009: 154) of *probabile* as the best estimate of the truth and as the basis for Cicero's embrace of certain Stoic-like "truths." It appears that Garsten need not have seen, as he does, Cicero's Stoic-like convictions as wholly departing from common opinion and showing no trace of skepticism.
28. To approve (*probare*) as likely true is often contrasted in Cicero with to affirm (*affirmare*) as true and sometimes with to assent to (*adsentiri*) as

true. Striker (1980: 61, n. 21) rightly notes "that Cicero does not always observe the terminological distinction between *adsentiri* and *adprobare*, but he emphasizes it in crucial passages." Thorsrud (2012: 145) reflects well on what Cicero does not appear to tell his readers about the relationship of the probable to the truth. On these terms and their likely basis for Cicero, see Lévy (1992a: 100–02). The one and only place where I have found a simple collapse of the general distinction between *adprobare* and *adsentiri* is at *Ac.* 1.45 where Cicero is explicitly summarizing the position of Arcesilaus. It is not unreasonable to conclude that this is intended, for Arcesilaus, who sought to disengage his followers from all judgments, may well have seen *adprobare* as a form of *adsentiri*. On the use of *probo* in Cicero's rhetorical works, see Glucker (1995: 129 n. 67). On the importance of this distinction to Carneades and likely also to Cicero, note Bett (1989: 74–75, 89).
29. *Ac.* 2.108–09; *Off.* 2.7.
30. To say this of Philo and Carneades is not intended to obscure the possibility that they embraced the criterion in different ways. On Carneades's *pithanon*, Bett (1989: esp. 71 f.)
31. One might conjecture that *probabile* brings more to the fore than *credibile* Cicero's interest in what one is able to approve (*probare*) and, thus, his interest, as opposed to that of "classical" skepticism, in judgments of what is likely true. Sedley (1983: 25, nn. 37 and 40) and Burnyeat (1983: 123) apparently regard "*probabile*" as an unfortunate translation. In a significant working paper, Burnyeat (1986: 6) indicates that his objection is not so much with what Cicero meant by *probabile* as with translations from that into the English "probable" or its equivalent and the concomitant modern meaning of "statistical frequency" or "evidential support" or "some combination of the two." Consider Lévy's limited disagreement (1992a: 104–06) with this observation of Burnyeat and his own discussion of *probabile*.
32. In this conception of probability's instinctual operation, Cicero and the New Academy, as he presents it, reflect "classical" skepticism's characteristic mode of simply accepting the inevitability of certain impressions, carrying us through the choices of ordinary life (Long and Sedley [1987:1.471; Tarrant: 1985: 16, 54 ff., 62, 65, 110]), and displaying a precursory notion of what Hume came to call natural or common belief (Olshewsky [1991] though he misses the force of *Fin.* 5.76 in his hesitancy [284] to find anything like Humean instinct in Cicero). Long and Sedley's (1987: 1.460) observation that "the most familiar modern strategy of simply not allowing philosophical scepticism to intrude upon daily life (e.g. Hume) is barely even contemplated in ancient scepticism" seems a misstatement, especially with respect to Cicero. Consider the interpretation of the end of *Academica*

later in this chapter. Long and Sedley's difficulty may be rooted in not fully appreciating that Hume seeks to explain "belief" as consistent with his comprehensive skepticism. Cicero's impact on Hume's thought clearly goes beyond the long acknowledged impact on his religious views. An argument for Hume's deep and thorough dependence on Cicero, and for the specific conclusion that Hume shares with Cicero a "moderate" rather than "extreme" skepticism, is found in Jones (1984: *passim* especially Introduction and Chap. 1), Laursen (1992: Chap. 6), and Olshewsky (1991). Allesandro Pajewski's recently completed study of Hume (2012) shows the depth of Cicero's impact on him and on many of the debates in which he engaged.

33. *Ac.* 2.66–68, 79 ff., 99; *Nat. D.* 1.12 and *Inv.* 1.57, where it is indicated that even the syllogism can yield no more than a probable conclusion. Here, too, Cicero reflects "classical" skepticism specifically in the comprehensiveness of its doubt; see Burnyeat (1984, esp. 239–40, 244) and Long (1988: 184, n. 14).

34. Note Lucretius's defense and counterattack against skepticism in *De Rerum Naturam*, iv. 469–521; a discussion of the passage is found in Sedley (1998: 85–90).

35. For discussion of the concept, *katalēpsis*, see *Ac.* 1.41; 2.17–18, 31, 144–45, and especially an old but very illuminating essay with respect to Cicero: Sparshott (1978: 284–86, 290 n. 1). Also, Hankinson (1997: 168–70, 181 n. 39, *passim*), Long and Sedley (1987: 1: 257), Long (1988: 183 n. 11, 186–87), Lévy (1992a: 98–100, on Cicero's distinctive use of the term); Sedley with observations on Cicero's refinement of the term in various uses (1998: 43–44), Frede (1987: 152 ff., 1999: 298–99), Tarrant (1985: 6 ff.), Shields (1994: 355 ff.), Barnes (1989: 72 f.), Striker (1997: 258–59 n. 1), specifically with respect to Cicero, Görler (1997: 47–50, 52 f., 56–57) and Algra (1997: 132 n. 60). Perception in this sense, of assured knowing, is not for the Stoics limited to sense perception.Michael Frede has argued that Stoic epistemological claims are not broad claims to knowledge on the part of the Stoics. The Stoics were in no mood to make such claims. But the Stoics did claim some expertise, and on the authority of this expertise tried to put forth views as to the nature and the material content of the knowledge Socrates had been looking for in vain. Hence the central role of the notion of a dogma and the charges of dogmatism in skeptical attacks on Stoicism (1987: 170, also 151, 176). One wonders if Frede's interesting distinction between being broadly dogmatic and being dogmatic only with respect to the conditions of knowledge applies to most Stoics. Cicero seems unaware of such a distinction and overall finds the Stoics dangerously dogmatic. See Chap. 3 in this book for some discussion of the nature of the knowledge claimed for the Stoic exemplar or Wiseman.

In support of Frede's view, at least to the extent of indicating which Stoic claims most disturbed the Academics, is the presentation of the views of the Stoic founder Zeno in *Academia Posteriora* and Cicero's *prooemium* in *Academica Priora*, specifically *Ac.* 2.7–9.
36. *Tusc.* 1.47. Here Cicero says that only after the soul's separation from the body will unhindered and true perception be possible. This statement is made by a person designated M in the text, probably standing for "Marcus" or "*magister.*" Internal evidence in *Tusc.* makes clear that M, the major voice throughout the disputations, is Cicero himself. As the following Chapter indicates, M, as Cicero *persona*, speaks to counter and refine a student's opinion and may not always reflect the view of Cicero the author. Apparently the M and A (*adolescens*) designations for the speakers in *Tusc.* are not found in the earliest manuscripts; see Douglas (1985: 16, n. 48, 1995: 198).
37. Burnyeat has overall persuasively argued that Descartes's doubt also differed from that of ancient skepticism because ancient skepticism never doubted the existence of an external world however much it doubted the reliability of the senses and the human ability to know the world (1982: esp. 18–19, 36–40). See Williams (1988: 87–88) for his differences with Burnyeat on this matter.
38. Alain Michel aptly observed, "Mais Cicéron n'est pas un Stoïcien. Il croit après Platon qu'on ne peut jamais dépasser l'opinion" (1992: 81).
39. A version of this objection is expressed by Lucullus apparently summarizing Antiochus's critique of Carneades in *Ac.* 2.33; see also *Ac.* 2.61–62. This problem seems foremost in mind when it appears that Hortensius is portrayed, in the work named after him, as aggressively challenging philosophy for explaining ambiguities with ambiguities and bringing an extinguished light into the darkness. (*Nam hoc est in tenebras extinctum lumen inferre*). Grilli (ed.), fr. 24, p. 25. Lucretius (iv. 469–85) makes a similar point. As one might expect, Augustine's objections to Academic skepticism seem to be drawn from Cicero himself.
40. Bett (1989: 74 f.) defends Carneades against the possible charge that his understanding of the criterion "appeared to reduce all action to something like instinctive behavior."
41. *Ac.* 2.32.
42. *Ac.* 1.44–45. The phrase attributed to Democritus is "*in profoundo*"; Arcesilaus, in the following sentence, is said to find all things "*in occulto,*" a phrase Cicero uses to describe his own view regarding truth in *Orat.* 237–38. Tarrant (1985: 58, 150 n. 29) observes the basis in the Platonic tradition for Cicero's and similar views.
43. Annas and Barnes (1985: 14) claim that Cicero, here, incorrectly sees Arcesilaus as "dogmatic" insofar as he is presented as asserting the truth

that knowledge is inaccessible. Shields (1994: 345 ff.) explores thoroughly and chiefly through the texts of Cicero the nature of Arcesilaus's redirection of the Academy and the manner in which he might have reconciled "dogmatism" with the withholding of assent or *epochē*; also, Annas (1994: 338–40). See *Att*.13.21 for Cicero's discussion of *epochē* as a usage of Carneades; also, Lévy's commentary on the passage (1992a: 97–98).

44. The dialectical strategy that Arcesilaus exemplifies is sometimes defended not, of course, in terms of it leading to any assertions of truth but in terms of its power to liberate from distorting dogmatisms. Though Cicero is not finally content with such negative skepticism, it should be noted that the Academic "classical" skepticism of Arcesilaus shares with the "classical" skepticism of Pyrrho a moral goal that is a type of integrity, if not peace, of life to which the suspension of belief is instrumental. See Sedley (1983: 14–16, 21–22), Long and Sedley (1987: 1.17 ff., 468–88), Frede (1987a: 185), Williams (1988: 547, 564–65) and Annas (1988: 103–08, 1986: 17 ff., 23 f). Burnyeat (1984: 241, 1982: 24 f.) captures this aspect of Pyrrhonism in concluding that its

> great recommendation...is that suspension of judgement on all questions as to what is true and false, good and bad, results in tranquillity—the tranquillity of detachment from striving and ordinary human concerns, of a life lived on after surrendering the hope of finding answers to the questions on which happiness depends. ... In its own way, Pyrrhonian scepticism offers a recipe for happiness to compete with the cheerful simplicity of Epicureanism and the nobler resignation of the Stoic sage.

Annas (1993: Chap. 17 and 430–31) describes this approach to happiness and questions its adequacy.

45. Williams (1988: 587) describes Pyrrhonian skepticism as standing "for the possibility of life without philosophy: for getting on with living while dispensing with large-scale explanations, justification or guiding principles." Also, Laursen (1992: 35). Nussbaum highlights the tension between skepticism as a "solution" to the problem of human happiness and the Socratic/Aristotelian striving for truth, noting at one point that skepticism entails not taking "control of life with thought" (1994: 321, also 304, 308 ff., 492–500).

46. In this, Cicero clearly stood with Philo if not also with a longer-standing practice of the Academy (Tarrant 1985: esp. 9–10, 43, 106–07). On the Academic commitment to searching for truth, see Annas (1983: 315), Shields (1994: 361), and Barnes (1989: 73–78). Lévy, while bringing to the fore concrete political reasons for Cicero's steadfast attraction to the

New Academy, emphasizes, too, the real issues of life that draw Cicero to the free, critical inquiry that characterizes the Academy (1992: 6121–22, 629 ff.)
47. *Div.* 2.3; also *Leg.* 1.32, 58; *Tusc.* 2.13, 28.
48. *Tusc.* 1.1, 64; also *Inv.* 1.1.
49. *Div.* 2.1, 4–5.
50. According to Tarrant (1985: 107), Cicero's expectations were widely shared in the Academy of his time where it was not thought "that life without assent would be desirable" nor "that it was possible to be a teacher of philosophy and offer no positive advice on how one should live one's life." Barnes (1989) confirms this.
51. *Leg.* 1.32, 37.
52. Earlier at *Leg.* 1.21, there is a playful indication by Atticus that the conversation is going in directions not welcome to his Epicurean associates; also Görler (1995: 87–88).
53. The issue of the adequacy and fairness of Cicero's representations of the Epicureans (to be considered more fully in Chap. 4) has been raised at various times since Cicero wrote. Cicero acknowledges that he is being challenged in this respect, *Tusc.* 3.37–38, 49–51. Tarrant (1985: 127, 129) describes the philosophical context for such a dismissal, observing that "there was not enough common ground between Academic and Epicurean for a good dialogue to develop, nor enough mutual respect." On the Epicurean rejection of Socrates as an exemplum of the philosophical life, see Vander Waerdt (1994: 7–8 and n. 24).
54. *Leg.* 1.38–39. At *Tusc.* 3.51, Cicero has M remark that if the Epicureans hold the truth, it is not such as can be publicly stated in general or in politically responsible bodies and it is not a truth that will win public acclaim. See also, *De Or.* 3.64; *Tusc.* 1.24; *Fin.* 2.74; *Brut.*131. A fuller discussion of Cicero's suggestion that the Epicureans may be speaking the truth and his banning them only "for a while" or "for now" from all the bonds of political community follows in Chap. 3.
55. *Rep.* (3.8) also reveals an uneasiness with the contribution to the discussion from the Academic school even while the method characteristic of the Academics is embraced. At 3.32, Laelius apparently reacts to the speech (*oratio*) of Carneades by saying that it is "monstrous" (*immanis*), that Carneades probably does not believe it, and that it should not be heard by the young. Noting this, however, does not constitute an endorsement of Schofield's suggestion that Cicero's Academic attachment is not in evidence in *Rep.* and *Leg.* (1986: 47). Lévy's discussion of *Rep.* 3 in this context (1992: 515 ff.) is more compelling. My reasons for this judgment follow in the text and notes.
56. It would seem from what has already been said (especially in preceding notes) that Arcesilaus should be more feared because he is more akin to a

Pyrrhonist and that Carneades is more akin to Cicero, but both, after all, are questioners, dialectical probers. Cicero does not want his Carneadean self forward at this point. Furthermore, as Brittain has observed (2006: xxiv, xxvii n. 46), "our sources for Arcesilaus and Carneades disagree radically about the form and extent of their scepticism" and the consistency of their "radical scepticism...remains controversial." Consider that the views of Carneades are, apparently, known only in oral traditions: see Ferrary (1977: 153–55).

57. That Cicero did not affiliate with the New Academy during the 50s is argued by Glucker (1988). He concluded (53), "Cicero, then, changed his affiliations twice: once, from a youthful enthusiasm for Philo of Larissa and Academic Skepticism to Antiochus' 'Old Academy'—albeit with reservations and with a lingering respect for the Sceptical tradition—and then, some time in 45B.C., back to the Scepticism of Carneades and Philo." Working independently of Glucker but reaching essentially the same conclusion in this matter is Steinmetz (1989: 1–21). Glucker characterizes Steinmetz's work in relationship to his own a few years later (1992: 134–38). Paul MacKendrick (1989:125, n. 14), while citing, it appears, an earlier unpublished version of Glucker's initial "Philosophical Affiliations" essay, observes that Cicero reverted to "dogmatism in the 60s and 50s." Likewise, in 1986 and drawing from and supporting Glucker's unpublished paper, Schofield (1986: 47) contends, (it seems to me without sufficient nuance) that in the *Rep.* and *Leg.*, which Cicero wrote in the 50s, "there was no sign of allegiance to the sceptical Academy." The most compelling evidence Glucker cites for such a switch is the exchange between Varro and Cicero in *Ac.* 1.13. Here Cicero is explicitly asked about his having left the Old Academy for the New and responds in a playful way of the right to move from the Old to the New as Antiochus had migrated from the New to the Old. Then Cicero, with apparently more seriousness, reminds Varro of Philo's view that there are not two Academies. Later in *Ac.* 1.43, Varro calls on Cicero to speak as one who abandons (*desciscis*) the old way for that of Arcesilaus and thus is able to explain the fundamental break (*discidium*) in the Academy. I think that these passages in *Ac.* 1 are calling attention to Cicero's association with the position of Arcesilaus perceived as a break in the Academic position rather than as a personal movement of Cicero from one school or strain to another. Cicero, in other words, is called upon to speak for the "secession" movement even though he is himself inclined to see its continuity with Socratic foundations. In other words, he holds steadily to Philo's view, and that which characterized the "Fourth Academy" (Tarrant), that there is a single Academy. There clearly is a tradition of understanding Cicero's philosophical affiliation that is supportive of Glucker's view. It is evident in John of Salisbury's *Policraticus* (prologue and vii. 1), where he twice speaks of Cicero turning

to the New Academy late in his life (1990: Nederman trans. 7149–50). John Henry Newman's study as a young man of Cicero (1873: 247, 271) indicates a then prevalent belief that late in life Cicero "relapsed into the sceptical tenets...." On the other hand, Glucker himself brings together (1988:38–39 n.18) much of the nineteenth and twentieth century scholarship that essentially concluded that Cicero was an Academic skeptic throughout his life, and he once interpreted the passages (1978: 104–05) at issue in this note essentially as I have done. Glucker also softens his thesis in a note by observing (1988: 53 n. 60) that "even during his Antiochean period, Cicero did not go so far as a wholesale repudiation of the Skeptical Academy." Then in his revisit to his initial piece and with exemplary openness to argument and evidence, Glucker draws attention to Cicero's taking Antiochean positions in his late period of identification with the New Academy (1992: 138). This brings him very close to those who are making the case in recent scholarship for the life-long continuity of Cicero's loyalty to the New Academy—a loyalty to an Academy that Cicero's sees as allowing him to take positions that are appropriately tested.Such scholarship seems persuasive and is, in some cases, specifically supportive of the interpretation of the key passage in *Leg.* in this chapter. Lévy (1992: 116–17, 126, 515 where he specifically focuses on *Leg.* 1.39, 629 ff.) and Görler (1995: *passim* but especially 107 ff.). At 111–12, he observes that while Cicero "was a sceptic continuously and incessantly," his skepticism is more in the foreground in his later works. In this vein, I think Cicero in his last years sees the need to be more open and explicit in defending how his Academic method can be combined with substantive or "dogmatic" conclusions. See also Griffin (1995: 334 f. and especially n. 42), also her later work (1997: 7, n. 24), and Englert (1990: 120 n. 13). Thorsrud (2012: *passim*), in what is likely the most recent consideration of this question, argues persuasively not only that Cicero was always an Academic skeptic but also that he was always a mitigated skeptic.
58. It is hard to factor in to this analysis the significance of the fact that the *Leg.* did not appear in a public way or was not published in Cicero's lifetime. It does not appear in Cicero's review of his philosophical writings including *Rep.* in *Div.* 2, less than two years before his death.
59. *Leg.* 1.36.
60. Titus Pomponius Atticus is here addressed by his forename.
61. The beginning of this book includes an observation (*Leg.* 1.4) by Cicero that some traditions and beliefs can be inquired into too diligently.
62. Hortensius, the orator-statesman in Cicero's *Hortensius*, appears to have seen philosophy as closely associated with a disabling skepticism and too far removed from a love of truth, which is the basis of wisdom and is granted to human nature itself (Grilli [1962: 8], also frs. 51–52, p. 31). Ruch, in his commentary on *Hortensius* (1958: 169), argues that skepticism was not

defended as philosophical in this work though the challenges and struggles of philosophy were presented as great.
63. *Ac.* 2.63.
64. *Ac.* 2.64. At *Fin.* 3.8–9, Cicero also refers to Lucullus with much admiration, including the observation that he had been one in thought or opinion (*sententia conjunctus*) with Lucullus. In his correspondence, Cicero shows himself aware that the actual historical Lucullus did not have the philosophical expertise he attributes to him in this dialogue; see Griffin (1989: 14) and Zetzel (1972: 175–76).
65. *Ac.* 2.10. See Burnyeat's discussion of the term and passage (1997: 278–79, nn. 4–7).
66. Görler (1997: 37 f).
67. *Ac.* 1.13–14; 2.10; *Att.* 13.16,19,22. These provide the basis for the conclusions drawn about the structure and personnel of the *Catulus*. See Glucker (1978: 86, n. 236) for a discussion of the possibility that Cicero suppressed the *Catulus*.
68. This discussion is set at the villa of Hortensius at Bauli not far from Cumae where, at the villa of Catulus, the first day's discussion occurred. Hortensius, like Catulus, is a prominent public figure; he is especially known for his oratorical ability, admired by Cicero and his chief rival for the crown in oratory in their lifetimes. Hortensius, as noted, has championed Antiochus on the first day; so the discussion has moved from the home of a defender of Carneades to one of a defender of Antiochus. There is no evident significance to this move save, perhaps, that the first day was, apparently, chiefly given to a defense of Carneades just as the second is given to the exposition and defense of the thought of Antiochus. There is perhaps significance in this initial version of *Academica* taking the same cast of characters utilized in the *Hortensius*. If Hortensius was converted to philosophy, as appears to be the case in the work by his name, the *Academica* may have been partly conceived as exploring how the conversion to philosophy as love of wisdom is threatened by skepticism.
69. Griffin (1997: 7); on the relationship of *Fin.* and *Ac.*, see the excellent discussion of Lévy (1992: 2–3 and Part IV).
70. Interpretations of the end of *Ac.*, in varying ways partly overlapping and partly differing from the one that follows in this chapter, are Görler (1997: 54 ff.), Lévy (1992: 177 ff., 274–75), Olshewsky (1991: 283), and Burnyeat (1997: 300 ff.)
71. *Ac.* 2.148. The variant textual readings for *comprobans* as *non probans* or *improbans* would turn around the meaning of the first part of the sentence and have Catulus disapproving suspension of assent with respect to all matters. This turnabout, though it would result in an internally consistent— albeit uncharacteristic—statement of the Academic position here, would not affect the interpretation that follows above, concerning how "*vehe-*

menter adsentior" is itself out of character with the kind of skeptical affirmation articulated and defended earlier in this work. In fact, *comprobans* does accord better with the mainline Academic teaching as summarized by Cicero at *Ac.* 2.104. See also Olshewsky (1991: 283 n. 23), Görler (1997: 54 n. 29), and Lévy (1992: 274 n. 97).

72. Striker's comments on Cicero's use of *adsentiri* and *adprobare* (note 28 above) only emphasize the startling character of the Academic position being expressed in the term *vehementer adsentior*. Startling though it is, we have been partly prepared for it by Cicero's confession earlier (*Ac.* 2.66–67) that he, not being the model Wiseman, gives way to assent. Frede comments on the dogmatism of this expression (1987b: 212–13, 215–16) and uses it to illustrate his distinction between classical and dogmatic skepticism (above, n.15). He calls Cicero a dogmatic skeptic but one aware, as the close of *Ac.* 2 indicates, of the classical form of skepticism and thus of another way of interpreting the Carneadean tradition (218, 220–21). It does not seem necessary to interpret Catulus's *vehementer adsentior* as Frede does (212–13) as being attributed to Carneades, or Cicero's subsequent remarks as a statement denying that this is Carneades's view. For a discussion set within the Pyrrhonist tradition, of assenting with the assurance that Catulus manifests, see Long and Sedley (1987: 1.472–73). See Thorsrud's wrestling with this passage (2012: 151 n. 23).

73. *Ac.* 2.59–60. Yet Cicero, on at least one occasion, seemed to see Arcesilaus slipping into "dogmatism" in the same way.

74. *Ac.* 2.10. *Ac.* 2.61 indicates that Lucullus is drawn to one of the less dogmatic formulations of Antiochus's teaching.

75. In *Brut.* 315, Cicero speaks of Antiochus as "the noblest and most prudent philosopher of the Old Academy." See also *Leg.* 1.54. Here in the *Academica*, Cicero speaks of the love between himself and Antiochus, refers to him, when addressing Lucullus, with the friendly if not intimate possessive *noster*, and describes him as "the most refined and acute philosopher" within his direct experience, *Ac.* 2.113,137,143. Barnes (1989: 61) finds Cicero a "profound student" of Antiochus but properly cautions that this and "mutual love" do not imply "philosophical assent." "Cicero was no Antiochean." Earlier, Horsley (1978) treated Antiochus as a key source for Cicero, and Kesler thought (1985:67 n. 38) that Horsley went too far in this.

76. With mostly the *Academica* in mind, Schmitt (1972: 84) notes the genuine philosophical or inquiring character of Cicero's dialogues in contrast with scholastic disputations. Griffin (1997: 5) looks at the work as setting the "aporetic tone" for the whole cycle of Cicero's major works.

77. Before the closing segment of *Ac.* 2, but near the end of his speech while treating issues in logic involving the Stoics and others, Cicero's frustration

with such highly refined discussions devoid of practical import is evident. At *Fin.* 5.76–77 Cicero, in his own name, backs away from a discussion of the differences between his skeptical approach to knowing and the way of the Stoics. He claims that this does not amount to a significant difference (*magna dissensio*) and would require "a very lengthy and quite contentious debate." At *Off.* 1.19, Cicero warned against giving too much effort to inquiry into matters obscure, difficult, and unnecessary. In *Fin.* 5.15, Piso makes the point that there are matters one can tolerate leaving unsettled or unknown, but one must not accept ignorance on the issue of the chief good. At *De Or.* 2.17–18, Cicero has his major character in the dialogue criticize the "Greek" tendency to enter into subtle arguments on unnecessary points without sensitivity to the occasion. Diderot's similarity to Cicero's stance is worth noting. See Lom (2001: 61–62).
78. On the issue of the criterion, Cicero seems, then, to follow what Bett describes as the middle way of Carneades (1989: 74 f., 86, 89).
79. *Div.* 2.1–4.
80. Discussions of the *Academica* in Cicero's letters indicate that his reworking was primarily motivated by his felt need to involve Varro in the dialogue and thereby pay a debt and a form of tribute to him. That this recasting did not involve a significant rewriting of the dialogue is Glucker's position (1978: 414–15), though his thorough excursus in the same place on "Sources for Cicero's *Lucullus*," 391–423, contain indications of Cicero's own struggle with what it means to follow Carneades and Cicero's elevation of the greater importance of *Finibus*. More weight needs to be given to Cicero's claim (*Att.* 326) that he used "unsurpassable care" (*sed ita accurate, et nihil posset supra*) in his reworking. Additional discussion of the two versions of *Academica* and the process of composition are found in Lévy (1992: 4, 129 ff.) and Griffin (1997).
81. Görler (1997: 38–39, 44–45) discusses Cicero's relative disinterest in the complexities of epistemological issues.
82. Cicero's concluding wish for future discussions on goods and their contraries (*Ac.* 2.147) has been preceded by clear indications that the most important work for philosophy, in the Academic manner, is inquiry into that which gives form and direction to life. *Ac.* 2.65,129,132.
83. *Off.* 1.4–7; 3.33; *Fin.* 1.11; 5.14–16 (here Piso is giving the Peripatetic position with which Cicero, on this matter, clearly agrees).
84. *Hortensius* (Grilli 1962: frs. 58–59, p. 33). *Fin.* 5.86 sees Piso recalling the universal desire for happiness; also, see *Fin.* 2.42, 86. Both *Finibus* and *Tusculans* in their entirety assume that all seek happiness as the supreme good; the primary issue is in what happiness consists.
85. Nussbaum (1994:15, 42, *passim*) treats the "broad and deep agreement [among the Hellenistic philosophical schools] that the central motivation

for philosophizing is the urgency of human suffering, and that the goal of philosophy is human flourishing, or *eudamonia*."
86. *Tusc.* 5.10; *Brut.* 31. That Cicero's appreciation for "the Socratic turn" is found in its providing a basis and goal for philosophy, not in its confining philosophy to moral and political concerns, is argued in Nicgorski (1991). Schofield is right (1986: 49 n. 5) overall on Cicero as he cites *Ac.* 2.127–28 in contending that Cicero is not opposed to studying physics as some scholars have suggested. See the precedent in Stoicism, Long and Sedley (1987:1, 60A at 309).
87. Glucker (1995: 130 ff.), following Sextus Empiricus on the Academic tradition, writes of a "second criterion" applicable in inquiries and distinct from that applicable in sense perception. He considers speculative ("speculates about" or "considers speculatively"?) whether Cicero himself extended the Academic procedure to compare the positions of philosophical schools to determine that which is *probabile* or *veri simile*. William (1988: 561 ff.) discusses the two criteria in Sextus. Also Tarrant (1985: 110).
88. *Ac.* 2.66. See Görler (1995: 91–96) on the different kinds of "rational" testing operative in Cicero. Also Algra (1997: 132, nn. 58, 59; 138); I am not in agreement with Algra's reading (133–34), suggesting that the ethics section in *Ac.* is approached from an epistemic perspective.
89. Cicero seems to regard Epicureanism as "the philosophy" easiest to comprehend and easiest to dismiss. *Fin.* 1.13, 27; 3.1–3; *Tusc.* 2.7; 4.6–7; 5.108; *Ac.* 1.5. Also, Inwood (1990: 143–44). As in *Nat. D.* where Cicero is systematically testing the positions of the major schools, so here in *Fin.*, Cicero takes up the Epicureans first. This may be because of the widespread popularity of the school in Cicero's time (*Fin.* 1.13; *Tusc.* 4.6–7). This popularity seems to be related to their appeal to pleasure and, perhaps, especially the subtle pleasures entailed in their masking pleasure in the garb of the virtues, the attraction to the good and the pleasurable both being satisfied, *Fin.* 2.44–45. Cicero's decisiveness, however, with respect to the Epicureans gives his treatment of them something of the character of "let's get it out of the way, so serious philosophical discussion can begin."
90. The moral horizon's prior or fundamental character for Cicero seems to be suggested in the Latin terminology: what is approved (*probatus*) is that which is *probus* and represents *probitas*, that which is choiceworthy or excellent, the most decent course. Woolf (2015: 86, 140) seems aware of a verification standard in Cicero that might be called "wholistic."
91. Neal Wood's treatment of Cicero's political philosophy (1988) takes this approach; see especially 45, 79, 96–97, 160, 208–09.
92. In this respect Charles Kesler's description of Cicero's approach to philosophy should be considered: He describes it as a "learning from gentle-

manship in the act of questioning it.... Philosophy would be transformed into political philosophy" (1985: 102).
93. The actual holding of office and exercising of leadership may not be a requisite for this perspective, but Cicero clearly sees it as an advantage for attaining or maintaining this perspective, *Rep.* 1.12–13, 31–37; *Leg.* 3.14. Glucker tends away from attributing any specific political dimension to *consulares philosophi* and to understand the phrase as meaning "first-rate philosophers" or the family of Socratic followers (1965: 229–234). Glucker is responding to Ruch (1959: 99–102). In these pieces and in Ruch's edition of the *Hortensius* (1958: 149–51), one finds some consideration of all of Augustine's uses of this concept attributed to Cicero. In the light of these *consular* philosophers being seen as marked by a notable integrity (*honestate*) and their positive inclination on the question of personal immortality, they may well be intended to represent a philosophy, or approach to philosophy, that considers thoroughly and sensitively the fullness of the experience of human life. Of course, to be or to have been a consul is not necessarily to be truly *consular* (*Phil.* 7.4). It seems that they are intended to be contrasted with "plebian philosophers" (*Tusc.* 1.55) or "small-minded philosophers" (*minuti*—*Sen.* 85), among whom Cicero would have placed at least "run-of-the mill" Epicureans.
94. The practical perspective in Cicero's thought bears a resemblance to the fundamental criterion of reasonableness, *eúlogon*, in the Stoic and Academic schools. Exploring this and differentiating Cicero's practical perspective must start with the work of Couissins (1983: especially 47 ff.); Burnyeat (1983: "Introduction," especially 7), in his Carneades paper (1986: especially 61 ff.), Bett (1989: 63 ff.), and Long and Sedley (1987: 1.69 B, E at 450–53 and 458–59). Glucker (1995: 137) speculates that in philosophical judgments, Cicero's effective criterion is "what accords better with what happens in real life—even where it may be logically inconsistent ...." Cicero's thought can be seen as a part of a movement to get over the long tension rooted in epistemology between Stoics and Academics, a tension that surfaced between Cicero's teachers Philo and Antiochus, a tension that Hankinson (1997: especially 212–13) suggests is quite fully resolved in Galen, more than a century after Cicero. Lévy differentiates (1992: 289–90, 491) Cicero's criterion from *eúlogon* and *pithanon,* claiming to be unable to find in these concepts a confidence in the reality of truth; for Cicero the criterion is not to imply some kind of relativism with respect to truth (1992a: 105).
95. Again consider the appropriateness of the Kesler characterization in note 92 above.
96. Note how this operates for Piso as presented by Cicero in *Fin.*5.16–22. See also *Rep.* 1.12–13, 31–37; *Leg.* 3.14. Consider Aristotle in the *Nicomachean Ethics* (1151a15–19):For virtue and vice respectively preserve and destroy

the first principle, and in actions the final cause is the first principle, as the hypotheses are in mathematics; neither in that case is it argument that teaches the first principles, nor is it so here—virtue either natural or produced by habituation is what teaches right opinion about the first principle.

97. "Prudence," or at least a formal analog of prudence in the Aristotelian sense, which appears to be Cicero's sense, is a key notion in Hellenistic philosophy. Consider the following from the writings of Epicurus: "Of all this the beginning and the greatest good is prudence. Therefore prudence is even more precious than philosophy, and it is the natural source of all the remaining virtues: it teaches the impossibility of living pleasurably without living prudently, honorably and justly ...." *Letter to Menoeceus*, 127–32 in Long and Sedley (1987: 1.113–15). For Zeno of Citium and the Stoic tradition on prudence, see also Long and Sedley, 1.377 ff. On the "hedonic calculus" as "practical wisdom" in the Epicurean tradition, see Stokes (1995: 153, 163 ff., 168).

98. *Off.* 3.71 and *Fin.* 5.67–68 where prudence is explicitly defined.

99. At *Tusc.* 3.37, prudence is personified and portrayed as making the choice regarding what constitutes good and happy life.

100. Sextus Empiricus (1967: I.231, p. 134). Stough (1969: 50) describes the Pyrrhonic solution to the issue of the criterion of truth for practical purposes as "merely following the dictates of social convention without commitment or belief...."

101. Sextus Empiricus, 1967a. VII.181–85, pp. 97–101. For Sextus, then, Carneades and the New Academy are seen on the "dogmatic" side of the skeptical tradition; Glucker (1995: 135, n. 84). Also, see Nussbaum (1994: 295) on Sextus and the distinction between Methodist and Empiricist schools of medicine.

102. *Ac.* 2.123–24,127–28. See also *Tusc.* 1.17, 48, and 78, which reveal Cicero's awareness about how his way of probability stands in contrast to an insolence in philosophy, claims of wisdom and overconfidence in obscure matters. Perhaps, Cicero must, above all, distinguish his philosophical response to skepticism from that of the Stoics because he shares so much with them. Görler (1997: 51) considers how a broad understanding of Cicero's probability criterion can lead him to accept, or at least respect, certain Stoic views in cosmology and physics. Hookway concludes his book (1990: 240) on skepticism by wisely observing that "[a] philosophical response to scepticism, which recognizes the contingency of our confidence without denying its legitimacy, must undermine the attractiveness of that [skeptical] project." Cicero does seem to have such a philosophical approach and not merely a psychological one. Cicero seems to fit, then, the eloquent description of the skeptic which Frede gave (1987a: 200): "The

skeptic saw his task as, on the one hand, not giving in to the temptation to expect more from reason and philosophical thinking than these can provide without, on the other hand, coming to hold reason in contempt." It is doubtful that Frede regards Cicero or Philo as such a skeptic; much depends, of course, on what is "more" than "reason and philosophical thinking...can provide."

103. Consider *Nat. D.* 1.60, where Cotta as a spokesman for Academic skepticism illustrates the comparatively greater difficulty in matters of physics and theology of even making assured judgments of probability. Earlier (*Nat. D.* 1.12), Cicero, in his own name, describes the capacity of an Academic to draw wisdom for the direction of life with the standard of "the probable." See the elevation of the distinction between that in physics and that in morals in Ferrary (1974: 749–50, n. 7).

104. Above, p. 24, n. 82.

105. *Fin.* 2.15, 37. Since human attunements or orientations measure what constitutes happiness, one can understand Cicero saying, as he apparently did say, that to get what one wishes is misery rather than happiness if one wishes for what is unbefitting (*non deceat...non oporteat*), *Hortensius* (Grilli, 1962: fr. 59a, p. 35).

106. Brittain (2006: 111) translates fragment 33 from *Academica* as uttered by Cicero who is using the standard of what is persuasive or truth-like and saying "a wise person should be an investigator of nature, not a creator of terms...." With respect to God's existence and the nature of the gods, David Fott's interpretation of *Nat. D.* (2012: 157) draws attention to how Cicero formulates his judgment at the beginning and end of this dialogue: "In his prologue Cicero observes that most people have said that gods exist; and that view, Cicero remarks, is the one 'that most appears to be true and to which we all come, led by nature' (*Nat. D.* 1.2). Cicero judges at the beginning of the work, as well as at the end." Ronald Beiner drew to my attention an important observation of Alasdair MacIntyre, which characterizes the relative assurance of moral judgments in ancient and medieval thought in a way that would seem to encompass clearly the Cicero emerging in this book. MacIntyre wrote that it is distinctly "modern" and not faithful to the structures of ancient and medieval thought to see "ethics and politics" as

> peripheral modes of enquiry, dependent in key part on what is independently established by epistemology and by the natural sciences (semantics has now to some degree usurped the place of epistemology). But in ancient and medieval thought, ethics and politics afford light to the other disciplines as much as vice versa. Hence from that standpoint, which I share, it is not the case that *first* I must decide

> whether some theory of human nature or cosmology is true and only *secondly* pass a verdict upon an account of the virtues which is 'based' upon it. Rather, if we find compelling reasons for accepting a particular view of the virtues and the human telos, that in itself will place constraints on what kind of theory of human nature and what kind of cosmology are rationally acceptable.

  Cited in Beiner (1989: 38–39).
107. *Div.* 2.1. At *Tusc.* 2.4–5, it is clear that Cicero distinguishes the "selectivity" of his Academic approach from the drive for consistency and the obstinacy of the other philosophical schools. One might say that philosophy in the Academic school of Cicero, or in the Socratic sense, is paradoxically seen as distinct from the school-approach to philosophy. See also *Tusc.* 4.7; 5.33–34; *Ac.* 2.114–15,119–20; *Inv.* 2.5.
108. Harris (1961: 32). In a similar vein, Görler (1995: 102) sees "Ciceronian skepticism," unlike "Carneadean," as a "constructive skepticism." Recall Barnes's distinction between the eclectic and the syncretic, noted in n. 10 of the Introduction to this book.
109. Burnyeat observes (1982: 25, 30, 40 and n. 57) that the "practical orientation" of both Pyrrhonian and Academic skepticism means that the existence of the external world and one's impressions of it do not become problematic for living. He writes, "[T]hat ancient skepticism even at its most extreme did not seriously question that one can walk around in the world." Earlier: "It goes without saying that a recipe for happiness is addressed to people who can live in the world and enjoy their happiness." An apt formulation, especially as it pertains to uncertainty at the level of perception, is found in an eighteenth century observation by Richard Bentley (1743: 249) on the force of the probable for Cicero's practical decisions:

    > [Cicero's] *Probable* had the same influence on his Belief, the same force on his Life and Conduct, as the Others *Certain* had on theirs. Nay within his own Breast he thought it as much Certain as they; but he was to keep to the *Academic* Stile; which solely consisted in that Point, that nothing was allow'd *Certum, comprehensum, perceptum, ratum, firmum, fixum;* but our highest attainment was *Probabile et Verisimile.*

110. *Tusc.* 4.82.

CHAPTER 2

The Critical and Rhetorical Modes of Philosophy

For if wisdom is attainable, we should not only overtake it but also delight in it; and if this is difficult, there is nonetheless no limit whatsoever on the pursuit of truth save the finding of it, and growing weary in inquiry is base when what is sought is the most beautiful of objects. (Cicero, *Fin.* 1.3)

…the relieving of anxieties, fears and desires, which is the greatest fruit from all of philosophy.

And philosophy is cultivation of the soul; it extracts vices by the roots and readies souls for seeds and commits to souls those seeds, or as might be said, sows those which upon maturity will bear the greatest fruit.

O philosophy, guide of life, pursuer of virtue and expeller of vice! (Cicero, *Tusc.* 1.119; 2.13; 5.5)

Cicero appears to have two distinct expectations or goals, and, hence, two basic tasks for philosophy. Both are represented in the passages just above. One of those expectations and tasks defines philosophy as the seeking of the truth. The truth is understood to be any and all truth but especially the comprehensive truth or truth of the whole, and the process of seeking is taken to be an unsettling, contentious, and arduous one. In this respect Cicero's understanding of philosophy is one with that of many philosophers from Plato to the present. He is aware of the difficulties and painful struggle of a climb from the cave to that goal of the apprehension of truth.[1] Cicero's commitment to this task appears to account for his allegiance to the philosophical school of the New Academy. This school's method of inquiry and qualified skepticism constitute for Cicero, as we have seen, the most authentic philosophical way.[2]

The second expectation and task for philosophy is to guide and comfort in the conduct of life. Besides the agricultural metaphor of cultivating the soul, planting the seeds of virtue, and weeding out vice, Cicero is also drawn to that of the healing art of medicine to portray this task. Philosophy is the physician or medicine of the soul.[3] In a literal vein, Cicero describes philosophy as the art of life, the most fruitful (*amplissima*) of arts, providing the discipline for living well.[4] In every time of life, writes Cicero in *De Senectute*, philosophy can free a person from anxiety.[5] Cicero's emphasis on philosophy as a guide and comforter probably accounts for some of his difficulties in commanding respect as a philosopher. The tension between this expectation for philosophy and the often unsettling critical process necessary for the pursuit of truth was not lost on Cicero, as was seen in the previous chapter.

Cicero seems, then, to be something more or something less than a philosopher of the New Academic strain. Cicero's ambivalence about the Academic approach to philosophy can be seen to reflect a personal tension between the two tasks for philosophy—discovering truth and guiding life—and, likewise, between two modes for practicing philosophy deriving respectively from the two tasks. These modes will be called here the critical mode and the rhetorical mode. The latter should be understood to include philosophy in what might be called the exhortative and the consolatory modes.[6]

Despite his awareness of the tension, Cicero is able to embrace both the tasks and both the modes. His explicit model in this is Socrates, who is perceived by Cicero and most others of his time as the source and ultimate authority of the Academy to which Cicero gives his allegiance. Cicero, in other words, accepts Academic skepticism in a Socratic framework. Socrates is for Cicero an instantiation of the critical doubting and questing spirit of philosophy, with the realization of the fruit of philosophy in truths of a way of life.

Cicero understands himself as a Roman Plato, not in the sense that he claims the philosophical acumen and range of Plato but in the sense that his objective in writing philosophical works is to perpetuate Socratic philosophy for the Latin-reading Romans in the way Plato did it for the Greeks. Though Cicero takes notice that Socrates himself did not leave writings and that earlier Roman Socratics fostered philosophy more by their lives than by writings, he takes up as his mission "to elucidate in

Latin letters that old philosophy stemming from Socrates" (*philosophiamque veterem illam a Socrate ortam Latinis litteris illustrare*).[7] That "old philosophy," as manifested in its founder Socrates, consists in a method of inquiry and a way of life. Method of inquiry and way of life are the bases of Cicero's attraction to Socrates.

Socratic Method

At the start of *Finibus* 2, Cicero makes it clear that even this philosophical school of his choice, the New Academy, now falls short of complete fidelity to the Socratic model of good method. It was not Socrates, reports Cicero, but his frequent opponents the Sophists who developed the tradition of the formal lecture or exposition (*schola*). For he (Socrates) followed the custom of eliciting the opinions of those with whom he was conversing by thorough questioning, so that whatever seemed so to him appeared in his response to the answers they gave. Although this manner of philosophy was subsequently abandoned, Arcesilaus revived it, making it the practice that those who wish to hear him not put questions to him but say for themselves what they thought; then when they had spoken, he argued to the contrary.[8]

Cicero observes that Arcesilaus, whose renewed Socratic manner attracts him, has not prevailed among the philosophers of the day. Their practice, even in the Academic school of Cicero's time, is to give lengthy monologic discourses (*perpetuae orationes*) in response to a student's question or expression of an opinion. Cicero complains that this does not produce a real statement of contrary views. Better to do what Torquatus, the Epicurean spokesman in the first book of *Finibus* is made to do, namely, not just to announce a contrary opinion or put a question but also to develop the contrary view by giving reasons for it. A full response to Torquatus, then, would result in developed statements of contrary views, what might justly be called the adversarial approach. This approach characterizes not only the *Finibus* but also Cicero's *Natura Deorum* and *Divinatione*.[9]

Not all of Cicero's works, however, are characterized by providing for a full and continuous statement of contrary views. The *Tusculans* explicitly and largely takes the form of the Greek *schola*, the monologic response to a student's question, which Cicero complained about in *Finibus*.[10] This characteristic of the *Tusculans* is explicitly noted by Cicero in the early pages of his *De Fato*. He confesses that the *Tusculans*, though following "the Academic custom of disputing whatever is proposed," are not in the preferred form, which mark his works on the nature of the gods and divination.[11] Cicero, nonetheless, associates the procedure in the *Tusculans* with Socrates by describing it as "the old Socratic way of arguing against the opinion of another; for in this way Socrates thought that what is most likely true (*veri simillimum*) is readily able to be discerned."[12]

The important statement at the start of *Finibus* 2 also makes it clear that Cicero finds yet another form of discourse even more preferable, before both that of the full and continuous adversarial speeches utilized in *Finibus, Natura Deorum,* and *Divinatione* and that of lengthy monologic discourses in response to questions or opinions as illustrated in the *Tusculans*. Observing how delighted he was with the long speech of Torquatus (*perpetua oration*), Cicero remarks that it is

> nonethelesss more beneficial to stop at each point and assess what a person is conceding and what he is denying and to draw what you wish from those concessions toward an appropriate conclusion. For when a speech like a rushing stream (*quasi torrens oratio*) is moved along, it is apt to drag along all sorts of things, yet one cannot hold onto or save anything, nor in any way check such a flowing declamation.[13]

This apparently highest preference of Cicero—this preference for real dialogue, for short answers and responses,[14] for what we would call "give and take" or probing dialectic—is associated with Socrates not only in the passage from *Finibus* 2 quoted just above but also in Cicero's earliest extant writing, his *De Inventione*. Here, when explaining Socrates's customary form of argument by analogy and induction, and by gaining consent each step of the way, Cicero observes that "Socrates was especially drawn to this type of exchange (*sermo*) because he wanted to make no argument of his own" but preferred to establish whatever he could from what his interlocutor had to concede to him.[15]

Since Cicero explicitly asserts the Socratic character of three different dialogue forms (the *schola* in response to questions or statements as in the *Tusculans*, the full and continuous statement of contrary views as exemplified in *Finibus*, and the preferred short exchanges which appear here and there in Cicero's works but never dominantly characterize one), one can specify and understand better the presumed Socratic dimension by isolating what is common to the three and examining the hierarchy among the three that allows Cicero to say in one instance and to imply in another that one approach is more Socratic than another. The common feature and apparent essence of the Socratic approach is that the speaker (Socrates) or writer (Cicero) proffers no view of his own and seeks to facilitate a free and informed judgment by the listener or reader on the matter under consideration. Thus, even in that minimally Socratic form, that of the *schola*, an argument is made against a given opinion or in response to a question in the interest of discerning what is most likely true. The argument does not necessarily represent the view of its proponent. In the maximally Socratic form of close dialogue and short exchanges, the primary speaker or teacher is limited to asking questions and allowing the intelligence and perception of the one questioned to attain whatever conclusions can be reached. The questions would, of course, presumably directly challenge assumptions implicit in definitions or statements insofar as that is warranted and as such statements are made.

It seems, then, that Cicero understands the three distinct dialogue forms to be true to Socrates in that all involve a way of teaching and inquiry in which the teacher does not proffer his own view or use authority otherwise to interfere with the listener's judgment.[16] One form is more Socratic than the other in the degree to which it facilitates a free and informed judgment by the listener. The *schola* does this least of all, for only one position is developed, though it tends to be that which the listener needs most to hear, namely the contrary of his own position or of that to which he is inclined. Full and continuous speeches on both sides of an issue provide an even better condition for a listener being informed and being able to compare arguments. And finally and best of all, the questioning and testing each step of the way in an argument provides the opportunity for forcing a close comparison of arguments and drawing out of what can be said on behalf of each position.

Socratic Irony and Socratic Skepticism

If the very core or basis of the Socratic method is, as Cicero perceives it, Socrates's refusal to assert his own view and authority, the legendary Socratic irony is understandable. That irony would be necessarily entailed in teaching properly. Socrates, then, and any teacher who would follow his method must be a dissembler (*simulator*), as Cicero terms Socrates in the *Officiis*.[17] In another work, Cicero has Atticus describe that irony (*ironia*) as Socrates's practice of denying wisdom to himself while attributing it playfully to those, such as Protagoras and Gorgias, most anxious to claim it.[18] Cicero seems clearly, then, to accept irony as a dimension of Socrates. The significance of this is that Socrates's statements of his own ignorance, at least some of them, are taken not literally, but as irony, as, in other words, pretenses or dissemblings of ignorance.

The alternative would be to take these reports on Socrates as true professions rather than pretense of ignorance. This is not as unreasonable as might first appear when one considers that Socrates is looked to by Cicero and others as the founder and continuing inspiration of Academic skepticism. Are not Socrates's uncertainties so pervasive and profound that there is really nothing of pretense in his professions of ignorance? That this possibility was not lost on Cicero is evident in a passage in his *Academica Priora*, where Cicero has Lucullus dispute the New Academy's view of the history of philosophy and specifically deny that the reform of Arcesilaus could be taken as a revival of the Socratic way.[19] Lucullus claims that Arcesilaus incorrectly takes what is, in fact, irony in Socrates for evidence of the denial of the possibility of perception and knowledge.

Cicero, not taking all of Socrates's professions of ignorance literally as direct manifestations of skepticism, affirms both the irony and the skepticism in Socrates. To seek Cicero's understanding of how method, irony, and skepticism relate in his model, Socrates, brings one back to the importance of Cicero's finding in Socrates the authentic source for the type of qualified skepticism that he embraced. This form of skepticism seems to give rise to the Socratic method, which is primarily a way of philosophical inquiry and teaching. The Socratic method as an inquiry would not be consistent with a skepticism that disabled, that undermined the discovering work of philosophy, that, in other words, rendered inquiry pointless. As Gregory Vlastos once trenchantly observed, "If after decades of searching Socrates remained convinced that he still knew **nothing**, would not further searching have become a charade—or rather worse, for he holds that virtue 'is' knowledge: if he has no knowledge, his life is a disaster...."[20] So, too, the Socratic method as a way of teaching entails irony meaning a pretense of ignorance, such a pretense being inconceivable where there is that total ignorance represented in an absolute skepticism like that of Metrodorus and that to which Arcesilaus tends.[21] In a Socrates who is both dedicated to the inquiring work of philosophy and capable of irony as a teacher (which implies his having knowledge), Cicero can find a unification of the two tasks of philosophy—its discovering work and its guiding and consoling work—both of which Cicero so clearly embraces.

The tension and apparent inconsistency in Cicero's holding to both these tasks and the corresponding critical and rhetorical modes is overcome once one recalls the role that Socratic skepticism appears to play in his unification of these tasks. This overcoming or reconciliation of the tension by the Socratic New Academy seems to be a matter of common sense, for the procedure of this school, as we recall from the preceding chapter, is to require the testing of all views, to refuse to affirm with certainty anything, and yet to insist on judgments based on what is most likely true. The reconciliation that suggests itself would, then, have the form of understanding philosophy as the seeking of truth and in its critical mode, as primary, both logically and chronologically, and philosophy as a guide and comforter and in its rhetorical mode, as secondary and derivative. This reconciliation, then, entails understanding philosophy (and the philosopher) as critically seeking the most trustworthy approximations to the truth and then utilizing these for guidance and support in life. Such utilizations, providing the basis for the rhetorical mode of philosophy, could be seen, as they clearly were by Cicero, as the fruit of philosophy.[22]

Such a reconciliation of the apparently divergent tasks of philosophy explains and illuminates much about the relationship of the critical mode and the rhetorical mode in Cicero as well as in Socrates. Yet, the reconciliation is simplistic in a way that is likely to mislead and, ultimately, to provide an obstacle to appreciating the complexity and coherence in Cicero's thought and works. The oversimplification in the reconciliation can be exposed by noting that it seems to understand the full work of philosophy in two stages: a first stage where we get at the truth as best we can, and a second stage where that "truth" is applied to the business of life. The oversimplification precisely consists in the suggestion that the passage through stage one to stage two constitutes an overcoming of skepticism and ignorance; it does, in a sense, constitute such an overcoming, but the danger consists in this "overcoming" obscuring or leading us to forget the depth of the ignorance and skepticism professed by both Socrates and Cicero, an ignorance that remains present in an important way in stage two.[23] Likewise, it is oversimplification to understand stage one as beginning in total skepticism or ignorance, a *tabula rasa*; rather, reliances or assumed knowledge of some sort are present, entailed in the very method and life of inquiry that characterizes Socrates and the New Academy of Cicero.[24] Put simply, neither Socrates nor his follower Cicero understands the work of philosophy as a passage from ignorance to certainty. Philosophy does not begin from an abyss of total skepticism and does not end free from an important, underlying residue of skepticism.

Cicero's texts show an awareness of this deep and persistent skepticism in Socrates as well as of various statements of Socrates which indicate that he could hardly be said to be without knowledge.[25] Putting the words in his own mouth near the very end of the extant portion of *Academica Posteriora*, Cicero indicates that Socrates's confession of ignorance (*confessio ignorationis*) is derived from the darkness or obscurity of reality (*earum rerum obscuritate*) but that Socrates had, contrary to Arcesilaus the founder of the New Academy, saved from skepticism the very teaching that nothing can be known.[26] Earlier in the same work, Cicero has Varro report that Socrates was always found arguing in such a way "that he himself affirmed nothing" (*ut nihil adfirmet ipse*), "that he rebutted others," and "that he claimed that he himself knew (*scire*) nothing other than that truth itself."[27] Likewise, in the first of the *Tusculans*, Cicero notices the tension between Socrates's ignorance and Socrates's assurance. Here, in a remarkable reflection on the closing lines of Socrates's final speech in Plato's *The Apology of Socrates* ("But the hour is now at hand for me to depart, for I must die, and you must continue with business of life. Which of these, however, is the better the immortal gods know; no human being, I find, does know."), Cicero observes that Socrates does know (*scit*), in the light of what he says earlier in the *Apology*, that very thing which he denies—that any except the gods know (*scire*). But, Cicero continues, Socrates stood by his position of affirming nothing to the end (*nihil ut adfirmet*).[28] Again, Socrates's professed ignorance is coupled with an acknowledgment that it does not extend to his knowledge of that very ignorance.

Cicero does more than simply notice the tension between Socrates's skepticism and his claims to knowledge. He associates himself with that Socratic outlook. The truth itself, he writes in the *Orator*, "lies hidden" (*in occulto lateret*); thus the judgments he makes even on the most important matters must rest on nothing more "than whatever would seem to me as most like the truth" (*quam id quodcumque mihi quam simillimum veri videretur*).[29] The phrase, *simillimum veri*, reminds us that this was the standard for judgments that Cicero specifically attributed to Socrates in the *Tusculans* and that it was, of course, central to his own understanding of his allegiance to the Academic school.[30] Not merely, then, in some loose way does the Academic school link Cicero to Socrates; rather, the line of descent in that school represented by Carneades is taken by Cicero as the proper one, the Socratic one. Socrates had struck the right balance between skepticism and knowledge, between the limitations and possibilities of human knowing. His method, inclusive of the *simillimum veri* standard of judgment, made sense only in the light of such a balance. Within the tradition stemming from Plato, that balance was regularly upset or threatened by those like Zeno, the Stoic founder, who turns to the assurance of dogmatism and, on the other hand, by those like Arcesilaus, whose skepticism was so total as to disable, in Cicero's view, those who embraced it.

Cicero had seen in the Academic tradition what Immanuel Kant later saw in a much larger segment of the history of philosophy, namely a struggle between dogmatism and skepticism marked by the alternating dominance of one and then the other. For Kant, it might be said that the dialectic between dogmatism and skepticism posed the essential philosophical problem to be worked out by critical philosophy. For Cicero, the tension was not to be resolved in a solution but was to be maintained by fidelity to the Socratic balance between knowing and doubting.[31]

The Socratic Way of Life

One thing that Socrates does seem to know is how to live. Cicero not only regularly draws attention to this dimension of Socrates's teaching but also looks to Socrates as a moral exemplar.[32] In the passage from the *Academica* cited just above, Cicero has Varro continue by observing that despite Socrates's constant repetition that "it is the mark of human wisdom not to think that one knows what one does not know," his entire discourse was given "to praising virtue and to exhorting people to the pursuit of virtue...."[33] So here too, as in Cicero's *Tusculan* reflection on Socrates's last speech in the *Apology*, Cicero is aware that Socrates claims to know even more than his ignorance. As the comment of Varro indicates, Cicero finds in Socrates an active promoter of virtue as well as a moral exemplar.

What is the status of these moral truths that Socrates promotes and that shape his way of life? Are such truths (the traditional virtues as, for example, reflected in Socrates's simple living marked by a scorn for wealth and diminishment of the ordinary pleasures, his equanimity in the face of death) the results of inquiry and, thus, findings, according to the standard of *simillimum veri*? Or are they simply conditions of and implied in and thus potentially derivative from Socrates's commitment to the philosophical life? Could they rest on both these grounds, such that they commend themselves as *simillimum veri*, partly because they are supportive of, if not necessary for, the life of philosophical inquiry? Insofar as the truths of the Socratic way of life are thus supported or derived, there remains the question of the status or ground of the fundamental, formative commitment of Socrates—the commitment to philosophy itself. Cicero's various considerations of Socrates do neither sort these foundational matters out explicitly nor answer these questions directly. It appears, however, that Cicero sees Socrates as operating within, if not the decisive founder of, the framework that we saw Cicero himself employing, in the previous chapter, when he builds a positive philosophy up from his skeptical outlook by setting a foundation in a choice among ends (*fines*), a choice that then functions to illuminate that most important fruit of philosophy, duties (*officia*), as well as all the inquiries of philosophy. Viewed in this framework, Socrates's fundamental choice, his choice of end, is to live virtuously and that includes, if it is not centered around, living the philosophical life. In the *De Oratore*, Cicero has the sage and aged lawyer Scaevola report that Socrates regularly thought his work complete when he had persuaded men to want virtue above all goals and to pursue an understanding of it and capacity to recognize it.[34]

What, then, justifies the fundamental choice of Socrates, and what is his criterion in determining that such a life is most likely or most probably the truly human life? Here too—though our task is not and cannot be to provide some authoritative interpretation of what the historical Socrates thought on this critical matter—it is provisionally plausible that Socrates was a model for Cicero and thus was seen as responding like Cicero did, namely with a multifaceted criterion drawn from the perspective of practice and reflecting the inner and outer sides of human experience, namely, what is congruent with who we are as humans as known through self-examination and the experiences of human life.[35]

Though the precise genealogy of the truths of the Socratic way of life is not delineated by Cicero, he is clear and explicit in appreciating Socrates's teaching that speech and action flow from the disposition of the soul (*animi adfectus*). Cicero recalls this teaching of Socrates in Book 5 of the *Tusculans*, when he is fixing attention on that seemingly primary disposition of the soul—the common desire for complete happiness. At least a part of his intention in this text is to argue that any more specific disposition of the soul (e.g. toward virtue) and the life of speech and action (presumably including the action of inquiry or thought) that flow from it are to be taken as expressions of the desire for happiness.[36] Socrates, for Cicero, exemplified a life of inquiry that was to mark and affect the soul and thereby form the way life was lived. Cicero's often noted appreciation for "the Socratic turn"—for the priority Socrates assigned to moral and political inquiry—reflects a concern that inquiry be fruitful for life.[37] More clearly and more pointedly, however, Cicero's appreciation for the Socratic way of life is implicit in his criticism, in the second of the *Tusculans*, of philosophers whose work does not touch their souls and character. Most of the professionals, he finds, see their discipline as an exhibition of learning (*ostentatio scientiae*) rather than a rule of life (*lex vitae*).[38] It is, then, the very integrity of the Socratic way of life that appears to attract Cicero. This is an integrity that includes philosophical inquiry that grows out of and is defended in terms of human experience in its fullness, that is, in other words, itself a part of virtue, and that expects inquiry and thought to bear the fruit of virtue in human life.

It is against the backdrop of Socrates as a model of reconciling in himself the two tasks and the two modes of philosophy that Cicero's embracing both those tasks and modes is best understood. Socrates is seen as both a questioning inquirer and a teacher of truths—truths that bear their fruit in the formative effect on his way of life and potentially on the lives of others. Socrates's form of skepticism, one that allows knowing and hence irony, provides the basis for the reconciliation. Socrates's irony, properly understood as pretense of ignorance, clearly masks at least this: his knowledge of the nature and goodness of philosophy, his knowledge of the nature and goodness of various human virtues, and apparently his knowledge of the favorable prospects after death for the good person. Socrates's major claim to knowledge—his most insistent one and the one on which Cicero especially focuses—is that what he knows beyond doubt is that he does not know. Perhaps the specialness of this claim is found in that it sums up the specific kind of skepticism which Cicero shares with Socrates, for the claim asserts the literal truth that one cannot know and yet in itself opens the door to knowing in some way and thus to the possibility of irony.[39] To know that one does not know is to understand reality sufficiently that one grasps the limits of one's comprehension; this implies knowing both what it would be to know and all the forms of reliances or limited knowing that allow one to know a standard for knowing. This key Socratic claim of knowing that he does not know allows or makes possible philosophical inquiry that can be fruitful, as was exemplified in Socrates's way of life.[40] Like Socrates, Cicero insists on the need to make defensible judgments about the true and the good and claims, thereby, knowledge in some form. Cicero is prepared, as indicated in the previous chapter, to find ordinary perception as reliable, and he specifically denies that all matters of inquiry are buried in the same degree of "obscurity."[41] He thinks, we recall, that the inquiry into ends promises the greatest assurance among philosophical topics and a very foundation for philosophy.

In preparation for considering how the modes of philosophy function in Cicero's writings, it is useful to emphasize that the skepticism, which Cicero shares with Socrates, is never totally overcome after critical inquiry and at the point when one might ordinarily expect to be switching to the rhetorical mode. The Socratic refusal to affirm with certainty persists throughout all the achievements of philosophy. Likewise, critical inquiry does not proceed outward from some sure ground—from some decisive Archimedean point that stands outside the world to be known and the pervasive uncertainty therein. The rhetorical mode may, then, have to precede the critical in some ways and to play an important role in stirring such inquiry. In other words, an important dimension of Socrates's example is his making a case for philosophy—a case that involves in a decisive way exhortation to philosophy.[42] What could be the ground or philosophical basis of an argument that makes the case for philosophy?

The Mixed Modes of Cicero

When one considers Socrates as a philosophical model for Cicero, both the complexity and coherence of Cicero's understanding of philosophy and, in turn, the nature of his philosophical writings become more comprehensible. The troubling tension, with which this chapter began, between different goals for philosophy and between the derivative critical and rhetorical modes can be focused on the question "How is one to regard the evident rhetorical dimension of Cicero's philosophical writings?" Is this simply the by-product of Cicero's practical mastery of the art of rhetoric—an intrusion of his specific history into the work of philosophy? Does it represent a mitigation of philosophy, so that one would be, one might say, less of a philosopher for the employing of this mode? Or does the rhetorical mode in philosophical matters have a properly philosophical defense?[43] Is the rhetorical mode necessary to the fullness or completeness of the practice of philosophy? Is this mode proper to a Socratic literary tradition that Cicero seeks to develop in Rome?

In the eyes of Cicero, his model Socrates has done more toward the reconciliation and union of philosophy and rhetoric than simply lay a basis for it by his qualified skepticism with its room for "knowledge," irony, and life-forming truths. From such a basis, Socrates himself put rhetoric to use in the service of philosophy, and he did so consciously, as evident in Plato's *Phaedrus*, a work in which Socrates is shown explicitly and thoroughly examining the true grounds of reconciliation of philosophy and rhetoric, and a work for which Cicero has a special appreciation.[44] In a general sense, then, Cicero the Socratic needs no apology for the rhetorical dimensions of his philosophical work.

Cicero is very much aware of these dimensions of his philosophical work. He does not simply fall or slip into rhetoric. This awareness was already in evidence in this chapter's earlier consideration of Cicero's embrace of the Socratic method. Cicero, as we have seen, held up short exchanges, real dialogue in the form of "give and take," as Socrates's and his own preferred mode of inquiry and teaching. This form of exchange is described as "more suitable" (*commodius*) than others that involve longer speeches.[45] It is more suitable, it seems, in the sense of a more reliable way to get at the truth (*simillimum veri*): the objective which has set the context for Cicero's reflections on the various types of exchanges or forms of philosophic discourse. Strangely, however, Cicero's philosophical writings are dominated by exchanges in the form of long discourses, like that of the *Finibus*, or by monologic discourses, like that in evidence in the *Tusculans*.[46] Only now and then does Cicero provide exchanges of the sort that he calls more suitable. At the same time that Cicero, for whatever reason, departs from the philosophically preferred form of discourse, he often appears to be using forms that retain the essential Socratic features of presenting a challenge (as in the *Tusculans*) or an encounter of positions (as in *Finibus*) without the interference of the authority of the teacher, being in this case Cicero as the author. In a strict sense, of course, Cicero would seem to be masking his authority only as long as he does not make himself a *persona* in the philosophical exchange or otherwise closely associate his authority with one of the characters he has cast in the work at hand. More consideration of such complications in understanding his authorial role will follow.

Clearly, the longer discourses to which Cicero tends are in the rhetorical mode, but Cicero distinguishes between a philosophical rhetoric, which is to characterize at least his own (as *persona*) long discourses in the *Finibus*, and forensic or legal rhetoric, which is said to be popular (*popularis*) and thus sometimes a bit heavier or duller (*hebetior*).[47] Discourse in the rhetorical mode, whether in the philosophical or popular form, is set, at times, within the framework of a writing primarily in the critical mode; for example, the long defenses of and attacks on the Epicurean and Stoic teachings respectively in the first four books of the *Finibus* are presented in the name of critically exploring the key teaching of these schools. Thus the conscious adoption by Cicero of the longer forms of discourse in a philosophical work is one instance—probably the simplest and most straightforward—of his mixing of modes, in this case of letting rhetoric play a role in the context of critical philosophical inquiry.

Cicero presents readers, however, with more complex mixtures of modes. His prefaces to dialogues, as in the case of the *Finibus* and the *Re Publica*, result in writings where he does show his authority, often using these to make a very strong argument on one side of an issue that is to be explored in the dialogue to follow. And as already indicated, he appears to reveal his position (or lead the reader to believe that he has) by inserting himself as a *persona* into the dialogue, as he does in the *Legibus*, but Cicero as a *persona* may not always be Cicero as an author, a possibility all the more to be considered because Cicero is a follower of the New Academic school whose advocates are known to represent views they do not personally embrace. Furthermore, there are dialogues where the issues under discussion or some of them are not clearly resolved, even though Cicero is involved, as in Book V of *Finibus* and at the end of *Academica, Natura Deorum*, and *Divinatione*. How strongly Cicero affirms what he seems to affirm, then, becomes an issue of interpretation; he appears able to mask his views and follow the Socratic way even at the end of long exchanges. For yet another stage of complexity, Cicero may give reason, as he does in the *De Oratore*, in his preface and/or in some other way for associating his own view with that of one of the speakers of the dialogue. Cicero confesses that in some works, he has sought authority for his views by putting them in the mouth of respected figures in the Roman tradition, like Cato major and Laelius.[48]

Within a given work, there may be a mixture of short exchanges, which match the preferred type of Socratic discourse, and of the different kinds of longer exchanges, such as were exemplified in the *Tusculans* and the *Finibus*.[49] Then, too, some philosophical works are quite directly and substantially rhetorical, such as his exhortative writing on ethics, *De Officiis*, which is formally addressed to his son but clearly intended as a philosophical writing for a larger audience. Cicero's *Hortensius* is characterized by him as exhortation to the study of philosophy (*cohortati sumus...ad philosophiae studium*) though it, apparently, entailed alternating long exchanges as well as some dialogue.[50] A work substantially in the rhetorical mode may be found utilizing the critical mode to get at the truth of an application or a fine point. Thus, Cicero in the *Officiis* will present divergent views on a specific moral dilemma in a context of arguing forcefully that the right must always be done and the useful or expedient is to be understood only in terms of the right. Cicero shows an awareness of this mixing of modes regularly and with sufficient frequency his mixing must be seen as an intended dimension of his various philosophical works.

Cicero's intentionality regarding the rhetorical dimension of his philosophical work makes it plausible for the reader to seek to make sense of this dimension, to seek to understand its rationale. Ultimately each philosophical work of Cicero calls out for understanding in itself and with respect to its specific mix of the rhetorical mode with the critical mode. Though this aspect of interpretations of given works will surface now and then throughout this book, such understandings of Cicero's mixing are all the more credible if they are consistent with and even follow from a general theory of the mixing of modes, which Cicero has revealed at one point or another and to which attention is now directed. Such a theory is more than implicit in Cicero's understanding of philosophy, an understanding shaped, of course, by his model, Socrates, but an understanding not entirely clarified here up to this point.

PERFECTA PHILOSOPHIA

Cicero reveals the key to such a theory, when, in his preface to the first of the *Tusculans*, he writes of philosophy completed or matured (*perfecta philosophia*): a phrase that could plausibly be rendered as "integral philosophy" and understood as efficacious philosophy.[51] Following a theme that he had earlier developed in his *De Oratore* and that is consistent with his expectations for philosophy throughout his writings, Cicero introduces the idea of *perfecta philosophia* as a way to speak of a union of philosophy and rhetoric, in which the art of rhetoric is incorporated in the very work of philosophy and rhetoric is, thus, in the service of philosophy. Philosophy's own development to its end requires in some way the rhetorical art.[52] The phrase and idea specifically appear in this text after Cicero observes with praise that Aristotle sought to teach the art of speaking in order to have the young "join practical wisdom to eloquence" (*prudentiam cum eloquentia iungere*).[53] Cicero then indicates that he sees himself in this tradition which Aristotle sought to develop, for he is not about to set aside his earlier devotion to the art of rhetoric.[54] Rather, he will put that art in the service of "this greater and more fruitful art" (*hac maiore et uberiore arte*) of practical wisdom.[55] "For," Cicero adds, "he has always determined this to be mature philosophy (*perfectam philosophiam*), which is able to discourse in an ample and well-adorned manner on the most important questions" (*de maximis quaestionibus*). The disputations that follow, here specifically identified with the *schola* of the Greeks, which we know is elsewhere associated by Cicero with Gorgias and the Sophists, are presented as Cicero's own efforts toward *perfecta philosophia*.

If philosophy completed or matured is manifest or approximated in such discourse (*schola*), has not Cicero contradicted his clear preference, following Socrates, for the method of short exchanges (*sermo*), namely for dialectical rather than rhetorical exchange? Earlier in this chapter, he was seen as assessing the *schola* as the least preferred of three distinct Socratic methods of inquiry. This difficulty or apparent contradiction brings the fundamental tension in Cicero's philosophical work, the thematic concern of this chapter, back into focus. With respect to determining the truth, or, more precisely, to determining what is most probably true (*simillimum veri*), with respect to this task of philosophy in its every manifestation, the critical mode of inquiry is called for and the testing of "truths" and arguments that this entails is best done through short exchanges, where the teacher, or Socrates, is more the midwife or facilitator than commanding authority. With respect, however, to the end or completion (*perfecta*) of philosophy, a clearly more rhetorical mode is preferred. It appears that determining the truth belongs to philosophy but does not constitute the end or completion of philosophy itself. Philosophy comes to completion, or, one might say, reaches fruition, in the fruits of a proper way of life. The second task of philosophy, that it guide life, apparently incorporates the first. The Socratic model, for Cicero, has prepared us to expect philosophy to be fruitful in this way. Philosophy, for Cicero, is not simply the finding of truth; it is also, in its completeness, the living of truth.[56] Thus the work of philosophy, including the use of philosophy's various modes, stands itself under a moral horizon even as it can reveal that very horizon.

The interpretation of *perfecta philosophia* as the realization or living of a right way of life draws support from other statements of Cicero.[57] In *Senectute*, Cicero has Scipio (Africanus minor) address the staunch and renowned Cato (Cato major) as one marked by a complete or mature wisdom (*perfecta sapientia*).[58] Here, as well as in *Amicitia*, it is made clear that Cato came to possess the cognomen of "wise" (*sapiens Cato*) through his good judgments learned through experience and displayed in the Senate and forum.[59] Cicero speaks directly of Cato as unmatched in practical wisdom (*nemo prudentior*).[60] Cato is wise, then, because of the actualization of virtue in his life. One manifestation of this wisdom is the way he handles old age, not theoretically, but as he lives it out. Significantly, Cicero reveals an awareness that Cato's reputation for wisdom was not associated with inquiry and learning. Such inquiry and learning were, on the other hand, associated with Socrates's wisdom and were being taken as the marks of wisdom for Laelius and presumably others in "the Scipionic Circle," among whom the Socratic spirit first took hold in Rome.[61] Despite the awareness that before and after Cato "wisdom" is taken as closely tied up with inquiry and learning, the ultimate test of the presence of wisdom is described as the same for Cato and for a Socratic-like Laelius. It consists in having within oneself the essential means of happiness, insofar as one finds that happiness in virtue, and then in meeting the challenges of fortune and life accordingly, from the wealth of that master possession.[62] Cato was no philosopher; in fact, he was wary of those philosophers from Greece, but the complete wisdom of Cicero's Cato is the measure of complete philosophy for Cicero. It is this same measure of wisdom as virtue actualized that is in evidence in the often-cited passage early in *Re Publica* where Cicero stresses that one cannot possess virtue as an art that one might not be currently utilizing, and that virtue is present only in its use or practice and virtue is the realization of the thoughts and words of philosophers.[63] Complete wisdom (*perfecta sapientia*) is the end of philosophy (*perfecta philosophia*) and is found in the practice of virtue. This human peak for Cicero seems another way to speak of consular philosophy or what it is that those leaders have who are marked by *humanitas*.[64] These appear to be the qualities of what we, here, later find that Cicero means by the perfect orator or model statesman. With all these concepts of completeness or perfection, Cicero appears to be striving to overcome in Roman garb the separation of tongue and mind, for which he once seemed to hold Socrates responsible.[65]

This passage (*Rep.* 1.2) as a whole makes clear that Cicero means by this "practice of virtue" moral virtue and, above all, its political manifestation in statesmanship. It is not that Cicero as a follower of Socrates fails to appreciate the thinking and discourse of philosophers. Such activity is central to the Socratic way of life, which Cicero embraces in his specific context. Yet, the significance of "the Socratic turn" for Cicero and his emphasis on the fruit of philosophy in a way of life are indications that Cicero does not think in terms of intellectual virtue as distinct from moral virtue but rather looks at the proper exercise of the mind as one manifestation of moral virtue. For Cicero, such exercise is proper or fitting and, hence, truly of human virtue only in relation to the context and needs of human life. In other words, a specific activity or action is virtuous only if it is part of overall human virtue. Cicero's apparent subordination of the theoretical life to the life of moral practice will become more understandable in the light of his direct examination of the tension between the life of the philosopher and the life of the statesman and his appreciation for necessity and utility in determining moral virtue. These considerations are taken up in the next chapter.

But where, one might ask, has the art of rhetoric gone as this fuller view of Cicero's *perfecta philosophia* has been developed? Understanding rhetoric's relation to philosophy was the object in turning to Cicero's view of philosophy as expressed in the phrase, *perfecta philosophia*. What came to light initially in this pursuit was rhetoric's union with philosophy, in the form of incorporation in the work of philosophy, specifically in the service of philosophy's seeking virtue, seeking to guide and comfort in the conduct of life. From the beginning of this chapter, there has been the easy, seemingly natural, association of the rhetorical mode with that second, and now seen as the final (*perfectum*), task of philosophy, namely developing and sustaining virtue. What, however, does rhetoric have to do with virtue? How does rhetoric serve philosophy aimed at human virtue? Only more articulation of how rhetoric intersects with philosophy will, possibly, yield the general understanding or theory that might help one make sense of Cicero's mixing of modes in his work.

This mixing of modes by Cicero, this incorporation of rhetoric into the work of philosophy, is initially comprehensible in the light of two dimensions of his thought, namely his underlying skepticism and his moral focus and prospect for philosophy (*perfecta philosophia*). His skepticism, as Chap. 1 brought out, was such that judgment concerning the truth—the likely truth—was always expected. This expectation is wholly consistent with, and probably derives from, his insistence that philosophy be fruitful in the form of a life of virtue. The weight of this responsibility to judge would account for the fact that Cicero's opinion on the matter at hand in his various philosophical writings is always brought out in one form or another, including his direct statements in *prooemia* or prefaces. Cicero, in other words, does not mask his authority. He lets his judgment show in different ways and in different degrees in his various philosophical works. Accordingly, even as Cicero teaches about, portrays within some dialogues, and appears to admire a Socratic method characterized by a speaker or teacher proffering no personal view or opinion, he, as a writer, does not adopt this stance.[66] Nor does he introduce himself as a *persona* within his writings in a manner that associates his name with a position he does not hold.[67] Cicero never appears to allow his own *persona* to be used simply to advance the argument or for heuristic or pedagogical purposes.[68] When Academics like Philus in *Re Publica* and Cotta in *Natura Deorum* are cast by Cicero into such roles, they draw overt attention to their role, unmasking themselves, then, to some degree, and in the case of Philus he actually makes clear that his Academic commitment entails his defending a position that he finds despicable.[69] It appears that however strong the encounter Cicero presents between contending positions at certain points within his works, he is not content to write in a mode of pure critical inquiry when the given philosophical work as a whole is considered.[70] Cicero's philosophical works are not, then, primarily the acts of an Academic philosopher in the course of inquiry or in the form of contending by taking up an opposing position as Arcesilaus was known to do. They are works about philosophical positions, including the Academic one of the philosophical method, embedded in a context of judgments that Cicero has made through his own philosophical inquiry.

The rhetorical mode, then, enters Cicero's work both directly and indirectly. Indirectly insofar as Cicero assigns speeches and long discourses to various characters in his dialogues and these writings function as descriptions and source books that simply reflect the way philosophy is practiced, especially in the Academic camp (where, we recall, the *schola* then prevails and where Cicero seems to be encouraging an Arcesilan reform that would cultivate adversarial, hence quite rhetorical, encounters between and among schools). Cicero's direct embrace of the rhetorical mode as an author is found insofar as he uses continuous long discourses in his own name and manifests his judgments on issues under consideration. He does this though he recognizes, as has been shown, the claims of proper philosophical method or pure Socratic critical mode characterized by short exchanges and by the masking of the authority of the teacher. In a sense, the distinction between a direct and an indirect embrace of the rhetorical mode by Cicero is inadequate, for all his written work, of whatever form, is shaped by a rhetorical intent. His use of the dialogue form, whatever its internal configuration in terms of long or short speeches and including his highly conscious choice of dramatic detail, is primarily, as A.E. Douglas has said, for rhetorical effect.[71] His dialogues can be seen as the most artful fusing of the rhetorical and critical modes, with the former dominating.[72] For Cicero himself, the very presentation of philosophy to Romans, the commendation of a certain philosophical method, that of the Academics, and his emphatic highlighting of the judgments emanating from his own philosophical inquiries are moral acts—fruits of philosophy. In his context, Cicero apparently holds the rhetorical effort to foster these objectives, wholly appropriate and consistent with Socrates.

It appears, then, that the Socratic way of life was more the polestar and more formative for Cicero than the Socratic method understood as the pure critical mode of inquiry. In fact, Cicero himself recognized the pure critical mode as an idealized or false conception of the Socratic method as actually practiced by Socrates.[73] It would be an error to push this recognition of the impact of way of life over method to the point of underestimating the genuineness of Cicero's own philosophical inquiry including his admiration and elevation of the critical mode. That his inquiry was genuine seems clear both from the depths of skepticism he shares with Socrates and from the honest and vexing encounters between philosophical positions he describes and leaves in some cases (as at the conclusions of the *Finibus* and *Natura Deorum*) in what appears to be a not altogether settled state of mind. Cicero, we recall, was drawn to the New Academy primarily because it represented better than any other school a commitment to procedure that captured the critical mode that was associated with Socrates. Despite its tendency, at its best, to conduct philosophical inquiry through contending speeches, he and any orator, claims Cicero, gains precision or acuteness (*subtilitas*) from this school.[74] The clearly dominant mode of the writer Cicero is, nonetheless, one in which he brings his rhetorical power to bear both in the exposition of philosophy, including the very commendation of the Academic method, and in support of a virtuous way of life in its various other manifestations.

Why the rhetorical mode is dominant in Cicero's own work is a question whose answer can be approached only with a deeper penetration of how Cicero's skepticism and his goal for philosophy revealed in the measure of *perfecta philosophia*, namely real or actualized virtue, shape his work as a philosopher. The interaction of these two Socratic dimensions result in a situation where philosophy's need for and use of rhetoric make sense.[75] The embrace of philosophy requires for most, if not all, exhortation to and defense of philosophy.[76] This choice of philosophy as well as other moral choices cannot, for Cicero, be made from the position of certainty, a kind of decisive illumination, and as moral choices they will involve pressures and pulls away from what seems good and right.[77]

These Socratic dimensions that influence Cicero can, when understood, make the alleged Socratic formula, "knowledge is virtue," more plausible: they bring it closer to ordinary moral experience. Since the Socratic or Ciceronic perspective is that knowledge is never certainty or decisive illumination, the capacity of such "knowledge" to direct and form a person's actions is dependent on that person's readiness or disposition to pursue the way to which the understanding attained points. Knowledge, then, is virtue only for the ready or prepared souls. Against this background, rhetoric may be called on to vitalize or vivify what is known.[78] Rhetoric may also be called upon to strengthen the dispositions that welcome the seed of philosophy and contribute to its fruitfulness. Cicero himself, at least once, invokes a version of the formula, "knowledge is virtue," when he writes that "understanding the right way of living makes one better" (*recte vivendi ration meliores efficit*).[79] The context for this statement makes clear that this becoming better will happen only if one avoids the blinding corruption of bad habituation.[80] Furthermore one needs not only to choose the virtuous way but also to be regularly sustained in that course, a need especially great for those in public life.[81]

Cicero thought that rhetoric, at the least, must be available to counter rhetoric, for even the modest and decent man (*pudens*) can be corrupted by speech. The *orationes* of the Academics were seen, even by Cicero the Academic, as dangerous under certain circumstances.[82] Thus persuasiveness and the rhetorical mode have a rightful place in a philosophy focused on and aimed at moral action. Cicero's use, then, of the rhetorical mode, for example when and how he uses long speeches and discourses and when and how he manifests his authorial voice, is subject not only to this aim, this fruitfulness expected of philosophy, but also in the pursuit of that, subject to the circumstances of context, especially that of interlocutors or audience. Cicero is ever acutely aware of his Roman audience and its dispositions and inclinations.

To speak of "a rightful place" for rhetoric is to reveal what is everywhere in evidence in Cicero, namely that the possession and use of the art of rhetoric entails moral choices. Thus the possession and right utilization of rhetoric is itself a part of *perfecta philosophia*, the most evident point being made when this phrase was first noted above. Rhetoric, in other words, has its place in living well. It is both a fruit of philosophy and the instrument of attaining other fruits. At several points in the *Tusculans*, while showing a high awareness of the rhetorical mode in this very work, Cicero indicates that he brings a moral horizon or framework to the rhetorical mode. What is especially noteworthy is that this moral perspective does not simply represent a restraint on rhetoric, keeping it to rightful or appropriate usages, but that it also involves a moral impetus or responsibility to embrace the rhetorical mode. He refers at one point to his own effort to join eloquence to philosophy in his writings, in contrast to those Latin writers whose ineptness leave their writings accessible only to their own followers and who thus misuse leisure and the power of writing (*otio et litteris*).[83] Overall, then, it is not with regret that Cicero sees the Academic school accommodate rhetoric and foster philosophical encounters in the adversarial form, that is between full-blown speeches by representatives of the contending schools. Philosophy in the Academic tradition encouraged the simultaneous practice of oratory, a feature that attracts Cicero partly, no doubt, because the requisites of public leadership and his own specific genius call him to cultivate rhetoric but partly also, as can now be seen, because philosophy must be wedded to rhetoric for its own purposes.[84] In fact, Cicero thought himself peculiarly suited, by dint of his talent as an orator, to do better than the ordinary run of Academics and to bring philosophy to its effective fullness.[85]

There is one point where Cicero, after carefully clarifying terms with the "oars" of dialectic, literally "sails" forth with the winds of rhetoric. Here, in the fourth of the *Tusculans*, the specific joining of dialectic and rhetoric is reminiscent of the teaching of Socrates in Plato's *Phaedrus*. Cicero is portrayed as approving this joining as "more correct" or "more right" (*rectius*), for it promises a more complete (*perfectius*) treatment of the entire matter.[86] Then, early in the fifth and last of the *Tusculans*, Cicero approvingly distinguishes the way philosophers proceed from the way of mathematicians, noting that the former mount up all relevant considerations rather than settling a matter by demonstration, building on what has been proved, and then moving on to another point. Philosophers—and Cicero makes clear he has in mind those concerned with moral choice and whose inquiry thus reaches fruition in a way of life—must treat every matter, especially that most important one of the end (*finis*) or happy life, "with its own proper arguments and promptings" (*propriis enim et suis argumentis et admonitionibus*).[87]

What Cicero has all along said is foundational for philosophy—the decision on the end or goal of life shows, in a special way, the necessary rhetorical dimension of philosophy as understood and practiced by Cicero.

For philosophy as well as the entire life of virtue, of which it is a part and which is exemplified by Socrates, entails recognition and choice of the virtuous way of life. This decision does not emerge from some incontrovertible proof or a single and decisive dialectical exchange. Rather, the decision is made and then again regularly sustained by the mounting up of relevant considerations including appropriate arguments and appeals to human inclinations. These considerations constitute the effective criterion for Cicero's work on the foundational question of philosophy. The question involves what fits with the basic orientations and experiences of human existence, with what might be called human nature. The question itself requires of a response prudential choice and the kind of assurance that can come in that realm. A practice of philosophy that emphasizes its rhetorical mode seems, then, especially consistent with Cicero's conception of what is foundational for philosophy.

The concern in this chapter, insofar as it takes up rhetoric, is primarily with the rhetorical mode in Cicero's philosophical writings, with Cicero's understanding of rhetoric's place in the work of philosophy, not with whatever general teaching he might have on the place and limits of rhetoric in human life. What does emerge from his rhetorical writings, the chief of which being the *De Oratore*, *Orator*, and *Brutus*, is wholly in accord with these preceding passages from the *Tusculans*. Attention to rhetoric is mandated by the condition of human life: like all human action, rhetoric is to be utilized in a proper (*decor*) and befitting way.[88] What is proper and befitting in speaking and writing—the very goal of rhetoric—is dependent on variables in each context such as topic, purpose, audience, and qualities of the speaker/writer. In fact, from the perspective of the art of rhetoric, philosophical speech in both its long and short forms is but one type of rhetoric, and the principles of the art would direct one as to when, where, and how to utilize such speech.[89] From this perspective, one might have organized this chapter not around the critical and rhetorical modes of philosophy but rather around some polarity like the more philosophical and the more popular modes of rhetoric.

There is ample evidence that Cicero understands this perspective, but it is decidedly not his. It is philosophy that he explicitly takes as the mother of the arts and therefore the director of them and arbiter between them. It is, as noted in the prior discussion of *perfecta philosophia*, philosophy which incorporates rhetoric and utilizes it toward its goal. And this priority of philosophy is consistently asserted even in his rhetorical writings, where Cicero defends the art of rhetoric and shows himself sensitive to an apparent slight of rhetoric by the Socrates of Plato's *Gorgias*.

The priority of philosophy—philosophy exemplified by Socrates—is not, however, a claim that philosophy can be done somehow prior to social and political interaction and the communication and interdependence that characterize social and political existence. Philosophy is not seen, then, as prior to rhetoric in that it proceeds from some sure ground, some Archimedean point, outside the realm of uncertainty. It is going too far to say that Cicero would regard philosophy as simply a specific artifact of a given culture, time or place, yet Cicero seems aware that most must be turned to philosophy by the power and art of others, and in being the instrument of that turning, rhetoric claims its own form of priority to philosophy. Cicero's philosophical work is deeply affected by his assuming a responsibility for that turning to philosophy in Rome, by his embrace, in other words, of the vocation of a literary Socrates in Rome.

Notes

1. Cicero observes the unlimited character of the call to philosophy: *Fin.* 1.2; *Tusc.* 2.1; 3.68–70. In a similar vein, Allan Bloom properly observes (1991: 338) that Plato's *Republic* "beginning with justice, must be a comprehensive book. In being forced to defend justice, Socrates is forced to enter forbidden realms and to expound novel conceits. Innocence once lost cannot be regained; the substitute is philosophizing in the fullest sense."
2. Philosophy, for Cicero, requires disputation, must war against ready assent, and follows reason rather than authority in its disputations. See, for example, *Tusc.* 2.4–5; *Off.* 2.8; *Ac.* 2.7, 108–09; *Nat. D.* 1.10. At *Nat. D.* 1.4, Cicero notes that none of a set of conflicting positions may be true (*vera*) but clearly no more than one of these positions can be true. With respect to natural philosophy, simple and clear language is more essential to getting at the truth than any rhetorical embellishment; see *Fin.* 1.13, 15; 3.19. Annas (1993: 351) properly points out a difference with respect to the unsettling character of philosophy between the tradition of the Academy, with which Cicero identifies, and that of Sextus Empiricus: "The Academic sceptics who do stress inquiry and philosophical argument, do not claim that tranquillity will result from this: they do not, indeed, represent it as having any further point beyond itself."
3. *Tusc.* 2.11; 3.1–2, 6, 13, 55–56. The extensive use in Hellenistic philosophy of the medical metaphor for the work of philosophy informs important parts of the work of Nussbaum, notably *The Therapy of Desire* (1994); see

Sedley's acknowledgment of this and concern that, while its pervasiveness for all of ancient philosophy be appreciated, its distinction from dialectical inquiry not be exaggerated, (1994: 9–10). See Gorman (2005: 69, n. 59). The agricultural metaphor in its varied forms in Cicero, the Stoic tradition, and subsequently in the Western tradition through the Renaissance is explored in Horowitz (1998).
4. *Fin.* 3.4; *Tusc.* 4.5–6; 5.5.
5. *Sen.* 2.
6. At *Div.* 2.7, Cicero claims to console himself and serve others with philosophy. Philosophy in the consolatory mode is taken as exemplified in *Tusc.* through the assurance given in the face of death and in the experience of pain; likewise in *Sen.* in the face of aging. For the consolatory tradition in ancient philosophy and Cicero's place in it, see Ochs (1993). Philosophy as consolation in this sense is not always clearly distinguishable in Cicero, if not in general, from philosophy as something to do, as a distraction from suffering or troubles. In finding the latter in Cicero as others have also done, Newman (1873: 264) seems to carry the point too far in his specific interpretation of *Tusc.* 5.5: "This was mainly the philosophy of the great Tully, except when it pleased him to speak as a disciple of the Porch.... If we examine the old Roman's meaning in '*O philosophia, vitae dux,*' it was neither more nor less than this;—that, **while** we were thinking of philosophy, we were not thinking of anything else; we did not feel grief, or anxiety, or passion, or ambition, or hatred all that time, and the only point was to keep thinking of it." Cicero has Piso, at *Fin.* 5.53–54, explain the consolation of philosophy in essential accord with this understanding. White (1995: 223–24, n. 9), in examining Cicero's self-therapy in turning to writing philosophy after the death of his daughter, sensibly cautions that "the initial impetus" for turning to or back to philosophy may not exhaust the reasons for a concern with and consolation in philosophy. It appears that there is another form of consolation that is not merely or not primarily distraction but is also, if not primarily, an application of truths or beliefs to the situation at hand, a form of rhetoric in the service of philosophy. Further, one might wonder if philosophy can absorb and, hence, distract only if it is thought to be a significant activity, not just an exercise or a game; one might, in other words, wonder if philosophy can absorb and hence distract only if it is capable of yielding fruits like the assurances in *Tusc.* At *Tusc.* 3.34 ff., 55–56, there is an explanation on how such consoling is accomplished. Cicero seems to see poetry in a somewhat analogous way (*Arch.* 16) for though it might be understood as mere entertainment and distraction from troubles, its real fruit and greatest justification is found in aiding humankind in "thoroughly grasping and cultivating virtue" (*ad percipiendum colendamque virtutem*).

7. *Ac.* 1.3; *Div.* 2.150; *Tusc* .4.5–6; at *Tusc.* 1.1,5–6, Cicero, without directly using the name of Socrates, proclaims his own task to be that of giving Latin literary expression to Greek philosophy concerned with the right way of living (*rectam vivendi viam*). Specifically on Socrates not writing, see *De Or.* 3.60. See also *Off.* 1.2; *Nat. D.* 1.11; *Tusc.* 5.11 and *Att.* 23, where he applies this Socratic way to personal and tactical political deliberation. At *Tusc.* 4.6, Cicero describes Socrates's philosophy as true (*vera*). Sedley (1997: 118 ff.) reflects on this fundamental loyalty to Socrates and his way and its primacy with Cicero, even over his respect for Plato and the claims for Plato's authority.
8. *Fin.* 2.1–2. Long and Sedley (1987: 1.448), in the course of contrasting Arcesilaus and Carneades, interpret arguing "to the contrary" by Arcesilaus to be a using of the opinion expressed "as the basis for an elenchus, just like the Socrates of Plato's early dialogues. But Carneades was prepared to take opposite sides on the same subject himself...." Gorman (2005: 90) clarifies well what Cicero takes from the work of Arcesilaus, namely an interrogative rather than a contradictive form of presentation, hence, in accord with the Socratic elenchus (the intellectual equivalent of wrestling hold).
9. *Fin.* 2.2–3. In *Fat.* 1, Cicero explicitly names *Nat. D.* and *Div.* as being characterized by the presentation of *perpetuae orationes* on each side of a question so as to facilitate a judgment by the listener as to what is most probable. In *Off.* 2.51, Cicero embraces the adversary procedure at trials as one that custom sanctions as a way of attaining the truth in a case. This appears to be a practical application of the method of the Academy. There has been a tendency for some to see adversarial practice in the law and the Aristotelian-rooted practice in rhetoric of arguing both sides of a matter as giving rise to Cicero's attraction to the Academic skeptical method. For an example of a mild version of this, see Garsten (2009: 150–51) though it seems that even he goes too far in diminishing the force of Cicero's philosophical interest in the Academy and suggesting that his Stoic defense of republican institutions "arose" out of his sense of "the interest of orators and oratory."
10. Cicero draws attention to the *schola* form of this work at *Tusc.* 1.7–8; 16–17. This first disputation openly moves from an effort at dialectic through short exchanges to continuous monologic discourse. *Tusc.* 2 moves more directly to use of *perpetua oratio*. At *Tusc.* 4.8, Cicero opens the disputation for the day with the very formula associated with Gorgias elsewhere in his work and by tradition: "Let whoever wishes so pick the subject for discussion." Background on the *schola* form and its relationship to diatribe is found in Douglas (1995: 202 ff.). Gorman (2005: 66–67) comments on Cicero's use of the *schola*.

11. *Fat.* 1, 2 and 4. Richard Bentley, the eighteenth century commentator, observes (1743: 237) "that there's a vast difference in the Manner of Dispute that's exhibited in the *Tusculans*, from what appears *In Academicis* [sic], *De Finibus, De Natura Deorum*, and *De Divinatione*. In the latter no man concedes; in the *Tusculans* no man resists. These last were *Scholae*, as Cicero **from** the **Greeks** calls them, discourses without an Antagonist; rather **Audiences**, than **Conferences**."
12. *Tusc* 1.8. We can now understand better why the voice of M later in *Tusc.* cannot always be taken to speak the opinion of Cicero himself. Recall Chap. 1, n. 36.
13. *Fin.* 2.3. At *Ac.* 2.8, Cicero comments on how the power of *oratio* leads some to dogmatic attachments to teachings of the schools other than the New Academy. Both Torquatus and Cato (Epicurean and Stoic spokesmen, respectively) in *Fin.* prefer uninterrupted discourse as the more effective way to present the appeal of their schools. Respecting the Stoics, Gorman (2005: 168 ff.) brings out their sense that the overall coherence and power of their "systematic philosophy" is best presented in such an *oratio* and that this appeal of Stoicism reaches to Cicero himself.
14. Described by Douglas as "a curious hankering after an authentically 'Socratic method,'" the entire passage and its context is examined in his Appendix (1995: 205, 215–18).
15. *Inv.* 1.52–53. This preferred or maximally Socratic form seems a way of describing what has now come to be called the Socratic "elenchus." The concept, its history, and scholarship on it is discussed by Vlastos (1982), and in the exchange between Kraut and Vlastos, which follows that essay as well as in Vlastos's subsequent book (1991: Chap. 4 and *passim*). See also Gorman (2005: 84 ff.).
16. This interpretation of what constitutes the essence of the Socratic method is supported by *Nat. D.* 1.11; *Ac.* 1.43 ff.; and *De Or.* 3.67 (Crassus speaking). Gorman (2005: 92–93 and *passim*) emphasizes "sincerity" or "say what you believe" as a critical condition of Cicero's use of the Socratic method in moving to the truth; he notes that this expectation "informs" Cicero's philosophical writings. He relates sincerity (114–25) to the specific kind of serious appeal that Cicero is thought to intend to make to Romans with his philosophical arguments.
17. *Off.* 1.108.
18. *Brut.* 292. In *De Or.* 2.269–70, Cicero has Julius Caesar Strabo, in a discourse on wit, present Socrates as the age-old master of irony. At *Ac.* 2.74, Cicero speaks of the irony of Socrates as a permanent (*perpetua*) feature of his way and as one supported by Plato.
19. *Ac.* 2.14–15. From the perspective of Lucullus, who is representing the position of Antiochus, what Arcesilaus does is translated better as "revolu-

tion" than "reform" (*Arcesilaus qui constitutam philosophiam everteret*). As evident above, Cicero's view of the reform or refounding of the Academy by Arcesilaus is more appreciative (see also *Ac.* 1.44; 2.76–77). Arcesilaus is seen to bring back the essential dimension of the Socratic method. However the fact that Arcesilaus employs the second-best of Socratic methods seems to be related to the fact that, in Cicero's view, Arcesilaus carries skepticism too far and beyond Socrates himself, for Arcesilaus is interested in relieving his hearers and students of the need to make judgments rather than bringing them, as Cicero would, to make judgments of the probable or likely true. Long (1988: 158–60) indicates that there was no "rigorously skeptical Socrates prior to Arcesilaus" in the tradition of Hellenistic philosophy. He speaks of Arcesilaus as "the discoverer of the skeptical Socrates." Vlastos (1991: 4, 82–83 n. 4, 114 n. 35) does not correctly interpret certain passages in Cicero in their contexts when he infers that Cicero sees Socrates in the tradition of the radical skepticism of Arcesilaus.

20. Vlastos (1985: 6). In the same vein, Burnyeat (1997: 290) has aptly remarked that Socrates must have some knowledge if he is to be "a philosophical hero."
21. The argument concerning Socratic irony throughout this section can also be stated and elaborated this way: Cicero has implicitly made a connection between this irony and Socratic/Academic method in that fidelity to the method as a form of personal inquiry entails irony when the method is employed by a teacher. In other words, the Socratic/Academic method of pursuing or "doing" philosophy permits the teacher of philosophy to stimulate the inquiry and to lead one along in it but not to draw for anyone else but himself the conclusions that appear true. Furthermore, since Cicero takes Socrates's irony as pretense of ignorance, he sees in Socrates one who possesses knowledge in some way and who, thus, possesses a basis for the rhetorical mode, for persuasion, consolation, or exhortation from the standpoint of that knowledge. Irony as a pretense of ignorance could itself be a rhetorical strategy, that is, it could be motivated more by the desire to bring a person to a certain truth (so one gets out of the way as a parent might remove herself from being a psychological obstacle to a child drawing her own conclusion) than by the desire to simulate in teaching the best method of critical inquiry.

    Vlastos credits Cicero (1991: Chap. 1, esp. 28–29, 43) as the first to capture the distinctive character of Socratic irony freed from the earlier Greek notion of intentional deceit. Cicero sees, then, that there is a sense in which Socrates does not know. Vlastos suggests, however, (and not correctly in my view, see n. 19 above) that Cicero misses the sense in which Socrates knows and that he regards Socrates as a radical skeptic. Gorman,

however, sees clearly that Cicero accepts irony as dissembling as a Socratic way of teaching, which he himself can embrace (2005: 48-50, nn. 31-32, p. 96 ff.).
22. At *Tusc.* 1.17, Cicero indicates that what he here speaks continuously and rhetorically rests on probability not certainty. Bentley (1743: 250), noting that Cicero is true to his perception of Socrates in taking the probable as the practically certain, makes the interesting observation that "if we seek therefore for **Cicero's** true Sentiments, it must not be in his Disputes against Others, where he had license to say any thing [sic] for opposition sake: but in the Books where he dogmatizes himself; where allowing for the word **Probable**, you have all the Spirit and Marrow of the **Platonic**, **Peripatetic**, and **Stoic** Systems; I mean his Books, *De Officiis, Tusculanae, De Amicitia, De Senectute, De Legibus....*"
23. Above, Chap. 1, 19-20.
24. Mackenzie brings out the fact that Socrates's elenctic practice (see n. 8 above) entails internal or self-knowledge, in the sense that Socrates must know what knowledge is, and she concludes that we cannot then call Socrates a skeptic (1988: 331-50). That Socrates is not an absolute or radical skeptic does not mean that he is not a skeptic in a certain sense, as both Cicero and Vlastos contend.
25. Tarrant (1985: Chap. 4) brings forward that tradition in the Academy of seeing both Socrates and Plato as neither totally and radically skeptical nor as dogmatic; also see Long (1988 150 ff).
26. *Ac.* 1.44-45.
27. *Ac.* 1.16. John Glucker notes the force of *adfirmare* in the texts of Cicero with respect to Socrates: "What matters is that it appears that one can ascribe to Plato, or his Socrates, the expression of positive views, as long as they are not accompanied by *adfirmatio*" (1997: 59-60 n. 6).
28. *Tusc* 1.97-100. In this exhortative and rhetorical work, Cicero seems to indicate some impatience or perplexity with the tension between Socrates's professed ignorance and apparent assurance. In the sentence (*Tusc.* 1.99-100) that immediately follows his observing that "Socrates stood by to the end..." (*tenet ad extremum*), Cicero writes, in the form of direct contrast, (*Nos autem teneamus, ut nihil censeamus esse malum...*) "We, however, take the position that we should think nothing evil which nature provides for all...." Death, then, for Cicero, cannot be considered an evil. What Cicero here confesses to "hold" or "know," may well also be his understanding of an important part of Socrates's "knowledge" as evident in the *Apology*. Consider that throughout the *Apology* (note especially 29a-b), Socrates stresses that doing injustice is a known evil and the nature of death is unknown; then in his last speech he sets out to tell "how great a hope there is" that death is good, for it must be "either of two things," neither

of which entail evil at least for *the good man*. Near the end (41c–d) he tells the judges that they too "should be of good hope toward death, and you should think this one thing to be true: that there is nothing bad for a good man, whether living or dead, and that the gods are not without care for his troubles." Translation of *The Apology* in this note is that of T. & G. West (1998). The *Phaedo*, which is also explicitly referred to in *Tusc.*, provides additional support that Cicero is here a faithful interpreter of an apparent tension in Socrates's position. Note especially at 63b–c, where Socrates, reflecting on the afterlife, asks his listeners to "be assured that I hope I shall find myself in the company of good men, although I would not maintain it for certain; but that I shall pass over to gods who are very good masters, be assured that **if** I would maintain for certain anything else of the kind, I would with certainty maintain this" (bold is mine). Socrates then indicates his overall conclusion, "I have good hopes that something remains for the dead, as has been the belief from time immemorial, and something much better for the good than for the bad," trans. Rouse (1956). Socrates is clearly indicating that his good hopes are relatively reliable ones, that, in other words, *if he were to maintain anything as certain* (which he does not do), his conviction about the afterlife would be among such certainties. Socrates, as one might expect of the father of the Academic school, then, knows and does not know at the same time, and this is no contradiction because it involves an equivocation in the use of "know," as has been well brought forward in the work of Vlastos (1985: 2, n.5, 3–4, 11 ff.; 1991: 4, 13). Socrates does not know in the sense of having absolute certainty, but he knows in some way, for only that allows him to claim that he knows that he does not know and to avoid a disabling skepticism. In returning to the text of *Tusc.*, from which this note began (*sed suum illud, nihil ut adfirmet, tenet ad extremum. Nos autem teneamus, ut nihil censeamus esse malum, quod sit a natura datum omnibus....*), one can see this passage as expressing agreement rather than impatience or perplexity with Socrates. The contrast is not between Socrates refusing to affirm anything and Cicero affirming the specific truth that death cannot be bad. The contrast seems more to be between a refusal to affirm (*affirmet*) and a willingness to opine (*censeamus*), to hold some views sufficiently reliable that one might even call them knowledge. Thus, to say (*Nos autem teneamus, ut nihil censeamus...*) "We, however, hold the view that we should think nothing evil..." can be seen as consistent with an insistence that nothing is to be affirmed. This is, after all, Socrates's position in the *Phaedo*.
29. *Orat.* 237–38; *Ac.* 2.32.
30. *Tusc.* 1.8.
31. The defense of philosophy in the *Hortensius* appears to involve the claim that happiness is found in searching for wisdom while remaining free of the

trap of affirmation. It seems that such searching would be satisfying only if it were it some way fruitful, that one came in some sense to possess wisdom, but clearly it is to be a wisdom without the assurance that affirmation entails. See Grilli (1962: frs. 106–07, pp. 49–50). Also, *Tusc.* 5.68 ff.
32. *Off.* 1.90, 148; 2.43; 3.11; *Tusc.* 1.71, 100; 3.8, 31; 4.80; 5.26, 47, 91, 97; *Fin.* 2.90; *Inv.* 1.90; *Leg.* 1.33–34; *Att.* 363.
33. *Ac.* 1.16.
34. *De Or.* 1.204.
35. Vlastos's elaboration of the difference between moral certainty, which Socrates has, and epistemic certainty, which he has not, is pertinent to the effective criterion discussed in Chap. 1 (1985: 6–7, n. 14; 1991: 269–71).
36. *Tusc.* 5.47–48; *Fin.* 2.86.
37. Above, Chap. 1, 30–31, n. 83.
38. *Tusc.* 2.11; see also *Ac.* 2.65, where vices like obstinacy and contentiousness are shown to be out of character with the high calling of philosophy. Similarly, Cicero criticizes historical interest that is driven by mere curiosity, devoid of any moral interest; *Fin.* 5.6. The scandal of professional philosophers was commented on by Cornelius Nepos in an apparent communication to Cicero where, among other things, he says that, given their practices, philosophers more than anyone have need of learning how to live (Rolfe trans. 1966, 696).
39. Above n. 21.
40. Recall from Chap. 1 that Antiochus, who is known to have emphasized the positive teaching of Socrates, is much appreciated by Cicero. Assenting, at least, to the truth that we do not know is where the Academic position appears to rest in *Ac.2*.
41. *Fin.* 2.15.
42. Scaevola's comment (*De Or.* 1.204) on Socrates cited just above describes the essential work of Socrates in terms of exhortation (*concitatus cohortatione*) and persuasion (*id persuasum esset*) to the philosophical life, understood as the pursuit of life-directing virtues.
43. Garsten (2009) offers an excellent exploration of such questions in the history of Western political thought. His book seeks to restore respect for persuasion, rhetoric, and judgment in politics.
44. *De Or.* 1.28; *Orat.* 14–15; *Fin.* 2.4. In this respect, see the interpretation of the role of the *Phaedrus* in *Leg.* 1 by Benardete (1987: esp. 308–09).
45. *Tusc.* 1.112 is another instance of Cicero's apparent constant awareness of his use or non-use of the rhetorical mode. Other instances follow in this chapter.
46. J.S. Reid, amid certain misjudgments many years ago, did rightly observe (1885: 25) that Cicero's dialogues are "of the later Greek type, and not of

the kind with which we are so familiar from the work of Plato." That form is said "to have died with Plato," and the later form is said to be "much less dramatic" and to contain "much less of question and answer and of repartee, and much more of continuous exposition." He adds, "The conversation between the characters was confined to a few episodes, and the various conflicting views of the subject discussed were delivered in uninterrupted, or scarcely interrupted speeches of considerable length." A probing of these features of Cicero's dialogues and a partial explanation in terms of sources is found in Zoll's thorough study of Cicero's dialogue form (1962). Note Lévy (1992: 322–24) on what is, in effect, the mixed modes pervading Cicero's philosophical works; also Buckley (1970: 144 ff.). Inwood (1990: 151–53, 162) discusses what Cicero loses in philosophical acuteness and what he might gain from his overall commitment to "rhetorical philosophy." A recent and excellent exploration of rhetoric's role and Cicero's preferred Socratic method in his works is found in Gorman (2005: esp. 66, 73–75, 79, 131, 142, 176).

47. *Fin.* 2.17; the statement, here, on philosophical rhetoric is directly intended to apply to Cicero's response to Torquatus which follows in *Fin.* 2, though it very likely also applies to Cicero's later response to Cato in *Fin.* 4 and to Piso's discourse in *Fin.* 5. At *Orat.* 62–64 Cicero gives a more extensive comparison of the characteristics of philosophical speech and oratorical speech, the latter appearing to be the same as forensic or popular rhetoric described in *Fin.*. At *Orat.* 64, Cicero says that although all speech (*omnis locutio*) is *oratio* in a generic sense, that which the orator exercises is properly called *oratio*; philosophical speech should properly be called *sermo*, the same term used to describe Socrates's preferred form of short exchanges above. "Philosophical rhetoric," then, as exemplified in Cicero's discourses in *Fin.*, would seem to share something of the quality of *oratio* in the specific sense (being actually called *quasi torrens oratio*) and something of the quality of *sermo* insofar as it is philosophical. Among the qualities of *sermo*, according to *Orat.* 62–64, are that it is a speech with which the learned (*cum doctis*) aimed more to settle souls than to arouse them (*sedare animos …quam incitare*)—that in considering less stirring matters, it seeks to teach rather than captivate—and that it is gentle and erudite. See Zoll's discussion (1962: 52–60) of Cicero's combining of *disputatio* and *sermo*. Also see especially Remer's illuminating discussion of *sermo* along with the argument that such discourse is, in a broad sense, to be action oriented for Cicero (1999: 43–49). Note the internal dialectic as in a soliloquy which can characterize an *oratio*; such is exemplified in Cicero's speech against Epicureanism in *Fin.* 2. Regarding *oratio* in the generic sense, Cicero at *Fin.* 5.84 describes the speech of Socrates and Plato as *honesta oratio*. At *Off.* 1.3 Cicero observes that he has at least tried for what has been rarely

achieved, namely distinction in both forms of *oratio*, forensic as well as philosophical speech.
48. *Amic.* 4–5.
49. Gorman (2005: 66), commenting on the *Tusculans* as a possible instance of Cicero "confusedly mixing two incompatible types of discourse," observes that "[a] closer look will show that the two types of philosophical speech have been combined with some skill and reinforce each other to produce Cicero's desired effect." Also, see 73–79 in this same work.
50. *Div.* 2.1. Both the Ruch and Grilli reconstructions of the *Hortensius* provide the basis for this inference about the mixed character of the exchanges.
51. *Tusc.* 1.7.
52. Douglas (1995: 200–01) sees *Tusc.* 1.7 as a key to understanding Cicero as advancing "rhetoricized philosophy" rather than "philosophical rhetoric." This theme is elaborated in a very significant passage at *Leg.* 1.58–62, where Cicero indicates that wisdom comes to embrace the rhetorical mode once it comes to understand the political nature of human life (see Benardete 1987: 308). See also DiLorenzo on *perfectus orator* in Cicero and on Ciceronianism as a conception of philosophy (1978: 248–52, 259; 1982: 172–73).
53. See also *De Or.* 3.71–73; 2.35.
54. Long (1995: 52 ff.) examines Cicero's attraction to Aristotle as a student of rhetoric. Making arguments on each side of a matter (*in utramque partem dicere*) which Aristotle emphasized for the development of the rhetorical art fits well with the role of arguing pro and con, as in Carneades and Philo, in the tradition of Academic skepticism. See both Buckley's discussion (1970: 145 ff.) of the Socratic heritage in these developments and Nicgorski (2013).
55. A measure of Cicero's success is found in a tribute Montesquieu pays to him in his "Discourse on Cicero" (Fott trans. 2002: 734), "[Cicero] does not give precepts; but he makes them felt. He does not exhort to virtue; but he attracts to it."
56. In Aristotle's terms, Cicero's *perfecta philosophia* is practical philosophy having attained its proper end—the actual practice of virtue. *Nicomachean Ethics*, 1095a4–5; 1179a35–b3.
57. See especially *Tusc.* 2.47 ff., where the nature of *perfecta virtus* is discussed, and *Leg.* 1.58, where wisdom (*sapientia*) is presented as the object of philosophy and the mother of all good things, including the law which is to provide the guiding principles of life, deterring humankind from vice and drawing them to virtue. *Fin.* 2.23–24 for Cato (minor), explaining the Stoic *perfecta ratio*, and *Fin.* 5.38 for Piso, giving Peripatetic support to the idea that the perfection of reason is found in virtue. Cicero, writing this Cato his peer in 51 (*Fam.*110.16), invokes their common dedication and

endeavor to bring "that true and ancient philosophy" (*philosophia illa vera et antiqua*) into political life.
58. *Sen.* 4.
59. *Sen.* 5; *Amic,* 6–7.
60. *Amic.* 5.
61. *Amic.* 6–7; *Rep.* 3.5–6. In fact, Cato major is thought to be behind the Roman Senate's decrees allowing the expulsion of teachers of philosophy and rhetoric (161 B.C.) and ejecting the "ambassadors" of philosophy in 154 (Diogenes, Carneades, and Critolaus). William Stahl summarizes the various forms of Cato's hostility to Scipio and the Greek influences on Roman ways in the second century B.C. (1962: 73–74).

"The Scipionic Circle" has been a traditional way of speaking of a second-century political-cultural group centered around Scipio and Laelius and is thought to include the Stoic Rhodian teacher Panaetius and the Greek historian Polybius. Zetzel (1972: 173 ff.) doubts its actual historical existence, finds little to no evidence that Cicero himself is asserting its actual existence, and draws attention to the differences between Cicero's portrayal of key characters in his dialogues (e.g. Cato major) and historical truth. See also his "Introduction" to his *Rep.* translation (1999: 12–13). See also MacKendrick (1989: 54), 328 n. 27. This "Circle" might be understood as one way to speak about a given historical cluster of learned statesmen in the wider field of "*consulares philosophi,*" considered above in the Introduction and Chap. 1.
62. *Amic.* 7; *Sen.* 4.
63. *Rep.* 1.2.
64. Above, n. 61's last sentence and directions to earlier considerations of the topic.
65. Crassus is made to bring this charge against Socrates in *De Or.* 3.60. Years ago, Buckley (1970: 147) commented, "Cicero envisaged his own career as a recapitulation of the efforts of Aristotle in the reuniting of rhetorical and philosophic excellences."
66. When Cicero, in *Tusc.* 5.11, talks openly about his masking his opinion in the conversations at Tusculan recorded in the work, he has ceased to mask his opinion at least to the same degree he presumably did in direct and spontaneous conversation. Annas, while properly noting that Cicero's Academic affiliation leads him to present various positions with which he does not necessarily agree, goes too far and surely beyond what we can know, in her claiming that "in none of his philosophical works does he put forward arguments (as opposed to incidental remarks) for a position which represents what he the individual Marcus Tullius Cicero thinks" (1989: 172).
67. In this respect, however, note the distinctive character of the *Tusculans*, above, Chap. 1, n. 36.

68. Though caution, as to just what Cicero's position is, is called for, Mary Beard on *Div.* goes too far in arguing that "no weight is added to the arguments against divination because they are spoken in the dialogue by the character of Marcus himself" (1986: 35). Levine has argued with respect to *Nat. D.* that the limited role of Cicero-*persona* in this dialogue, compared to his other philosophical dialogues, is among the effects of a revision or change in design of the dialogue as Cicero worked on it. In moving the principal role from his own *persona* to Cotta, Cicero was apparently alert to the authority that his *persona* would carry, and he possibly sought either to disguise his view on the sensitive matter of the gods or to indicate that in a critical respect he did not agree with the Academic position that Cotta represents though he might agree with much else that Cotta has said (1957: 16 ff.).
69. *Rep.* 3.8; *Nat. D.* 1.57, 60; 3.1; at 2.168, Balbus, within the dialogue, draws attention to the Academic commitment of Cotta to foster arguments on both sides of issues even if it allows taking up a view that is not one's own.
70. Thus, I reach a point of apparent disagreement with the observation of Bentley (above, n. 22), and find myself more in accord with Tarrant (1985: 35-36) who comments on Charmades, student of Carneades, and his role in an Academic tradition that does not argue *pro* and *contra* without holding an opinion—an opinion often revealed in the structuring and comparative intensity of the *pro* and *contra* formulations. Cicero's views are, at the most, only comparatively, never totally, masked in his writings. As to the possible presence of circumspect or even esoteric writing in Cicero, it should be noted that comparative or relative masking allows for this. Writing can, of course, be recognized as circumspect or esoteric only if there are internal indications of the author's true views.
71. Douglas on the intent of Cicero's dialogues, (1985:12-13; 1965:140 f.; 1962:46-48). In this last reference in particular, Douglas notes Cicero's careful attention to dramatic detail. Also Levine (1957: *passim*). Looking at particular dialogues, MacKendrick (1989: 42, 83) sees the dramatic details as chosen to add "authority" and "seriousness" to dialogues.

Cicero's letters make clear not only that he is giving serious attention to the dramatic details of his dialogues, as he writes and revises them, but also that his rhetorical intent can encompass enhancing his own authority in the political and intellectual circles of Rome as well as advancing the intended message of the dialogue. Thus, in a letter to Atticus (*Att.* 326) late in his life (45 B.C.), Cicero shows an awareness of the impact on the authority (today we might speak of "image") of contemporaries, including himself, being given a presence and a certain kind of role in his later dialogues. The later dialogues are here explicitly seen as after "the custom (*mos*) of Aristotle"—meaning that the principal part goes to the author—in contrast with those major dialogues (*Rep.* and *De Or.*) written and made public in the 50s in which, Cicero notes, a role for him would have been anachronistic and inappropriate.

I have come to conclude, against what I have written earlier (2012, though originally written in 1978: 249), that Cicero's turn to the dialogue is not primarily a way of following Carneades and the New Academy by serving as a means of concealing his own opinion. This change of interpretation toward seeing his presence or absence in a dialogue in terms of intended rhetorical effect removes the difficulty with which I struggled in the "Rebirth" piece, namely that Cicero reveals his position in the author's *prooemium* even in those dialogues where he does not personally appear. In an earlier letter to Atticus (89) Cicero claims, as he works on *Rep.*, that he is following Aristotle's model in his exoteric books (apparently Aristotle's now lost dialogues) by writing a *prooemium* to each book of the work. The letter to Atticus and the variety of dialogue and other forms utilized by Cicero all along make unlikely the conjecture of Rawson (1974: 233) that he lost interest in the dialogue form in his last writings. Rather, Cicero is better seen throughout his writings as a highly conscious adapter of established forms (primarily the Platonic and Aristotelian dialogues) to his specific rhetorical objective in the work at hand.

Aristotle's dialogues appear to have been a major influence in Cicero's shaping of his own dialogue form. See above, n. 46 where Reid writes of the "later Greek type" of dialogue, which is apparently the Aristotelian dialogue and possibly that of a contemporary of Aristotle, Heraclides, who is mentioned several times in Cicero's correspondence. Zoll gives substantial attention to the impact of the Aristotelian *disputatio* on Cicero (1962: 36, 52–60, 146). In an earlier letter, written as he completed *De Or.* (*Fam.* 20.23), Cicero says that he has written this work according to the way of Aristotle (*Aristoteleus mos*)—meaning here, I believe, that he uses longer speeches, for he himself is not cast as a participant in this dialogue. Jaeger has made a precise and discerning statement on the three distinct Aristotelian precedents respecting the dialogue form that Cicero cites in his correspondence (1934: 29–30 n. 2).

Two notes of caution are called for while recognizing Cicero's more Aristotelian and less Platonic approach in his dialogues. First, Platonic dialogues do, indeed, seem more genuinely philosophical than Cicero's (in the terminology of this chapter, more in the *critical mode*), and it is understandable that Douglas (above) and others have seen Plato actually in the process of working out the solution to philosophical problems in his dialogues. Even for Plato, however, to write the dialogue is to step back from the openness and spontaneity of philosophical dialectic (which presumably Socrates exemplified in a practice without writing) and to step into a conscious rhetorical mode—at the minimum, perhaps, being an effort to portray and thereby commend a genuinely philosophical conversation (consider in relation to n. 65 above). The second and related note of caution is not to confuse Cicero's overriding rhetorical purpose and use of longer discourse with philosophical ineptitude or an inability to appreciate the power of alternative philosophical positions. Cicero's dialogues do not feature "the straw man"; see Schmitt (1972: 84). It is also significant to note that long speeches can contain a very real internal dialogue, as in *Fin.* 2 and as in cases where Socrates sometimes takes up the role of interlocutor and asks questions of his own position. How we miss Aristotle's dialogues! It appears that the Aristotle Cicero knew was notably more eloquent than the Aristotle we now have.

72. Thomas Tarver (1997: 162-63) observes, "Cicero exploited a marriage between the sceptical intellectual stance of the New Academy and the possibilities of the rhetoric of the dialogue."

73. Above, including n. 42 where Socrates as a person is characterized by an effort at persuasion to a way of life. Cicero, speaking chiefly through Crassus, notes that Plato and his Socrates in the *Gorgias* show masterful rhetoric to, as it were, clip the wings of rhetoric, *De Or.* 1.47; 3.60, 129. Also, insofar as the irony that characterized the practice of Socratic method implied knowledge, the critical mode of inquiry, is likely to be strategic rather than pure and to be employed to the degree that the context warrants; above, esp. n. 21.

74. *Fat.* 3.

75. Lorenzo Valla and other Renaissance humanists are said to appreciate the integral relationship between Cicero's skepticism and his commitment to rhetoric; see Jardine (1983: 253-89). Jardine observes at one point (254), "[I]f Cicero is viewed as consistently taking a skeptic's stand, it is possible to bring together his philosophical and oratorical [rhetorical] works in one coherent reading." In this respect, see Garsten's discussion of Erasmus (2009: 40-41).

76. *Fin.* 5.6,43. In 5, 43, Cicero portrays Piso describing how the reasoning of the philosopher must be ignited (*accendere*) from an inborn spark. Plutarch (1960: 143-44 [3.1, 4.1]), in reporting on those who significantly influenced Cicero's philosophical education, introduces Philo as one whom the Romans "admired for his eloquence and loved for his character" above other Academic philosophers and Antiochus as one "whose fluency and elegance of diction" much attracted Cicero.

77. Cicero's awareness of the fundamental moral choice that philosophy itself involves is, according to Lactantius, highlighted in his *Hortensius*, where a disputation over whether philosophy should be pursued is taken, as itself, an inherently philosophical and moral choice, Grilli (1962: fr. 54, p. 32).

78. Cicero understands true eloquence as a dressing up—making vivid and attractive—that to which we are drawn by reason; *Inv.* 1.3. Consider Platonic myths as rhetoric in this vein; in the *Phaedo* (114d), the myth of the afterlife is explicitly presented with the intent to build the confidence of the listeners for what has already been argued. Relevant to this and the myth of Er in the *Republic*, see above, n. 28 for a reflection on the nature of the assurance Socrates has regarding the afterlife.
79. *Leg.* 1.32.
80. See *Tusc* 2.13, where the "magister" (likely the view of Cicero here) says that "all cultivated fields do not bear fruit" (*frugiferi*) and argues that Accius the tragedian is wrong in saying that healthy (*probae*) seed will bear *fruges* even when set in poor soil (*in segetem deteriorem*). Direct application of such terms as *probus, frux,* and *deterius* to matters of character and morality is common in classical Latin. See also *Tusc* 4.60–61 where different moral dispositions are shown to set limits on what a philosophically informed rhetoric can accomplish.
81. *Tusc.* 5.104–05.
82. *Rep.* 5.11.
83. *Tusc.* 1.6. Gorman (2005: 191) concludes his important book with an emphasis on Cicero's concern that philosophy be persuasive and effectual and, thus, overcome the limits of close dialectic.
84. *Tusc* 2.9. Smith (1995: 301–23) emphasizes Cicero's view that philosophy requires rhetoric, as she explores the dangers of the bringing together of philosophy and rhetoric in Cicero.
85. That fullness which is true eloquence is that of the perfect orator, namely, wisdom joined to the complete mastery of rhetorical technique, *De Or.* 3.55; consider also *Off.* 1.2–4. At *Fat.* 3, where Cicero speaks of the Academic school supplying the orator with *subtilitas*, he notes that he as an orator contributes "fertility and lustre" (*ubertas orationis et ornamenta*) to the philosophical work of the school. Recall that at least one contemporary of Cicero, Cornelius Nepos, shared (Rolfe trans. 1966: 696) Cicero's self-perception that he brings eloquence and finish to philosophy.
86. *Tusc.* 4.9–10, 33.
87. *Tusc.* 5.18–19.
88. *Off.* 1.93–94; *De Or.* 1.132; 3.212.
89. At *De Or.* 2.62, 64–70, Antonius notes the bearing of the art of rhetoric on writing history, teaching, warning, and comforting. His claim is that even if the formal art of rhetoric as developed does not specifically extend to these forms of expression, one who knows the art will possess the principles for appropriate expression in these forms.

CHAPTER 3

Duties and Virtue

> Were those terms [right and justice, *honestas et justitia*] not employed by philosophers, we would have no need at all for philosophy. Through love of those very ideas of wisdom, courage, justice, and temperance, so rarely mentioned by Epicurus, men of the greatest talents have devoted themselves to the study of philosophy. (Cicero, *Fin.* 2. 51)
>
> And Socrates properly persisted in condemning that man who first separated the useful (*utilitatem*) from the right (*jure*), for that, he charged, was the source of all moral disorder. (Cicero, *Leg.* 1. 33–34)

Socrates's way of life entailed an answer to the question that was explicitly foundational for Cicero, the question of ends or of true happiness. Socrates's answer, that this happiness consisted solely in virtue, deeply attracted Cicero and seems chiefly to account for Cicero's high regard for the Stoics, the school that, in his eyes, was most faithful to Socrates regarding the supreme good. Cicero's reasons for following Socrates and the Stoics on this fundamental matter were rooted in his practical perspective.[1] This attraction to the Stoics does not mean that Cicero found the school in all respects the true heir of Socrates, nor that he thought its teachings entirely adequate to the practical perspective.

To claim that Cicero has reasons for choosing the path of virtue is not, of course, to say that he had attained certainty about this fundamental choice or that he had even thought that the correctness of such a choice could be demonstrated in some absolutely conclusive way. Quite to the contrary for Cicero the skeptic. In fact, this choice, even for Cicero and surely for many of those he sought to influence in his writings, seemed to require rhetorical support and reinforcement such as that provided by the examples of virtuous lives of Roman heroes and statesmen. Thus, even at this foundational level, mixed modes of discourse were appropriate. Though this basic choice was to be an examined or philosophically informed choice, it entailed justifying philosophy even as it utilized it. Lack of absolute certainty on the rightness of this choice must not, however, be allowed to obscure Cicero's conviction that a relative assurance on its correctness is possible. In fact, the choice of the supreme good can illumine all of philosophy.[2] It is the point of greatest possible assurance among all the potential "findings" of philosophy. This fundamental choice appeared for Cicero not only to justify philosophy but also, by providing an anchor for all knowledge, to make philosophy—in any meaningful sense of a pursuit of wisdom—possible.

What does it specifically mean for Cicero to follow the path of virtue—to have concluded that happiness is found in *perfecta philosophia*? To choose the path of virtue, presumably, means more than to embrace this central Stoic teaching as a truism or to pick the path of an abstraction, an edifying but empty concept. The fundamental choice would hardly be illuminating unless virtue is understood in ways that provide more specific guidance in the pursuit of happiness. What are the tasks or duties of a virtuous person? Cicero most directly addresses this question in his work on duties, *De Officiis*, a writing once described by a thoughtful statesman as doing honor both to human understanding and to human heart.[3] *Officiis* draws openly, though critically and apparently selectively, on a form of Stoic ethics presented earlier by Panaetius (185–109).[4] *Officiis*, the last of Cicero's philosophical writings to be completed, takes up the question of duty as it appears in the common moral horizon and with an explicit commitment to use the ordinary language in which the dilemmas and perplexities of moral choice arise for most people. In these respects, Panaetius clearly appears to have been Cicero's model.[5] This horizon, from which inquiry proceeds—and the language of *Officiis*—not only appears appropriate for Cicero's son, the formal addressee of the work, and for all Romans who might benefit from this endeavor but also seem to be Cicero's own, being entirely suitable to a public person of action.[6] The horizon is framed in terms of a common human concern to act in accord with the right and the useful, the moral and the expedient, with special attention to situations where the right and the useful pull in different directions.

In the *Officiis*, then, the question of ends and the supreme good is located by Cicero in relationship to ordinary moral choices: "[E]very inquiry into duty," writes Cicero, "has two major parts," one of which concerns the supreme good (*finis bonorum*).[7] The question of the ends is encountered here, not as in *Divinatione 2* as one topic—though a central and illuminating one—in a program for philosophical inquiry but as an ineluctable center toward which choices point and from which they are illuminated and directed.[8] Some questions, writes Cicero, such as asking about priority between conflicting duties, directly require an understanding of the supreme good for resolution. For Cicero, then, a practical orientation or perspective elevates the importance of the fundamental choice of the supreme good in a fashion very similar to that long before exemplified in the opening paragraphs of Aristotle's *Nicomachean Ethics*.[9] The emphasis, however, in Cicero's *Officiis*, is not—nor for that matter is it for Aristotle—on a teaching about the supreme good or happiness that can be tapped to offer solutions to quite immediate moral choices. Cicero is not teaching that one strictly deduces duties or morality from a conception of the highest end or good.

For Cicero, duty is what is right in the sense of what is to be done;[10] virtue consists in choosing the right, thus seeking to do it. The duties that Cicero claims to explicate and examine in the *Officiis* are precepts for governing everyday life.[11] When Cicero observes that "though these duties are related to the supreme good, this is nonetheless hardly in evidence," he gives an indication of the complex nature of the relationship between ordinary everyday responsibilities and an understanding of the highest good. Ordinary duties (*communis officium*), also called by him "mean" duties (*media officia*), are those which can be argued for (*ratio probabilis reddi possit*).[12] An argument for seeing some action as a duty means an argument as to why that action is to be done. Such an argument, presumably, would take into consideration a conception of the supreme good when one is shared in the context of argument and does not have to be established. Even in such a case, the specific action before one, involving, as it might, issues such as telling the truth or taking life in a given context, chiefly requires an argument to establish the character of the action proposed.[13] In seeking to establish the character of the action as according to or against nature, right or wrong, useful or not, the argument might appeal to many different considerations including various ways of reading nature and such inclinations and principles that appear to emanate from an *a priori* voice of conscience. Only, however, when an action characterized in some way is brought under the rubric of the supreme good can it be seen clearly as that which should be done and be fully embraced as duty.[14] So it seems for Cicero that the concept of the supreme good is central to moral action but, because so much argument in ordinary moral choice is over the character of a proposed action, it hardly comes into view in deliberation.[15]

Duties, in some form, appear for Cicero to precede in human awareness the notion of the supreme good.[16] This precedence is clearly revealed when Cicero observes that though philosophy is to bear fruit in teaching duties, some schools of philosophy undermine the entire notion of duty (*officium omne pervertant*) by their conceptions of the greatest good and greatest evil.[17] By way of example, Cicero points to that man who "constitutes the supreme good so it would in no way be connected with virtue and defines it in terms of his own conveniences (*suis commodis*)" rather than in terms of goodness or virtue itself (*honestate*).[18] That Cicero has most in mind here the Epicureans becomes unquestionably clear in what immediately follows. Cicero says of that man who measures the good by his own conveniences that if he maintains consistency and is not, along the way, overcome by the goodness of nature (*naturae bonitate*), he is unable to cherish and embrace (*colere*) friendship, justice or liberality; nor could he in any way be brave who set pain as the greatest evil, or temperate while holding pleasure as the greatest good.[19] Cicero, here, indicates that certain commonly perceived goods and virtues, such as friendship and courage, both much esteemed in the Roman tradition, are seen as the very test of the adequacy of a conception of the supreme good. Cicero holds that a philosopher whose teaching on the supreme good undermines duty is barren and, in fact, dangerous. Clearly, such a man would not be worthy of the name philosopher. Furthermore, in using the phrase, "overcome by the goodness of nature," Cicero makes his revealing observation that the Epicureans live better than their theories and points toward nature and nature's inclinations as the source for those commonly perceived goods and virtues and the ultimate check on "philosophers'" theories of the supreme good.[20]

There is a twofold significance in finding that Cicero holds our awareness of duties to be prior to any clear general conception of the supreme good, including that true one of virtue itself. First, it gives some indication of what may be available to supply the need when one draws the logical conclusion that the fundamental choice of virtue as the supreme good must be made with some understanding and awareness of what virtue consists in.[21] Attention to what is available and prior is a way of access to the very ground of Cicero's entire philosophy—of viewing and understanding the ingredients of that effective criterion that Cicero employs to determine the supreme good and to find what truth he can among the teachings of the various philosophical schools of his time. Second, the priority of duties to the conception of the supreme good itself means that there is a way of knowing what concretely is to be done by the person who would follow the path of virtue. The prior awareness of goods and virtues, then, not only gives one a basis for finding in a life of virtue the highest good but also provides specific direction to the person who has chosen the path of virtue.

Cicero saw his philosophical writings as a way to serve Rome, specifically as a way to shore up the faltering virtue of Rome.[22] Observing the dual significance given to the priority of duties, evident in Cicero's moral philosophy, opens a way to understanding how he appears to think of philosophy as an instrument for strengthening duty, or how, in other words, he could expect philosophy to be so fruitful. If one thing moral philosophy does is to inspect the scene or those factors in human nature and the human context that make the way of virtue credible as the highest good, it thereby can strengthen the attachment to virtue. That same inspection, which can strengthen the attachment to virtue as an end, also clarifies specific duties and virtues, namely what is to be done here and now in the light of an overall commitment to a life of virtue. Cicero's moral and political philosophy is always moving toward both these goals and, in the process, employs mixed modes of philosophy as appropriate. All that he teaches falls within this framework.

There seems to be good reason for looking at the *Officiis,* in the manner of some scholars, as a culminating and integrating philosophical work for Cicero.[23] Whether or not he so intended, it, clearly, can function that way in helping one see the structure of his thought. What, then, is the prior and, ultimately, constitutive of the supreme good, and what is also foundational to Cicero's own philosophical judgments, can best, and perhaps most persuasively, be approached by working from the horizon provided in *Officiis*—beginning with the common understandings of the right and the useful and the experience of tension between those conceptions.

The Right and the Useful

Inquiry into the right (*honestas et jus*) and the useful (*utilitas*) serves well as a description of Cicero's understanding of the nature of moral and political philosophy. Though Panaetius is Cicero's immediate and self-confessed source for thus casting moral inquiry in *Officiis*, this formulation likely reflects a long-standing and understandable tradition, which Cicero encountered in other sources. Some indication of how long-standing it was is witnessed in the accounts of Socrates, including Cicero's own, as seeing that the moral problem arises, for most people, in the terms of the right and the useful.[24] Aristotle, in the *Politics*, presents the power of speech and reason (*logos*) as distinguishing the human being from other animals and serving primarily to express "the expedient and inexpedient, and therefore likewise the just and the unjust."[25] Cicero's own rhetorical writings, including that product of his youth, *Inventione*, show him emphasizing the terms of the right and the useful, and the tension between them as formally constitutive of the horizon, for most people and thus for the audiences, which the orator would be seeking to persuade.[26]

Determining duty, or what is to be done, entails, as already indicated, establishing the character of an action proposed. An action would apparently qualify as duty only if it fell within the range of the right and the useful, the kinds of actions to which human beings are drawn. When a proposed action is found to be both right and useful, clearly an important step in determining duty has been taken. When, however, *honestas* seems to pull in one direction and *utilitas* in an opposite direction, then, writes Cicero, our deliberation is troubled and we are caught up in indecision.[27] The *Officiis* seems to regard such troubled deliberation as a common experience. Here, as well as elsewhere in Cicero's writings, there are indications of a perspective on moral development where the experience of tension and conflict between the right and the useful diminishes as one gains self-understanding in the context of nature as a whole. Piso, in the last book of *Finibus*, is portrayed stating, apparently in accord with Cicero's own judgment,[28] that we come into the world marked with a certain immaturity and weakness which makes us "unable both to see what is best and to do it."[29] From birth on, humans are drawn to goods (*prima naturae commoda*)[30] or primary needs of nature such as preservation and health of body. Only later, he adds, "does the radiance of virtue and a happy life, those two objects most to be sought, come into view. And only much later do they come to be seen in a way that their natures are clearly understood." Such a clear and developed understanding is obtained when one recognizes, as Cicero says in the *Tusculans*, that "there is no happy life which is not at the same time a virtuous or rightful (*honesta*) one."[31] This stage, fully realized, seems to be that of the Stoic perfect Wiseman who would, presumably, not only affirm, as Cicero does frequently, that happiness and the supreme good consist in the life of virtue, but also knows the natures of happiness and the right with such thoroughness, clarity, and certainty that he confronts none of the troubled deliberations which beset humans in general.

Although the *Officiis* is shaped by and comes to affirm as true the view that happiness consists solely or essentially in virtue and that there can be, then, no real conflict between what is useful and what is right, it takes seriously the ordinary search for duties and common problems of deliberation over duty. No one, in fact, stands where the perfect Wiseman allegedly stands.[32] The ordinary horizon is unfolded in *Officiis* in a more elaborate way than what Cicero apparently found in Panaetius. In finding duty—in determining what should be done—a person not only is drawn to the apparently right and the seemingly beneficial or useful and, sometimes, caught between their divergent pulls, but also faces the need to establish the greater right among two courses of action that seem right, and the greater utility among two courses of action that appear useful.[33] Cicero's bringing out this additional complexity to ordinary deliberation helps to make clear the need for understanding the grounds or bases of the right and the useful.

The structure of the *Officiis* follows from Cicero's understanding of the five basic questions that appear in ordinary moral deliberation. What is the right and what is the more right of two good ways are considered in Book 1; what is the useful and what is the more useful of two expedient courses are taken up in Book 2. Book 3 turns to cases of apparent conflict between the right and the useful. In seeking the bases for the right and the useful in the first two books, Cicero is uncovering the same resources that must be employed to deal with the questions of comparative "rights" and comparative "utilities." Understanding the true bases of the right and the useful also provides the illumination necessary to show, in Book 3, that conflicts between the right and the useful are always apparent and never actual conflicts. Without naming specific duties, which constitute an important part of the *Officiis*, one can summarize the overall teaching of this work as stating that whether a person begins with the useful or the right as her primary concern, a full understanding of either will reveal that the truly expedient is the right and that the truly right is the expedient. Already in this exposition, there have been indications that this understanding is attained, according to Cicero, by looking to and interpreting nature.

Nature, Natural Law, and the Virtues

It is not surprising to find Cicero, long recognized, in at least some respects, as a follower of the Stoics, seeming to turn to their maxim "to live according to nature" *(convenienter naturae vivere)* at the critical point of determining duty.[34] Close attention, in the light of Cicero's Academic skepticism, to how he proposes to understand nature provides the proper context for interpreting the concept of natural law which has been widely seen as making its first significant appearance in Cicero's texts, though it too is often traced to the Stoics. This law should be seen, not as a detailed legal code but, primarily, as an obligation, the highest and source of all others, to interpret with the power of reason and then to follow the way of nature.[35] Civil laws, customs, good traditions, and the ordinary virtues associated with decency are but partial articulations of this law, which precedes all of these in an important sense, though not in the sense of its being experienced and understood first.

If the Stoic tradition had not provided such apt formulations to satisfy the need to appeal to and follow nature, it probably would have made little difference to Cicero or to any other cogent thinker about the moral life before or since his time. Such formulations, or their equivalents, would, then, have had to be invented as they, in fact, have been outside of the high Western tradition in which the Stoics and Cicero stand.[36] The appeal to nature, though not the phrase "natural law," had a critical role in the thinking of Socrates, Plato, and Aristotle, whom Cicero held in respect above all other philosophers.[37] It seems that moral discourse requires, in some form, an appeal to nature, meaning the *given* of our being and context; the only conceivable exceptions to this common horizon for moral inquiry appear to be constituted by interventions of the supernatural. In terms of Cicero's search for duties in *Officiis*, just as that which appears to be duty can only truly be so if brought in relationship to the supreme good, so too that supreme good could support a duty as duty only if this end or good were defensible in terms of the kind of beings humans are in the very nature of things.

However, as we have seen, duties are not derivative from but constitutive of the supreme good, that is, they give the kind of specificity to this good to make it a choice-worthy and useful concept. So it is understandable that nature is given a predominant position not only in the *Finibus*, where it is to function as the guide in choosing between competing conceptions of the supreme good, but also in the *Officiis*, where it is the determining standard to bring to light the truly right and the truly useful when confronted with what appears right and useful. According to Cicero, then, all roads in moral inquiry lead to nature, more specifically to the necessity of interpreting nature so she can be followed. The "broad" considerations (*rationes...latiore specie*) raised in testing against nature the conceptions of the ultimate good or happiness in *Finibus* contain appeals to duties to friends and political community as commonly understood and to the ordinary sense of virtues, to, in other words, a moral tradition.[38] These are, it seems, ways to reach nature's measure.[39] In this "testing," in *Finibus*, the Epicurean position on the ultimate good or nature of happiness is taken seriously and their case is given a full hearing, though in a rhetorical rather than dialectical mode.[40] Yet in the *Officiis*, where duty is sought, and in *Legibus*, where the foundations of morality and law are being laid, the Epicureans are seen as a threat and are sent away. In a sense, the Epicureans are also dismissed in the *Finibus*, when after the testing of their position in the first two books, Cicero writes that pleasure can be set aside as not being a serious philosophical response to the question of the supreme good.[41] It happens, however, that what is at the core of the broad case in *Finibus* against the Epicurean conception of the supreme good is focused upon and directly approached in *Officiis*: it is that aspect of nature which the Epicureans so overlook or distort that their overall teaching comes to be at variance with the ordinary understanding of human needs and human decency, with the simple pull of *honestas*, the natural appeal of the virtues, virtues, which Cicero says, are rarely on the lips of Epicureans.[42] Thus the *Officiis* goes directly to those very grounds in nature that play a critical role in the judgments of the *Finibus*. Through the *Officiis*, one is given access to those aspects of nature that are not accommodated in the Epicurean understanding of happiness.

To determine duties, the *Officiis* directs attention specifically at the bases in nature for *honestas*. As already indicated, for Cicero there is no *honestas*, hence no duty and no real moral problems, if nature's only inclinations and teachings have to do with directions toward personal power and pleasures, whereby morality disappears into a calculus of personal advantage. However, to affirm the moral realm as rooted in nature, as Cicero does, is not to claim that interpreting nature's way so as to find duties and resolve moral problems is an easy matter. The difficulty of interpreting nature is evident in Cicero both in what he says of nature's teaching at the very start of *Officiis* and in his repeated indications throughout his works that our progressive and developing understanding of nature, and, hence, of right and duty is the very best to which human beings can aspire. In those paragraphs in *Officiis* (1.11–14), where Cicero first directs attention at nature as our guide, it is not presented as a book of duties or norms simply to be read. Rather nature seems to have endowed us, according to Cicero, with certain indications and instruments with which we might seek to know duties more specific than the general injunction to live according to nature.

Interpreting nature is, then, first of all recognizing and utilizing the signs and tools that nature herself has given for the task. Nature's indications and instruments include certain inclinations or tendencies, like those of seeking to preserve one's own life and body and offspring, and the power of reason (*ratio*) which most distinguishes humans from other animals.[43] It is noteworthy that when Cicero introduces this power of reason he does it by describing the human being (*homo*) not in this language of empowerment so familiar to us but by speaking of him as a participant or sharer in reason (*particeps rationis*). This sharing in reason allows man to transcend the immediate scene, to see the causes of things, and to take his whole life in view and make all necessary preparations for conducting it. Joined to this power to understand the causes of things is an inclination to know and understand all that is. Among nature's gifts that are said to distinguish humans from all living beings is the power to appreciate visible beauty, grace, and harmony of parts. This inclination, joined with the power of reason, brings the human being to expect thoughts, words, and actions to be characterized by "beauty, consistency, and regularity" (*pulchritudo, constantia, et ordo*). This expectation (later to be called the moral sensibility—*verecundia*) with its apparently innate standards, the other fundamental inclinations of nature, and the power of reason provide the elements for the understanding of *honestas* or right that can be attained.

Given what is entailed in finding the natural basis of *honestas* and in knowing this "rightness" in sufficient detail so that duties are known, it is possible to appreciate even more fully Cicero's emphasis that moral understanding—knowing the supreme good and duties—is at best a developing or progressive process. In the third book of *Officiis*, Cicero reemphasizes that "mean" duties are his concern in this work and, in contrast with the perfect Wiseman of the Stoics, what can be sought is not the right simply and perfectly grasped but approximations or semblances of it (*similitudines honesti*).[44] Such duties and, therefore, such understanding of the right is attained by many, adds Cicero, through a natural goodness (*ingenii bonitas*) and progress in learning (*progressio discendi*). A little later, Cicero comments that we ordinary mortals must hold fast to what understanding of the right we can achieve if such progress toward virtue which has been made (*ad virtutem est facta progressio*) is to be maintained.⁴⁵ There is no doubt that for Cicero, more is entailed in the progress toward virtue than growth in knowledge or understanding, for the latter passage's context and the emphasis on holding fast (*tuendum conservandumque*) to what falls to our understanding indicate that the constant practice or habituation in choosing the right, such as we understand it, over the useful is a part of a process toward virtue.⁴⁶ Yet progress in learning—improvement of our understanding—is clearly a critical element in moral development.

And what is to be understood is the way of nature. For Cicero, following Socrates, this is self-knowledge but such that points beyond the self and could be complete only when the self is understood in the context of nature as a whole. Quite aptly, Cicero has Piso in *Finibus* speak of the responsibility to search into the nature of things (*in rerum naturam*) and to seek to understand thoroughly what nature requires of us.⁴⁷ Only in this way, adds Piso, can we know ourselves, and the only path unto this way is through knowing the potential of the body and the mind (*vis corporis animique*) and following the way of life which would bring it to fruition. Thus, ever-deepening knowledge of nature, initially through rationally informed attention to one's own basic inclinations and through living in accord with the best attainable understanding of the right, is the difficult but alleged true way of progress which Cicero holds out.

The way of nature to which Cicero points as the guide and basis for duties, and which must be approached by a progressive understanding of nature, is but another way of speaking of nature's law or the natural law. Early in the *Officiis*, where Cicero forms a concept of *honestas* from various elements in nature, he describes this integrity or goodness as the way of right, "even if it is not ennobled" by humankind, as praiseworthy (*laudabile*), "even if it is praised by no one."⁴⁸ Shortly before in the same text, Cicero writes of the sense of self-determination of the mind that desires the truth and is well-formed in it by nature (*animus bene informatus a natura*): a person whose mind is so formed will subject himself to no counselor, teacher, or ruler except one acting rightly and justly (*juste et legitime*) for true benefit (*utilitatis causa*).⁴⁹ Thus, without, at this point, using the language of natural law, Cicero has spoken very directly about a standard of nature that transcends custom and ordinary law and is to be used to judge them.

On those occasions when Cicero does introduce the language of law to speak of nature's way, there is no need to conclude that he implies a clarity, completeness, and even rigidity that is often associated with codes of the ordinary positive law.[50] For him, nature's way is a law in that it obliges us to follow or to seek to follow it. It seems that he is also inclined to call it a law because the order that marks nature suggests an ordering intelligence which, by analogy, can be understood as like, though on a grand scale, a human lawgiver who provides for civil order.[51] The difficulty of knowing nature is not lost on Cicero: for him as for many in human history, the idea that there is a natural law is more certain and clear than many of the specific duties and norms that arise with a claim to be rooted in the natural law.[52] Quite properly then, the expression of natural law that best captures the flexibility that Cicero intends, and that is consistent with his overall restraint about comprehensive knowledge of nature, is the statement that the highest law which is imbedded in nature consists in the mind and reason of the prudent person (*mens ratioque prudentis*).[53]

The most cited passage in Cicero on natural law, and probably the most memorable passage in the rich history of natural law theory—that spoken by Laelius in the third book of the *Re Publica*.[54]—can be interpreted as consistent with the preceding paragraphs. The passage opens with the statement, "[T]rue law (*vera lex*) is in fact right reason in accordance with nature (*naturae congruens*) present everywhere, unchanging and everlasting...."[55] The passage closes with Laelius saying that he who will not obey this law runs from himself and denies his very human nature (*naturam hominis aspernatus*).[56] Nature's way is what obligates all, and it constitutes a law that, however poorly understood or resisted, as it is by the shameless (*improbi*), cannot be totally ignored or repealed. No ordinary political authority, like the people or the senate, can release one from this law; reason alone is the expounder and interpreter of this law.[57] Further, it is this law, as it is known and understood, that calls one to duty (*ad officium*).

Within the framework of *Officiis*., as we recall, the turn to nature's way arose in the effort to determine duties. That effort in the ordinary horizon confronts the need to understand the right and the useful, which present themselves as supplying the content of duty and which, at times, seem to pull in divergent ways. The natural law, then, comes to be expounded in terms of particulars through the very process of determining duties. Duties, articulated by the prudent person working from the ordinary horizon, are the specific and concrete expressions of the natural law. Cicero writes of finding the fundamental or natural law as a "choosing" from the way of nature, a self-imposed law or laws of aspects of the way of nature.[58]

This common practical horizon can unfold to philosophical inquiry into the whole of reality, and Cicero, at times, points in that direction, as in Piso's call to search into the nature of things in order to understand thoroughly what nature requires of us.[59] What checks such a dynamic or development, and a consequent freeze, of action until nature can be fully understood is both the limits of the human condition and the assets or gifts provided to cope with those limits. Life (or nature) does not permit escape from or postponement of practical, and hence moral, decisions. Nor does it, for Cicero, allow the complete and assured knowledge that comprehensive inquiry points toward and that the perfect Wiseman claims. Nature does provide, it seems, for the practical order by the seeds of virtue (*indoles virtutis*) inbred in humankind and the consequent attractiveness or luminosity of virtue when manifested.[60] Furthermore, over time, there has been provided from these seeds, and from the work of reason upon the powers and inclinations of mind and body, a moral tradition expressed in the form of certain basic or essential virtues. "A great force" (*magna vis*) are these virtues, writes Cicero, and they must be called upon.[61] Nature has, then, provided a way to find the right, to read its law, and to determine duties. The virtues are general or broad expressions of human duties, which humans are equipped to recognize and admire and which are developed and held up in the moral tradition of Socrates and his successors. The appearance of the virtues in Cicero's thought provides the locus for seeing the relationship between his skepticism and his traditionalism, specifically a moral tradition marked by appropriate historical *exempla*. It also provides the locus for many of his statements concerning the inherent sense of right given to all humans, the much noted appearance of the concept of conscience in Cicero.[62]

Thus, the established virtues of wisdom, justice, greatness of spirit, and temperance serve for Cicero as bases or sources for finding the right and determining duty.[63] These specific dispositions of the soul in accord with nature and reason, which is Cicero's way of defining the virtues,[64] can and do appeal on their own terms. As sources for the right (*honestas*), they appear to precede and, in fact, constitute the right. They are, thus, an instantiation of our earlier observation that duties, or specific instances of the right, must, in some sense, precede the choice of following the right as the supreme good if that choice is to make sense.[65] Put in the terms of virtue, one knows and is attracted to various virtues before one might formulate a general understanding of virtue and know it as the right, as the way of nature, and as the mode of action that constitutes the supreme good.⁶⁶ Looked at another way and put in the terms of duty, one can see Cicero teaching that the four basic virtues are the four essential duties; these virtues then are the first level of specification of that general duty to follow nature's way.⁶⁷

Conflict, or seeming conflict, between the requisites of the basic virtues is the highest level of conflict of duties and one that especially concerns Cicero in *Officiis*. Such conflicts between virtues, as that between wisdom and justice, appear to be seen by Cicero as the bases of all tensions between apparent duties, between what seem to be right courses of action.⁶⁸ To establish a hierarchy among the basic virtues in order to settle such conflicts, Cicero needs to turn to the very resources that allowed the development and, hence, justification of the virtues themselves as the basic ways or sources of the right. The resources are reason and the inclinations of human nature in the context of nature as a whole. These are aided by the inherent appeal of the right.

Cicero is, thus, drawn back in this process to an important if underlying truth, namely that virtue is one and that the common splitting of it into the four basic virtues is a function of ordinary discourse, which, however understandable and useful, can obscure the truth that such virtues are but partial manifestations of the one virtue, *virtus generalis* or *honestas*, which is living rightly or in accord with nature. One significant implication of the unity of all true virtues is that the commonly recognized basic virtues are so interdependent that it can properly be said that a person who possesses fully one virtue possesses them all.⁶⁹ Complete or perfect virtue, which belongs only to the hypothetical perfect Wiseman, is, then, the ground in which any single virtue reaches fullness or perfection. One could not, in other words, be an unqualified exemplar of temperance if one were not also an exemplar of wisdom. The essential unity of the virtues is the basis for the fact that now one and now another virtue seems like the overall virtue. Another important implication of the unity of all virtue relates to how this truth undergirds the "flexibility" of Cicero's teaching on duties, on what natural law concretely requires. Cicero's structure for all determinations of duties brings this out, for even those duties fundamental to all others—the duties to be wise, just, magnanimous, and courageous—yield to the overall duty to do the right. Prudential judgment is always the ultimate articulator of what duty is, of what natural law requires in a certain situation.

Overall virtue or right *(honestas)* is understood by Cicero as essentially propriety or appropriateness (*decus*). Among the primary virtues, temperance or moderation (*temperantia*) is the one most akin to the proper (*decus*) and right.[70] Virtue or right, then, is proper moderation in all things. Passivity in the face of wrongdoing or in an evident need in one's society, and a quiet resignation leading to failure to develop one's human potential and specific excellence—these are not instances of moderation but, really, excesses when rightly viewed. Moderation or temperance arises from a sense of and inclination to propriety (*verecundia*).[71] *Verecundia*, perhaps best translated as sense of shame or moral sensibility, is the basis and source for not only the specific virtue of temperance but also morality and right itself.[72] It is not simply negative but represents awe and respect in the face of human goodness. It is through *verecundia* that nature speaks, despite all human efforts to resist or not to listen. It is the name Cicero gives to that inherent sense of right or conscience—those inborn seeds of virtue—that allows some sense of duty and virtue even prior to the formulation of these concepts and to an overall grounding of duty and virtue in a more comprehensive understanding of nature. Thus, this moral sensibility accounts for the apparent presence of virtue in people and communities where there is no formal philosophical awareness or teaching concerning the virtues.[73] In Cicero's view, such was the status of virtue throughout much of Rome's earlier and glorious history.

Into the moral sensibility (*verecundia*) are woven various aspects or facets of human nature. These are the basic human inclinations nature has provided, including that of all living creatures for preservation: the inclination to human interaction or participation in society, and that most distinguishing human inclination—to seek the truth.[74] Some inclinations are quite directly sources for some specific primary virtues, as seeking the truth is for wisdom, but because virtue is one and unified, all the inclinations play a part in the constitution of the moral sensibility that is the basis of virtue itself. The inclinations are the material elements from which the human mind, namely reason, shapes an overall moral framework. When that shaping occurs naturally, in the sense of quite spontaneously and thus without much conscious effort, that moral framework is what has here been called moral sensibility or a natural sense of right and wrong. When that shaping is submitted to examination and the precision of philosophical inquiry, the overall framework comes to be expressed as the comprehensive right (*honestas*) or overall virtue or the law of nature, and nature's way is articulated in developed concepts of the basic virtues and the duties entailed in them.

The Norms of Utility

As in Book 1 of *Officiis* Cicero indicates the bases or sources for what is right, so in Book 2 he points out the sources for the expedient or useful. He does this after emphasizing that duties (*officia*) arise from considerations of not only what is right but also what is useful.[75] The sources for the useful are also human inclinations. Those inclinations toward, what is ordinarily called, the expedient or the useful are natural and good.[76] However indebted he is to the Stoics, Cicero has no patience for a Stoic tendency to sever the good and the right from what is ordinarily thought to be useful and necessary, like security and health.[77] However hostile Cicero is to the Epicureans, he will not, in the end, permit them alone to champion the useful and to appropriate it to their distinctive understanding of the human condition. To follow nature, Cicero insists, is not to look to some disembodied human nature as the model.[78] Rather, the pulls to the right and the useful, in the ordinary horizon of decision-making, are taken as revealing nature and as elements that must be considered in reason's determination of nature's way. Cicero can be seen to be upgrading *utile* rather than downgrading *honestum*, as has sometimes been claimed.[79]

Nature's way, then, is called the right (*honestas*), but this is a right fashioned in the light of appropriate utilities. Properly reading nature overcomes the apparent distinction and tension between the right and the useful. Thus, inclinations toward the useful not only are among the sources for the formation of a proper understanding of right but also will have duly entered the development of the moral sensibility of decent people.

The utility that is allowed by Cicero as entering into the right is, of course, not a simply pleasure-seeking utility but one that is consistent with the overall and true requisites of human nature.[80] Nor are the ordinary utilities, such as security and health, determinative in themselves of the right. Cicero urges that justice be based on nature rather than on utility in its common meaning.[81] In his view, many matters ordinarily considered useful, such as security, shelter, food, and arms, are part of the requisites of human nature. The natural needs of man require a concern for resources and power. To speak of a necessity or necessities, as Cicero does recurrently, is to describe a particularly compelling utility or requisite of human nature. The need for society, even the related need to pursue glory, the need for moderation, and the need for wisdom and the seeking of it are also among the requisites of human nature according to the full and capacious view of Cicero.[82] Cicero's writing that "the greatest necessity is to do the right" is a reminder that even as he incorporates common utilities in his determination of the right, it is following that right which constitutes the supreme good and, hence, the primary requisite of human nature.[83] Thus, a closer examination of those inclinations of human nature reviewed in Book 1 of *Officiis*, from which the right and the virtues are derived, shows them implicated with utilities. The useful and the right, under proper examination, come to be seen as one because their content is derived from common sources; they are the names given to different aspects of the overall requisites of human nature as revealed in its fundamental inclinations. Nature is being followed.

Cicero's incorporation of utility into the very notion of right and, hence, as a factor in the determination of duties marks an important point in his thought.[84] This is especially so for seeing how politics, law and political theory relate to his moral theory and the very foundations he sets for philosophy. Given the kind of beings humans are, attention to politics is itself a duty. One very important dimension of reason's attention to the requisites of human nature is working out determinations of nature's way or duties with respect to political-legal matters where utilities (needs and necessities), such as security and material supplies, loom so large.[85] This "working out" by reason will not yield a certain, comprehensive, and detailed political science—a veritable set of "blueprints" for action in different situations—because human nature, in the context of nature, cannot be known with that completeness and clarity. Following nature or doing the right in politics allows, however, some specification of what that right is. In other words, the work of reason on politics is an effort to clarify by specific requisites the very end being pursued. These requisites as duties or responsibilities are best seen, then, as partial goods or proximate goals rather than as the supreme good and the ultimate end.

As in non-political moral matters, reason in determining such requisites does not work from abstract human nature but draws what conclusions it can from nature revealed in practice, in other words, from experience and from what is often an authoritative and accumulated experience in the form of political traditions. Just as a moral tradition of both thought and experience holds up the four basic virtues as key duties, so are there political traditions such as the consent of the governed, constitutionalism, equality under the law, and the protection of property that command initial attention as reason seeks political duties or the politically right. In Cicero, as in his Greek forebearers, the political is quite inextricably bound up with the moral: to speak of political duties is, of course, to reveal their fundamental moral character. Moral duties can be said to comprehend and shape political duties. The political, however, appears for Cicero not merely one possible subset of the moral but a necessary and critical dimension of it. The moral dimension of life seems, in fact, dependent on the effectiveness of the political order. This necessary and critical role of the political manifests itself in the primacy Cicero assigns to the duty of political leadership and to the life of the statesman.

THE PRIMARY NEED: STATESMANSHIP

The primary importance of the work of the statesman is Cicero's most prominent teaching in his moral and political writings. Political leadership is the theme in Cicero's preface to the first book of *Republica*, his most direct and important work on political theory.[86] Here, and consistently throughout Cicero's writings, it is presented as the greatest necessity and the highest human calling, and accordingly such leadership allows for the greatest virtue consisting in the bringing into actuality, through the political community, the very goods on which philosophers merely discourse. The caring for the community that is statesmanship is seen as the human approximation to divine work.[87] Cicero points to the well-being of the Roman state as having been attained and protected by the response of men to this call to virtue. In the same preface, he notes the allurements and arguments that might draw one away from the struggles and difficulties attendant on a life of public leadership. Neither pleasure, nor personal tranquility, nor philosophy, concludes Cicero, should be allowed to draw the suitably talented from the high service of statesmanship. Cicero seems to be speaking chiefly, though not exclusively, to the widely popular Epicureanism of his time, which, he feared, would draw suitable leadership away from public responsibilities.[88]

Cicero's elevation of statesmanship to the highest duty is one form of his claim in *Officiis* that the duties deriving from justice (which requires actions for the common good)[89] are to take priority over those deriving from the virtue of wisdom. Here and elsewhere Cicero is aware that he is taking a stand on the comparative importance of the two lives that most attract him, the life of the statesman and the life of the philosopher.[90] Two paradoxes appear in Cicero's thought in connection with his claims for statesmanship and for the duties attendant on justice. First of all, Cicero insists, in the *Officiis* and throughout his writings, that wisdom is the highest and greatest of the virtues,[91] and thus it appears that at one moment justice is prior and then at another time wisdom is prior. A second paradox can be seen in the apparent fact that when inquiry into duties, in the light of the overall human condition, leads to the priority of the duties stemming from justice, coming to know this would seem to be a form of wisdom.[92] Thus, one might say that the wise person knows the priority of the claims of justice. Cicero's and the Stoics's teaching on the unity of the virtues would not allow these paradoxes, but in the perspective of ordinary discourse, which Cicero is utilizing, explicitly so in *Officiis*,[93] they do arise. In terms of ordinary discourse, Cicero's finding on this matter—his "wisdom," albeit practical wisdom—is that wisdom is the goal and peak of human existence and, hence, of the human virtues, but those duties to others and community, the duties of justice, can never be put aside in the interest of pursuing knowledge and understanding.

Cicero's defense of the priority of the life of the statesman exposes the compelling logic or common sense underlying his elevation of the duties emanating from justice. His defense is not presented in a single place as a tight philosophical argument; rather, it is evident in its various parts and in various ways throughout his writings, being, for example, exemplified in his understanding of his own course of life and in the lives of the characters, so often Roman statesmen and consular philosophers, chosen for his dialogues. The defense of statesmanship brings the idea of utility as a norm and, in the form of necessity, into clear and evident operation and provides an opportunity to see the inherent moral sensibility at work. Cicero's defense provides a grand instance of incorporating the useful and necessary in the determination of the right.

The way of nature, Cicero believes, establishes priorities among the various human activities or callings. Nature's teaching in this matter is founded on utility and follows what can be called the rule of necessity: To do what is necessary is to act in accord with duty, that is, to act appropriately; what is necessary is initially and generally indicated through an inherent or readily attainable prephilosophical understanding of human needs.[94] As already noted, Cicero has what might be called a large and deep view of human needs. He understands human society and, thus, political life itself to be formed out of need, not merely in the sense of security or "necessities of life" but in terms of the full requisites of human nature, the chief of which is virtue itself.

Humankind is not dependent on high learning or philosophy to recognize some of those requisites and, possibly, even to have some understanding of all of them. Cicero is impressed with great things, such as Roman social and political achievements, attained as a result of a certain practical sense, the utility element in the moral sensibility, rather than through philosophy.[95] Men in general, he thinks, are readily aware of the good and bad things of life.[96] Just as the man about to give a speech understands, according to Cicero, the necessity of speaking clearly without any art of rhetoric telling him so, so it is that whatever individual aims humans may hold dear, they are at once aware that the safety and sound ordering of their political community is a necessity of the first order. The best of human beings have always left their other pursuits and inquiries to come to the aid of their political community at a critical moment. Because the well-being of this community is the necessary condition for fulfilling all man's needs, it is the most important of his needs. Thus, those especially useful (*maxime utiles*) deeds of public service through public leadership are the mark of a divine-like human exemplar—the truly just, courageous, and great-souled person.[97] Philosophy for Cicero does not, then, seem necessary to make the case for statesmanship's priority or to assure rather notable accomplishments by statesmen. On the other hand, statesmanship is necessary to cultivate the political conditions that would allow philosophy to flourish and be efficacious.

Cicero's argument for the primacy of the politically active life is sometimes seen as a break with his prominent Greek teachers, Plato and Aristotle, and with their view that the philosophical life is the best and happiest of human lives. They so concluded while recognizing and acknowledging human dependence on the political community for attaining this happiness. According to this view, Cicero's claim of priority for the life of the statesman might be seen to violate the sound principle that the first in the order of necessity is not consequently the first in the order of importance or achievement. Cicero, however, has a way of thinking about the respective claims of the philosophical life and the political life that appears to save him from violating this principle. His claim, as previously noted, that wisdom is the greatest of the virtues signals the fact that Cicero accepts the classical teaching that philosophy for its own sake—search and contemplation—was the highest human activity. Necessity, however, determines right and duty. Impressed, no doubt, by the conditions of his own lifetime, Cicero sees the usual situation of men as one requiring primary emphasis on the service of political activity. In abstraction from the concrete historical conditions that men have usually known, inquiry and contemplation, clearly, constitute the most divine of activities and provide the greatest of delights. The philosophical life is, then, the fitting and fulfilling human activity after all public tasks have been completed or in the life after death. As a way of life, however, within the usual human condition, such philosophizing is contrary to the duties proper to human beings.[98] If Cicero's position on the claims of the philosophical and political life is not, in the end, essentially different from his Greek teachers, it does represent, in the attention given to the work of the statesman, at least a difference of emphasis. If Plato and Aristotle are interpreted, as some are inclined, to advocate or tolerate a kind of trans-moral autonomy for the philosopher, then Cicero's moral insistence on the priority of political leadership represents, on this question, a fundamental alternative within the tradition of classical political thought.

Cicero does not find that the fact that the responsible, contemplative man intends to and actually does come to the aid of his political community at critical moments is the basis for reconciling the high claims of the life of philosophy with the similarly important claims of the life of political activity. Those who scorn the political life for the life of philosophy are likely to find themselves ill-equipped and poorly positioned for offering any significant help to the community in a time of need. Political well-being is not generally served by part-time, *ad hoc*, and emergency thrusts into political life by the otherwise preoccupied.[99] Cicero seems to have as a target not only the powerful human tendency to avoid the turmoil and burden of politics but also the specific injunction of Epicurus, who is said to have written, "[T]he wise man will not engage in public affairs except in an emergency."[100]

As utility and necessity ever enter the determination of right and duty for Cicero and play an evident and critical role in the claim for the priority of the political life, so too do they shape the preparation and education for political leadership. The requisites of a life of public leadership provide the standard for determining the claims of various arts and fields of study, such as rhetoric and law. What is useful to a life of public leadership affects the determination of the rightful use of leisure and the very questions to be given priority in serious or even casual conversations. To proceed further along these lines will take us, in the following chapters, into a fuller and more detailed statement of a model statesman who is found in Cicero's writings and who sums up the various requisites for effective statesmanship. This model statesman emerges as the central concept or leading idea of Cicero's political philosophy. The nature or requisites of this statesman becomes clearer when his function in Cicero's best constitution comes into view. Thus, the politically right, which consists above all in the model or best constitution and which statesmen would find useful or need to have in mind in order to provide proper direction, will be explored before additional consideration of the requisites of statesmanship.

At this point, we have proceeded far enough to see how a reading of nature, in an effort to determine the right and the duties entailed therein, incorporates considerations of utility and leads to duties to the political community and specifically to the duty or high calling of service in the form of statesmanship. Experience—individual and collective—always plays an important part in determining nature's way; reflection on how we have lived seems critical in understanding human inclinations and proper ways to order and control them. Reason, then, works in tandem with experience in seeking as comprehensive and detailed understanding of nature's way as is possible.[101] When Cicero is seen finding more detailed and specific notions of the politically right (i.e. proximate goods) and of the model statesman in the following chapters, personal experience and the shared experiences of history seem ever more involved in determining the right. We have proceeded far enough to see the elements of what we have called the practical perspective emerge in a critical sub-foundational role in Cicero's thought. Drawn together, those elements can be described as the sense of good or right clarified in the experience of living. Chief among these elements is the moral sensibility, with its inherent sense of right and its attentiveness to evident human needs, and the moral and political traditions that represent the tested work of reason upon human nature. These elements constitute the effective criterion that seems operable in Cicero's choice of an ultimate good or end, a choice in his view of philosophical foundations.

The effective criterion indicates that to which Cicero seems to be appealing when he determines the true or credible from among the teachings of the philosophical schools he faces. It saves Cicero from a skepticism that would be disabling in the practical world. Now we are better positioned to look more deeply into how Cicero sorts his way through the different philosophical teachings of his time, being able to reject outright that of the Epicureans, hesitating between the Peripatetics and the Stoics on crucial foundational matters, notably turning his back on some tendencies and characteristics of the overall Stoic philosophy, and conducting this entire critical inquiry from that useful ground of a qualified Academic skepticism.

Before a closer look at his assessment of the various philosophical schools is taken in the light of the practical perspective, this is a fitting time to reflect upon one of the common reactions to Cicero and even to the Romans in general. Hegel's and Mommsen's distaste for the "prose" of Roman life, for their "unpoetic" and "dogmatical" temperament, for the oppressiveness of their rationalizing and organizing—the very talents and tendencies that give rise to systematic positive law—represents one classic expression of the sense that the Romans with their concern with overall utility-informed duty and service tend to confine if not crush the human spirit.[102] It is undeniably the case for Cicero that duty pervades every part of human life: from that critical responsibility of the talented to put public leadership first (over which he suffers to make even the slightest exception)[103] to the various uses of leisure and even topics of conversation. One might say that Cicero exemplifies, then, not the free spirit but the responsible spirit—the Roman spirit; yet this is the Cicero who loves learning so, who encourages and defends poetry, loves humanistic historical studies, and the fine arts, and who must endure the charges of "Greek" for his attraction to Hellenic learning and culture.[104]

All is duty for Cicero, which means that nature's way is to be followed in all matters. To act in any way other than appropriately (in accord with *decus*) is never excusable. All actions and things must be seen in their connection with being human. It is a caricature of Cicero's thought to presume that nature's way is known as some detailed code, like a system of positive law, or that he is calling for the imposition on human life of some sterile, abstract notion of right. Rather, human embeddedness in nature provides the basis for comprehensive morality and, in fact, the ineluctability of the moral horizon. For Cicero, the sphere of nature or morality is a human moral sphere in which, without comprehensive and absolute knowledge, duties are determined with reference to human needs, wants, ordinary pleasures, practices, and traditions.

Assessing the Philosophical Schools

There are a number of ways to explain Cicero's being drawn to assess the major philosophical schools of his time. First, insofar as Cicero is drawn to philosophy, it is quite unavoidable that he engages the major philosophical traditions which had been part of his own philosophical education. Second, insofar as Cicero works from a practical perspective or Socratic orientation, he brings to philosophy an expectation that it be fruitful for the way life is lived, and, accordingly, he is interested above all in the understandings and defenses of the supreme good in each of the schools.

In judging the teachings of the schools on the foundational question of ends, Cicero uses, as seen in Chap. 1, a prephilosophical standard, which has here been called the effective criterion of the practical perspective. Since Cicero is notably appreciative of what is known and accomplished only by means of this standard and hence without philosophy, it is possible that a third reason for Cicero turning to philosophy is to critique philosophy against what is commonly known by decent and experienced people, to protect, in other words, a sphere of natural prudence or untutored natural virtue from the faulty and ultimately corruptive teachings of the philosophical schools. All three of these reasons seem to be operating in Cicero's turning to assess the philosophical schools. Cicero does seek wisdom from them, but it is a certain kind of wisdom that he seeks, and this gives a very pointed focus to his inquiry—a focus on that which he regards as foundational and illuminative of all philosophy.

Cicero sees Roman history as evidence of Rome's having been beneficently endowed with a national treasure of utility-informed moral sensibility or untutored natural virtue. Nonetheless, it appears that such natural virtue can be strengthened and refined by that part of philosophy—moral and political philosophy—which develops prudence and is regarded by Cicero as a teacher of virtue.[105] The substance of the moral and political philosophy that Cicero develops can be understood as a clarifying, deepening, and extending of what is present in the inherent moral sensibility.[106] Cicero's interest in strengthening natural virtue is not only or primarily a theoretical interest, an abstract ahistorical interest. The political discord and decline during his lifetime were key indications for Cicero that the natural virtue of the Romans seemed to be failing and that philosophy was required to shore up sound traditional ways.[107] This explains, at least partly, the intensity of Cicero's work in philosophy in the years after 49 B.C.[108]

What Cicero, then, expects from philosophy is that it strengthen virtue and expel vice, as those are commonly known in the Roman tradition. The virtue that philosophy is to strengthen includes justice, which requires that the political community's good be foremost. Philosophy must, then, contribute to the safety and sound ordering of the political community. For Cicero, this would be done chiefly by its formative influence upon leaders and potential leaders of the community. No conception of the supreme good—no philosophical teaching—that undermines society by drawing the most talented away from political responsibility is acceptable to Cicero. No philosophical teaching may controvert the evident human need for society and the evident societal needs for dedicated leadership and a bond of virtue.

Regarding Epicureanism as a failure in these respects, Cicero readily and persistently eliminates it as a serious philosophical alternative.[109] He perceives this school's "supreme good" as eliminating duty and drawing its adherents either to retreat from politics and its "pains" or to effect those disasters that are always wrought when public affairs are administered by those whose only idea of good is their own personal pleasure.[110] Cicero's severe condemnation of the Epicureans and his ostracizing them from "every bond of the political community" in *Legibus* (1.38–39), which was initially noted in Chap. 1, can now be much better and fully understood.[111] There, Cicero not only bans them "for now" (*paulisper*) from the bonds of political community (*ab omni societate rei publicae*), of which, he asserts, they never knew or even wished to know any part (*cujus partem nec norunt ullam neque umquam nosse voluerunt*) but also makes the unsettling statement that they are to be ostracized even if they speak the truth, a matter not to be settled in this context of investigating and laying out the foundations of law.

In making self-satisfaction in pleasure the measure of the good and the right, the Epicureans, in fact, leave no place for any bonding, for any fundamental law of nature, and, hence, for any sense of duty that would function to restrain this pursuit of pleasure. In the Epicurean view, bonds and duties must be attachments calculated to serve a person's pleasure or tranquillity,[112] and Cicero regards such attachments as unstable and inadequate for most people. It is the incongruity of the Epicurean notion of the supreme good with such bindings, such apparent necessities, to which Cicero is drawing attention in saying that they neither know nor wish to know any part of such a community. They really have no business in a discussion of a basis in nature for law and law's binding force nor in a discussion of the political community regarded, in Cicero, as a union of many brought about "by agreement in right and by common advantage," where the "right" is grounded in nature and is not simply constituted by consent or agreement as in a form of democratic positivism.[113] A well-founded and stable legal and political order would, it seems, be able to go far in tolerating and protecting those with Epicurean convictions, but at a time of founding, or of crisis and refounding, such as Cicero is engaged in here in *Legibus*, the Epicurean teaching is particularly threatening and must "for now" or "for a while" (*paulisper*) be kept off the scene. In this respect, Cicero has stated in his case against the Epicureans a classic objection—not without relevance to certain modern contractarian approaches to politics based on the individual pursuit of security or pleasure—that such approaches, being at root amoral, remain inherently private and ultimately anarchical and apolitical in character.

What, however, could Cicero possibly mean by saying that the Epicureans may be speaking the truth about this matter and yet they must be ostracized? This, like the often troubling observation in the *De Or.* (3.63–4), that philosophies are not tested here with a view to which is truest but to which would be most befitting and useful to the orator or statesman, can be seen as revealing Cicero's understanding of the limitations of his own argument. Could it be that the Epicureans have the best of answers on the question of the supreme good and that we simply find ourselves in a world in which there is no political and legal order other than one that reduces to a system of private instrumentalities—that there is no basis in nature for political and legal restraints on individual desires and needs? Recall that, in another context, Cicero had explicitly entertained the notion, suggestive of latter-day existentialism, that no one but nature is to blame for burying truth in darkness and thus putting the norms we seem to need beyond our reach.[114] In conceding that the Epicureans may be speaking the truth, Cicero seems to be facing up to the fact that the basic incongruity between the Epicurean conception of happiness and a commonly felt need for moral foundations may be where we are finally left. Although Cicero does not think that the incongruity he highlights is in itself a decisive argument against the truth of the Epicurean view, or that a kind of knowledge is attainable which would allow an absolute and certain dismissal of this view as wrong, the incongruity has the character of many of his arguments as he seeks what is probably true among the teachings of the schools. Given the widely perceived need for moral restraints and for a legal and political order based on such restraints, drawing out the implications of the Epicurean teaching on happiness renders it a less credible—a less probable—view.

In saying that this is not the time or place for determining the truth of this teaching, Cicero appears to be admitting that much more can and should be said on the credibility of this view than simply noting, as he does here when writing primarily of legal foundations, that this teaching cannot be reconciled with a public order grounded in norms of nature.[115] The incongruity he highlights turns out to be but the surface of a deeper incongruity between the Epicurean teaching and human nature. The arguments establishing this deeper problem and, hence, the improbability of the Epicurean view are concentrated in the first two books of the *Finibus*. In those books are found not only more arguments of the kind made at *Legibus* 1.38–39 and arguments about apparent inconsistencies and obscurities in the Epicurean teaching but also a testing of the reading of nature—the entire setting of the human being in nature—that is used to support the critical teaching on the highest human end. A series of arguments and considerations, constituting what he appears to regard as "reasons of a broad sort" lead him to as clear and sure a view as is attainable on the important questions of philosophy and provide the basis for his rejection of Epicureanism.[116] At the heart of those reasons or, more precisely, what makes them work as reasons for Cicero and others is his effective criterion: that inherent sense of the good which carries with it the basis of an alternative reading of nature. This sense of the right and the good and the various needs incorporated in it would seem to be what is operating, in Cicero's view, to call Epicureans in practice away from the folly of their teaching, when they live "better" than their theories.[117]

Congenial as Cicero finds the Stoic school's formulation of the supreme good as living rightly or virtuously, there is much of its teaching and practice which does not seem to serve the need for public leadership and virtue throughout the community. The Stoics, not unlike the Epicureans in this respect, tend to draw potential statesmen away from the cares and anxieties of politics. A Stoic retreat from politics is not, of course, colored with the Epicurean language of pleasure and pleasure-based utility. It is, rather, encouraged by the Stoic emphasis on the contented happiness of self-mastery and self-resignation.[118] When Stoicism does not keep an adherent out of active politics, it can handicap him in the course of public life due to its self-regarding perfectionism. Crassus, the apparent spokesman for Cicero in *De Oratore*, finds a ridiculous scene when imagining the rigorous Stoic before a public assembly. Such a Stoic is doomed to failure in his attempt to persuade those with whom he cannot at all sympathize. He regards most men as slaves, madmen, and enemies, for they fall short of Stoic perfection represented in the Wiseman. Furthermore, the Stoic is unable to speak clearly, fully, and forcefully in the language and with the sense of the people in general. He is hampered by a cramped style of speech reflecting his exercises in the tight logic and dialectic that characterize the school, and he understands good and bad, honor and disgrace, and reward and punishment in a specialized way, different from the general understanding of these terms.[119] Cicero cannot, then, find in the old Stoic tradition rooted in Zeno an effective public philosophy.[120]

In *Officiis* as well as elsewhere in his writings, Cicero appears to be approving and utilizing a Stoicism that has come down to earth, a Stoicism that faces the commonly acknowledged claims of utility and necessity and that is concerned to give more specific moral and political guidance than the absolute but very general principles that seem to suffice for the Wiseman. The ordinary moral horizon, with its felt tensions between the right and the useful and multiple expressions of each of these, is not that of the Stoic Wiseman, who presumably knows and chooses the right without hesitation.[121] This horizon and ordinary language is, as we have seen, what Cicero explicitly adopts for the *Officiis*, and it reflects a moderating of Stoicism, a "humane turn," that had already taken place in Polybius, Panaetius, and Posidonius, thinkers whom Cicero clearly took very seriously and from whom he learned.[122] Insofar as Cicero is attracted to and utilizes the thought of the Stoic tradition, it is this less formalized Stoicism (the approach of consular philosophy) of Roman public men and heroes of the past, especially that represented in the alleged "Scipionic Circle" of the second century.[123] This is a Stoicism that not only accommodates but also appears to require a commitment to active public service and a willingness to suffer and work with the compromises and imperfections of ordinary political life.[124]

Cicero's essential difficulty with the Stoics shows up in his detailed examination of their position on the highest good or happiness, the very position paradoxically that especially attracts him to the Stoic school. Cicero welcomes the Stoics' unqualified elevation of the right (*honestas*) above all as giving virtue the greatest conceivable luster and providing direction to at least the core, if not the whole, of happiness.[125] The Stoic portrayal of the way of virtue as an unqualified good and the way of happiness is seen as a rhetorical plus. In this, the Stoics are seen as true Socratics.[126] The difficulty for Cicero is found in their artificial and unrealistic understanding of the right as something entirely distinct from certain commonly perceived "goods."[127] Cicero appears to work to open the Stoic teaching to an explicit acknowledgment of the Peripatetic view that there are other goods besides the highest good,[128] not because he believes that any "good" is ever to be chosen over the highest good but because he thinks that the right and virtuous course of action in concrete situations would be one that gives appropriate consideration to (and thus incorporates in the very determination of right or duty) these "goods," namely the matters usually called considerations of utility or expediency. As he is found, apparently, resolving this matter in the *Officiis*, Cicero does not believe that, taking the words literally, there are other "goods" besides the highest good, and that is at least partly why he is drawn to the Stoic formulation rather than the Peripatetic.[129] He does, however, hold that the highest good is to be specifically understood with an eye to the comprehensive requisites of human nature. No disembodied Stoicism for Cicero, yet he would not have that attractive Stoicism which has been brought down to earth seen as a lowering or compromising of the standard that the right is always first and is always to be chosen but as an insistence that the full range of human needs or utilities be appreciated in shaping the duties of an honorable and good life.[130]

Cicero also finds himself repelled by the extensive and dogmatic claims of Stoic natural philosophy, and this line of criticism seems primarily animated by a concern to defend philosophy in terms of human need as evident in the ordinary horizon to practical men. In this regard, the Stoics are the worst example of a failing that characterized to some extent all the schools except the Academic.[131] The Stoics abuse reason by their contrived effort to explain with certainty and consistency all things. This is especially evident in the Stoic explanation of origins, the heavens and divinities.[132] The Stoics confidently, in fact arrogantly, assert explanations of matters shrouded in obscurity for most intelligent people.[133] Cicero believes that Carneades, the Academic, saved philosophy by his famed attack on the Stoics and seems to understand his own philosophical interests beyond moral and political philosophy to have much the same immediate purpose.[134] The Stoics, by attempting to do more than is possible in the name of philosophy, bring philosophy into disgrace. By their unjustified assertions, the Stoics lose respect not only for their entire teaching but also for the activity of philosophy itself.[135] The cause of philosophy is important to Cicero because it is finally the cause of virtue. The defense of philosophy requires a purification of philosophy through a critique of the schools, especially the Stoics. When philosophy presents itself with its properly Socratic face and orientation, humbly acknowledging its ignorance in the most uncertain and obscure matters, then it is most acceptable to intelligent, practical persons like the leading men of the Roman past; then also it is more likely to be taken as a guide in man's most important search, the search for the way of nature as a rule of life; and then it is most likely to serve effectively to support natural virtue.

In the light of the common tendency to see Cicero as a Stoic, or at least to emphasize his apparent Stoic formulations in his writings and Stoic sources for them, it may be surprising to find that the Peripatetics or Aristotelians appear to meet with more overall approval in Cicero's assessments of the schools. Near the very beginning of *Officiis,* Cicero writes of his philosophy "differing very little from that of the Peripatetics, for both of us seek to be followers of Socrates and Plato...."[136] Like the Stoics, the Peripatetics suffer, in Cicero's eyes, from their approach to philosophy as a school with a systematic doctrine and from their ambitious explanations in natural philosophy.[137] Nor is their approach to the supreme good without troubling aspects for Cicero. He questions the consistency of certain Peripatetics, allowing external and other "goods" while placing happiness in the highest good of virtue.[138] On the other hand, Cicero takes the interest in and regard for the rhetorical art shown by Aristotle and in the Peripatetic tradition as a sign of their soundness.[139] They appreciate rather than scorn this important requisite as well as other needs of effective and wise public leadership.[140]

Despite his criticisms of both schools, Cicero appears to find much of Stoic and Peripatetic moral teachings supportive of natural virtue, essentially in accord with the moral sensibility, and therefore worthy of serious consideration in a way Epicureanism is not.[141] No doubt, with moderated Stoicism in mind, Cicero claims that it and the teaching of the Peripatetics makes for a decent public philosophy which is cast in terms befitting the work of the Senate and courts.[142] Only the Stoics, Peripatetics, and the Academics, insofar as these skeptics approve and adopt a position drawn from or akin to that of the other two schools, hold a view of the ultimate end that allows the formation of duties rather than mere calculations in the pursuit of personal security or pleasure.[143] The conflict between the Stoics and Peripatetics on happiness, or the ultimate end, is on the whole regarded by Cicero, as it was by Carneades, as more a difference in choice of words than a real conflict (*in rebus*).[144] Cicero does seem interested in which of these schools makes the more effective case for its formulation and hence for virtue. Insofar as a real rather than verbal difference is involved, this is an honorable and fascinating contest (*certamen honestum et disputatio splendida*), which requires one to probe how important virtue in itself is, and which is then fraught with significance for all of life.[145] On this key matter, as well as other aspects of their moral and political philosophies, Cicero is attentive to Stoic and Peripatetic thinking, sifting through their views as an Academic or, one might say, as a Socratic. What is acceptable or able to be approved is what is most in accord with that effective criterion—the moral sensibility that includes the practical necessity of public leadership. Not entirely settled on every detail, Cicero has worked out a position—a public philosophy—of his own.

Let us look back from this point of Cicero's assessing the teachings of the schools to recall how he has proceeded from his essentially skeptical stance. Understanding that skepticism and the way Cicero is able to work out a moral and political philosophy from it is critical to appreciating the coherence and persuasiveness of his approach to philosophy and his philosophical work. Regarding his own skepticism as that of Socrates, Cicero took it as the most credible philosophical stance and one very useful for getting at and teaching what was likely true. Like Socrates, and as exemplified in his way of life, Cicero expected philosophy to be fruitful in a properly lived or virtuous life. His skepticism would not be a despairing or practically disabling stance. It would be focused on practical or moral inquiry and would need to open to moral wisdom. In fact, Cicero thought that the critical or foundational question for all philosophy was in the sphere of practical philosophy, namely the question of the nature of happiness or the ultimate end. On this question, Cicero found the contention among the philosophical schools to be most significant, and his assessment of these schools is seen to rest primarily on how each handled it.

That happiness consisted essentially in virtue or doing the right was the response to the foundational question that Cicero adopted,[146] and in this too he saw himself following Socrates. That view of the ultimate end, thought Cicero, served to illuminate all of philosophy. Upon what, however, does this foundation itself rest? What illuminates and, hence, makes compelling or reasonable this fundamental choice? In reading Cicero with this question in mind, one comes to face the basic reliances—what have here been called the elements of the effective criterion—that determine his choice and allow this relatively assured step toward moral wisdom against the backdrop of a comprehensive skepticism. In fact, it seems that this step is thought foundational by Cicero because judgment is assisted by the inclinations, the very orientation of the human person toward happiness and the right in certain specific forms as well as by experience in pursuing this happiness.

That orientation, a prephilosophical moral sensibility that is attentive to basic utilities, also comes to light in Cicero's effort to determine duties and know nature's way, for one comes to know the right and understand this way as constituting genuine happiness through particular instances of it, not through some definitive grasping of a comprehensive notion from which one can then deduce specific duties for moral guidance. Thus, in his judgment of the schools on the ultimate good, and in his effort to specify duties, the elements of the effective criterion appear. Those elements, however commonly possessed, usually need clarification and extension of their implications through reflection, specifically on personal and vicarious experience. This clarification and extension is the work of moral and political philosophy. One is always in need of knowing more in the light of what is known, and if one is to act virtuously and so attain the very end of philosophy, one usually needs to be ever renewed in attachment to what is known, to the way of virtue, by this being rendered attractive to those very inclinations which point human beings to the right and the good. The process, of coming to know and do the morally and politically right, calls for both the critical and rhetorical modes of philosophy as indicated in Chap. 2. The nature of that process and the ground for judgments of the right indicate the good sense in Cicero's not separating, sequentially or too strictly, the critical and rhetorical modes.

NOTES

1. Above Chap. 1 and Vlastos (1991: Chap. 8) for the Socratic basis of the Stoic view of happiness.
2. *Div.* 2.2.
3. James Wilson as quoted in Richard (1994: 65).
4. Cicero takes pains to indicate (*Off.* 1.6; 2.7) that he is not following the Stoics or Panaetius in a servile way or as a mere translator, but in the fashion, it seems, of an Academic philosopher who will select what he judges appropriate. In fact, when he initially mentions Panaetius (*Off.* 1.7), Cicero faults him for failing to define duty in his work on the subject, and at several points later in *Officiis* he draws attention to inadequacies in the way Panaetius treated duties. Discussions utilizing Cicero's correspondence that deal with his dependence on and independence from Panaetius in *Officiis* are found in MacKendrick (1989: 254–56), Griffin (1991: xix–xxi), and Long (1995a: 219, n.14). Gill (1988: 169–99) has explored an aspect of Cicero's difference from Panaetius.
5. *Off.* 1.9; 2.35; 3.18; *Fin.* 4.23. Noting the great "renown and influence of *Officiis* "from the Renaissance to the nineteenth century," Long draws the interesting and persuasive conclusion that "through Cicero Panaetius might fairly be regarded as the most influential of all Stoic philosophers" (1986: 211).
6. For evidence of Cicero utilizing the framework and terms of moral analysis of *Officiis* on decisions in his own life, see Brunt (1986: 12–32) and Long (1995a: 218, n.13).
7. *Off.* 1.7.
8. See also *Fin* 5.15–16.

9. This is not to say that Cicero knew the *Nicomachean Ethics* in the form we have it, or if he did have it in this form, knew it to be Aristotle's; see *Fin.* 5.11–12, Rawson (1985: 290) and How (1930: 27). Long (1986: 212–13, also 10, 112) has noted the Aristotelian features of *Officiis*.
10. The fairly common practice of translating *officium* as duty is followed here. See Griffin (1991: xlv). Cicero himself directly ties *officium* to the Greek *kathākon* (e.g. *Att.* 417; 420), and this Greek source-term and its use in the Stoic tradition leads some to prefer rendering *officium* as "proper," "appropriate," or simply "human" "function." However, see Dyck (1997: 3–8). Long makes the case for "function" (1986: 188–89) by observing that Stoics applied *kathākon* to infants, animals, and plants and that it is hardly right to speak of the duty of such beings. What makes *officia* duties, he adds, "is the fact that they are functions of a rational being. Nothing in the moral sense obliges a non-rational creature to behave in a certain way. It is therefore best to translate *officium* by 'function' throughout...." Since Cicero's *Officiis* is limited to providing guidance for human action, and the term "duty" strongly connotes a moral sense, it seems to be the most effective and sensible English translation for *officium* in this book. Powell (1995: xvi–xvii) demurs on associating the moral sense with all of the right or appropriate behavior commended in *Off*. Walsh, in the recent Oxford English translation (2001), renders *officiis* as "obligations," in an effort to restore the moral sense that he thinks is diminished or lost in a translation as "duties." "Note on the Translation," liv.
11. *Off.* 1.7.
12. *Off.* 1.8; also 3.14 and *Fin.* 4.15 and Lévy (1992a: 104–05). *Medium officium* is here distinguished from *perfectum officium*, absolute or perfect duty, which is simply the fully right (*rectum*) in a self-evident sense, meaning, it appears, that no plausible argument (*ratio probabilis*) needs to be made for it; rather, it is simply unambiguously the right course as apprehended by one possessed of comprehensive knowledge and the proper intention. Such a one is the perfect Wiseman of the Stoic tradition. Though properly seeing the focus of *Off.* on "mean" duties, Kidd tends to go further than seems warranted in insisting that *honestum* belongs only to the perfect Wiseman and that "*officium* is not *honestum*" (1971: 160–62, nn. 49, 50).

Would such a perfect Wiseman have "duties"? What one would do as a result of that hypothetical comprehensive knowledge and virtue does not seem to have a character, specifically the moral sense, that, it seems, we should expect with duty in this case. Earlier Stoics may have avoided this difficulty. According to *Ac.* 1.37, Zeno, the Stoic founder, explicitly chose not to use *officium* (presumably *kathākon*) to describe the right action of the Wiseman. The traditional Stoic term for this right action, or the simply and fully right, is *katorthōma*, which Cicero renders as *perfectum officium*.

Mitsis has provided an exceptionally lucid explanation of the Stoic terms *kathākon* and *katorthōma*: He is inclined to see the Wiseman marked by *katorthōma* as yet having duties (1994: 4825 ff., 4830–31 n.46, 4843). This makes sense if the Stoic Wiseman or sage has neither detailed knowledge of what will produce the best results nor omniscience but has comprehensive knowledge in the sense of a firm knowledge of essentials—of the nature of the whole and his place in it. There is disagreement among scholars on the nature of the sage's knowledge, but there is a general agreement that the formal intention to act rightly is perfect and complete and independent of any assessment of consequences. See Mitsis (1994: 4826), Vander Waerdt (1994a: 274–77), Lévy (1992: 523–25), Frede (1987 :153–54, 170), Long (1986: 130), Bett (1989: 64–65), Kerford (1978:125–36), and Engberg–Pedersen (1986: 182–83). Relevant Stoic texts are presented and explored in Long and Sedley (1987:1:359–68, also 257, 345). See also Striker (1991: 37–40). *Officium* (*kathākon*) for humans seems, in Cicero's usage, usually co-extensive with what came to be called *medium officium* (*Fin*. 3.20–25). It seems that in the Stoic tradition, down to Cicero, *medium* came to be associated with *officium* because the latter was concerned with bodily and external advantages (for the Stoics, these were indifferent or intermediate [*media*] things, that is, neither good nor evil); see *Fin*. 3.58; 4.26; 5.69, and see Rist on *medium officium* and its relationship to "natural ends" which are "indifferent as to virtue and vice" and Sandbach's related suggestion (1969: 99, 102 n. 4). Also see Engberg-Pedersen (1986: 179), Irwin (1986: 234–35) and Reesor (1951: 102–110).

Rist (1969: 97 ff.) thinks that Cicero, specifically at *Ac*. 1.37, has the Stoic teaching wrong or muddled and believes that the Wiseman still has *media officia*, that, in other words, the Wiseman utilizes plausible argument (*probabilis ratio*) and is perfected morally but not with respect to certain and comprehensive knowledge. Without attempting here to sort out the complex history of Stoicism with respect to the distinction between *kathākon* and *katorthōma*, but strongly suspecting that Rist has portrayed it as clearer and more settled than it was, I find that Cicero consistently seems to take his bearings from there being a difference between these terms. Cicero also regards *katorthōma* or *perfectum honestum* as the product of perfect knowledge as well as an entirely proper disposition, an aspect that does not clearly come to the surface in Rist and in some other writings on the Stoic *kathākon*.

Rist is apparently not interested in whether Cicero's thinking on *officium* is consistent and coherent, for he fails to even cite *Officiis* in his chapter (Chap. 6, 97–111) on *kathākon* which begins with his criticism of Cicero. In a later chapter (Chap. 10, "The Innovations of Panaetius,"

197), Rist argues that Panaetius is not an orthodox Stoic with respect to *kathākon* and that *Officiis* 1.8 does not stem from Panaetius. Those conclusions should, it seems, increase interest in Cicero's own consistency and coherence, for his understanding of the matter may be the Stoic understanding, or a widely held Stoic one in his time. Mitsis dissents from Rist on this (1994: 4842–43 n. 82). Consider Long (1967: esp. 89–90).

13. *Off.* 3.18–19, 34. And consider 3.29 ff., 50 ff., 91–92.
14. Thus the importance of the concept of the supreme good to moral action, considered in an important way in Chap. 1.
15. At this point, fuller elaboration of an example may be helpful. Consider an impending decision over keeping a promise or maintaining a treaty in a specific context. Much argument and deliberation is conceivable on whether it is right or wrong to do so, but all the while it is assumed that doing the right is the supreme good or an important part of the supreme good. *Off.* 1.31–32, 39–40; 3.92 ff., 100 ff.
16. The notion that one might inquire into what is already in some sense known was discussed in Chap. 1. See also Engberg-Pedersen (1986: 178, 182).
17. *Off.* 1.4–5.
18. *Off.* 1.5; similarly in *Sest.* 23. Cicero elaborates on this statement in the paragraph that follows (*Off.* 1.6), where he makes clear that, opposed to an ethics of calculation, in the form of what later might be either crude or high-toned utilitarianism (in either case, a form of the "hedonistic calculus"), duty for him entails at least some precepts that are settled, stable, and based on nature (*officii praecepta firma, stabilia, conjuncta naturae*). For examples of such *praecepta* in the Stoic tradition, see Diogenes Laertius, 59E (in Long and Sedley 1987: vol. 1); see also Rist (1969: 101) and Engberg-Pedersen (1986: 180–81). The slide into a mere ethics of calculation, where convenience or interest is measured, can be averted and the notion of duty saved only by pursuing virtue alone (*sola honestatis*) or primarily virtue (*maxime honestas*) as the supreme good. Cicero finds such acceptable understandings of the supreme good only in the Stoic, Academic, and Peripatetic schools. A very similar statement of the argument in *Off.* 1.4–6 is found in the mouth of the Peripatetic Piso in *Fin.* 5.21–22. Also see *Off.* 3.33; *Tusc.* 5.119–120; *Leg.* 1.57. *Honestas* is Cicero's term for overall virtue, goodness, right, or integrity; *Leg.* 1. 44–45 and consider Annas (1993: 121 and n. 243); David Londey (1984: 144–45), assessing the difficulties of translating *honestas* and his choice translation as "moral integrity." *Honestas* characterizes the consular philosophers, treated in earlier chapters. An eloquent appreciation of the role of a "primeval, natural sense of justice" that functions as a check on a utilitarian slide of Cicero's "naturalism" is found in Arkes (1992: esp. 259, 272–74).

19. Cicero's use of the terms *sua commoda*, to describe the operative goal of those who he here thinks have no business teaching duties, accommodates well the various understandings of pleasure (*voluptas*) and tranquillity (*ataraxia/tranquillitas*), which are offered to function as the polestar or ultimate good in the Epicurean tradition. The basis of the Epicurean ethic is that individual benefit or convenience—in Cicero's view always reducible to sensual pleasure (*Tusc.* 3.41 ff.)—is the supreme good. Cicero's, and no doubt others', struggle for a clear understanding of Epicurus and the Epicurean tradition on the nature of the ultimate good is presented primarily in the first two books of *Finibus* (see especially *Fin.* 2. 36–37). As indicated earlier (Chap. 1 n. 53), there is a long tradition of protesting that Cicero misrepresents or treats uncharitably the Epicurean teaching. It includes Thomas Jefferson and extends to contemporary scholars. For a more direct extensive consideration of these charges in the light of the texts of Cicero, see Nicgorski (2002). On the reliability of Cicero's account of Epicureanism in *Fin.*, see Mitsis (1988: 7–8, 73). Overall there is much confidence in Cicero's account. See Stokes (1995: 145, 150–53, *passim*), who finds in *Fin.* "the fullest consecutive account extant" of Epicureanism. He claims that Cicero does not "misrepresent" Epicureanism and believes that is "not yet proved" that Cicero failed to pay careful attention to the extant texts of Epicurus. Similar confidence in Cicero's account is found in Lévy (1984: 111–17, 1992); Striker (1996: 196–208); Brunschwig (1986: 113–44, esp. 127) and Hossenfelder (1986: 245–63). Hossenfelder finds Cicero overall reliable except in one instance (257).

Not overall supportive of the adequacy and/or fairness of Cicero's account are Inwood (1990: 143–64); Long (1986) 30; Vander Waerdt (1987: 408). MacKendrick (1989: 146), taking what seems an indefensible position in the light of Cicero's writings and argument, but a position partly shared by Harris (1961: 17), claims that Cicero was selective in what he chose to use and attack among the writings of Epicurus and that Cicero is not "a safe source for understanding Epicureanism, chiefly because he assumes a viciousness not inherent in the doctrine." Inwood (144) reveals that the recurrent attraction of Epicureanism likely plays a part in the severe reaction one sometimes find to Cicero's critique of Epicureanism when he observes that "there is much in Cicero's treatment of Epicureanism which sympathetic modern students of the school find unfair."

Among a few contemporary scholars there is a specific sense that exists is an altruism in Epicurus's teaching on friendship and justice to which Cicero is blind. See Mitsis (1988: 97, 102 n. 7) for some explicit indication of his interpreting Epicurus in a way to find altruism and aspects of a virtue-based justice rather than simply a contractual or instrumental understanding of justice. Qualified support for the interpretive direction of

Mitsis is found in Annas (1993: 293, 448), Striker (1988: 177), (1996: 198 ff.), Nussbaum with respect to friendship (1994: 250) and Griffin (1997: 102). Opposing this interpretive direction are Inwood (1990: 157 n. 26); O'Connor (1989: 167, 182); Vander Waerdt (1987: 407 n. 22, 416 n. 56, 420–421). At 405, Vander Waerdt touches on the struggle over this matter within the Epicurean tradition; such differences are explored further by him later (1988: esp. 102–03).

20. *Fin.* 2.28, 35, 51, 80–81; *Tusc.* 5. 87 ff.; *Ac.* 2.37 ff.: on the powerful inclination to approve and act upon what is in accord with human nature, skepticism notwithstanding. One senses in Mitsis and others an uneasiness with this argument of Cicero and the suspicion that if Epicureans are thought to be living better than their theory, one may not, in fact, be understanding their theory adequately.
21. Recall above, Chap. 2 and Cicero's writing of the need of philosophy to treat the supreme good "with its own proper arguments and promptings."
22. *Div.* 2.5, 7. In the year 46, as Cicero is starting into that major set of philosophical writings of his last years, he writes (*Fam.* 177.5) urging Varro to join him in efforts toward strengthening the political community (*ad aedificandam rempublicam*), by studies and writings in the fashion of the most learned men of earlier times.
23. Hunt (1954: 187) and Tanner (1972: 109 ff). Also, consider the function of *Off.* for Arkes (1992). See Kries's interpretation of *Off.* as intended for two distinct audiences (2003: 377 ff.).
24. See epigraph from *Leg.* above, p. l; also, *Off.* 3.11. After noting these passages, *Off.* 3.34 can be seen as indicating that Panaetius is perceived to be following Socrates in respect to his view of the person who separates the useful from the just. Did Panaetius and/or other later Stoics renew this formulation of the essential moral problem, and was Cicero attracted to it because it engaged the Epicurean agenda and Epicureanism was then attracting a wide following? See Kries (2003) on the rhetorical intent of *Officiis*. For the centrality of utility to Epicurean ethics, see Long and Sedley (1987: 1:129–35) and *Fin.* 1. *passim*. Also, the very structure of earlier Stoic ethical thought strongly suggests a development that would pose the common moral problem in terms of the right and the useful, given the role in the Stoic tradition of the distinction between the right and intermediate or indifferent (*media*) things, bodily and external advantages (see n.10 above) to which humans are drawn by nature. The link is apparent in Cicero's concept of *utilitas* being at times expressed as *vitae commoditates* (*Off.* 1.9, n.16 above) or *commoda vitae* (*Off.* 2.9), the very terminology attributed to the Stoics when they set right off against advantages (*commoda*, *Leg.* 1.55; *Nat. D.*1.16; *Tusc.* 5.120). Griffin brought this

relationship to my attention in her suggestive comments (1991: xxxvi). For the struggle in the Stoic tradition to distinguish advantages from the right and yet tie them with the good, see Long (1986: 195 ff., esp. 203); also, Long and Sedley (1987: vol. 1: 345–46); Annas (1993: 397, 404–05). Consider Kries (2003: 384 ff.). This aspect of Stoicism enters upon the concerns of this chapter later in the segment on "assessing the philosophical schools."

25. 1253^{a}10–15, Benjamin Jowett, trans.
26. *Inv.*2.53–55; 156 ff.; *De Or.* 2.334; *Part. Or.* 89 f.
27. *Off.* 1.9.
28. Everything we know about Cicero's thought overall and the very structure and dramatic detail of *Finibus* make it reasonable to see Piso in this text as his spokesman in most, though not necessarily all, respects. Cicero indicates in other works his approval of a developmental perspective in attaining virtue, both personal (e.g. *Leg.* 1.60) and communal (e.g. *Rep.* 2). Piso is portrayed as a spokesman for the Old Academy, a type of Peripatetic, a Stoicizing follower of Antiochus, whom Cicero admires much and with whom he appears to agree on much. In the *Officiis* (1.2), as well as elsewhere, Cicero stresses the essential agreement between the Peripatetics and the Stoics. Here in *Finibus*, Piso has the last word, save for a guarded and limited demurrer by Cicero; Piso's position is thus treated markedly differently from earlier Epicurean and Stoic spokesmen whom Cicero rebuts.
29. *Fin.* 5.58; also 41.
30. *Prima commendatio naturae* is the phrase used at *Fin.* 5.40, 46.
31. *Tusc.* 5.50.
32. *Amic.* 18: the perspective of the perfect Wiseman is criticized and that *in usu vitaque commune* is commended.
33. *Off.* 1.10; though Cicero states this elaboration in these comparative terms, there seems to be no reason not to see such kinds of choice as inclusive of cases where multiple, rather than merely two, courses of right action or useful action are before one.
34. Though this maxim and in good part a similar one, *secundum naturam vivere,* first appears in *Officiis at* 3.13, it describes well his turn to nature at *Off.* 1.11 ff. in search of the basis of right. See also *Fin.* 1.11; 5.17,44. *Fin.* 5.20–22 shows Cicero claiming through Piso that the idea of following nature was among those matters of moral philosophy which the Stoics took from the Peripatetics and earlier Academics. Striker (1991: 12) provides a valuable and insight-filled exploration of this theme and its problems in the Stoic tradition. Her reconstruction of the basis for the Stoic view that the human end is to follow nature leads her to explicate a developmental conception of grasping nature's ways that seems clearly to have influenced

Cicero's own thinking and is well summarized in her statement "that the Stoics held the end to be what one should desire, not what every one of us does desire. The Stoic conception of the end does not arise as a natural continuation of one's concern for self-preservation, but rather as a result of one's reflection upon the way nature has arranged human behavior in the context of an admirable cosmic order." Long, earlier (1967: 59–90), had traced the discussion in the Stoic school of the concept of "living in accord with nature." See also 59B, 61 in Long and Sedley (1997: 1: 398).Striker's explication of a developmental conception of coming to know the self fully in the context of the whole is a way of describing a progressive realization of the Stoic concept of *oikeiōsis*, or of realization of how one is "situated." This concept, given varying expressions in the Stoic school and other schools, has clearly informed the philosophy of Cicero as it comes to light in this section of this chapter. See Powell (1990: 88). For some significant treatments of this concept: Engberg-Pedersen, (1986) and his subsequent book (1990); Wright (1995: 164–65); Kidd (1971: 164–67); Mitsis, drawing on Kidd, (1994: 4828); Schofield (1991: Chap. 3) and (1995a: 195 ff.); Striker, on the role of Antiochus in developing *oikeiōsis*, (1986: 200–01 n.16); Vander Waerdt (1988: 90–91, 95–106) on the limited admission of *oikeiōsis* to the Epicurean tradition.
35. *Inv.* 2.65 ff., 160–61; *Leg.* 1.19.
36. Chrysippus (c.281–208), a leading Stoic and the most noted head of the school after Zeno, the founder, captures the experiential ground of the Stoic formulations in saying "What am I to begin from, and what am I to take as the foundation of proper function [duty] and the material of virtue if I pass over nature and what accords with nature." Reported by Plutarch, 59A in Long and Sedley (1987: vol. 1: 359).
37. Cicero has been properly described as representing the Socratic position of a "natural articulation of justice and law" (Hathaway, 1968: 4). For warnings against reading back into Cicero's concept "subsequent ideas of natural law" and for arguments that Cicero's "position is not fundamentally different" from these notable Greek predecessors, see Crosson (1988: 5–6) and West (1981: 77 and *passim*).

Doubts that the early Stoics ever used the expression "natural law" or had much of a natural law theory are raised along with speculation that Cicero "may be the legitimate father of the natural law theory" in Fortin (1978: 182–83). Fortin claims that Cicero's appeal to the concept of natural law was "for political rather than theoretically valid reasons" (186); he holds that if this were not so, Cicero would be involved in "a substantial deviation from the teaching of his Greek masters" (183). Fortin's doubts about the Stoic use of natural law are based on the work of Koester (1968: 521–41). Koester notes (522) "very little evidence for the occurrence of the term 'law of nature' (*nomos phuseōs*) in classical Greek texts" and specifically concludes that the term natural law is (529) "almost totally absent from Stoic writings" and that "all evidence for the concept 'natural law' in Stoicism comes from Cicero or from Philo." Philo of Alexandria (30 B.C–45 A.D.) is claimed as (540) "most probably...the creator" of the "theory of natural law." In Philo's work, which is marked by a frequent use of *nomos phuseōs*, Koester finds (534) that "the fundamental Greek antithesis of law and nature is overcome...by virtue of the Jewish belief in the universality of the Law of God." As to explaining Cicero's use of natural law, it is for Koester (540) at the end a "still unanswered problem," and his best thought on a solution is that this use "developed independently by a productive misunderstanding and mistranslation of a Greek Stoic concept." The nature of the mistranslation was explained earlier (529), when he concluded from a review of likely Greek Stoic sources, "[W]hat actually corresponds to the Latin *lex* in the term *lex naturalis* is not the Greek term *nomos*, but the Greek *logos*." Horsley (1978) takes up the challenge of Koester's "unanswered problem" and more. He convincingly insists (36) that "the parallel passages on the law of nature in Philo and Cicero derive ultimately from a Stoic tradition on universal law and right reason...But this Stoic tradition had been reinterpreted by a revived and eclectic Platonism upon which both Cicero and Philo drew," and "the key figure in the Platonic revival and the thinker upon whom Cicero and (probably) Philo depend was Antiochus...." Horsley finds (57) Cicero on natural law, like Philo and presumably Antiochus, moving away from "the fatalism of Stoic materialism and determinism" and seeing "the true, universal reason or law as the mind of the divine Creator and Lawgiver—a divine mind which transcended the sense-perceptible creation and worldly affairs...."

Horsley's argument for Stoic elements in Cicero's concept of the law of nature properly drew attention to (39 f.) the sense of being bound by true or right reason and of being in one community as pervasive features of Stoicism before Cicero (see also, Long and Sedley (1987: vol 1: 435). The Stoic provenance, if not direct parentage, of the concept of natural law and Cicero's use of it is defended and carefully explored in Schofield (1991: esp. 70–73, 102–03). Schofield not only calls attention to the Stoic use of a concept of basic, fundamental, or natural law to express right reason but also emphasizes the authoritative prescriptiveness of this law and its focus on the social relation of gods and men. See also (1995a: 205 ff). Other recent arguments for this traditional view of a Stoic provenance are found in Vander Waerdt (1991: 195–97, 1994a, 1994b). Here, Vander Waerdt is interested in showing how Cicero, largely following Antiochus, used the earlier Stoic tradition to forge his own position. Mitsis (1994: 4843 and passim) sees more continuity between the early Stoa and Cicero in this

matter and less of an Antiochean influence. Also see Erskine (1990: 16, n. 13, pp. 119, 194), and Striker (1987: 80 ff). Ferrary (1995) emphasizes the unorthodox Stoic aspects of Cicero's understanding of natural law. Although the Stoic parentage of Cicero's concept need not, in my view, preclude his thinking on this topic being fundamentally informed by Socrates, Plato, and Aristotle (for much depends on how one understands the Stoic elements entailed in his concept of natural law), Striker, it must be noted, is one who argues that there is a significant difference between the natural law concept of the Stoics and Cicero and natural justice in Plato and Aristotle. Mitsis (4813 n. 1) essentially supports Striker in this, while developing an argument on the consistency of Cicero's teaching with the early Stoa's appropriation of Socrates (4815 ff.). On the "non-rhetorical" genuineness of Cicero's embrace of a Stoic appeal to nature, see Garsten (2009: 143–50, 155) on the probabilistic status of natural law for Cicero.
38. *Ac.*2.66.
39. See Mitsis (1994: 4841–43, n. 81, also, 4828) on the relationship of duties to natural law in the Stoic tradition.
40. On the rhetorical mode, see Chap. 2, and on the adequacy of his treatment of the Epicureans, n. 19 in this chapter.
41. *Fin.* 2.118; also 1.1–2.
42. *Fin.* 2.51. Cicero is aware that Epicurus and the Epicureans have accommodated the traditional language of the virtues. He thinks that this makes Epicureanism all the more appealing (*Fin.* 2.44–55). Epicurus once suggested that the virtues were a necessary means to pleasure, and this observation can surely suggest that they are so implicated with the end or goal of the truly faithful Epicurean that they might appear to be the end itself (*Fin.* 1.25, 45–46; 2.73; 5.74, 93; *Tusc.* 3. 48–49; 5.93 ff.; *Fam.* 216.2–3; *Off.* 3.118; Lévy [1992: 424 ff.]). Both Epicurus and Cicero, however, seem clear that pleasure is one thing and virtue is another, and Cicero describes Epicurus's view in a way that would seem acceptable to Epicurus, namely that the virtues are habitual practices instrumental to pleasure.

These practices or Epicurean virtues are developed from what I would call the calculative injunction, which is more commonly referred to as "the hedonistic calculus." In Epicurean ethics, this calculative injunction is second only in importance to the supreme end itself: pleasure. Near the end of the *Tusculans*, Cicero gives expression to this injunction: the Epicurean "wise man will use a kind of balancing (*compensatio*—literally balancing of account books—we would say 'looking to the bottom line') so that he will flee pleasure if it is likely to bring greater pain, and he will embrace pain if such promises greater pleasure...."(*Tusc.* 5.95). One can see in the calculative injunction an opening to forms of social contract thinking, to one kind of basis for patriotism and, in sum, to all actions, habits, and institutions that might take their bearings chiefly from the dominant way of understanding "self-interest rightly understood," namely maximizing pleasure in the long run.

It is important to notice Cicero's recognition of the virtuous—even ascetically virtuous—way of life of Epicurus as well as of the overall laudable, decent lives of his own Epicurean acquaintances and friends such as Atticus. It is important, because a common error is to suppose that the philosophical hedonism that is Epicureanism is one and the same with crass or vulgar hedonism which expresses itself in excessive and usually self-destructive indulgence in one or another or various sensual pleasures. It seems that at least some of those who think that Cicero "gets Epicurus wrong" believe that Cicero committed this common error. However, this is patently not the case, though Cicero has an argument of another kind, considered later in this chapter, that connects vulgar hedonism to philosophical hedonism.

Epicurus, writes Cicero, was a "good" and "kindly" and "humane" man (*bonus et comis et humanus*), a kind and attentive friend, who expressed many noble opinions. His virtue, according to Cicero, was even severe, judged against the moderate indulgence in sense pleasures custom generally allows. He never intended licentiousness in his teachings. The issue is not, insists Cicero repeatedly, his character but a deficiency in intellect with a resulting unsoundness in the doctrine he shaped (e.g. *Fin.* 2.80; *Tusc.* 3.46; 5.26–31). In a similar assessment, Cicero confesses in a letter (To Memmius, June or July, 51, *Fam.* 63.2) to have lost respect for Phaedrus, the Epicurean teacher of his youth, as a philosopher but to continue to hold him as "a good, amiable, and dutiful man" (*bonus et suavis et officiosus*) (also, *Fam.* 216.2–3). The doctrine is not worthy of philosophy; it is the mask of philosophy, plebian philosophy at best. The doctrine does not warrant the kind of life that was exemplified by Epicurus and certain others of the Epicurean persuasion. On Epicurus himself as philosopher, *Tusc.* 5.73; *Fin.* 1.26. On popular Epicureanism of Cicero's time, *Ac.* 1.5; *Tusc.* 4.6–7; Nicgorski (2002: n. 44). Cicero actually uses the phrase and concept of plebian philosophy in reference to thinkers who deny the Socratic/Platonic claims for the immortality of the soul. *Tusc.* 1.55; *Sen.* 85.

43. More on the interaction of inclination and reason is found at *Off.* 3.14–16; *Tusc.* 3.2–3; *Fin.* 2. 36–37, 44–45; 3.23; 4.47. Language apparently develops from a similar interaction (*Rep.* 3.3).
44. *Off.* 3.13–15.
45. *Off.* 3.17.
46. Recall above where the initial human condition is described by Piso as one in which we humans are "unable both to see what is best and **to do it**" (ut nec res videre optimas nec agere possint) [bold supplied].

47. *Fin.* 5.41–44. See Striker in n. 34. This, as we will come to see, is what Cicero expects of the true statesman as exemplified in Scipio.
48. *Off.* 1.14. Also, *Tusc.* 3.3; 5.104–05.
49. *Off.* 1.13.
50. Perhaps one has to concede, in Erskine's phrase, "a degree of rigidity" in Cicero's natural law (1990:16 n.13) insofar as some call "rigidity" any formulable guidance or real and useful content to the way of nature. Nature's way is found by Cicero to involve certain constant aspects that give rise to stable precepts; see n.18 above. *Inv.* 2.174 provides an example of what "seems" to Cicero a certain and permanent duty: to tend to personal and civic survival and safety but never to do so without attention to right (*honestas*). I do not think Cicero's texts allow an interpretation that he conceives of natural law as a "rigid and inflexible" detailed moral code; he does endeavor, primarily in *Officiis*, to determine specific duties that are both grounded in nature and necessarily formulated in the light of the circumstances of his time. Thus Watson (1971: 234) has been properly concerned that the ordinary understanding of law does not capture Cicero's understanding of natural law. He writes, "*Lex*, then, is not *lex* in any restricted law sense in the *lex naturae* contexts of Cicero. The whole phrase is often better translated rationality or morality. It directs man's response to his total environment, it is the guide of his reason." Inwood (1987: 98) is inclined to see in Cicero more of the rigidity that is customarily associated with the term "law." If Cicero understands natural law as I have suggested here, there would be less reason for those who see him as a genuine Socratic, endeavoring to distance him from the natural law formulations in his writings. See Nicgorski, (2012: 270–73). Also, Fott (2008: 158–60); however, consider Strauss writing "One may therefore call the rules circumscribing the general character of the good life 'the natural law'" (1953: 127).
51. Association of this intelligence with god is explicit at *Rep.* 3.33, *Leg.* 1.21–23; 2.8–10; *Fin.* 5.11. Fortin properly observes (1978: 180) that the concept of natural law is "fully intelligible only within the context of divine revelation." In saying "properly," I pay due attention to the phrase "fully intelligible," and think that it is a mistake to deny or underestimate the significant continuity between Stoic sources, Cicero's usage and later Judeo–Christian uses of the concept of natural law. Horsley seems on the mark in his appreciation (1978: 58–59) for the significance and character of the "transformation of the Stoic concept of natural law" represented in the texts of Cicero and Philo. He concludes by observing that "transformed by connection with the Middle-Platonic idea of a transcendent God who was the Lawgiver as well as the Father and Maker of the world, the concept of natural law could be harmonized with the biblical ideas of

divine creation and divine commandment as well as with belief in the transcendent Word of God." Schofield (1991: 65,103 and *passim*) has brought forward, with reliance on Cicero, the role of a "metaphysical theory of providence," meaning that the universe is created and provided for humankind, in the early Stoic tradition. At the very end of the book, Schofield notes that the idea of natural law comes to be "put to work in social ethics in contexts which make no appeal to the divine city or to a metaphysical theory of providence. In short, the stage is set for *jus naturale* as it appears in Cicero's *de officiis* and the *Digest* [Justinian] and in Grotius, Pufendorf and beyond." As to Cicero, this amounts to a suggestion that appeals to a divine mind and some sense of a creator disappear in his last work, *Officiis*. There is a degree of truth in this suggestion, but there are two caveats which need recording on this matter: Though Schofield's point about *jus naturale* concerns the later, more strictly secularized idea of the law of nature, the actual phrase *jus naturale* is not employed in the *Officiis*. More importantly, there is a passage which can potentially mediate between fuller metaphysical elaborations of the idea of natural law and Cicero's use in *Officiis*. At *Off.* 3.23, Cicero writes of *ipsa naturae ratio quae est lex divina et humana*. Also see Benardete (1987: esp. 312) as well as Caspar (2010: *passim*) regarding the descriptions of natural law in *Leg.* and the related role of piety and religion in political society.

52. We must depend, says Cicero, on "a sketch and semblance of true law and genuine justice" (*veri juris germanaeque justitiae...umbra et imaginibus utimur*), *Off.* 3.69. Supreme law (*summa lex*), which is the divine mind, is known only in that perfected reason of the Wiseman; *Leg.* 2.11.

53. *Leg*.1.18–19; 2.8. Nature is literally the source (*fons*) from which the mind draws in making judgments of the right; *Leg*. 1.16; *Off.* 3.71–72; *Fin*. 5. 17–18 (Piso speaking). See *Caecin*. 65, where Cicero acknowledges a distinction between equity (*aequum et bonum*) and the letter of the positive law. *Off.* 3.67–69 on positive or civil law being unable to reach to every wrong or to secure every good. Mitsis (1994: 4835–37) discusses the Stoic tradition's use of moral rules but claims that one does not find exceptionless rules. J. Atkins (2013: Chap. 5) affirms the critical importance of natural law to Cicero's thought while noting his "skeptical fingerprints" in approaching it.

54. *Rep*.3.33; the passage actually constitutes a fragment found in Lactantius and is not part of the partial manuscript of the *Rep*. we now have and which was first recovered in the early nineteenth century. See the discussion of this passage and its likely sources in Ferrary (1974). Ferrary (1995: 66–67) sees in the passage a "Christian reinterpretation" of Cicero's understanding of natural law.

55. Cicero describes the idea of natural law or law of nature in a variety of terms besides *vera lex* and *suprema lex*, for example, *communis lex naturae*

(*Rep.* 1.27), *jus naturale* (*Rep.* 3.13), *naturae jus* (*Inv.* 2.65, 161), *naturae lex* (*Off.* 3.27, 69), *naturalis lex* (*Nat.* D.1.36), *universum jus* (*Leg.* 1.14 and 17), *sempiterna lex* (*Leg.* 2.10). He does not appear to intend a distinction in meaning in his alternate uses of *lex* and *jus*; nor does it seem, overall, that the difference between these two terms can be given significance by considering the *personae* and dramatic contexts of their various uses. Philus, making the Carneadean attack on justice, is the speaker of *jus naturale* at *Rep.* 3.13. Law of nature, here, is in the universalist, determinist sense that appears in later Roman law and that comes widely to characterize modernity.

He also uses the term *jus gentium*, law of nations or all peoples, in ways that make it appear the equivalent of the natural law (*Off.* 3.23, 69; *Har. Resp.* 32); however, these passages when read along with his usage of the phrase at *Rep.* 1.2 seem to indicate that already in Cicero we find *jus gentium* used not simply as an equivalent of natural law but specifically as a referent to that portion of natural law generally if not universally actually in effect between and among the peoples of the world (*Q. Rosc.* 143; J. Atkins (2013: 220, 224). It appears that already in Cicero, who may have initiated the use of the phrase *jus gentium*, one finds "the ambivalent nature of *jus gentium*" which M. Zuckert discerned in prominent later Roman jurists (1989: 78, 76). Fortin has offered an interpretation of the meaning and significance of Cicero's *jus gentium* (1996) and (1996a: 143–44, 187). For an interesting and persuasive argument that *jus gentium* is best translated as natural or "universal law" rather than "law of nations" or "law of peoples," and that it develops within Roman law rather than from any "conscious search for uniformities in the laws of Rome and her neighbours," see Lee (1954: 35, n. 89 and p. 37). At *Tusc.* 1.30, Cicero uses *lex naturae* in the sense of that on which the nations (*gentes*) invariably agree.

56. Laelius is also the speaker (*Amic.* 85) where bad or unreflective choices in friendship are said to produce much serious suffering in life.
57. Here I am paraphrasing my own quite untraditional translation of *neque est quaerendus explanator aut interpres eius alius*. Other English translations interpret the passage as saying that natural law requires no interpreter other than oneself (Keyes, 1928, and Rudd, 1998) or that natural law requires no expert interpreter as Sextus Aelius, a legendary legal scholar who lived a century before Cicero, (Sabine/Smith, 1929, Zetzel, 1999, and Fott, 2014). My translation is "other than reason," and it seems justified in terms of the context both of the passage and of Cicero's thought as a whole. This translation is consistent with the evidence that Cicero does affirm human equality in terms of a minimal, humanity-defining level of rational potential yet says that the actual attainment of virtue depends on having the proper guide (*Leg.*1.28–30). This also seems consistent with

Laelius's fragmentary remarks which follow in *Rep*.3, defending a just inequality in human relations and institutions.
58. *Leg.* 1. 19. Nederman (1990: 629) gives a helpful explanation of how duties as prohibitions are related to the underlying way of nature.
59. Cicero in his own name points to such a program in *Leg.* 1.58–62 and *Tusc.* 5.70 ff.; 1.64.
60. *Off.* 3.15–16, 76; *Tusc.* 2.16, 58; 3. 2. Horowitz (1998) explores this metaphor of the gift of the seeds in relation to the idea of natural law in her first chapter.
61. *Tusc.* 3.36 ff.
62. Gwynn (1926: 74) has described Philo, Cicero's teacher in the tradition of Academic skepticism, as an "open skeptic in his metaphysical teaching" who "based whatever certitude he admitted on the testimony of moral conscience." On Cicero's role in Augustine's development of "his uniquely Christian doctrine of conscience," see Fortin (1996b: 67–68, 71).
63. Cicero's absorption of the virtue of courage in magnanimity is more fully explored in Fetter and Nicgorski (2008).
64. *Inv.* 2.159 (*Virtus est animi habitus naturae modo atque rationi consentaneus*). At *Leg.* 1.25, Cicero writes of virtue as nothing other than nature perfected and brought to its peak (*perfecta et ad summam perducta natura*). That the test of possessing a virtue is actions (*Rep.* 1.2), rather than thought or talk about virtue, is, of course, wholly consistent with these definitions.
65. *Fin.*2.37; *Amic.* 18, 28.

Rightly taking the *Officiis* as not "a weakening of the early Stoic distinction between 'perfect' and 'intermediate' [duties or proper functions]," and seeing the virtues as "dispositions to perform" such duties "perfectly," Long and Sedley (1987: vol. 1: 368) conclude that "it is legitimate to analyze 'proper functions' [duties] both ascendingly, by reference to the individual's evolving rationality..., and descendingly, by reference to the virtues which are their ultimate fulfillment and justification...." The latter, they claim, is the way of Panaetius, which they apparently find in the *Officiis*. In my interpretation, here, of Cicero's overall thought on the virtues as well as their specific role in *Officiis*, they have a role in the "ascent" to full rationality, and they often appear in this function as qualities of exemplars or traditional heroes, who are not necessarily "perfectly" virtuous. Philosophy might then develop or perfect the virtues (*Tusc.* 2. 10–11).
66. *Leg.* 1.17–19; 2. 13: law as the way of nature is made to precede justice in the sense that it is the source for justice and the other virtues. Virtues, then, can be seen as expressions of the natural law; so Cicero writes of *lex fortitudinis* at *Leg.* 2.10.
67. *Off.* 3.13. Zeno is reported in Diogenes Laertius (Long and Sedley 1987: vol. 1: 361 [59E]) to have said that it is always a duty to follow the way of

virtue but not always appropriate and, hence, a duty to engage in dialectical inquiry.
68. E. Atkins, in making her case for the importance and centrality of justice for Cicero, notes that Cicero compares only the claims of justice with those of the other virtues. The other virtues are not set against one another (1990: 260.) A form of such conflict is entailed in the limits of friendship. See the case of Blossius, *Amic.* 37–38.
69. *Off.* 2.35; *Fin.* 5.67; *Tusc.* 2.32–33. The unity of the virtues appears to have been a key Stoic teaching, see Long and Sedley 1987: vol. 1: 377–80, 384. Eloquence joined to the other virtues makes for a perfect orator. See *De Or.* 1.83 and Gorman (2005: 153–54).
70. *Off.* 1.93–94,100; *Hortensius* (Grilli 1962: fr.59a, p.35 where *non deceat* and *non oporteat* are ways of speaking of the lack of *honestum; Tusc.* 2.46.
71. Cicero, at times, uses *verecundia* as a substitute for or in pleonasm with *temperantia*. Schofield (2012: esp. 53 ff.) examines closely the two terms, notably as used in *Officiis*, and finds the fourth virtue being reoriented to *verecundia*.
72. *Off.* 1.148; 2.15; *Rep.* 5.6; *Amic.* 82. Note the consideration earlier in this chapter on the expectation of beauty, consistency, and regularity in human matters. Overall, *pudor* appears to be used as synonymous with *verecundia* as translated here (note especially *Fin.* 4.18). Both *pudor* and *verecundia*, as well as *honestas*, to which they give rise, entail for Cicero sensitivity to societal norms and the opinion of the good but are not simply socially induced and socially dependent. See Arkes (1992: esp. 252.) Brunt (1986: 16 and n.14) cautiously, to be sure, suggests otherwise with respect to *verecundia* and *honestas*.
73. *Leg.* 1.32; *Fin.* 2.28; *Fin.* 5.61–63. This might help explain why, according to Cicero, Epicureans live better than their theories and Academics live, it might be said, better than their queries.
74. *Off.* 1.11 ff.; 2.18; *Fin.* 4.18.
75. *Off.* 2.1; also a version of this that Piso provides at *Fin.* 5.69.
76. *Off.* 3.35; Long and Sedley (1987: vol. 1: 352–54) for Stoic efforts respecting the derivation of moral value from natural "impulses."
77. The Stoics are seen by Cicero as connecting duty as *officium* with utility but removing it from the realm of right or morality; see *Ac.* 1.37; *Fin.* 3.37, 58.
78. *Fin.* 4.26–27. Late in 45 B.C., Cassius, having converted to Epicureanism, writes to Cicero that it is very hard to convince people that virtue and the good are to be sought simply for their own sake (*Fam.* 216.2–3). Perhaps this is an opening to Cicero's state of mind before he begins work on *Off.* Utility in the ordinary sense, as distinct from right, is acknowledged by Cicero at *Leg.* 1.44. In this sense too, it masks itself behind the common

appeal of pleasure, *Fin.* 2. 44–45. At *Fin.* 2. 78–79, utility in this ordinary sense is set in tension with genuine friendship.

79. While properly seeing *Officiis* as an effort to reintegrate *honestum* and *utile*, Zerba (2012: 153 f., 161, 199, 201) uses the language of "downgrading" *honestum* and, like Colish earlier, sees Cicero as collapsing *honestum* into *utile*. Colish (1978: 86–89), in her attempt to work out the relationship between *honestum* and *utile* in Cicero, goes too far in concluding that Cicero makes *utile* "the norm of *honestum*," though she is right to see Cicero elevating *utile* and giving it ethical weight of its own. See Barlow's persuasive detailed response (1999: 629 ff., esp. 639–40) to this aspect of Colish's interpretation of *Off.* Long (1995a: 217) perceptively reads *Off.* as Cicero's attempt "to reintegrate" the *utile* and the *honestum*. Dyck (1997: 492) writes perceptively of Cicero's effort here to "reform the content of *utile*." See Remer (2009: 2, 15 and 21), where he observes that Cicero's "intermingling of the ethical and the useful" reflects "the fullness of our humanity."

80. Marrou (1956: 238) describes the traditional Roman education that Cicero inherited as marked by a moral training that could not be separated "from real life and its responsibilities." A fragment from Aetius (26A) in Long and Sedley (1987: vol. 1: 158) indicates that in Cicero's time, if not before, this high sense of "utility" was employed in Stoic circles.

81. *Leg.* 1.42–43; *Off.* 2.42. At *Off.* 3.99 Cicero writes of the Roman hero Regulus being able to distinguish the appearance of utility (*utilitatis species*) from the real thing. Cicero overall approves the Stoic view, expressed by Cato (*Fin.* 3.70), that a stress on utility can undermine friendship and justice. Though aware of the role of the "virtues" for the Epicureans, Cicero appears to think that the hedonistic calculus undermines rather than supports the virtues.

82. The following passages concerning the basis for justice and society show Cicero's tendency to view the virtues as "needs": *Off.* 1.54 ff., 158; *Rep.* 1.39–41; *Hortensius* (Grilli 1962: fr.110, p.51). The role of the pursuit of glory in all of this is considered in the final chapter of this book.

83. *Inv.* 2.173.

84. This interpretation of *Officiis* differs, then, from that of Kries (2003), who does not see Cicero resolving or intending to resolve the tension between the right and the useful.

85. Note *Att.* 425, where Cicero specifically endorses the use of *officium* with respect to political responsibilities. See Lévy (1962: 523). The degree to which Cicero sees political life in terms of the right and the useful is revealed in the definition (*Rep.* 1. 39) of the political community (*res publica*) as formed "by agreement in right and by common advantage" (*juris consensu et utilitatis communione*). When at *Rep.* 3.19–23, Philus in an Academic role is made to argue against justice being based on nature,

he does it chiefly by showing that what rulers claim to be just is in fact simply what is useful or advantageous for them. See Cicero's eloquent praise of the positive law in terms of utility, *Caecin.* 70 ff. That the Stoic tradition's use of *officium* extended to politics, see Vander Waerdt (1991: 186). Schofield claims (1991: 71) that reason, natural law, and, hence, duties in the Stoic tradition provide "dictates" that "are principally social or communal norms." This accords with Cicero's emphasis in *Off.*, though Cicero does say (*Off.* 1.4), and we have reason to believe that the Stoics in general also held, that duties are not exclusively social and other-directed.

86. *Rep.* 1.1–13.
87. *Rep.* 1.12, 33; 3.4–6; 5.8; 6. 13, 28–29.
88. Here too some protest, in effect, that Cicero is not providing a fair interpretation of the Epicurean position. In this respect, notable is Long and Sedley's (1987: vol. 1: 136–137) far from convincing defense of Epicurus and Epicureans regarding their alleged failure in citizenship and political leadership. They write: "What Epicurus prohibits (as does Lucretius in his more balanced moments) is not all forms of conventional social life, but active and willing involvement in competition for political office and popular renown." Later they add, "To the charge that his attitude to politics is irresponsible and complacent, Epicurus could reply that his philosophy offers an alternative way of organizing society, which...eliminates everything that promotes false conceptions of value and endangers people's happiness." They conclude, "When all the evidence is duly considered, Epicureanism would be better regarded as a radical but selective critique of contemporary politics, rather than the apolitical posture with which it is frequently identified." Focusing on Lucretius, Nussbaum (1994: 503–04) makes a similar case for the development of a more positive Epicurean political teaching. On the other hand, Schofield, (1991: 125) finds Epicurus denying to man a "social nature" that "generates an altruistic obligation to seek to strengthen the society in which he actually finds himself, by various means including political activity...." O'Connor argues that the "anti-political" implications of the teaching of Epicurus are overt and undeniable, that one cannot read altruism into the teaching, that it is egoistic but not selfish, thoroughly hedonist but worthy of attention, (1989: 167, 186, *passim*). At the same time, Fowler reviewed the evidence for the anti-political position of the Epicureans (1989: 122 ff.). See also Vander Waerdt (1987: 421).
89. At *Off.* 1.20, justice is said to consist in not harming another unless provoked and in using common or public things for the common good and private things for one's own good. These are clearly ordinary terms of understanding, not the Socratic understanding which insists that one never harm even when harmed or that the useful and just are one and the same. Cicero moves from this ordinary horizon and shortly (*Off.* 1.22) is found

saying that each of us and all of the earth's goods come into being for the common good (*communes utilitates*). At *Inv.* 2.160, he had provided a definition of justice more directly in Socratic/Platonic terms: Justice is "a disposition of the soul that, while protecting the common good, gives to each what is deserved" (*habitus animi communi utilitate conservata suam cuique tribuens dignitatem*).

90. Cicero's apparent lifetime vacillation and struggle between the two ways of life is thoroughly explored in Lévy (2012).
91. *Off.* 1.153; 3. 4; *Rep.* 6.1–20; *Tusc.* 1.44–45, 74–76; 5.66, 105, 111, 115; *Fin.* 4.18; 5.11 (here Cicero shows a clear comprehension that the Peripatetics regarded the life of inquiry and contemplation as the best human life, as possessing the highest virtue).
92. Wisdom is "the mother of all good things" (*Leg.* 1.58), including, presumably, the recognition of the priority of the duties stemming from justice.
93. Above, 3.
94. *Off.* 1.153–159; 2.9; 3.11; *Rep.* 1.39; *Leg.* 1.33, 43 ff.; *Inv.* 2.173–75; *Fin.* 4.24–26. Necessity as a norm of utility, for Cicero, is not a necessity that is mechanically determinative but is always necessity in terms of an end. At *Off.* 1.56, Cicero notes that humans admire justice and generosity most among the various forms of virtue. In these social virtues, common utility is presumably most evident.
95. *Tusc.* 1.1–6; 4.5; *Fin.* 4.24–26; *De Or.* 1.197 and 3.137 (Crassus speaking).
96. *Off.* 1.95; 3.16, 77; *Rep.* 3.4–6; *Tusc.* 1.89 ff.: *De Or.* 3.77–80 (Crassus speaking); *Fin.* 5.80–81; *Amic.* 18–19 (Laelius speaking).
97. *Off.* 1.66, 19, 28, 69–73, 92, 153–60; *Rep.* 1.1–3,8–11; *De Or.* 1.1–4, 3.64; *Tusc.* 5.72; *Ac.* 2.6; *Sen.* 11. Nederman has properly emphasized that the peak of "republican virtue" for Cicero is statesmanship and not military command, though my analysis here leaves me uneasy with Nederman's statement: "[T]he use of physical force may on occasion remain a necessity for civilized human beings, but it can never really be a virtue, according to Cicero" (2000: 17–29, esp. 22).
98. *Rep.* 1.19–20; *Fin.* 2.46; 4.12; *Ac.* 2.6,127; *Hortensius* (Grilli 1962: frs.55–56,106–110, pp. 32–33, 49–51). Fott's interesting commentary (2014: 9) on the Dream of Scipio brings out the claims for priority of the life of political leadership and that of contemplative philosophy.
99. *Rep.* 1. 10–11.
100. Cited by Seneca, *De Otio.* 3.2. As translated here by Basore (1935: in *Moral Essays* 2:185). Fowler (1989: 127 ff.) discusses this statement of Epicurus.
101. Long has written about a Stoic practice, as early as Zeno, to assimilate to and identify with traditional wisdom (1980: 164–65).
102. Rawson (1974: 306), (1985: ix), Habicht (1990: 92, 121–22 n. 29) and Nicgorski (2012: 252 ff).

103. "Perhaps" (*forsitan*) the superb genius devoted to learning should be allowed freedom from the responsibility of political leadership" (*Off.* 1.69–71); the larger context of this same passage makes sense out of Cicero's friendly and clearly limited tolerance (*minime reprehendenda ratio*) of the principled withdrawal from politics by his close friend Atticus (*Att.* 17). At *Off.* 1.155–56 and *Rep.* 1.12, Cicero, with Plato, Socrates, and Aristotle in mind, notes that such outstanding men of genius have often come to serve the political community by their writings and through those whom they have educated. See also *Off.* 1.28; *Fam.* 177.5. It is important to note that it is not the exception but the rule which requires attention to one's own specific nature in choosing a career (*Off.* 1.110); thus one must be suitably talented even to make applicable to oneself the rule that public service is a duty prior to philosophic inquiry and contemplation.
104. *Arch.* 18–19; Plutarch (1960: 143 [2.3]; 145 [5.2]).
105. *Leg.* 1.32; *Div.* 2.4; *Tusc.* 2.28.
106. See above, 100-01.
107. *Rep.* 1.31–32; *De Or.* 3.226; *Div.* 1.4–7.
108. Through philosophical writings Cicero understood himself to be exercising a form of public leadership; according to Plutarch (1960: 172 [40.1]), his work in philosophy gave him great power even as the normal channels of political leadership closed to him.
109. There has been consideration earlier in this chapter regarding the fairness and accuracy of Cicero's understanding of the "political stance" of the Epicureans. Overall, Cicero's argument in this respect against the Epicureans falls under the form of *via negativa* that Cotta, the Academic spokesman, states in *Nat. D.* (1.60, 57): "nearly in all matters but especially in natural philosophy I would have argued more readily what is false than what is true" (*omnibus fere in rebus sed maxime in physicis quid non sit citius quam quid sit dixerim*). That the Epicureans can be treated first in *Nat. D.* and *Fin.* because they are the easiest to dismiss, most manifestly wrong. Consider that the three separate dialogues that make up *Fin.* are not in chronological order by dramatic dates; rather, they are ordered by Cicero in accord with his philosophical and rhetorical purposes.
110. *De Or.* 3.63–64; see Garsten's comment on this passage (2009: 243–44, n. 21), where the Epicurean doctrine about retreat from politics is seen to undermine their very desire for tranquility; also, *Rep.* 1.1; *Tusc.* 2.27–28; 3.50–51; *Fin.* 1.23,71; 2.73 ff., 85,117–18; 3.40; *Fam.* 362.4. Cicero understands well the attraction of withdrawal from active politics. See Gildenhard (2007: 67) and Lévy (2012). Caspar (2010: 81) observes: "The Epicureans and the Skeptics must somehow reflect something permanent about human nature that is nevertheless unhealthy for sound politics, at least at the beginning of a regime when it is most politically vulnerable."
111. Chap. 1: 22–23.

112. For the scholarly disputes on whether altruism and some sense of a virtue-based justice can be found in Epicurus, see the last paragraph of n.19 above.
113. *Rep.* 1.39; a fuller discussion of this passage, along with textual evidence that *jus* here is understood as a binding in nature, occurs in the following chapter.
114. Above, Chap. 1: 20–21.
115. Similarly, regarding *De Or.* 3.63–4, the inappropriateness of a philosophy, in the light of the need for persuasion and public leadership, does not settle the question of its truth, but it becomes a factor in determining whether the philosophy is consistent with human nature. At *Tusc.* 5.82, Cicero is inclined to think those very courageous Stoic statements about the self-sufficiency of the virtuous life are also the truest. Perhaps the utility of such statements plays an important part in making them appear true; see also *Parad.* 23, where the truest is also found to be the most useful. Cicero does seem to be using something like overall congruence or what is fitting (see Engberg-Pedersen, 1986: 179–81); *eúlogon* in relationship to mean duties was considered earlier in this chapter and can be seen as the standard of truth; humankind is attuned by nature in a number of ways to this truth. Consider the following description of Carneades' criteria of truth and how faithful a follower of Carneades Cicero may indeed be:

> Criteria may be discerned rather than proposed, and there are indications that Carneades considered his criteria to be recommended by the virtue of actual use.... The point of the criteria seems to be not to provide a systematic doctrine of truth but to sketch an informal method actually employed for deciding whether a given assertion or belief should be regarded as true (whether assent is justified) **within the context of a whole network of beliefs already accepted as true**... Stough (1969: 63); emphasis is mine.

Newman (1873: 271), a century earlier, described Carneades with these words:

> ...[Y]et, by allowing that the suspense of judgment was not always a duty, that the wise man might sometimes believe though he could not know; he in some measure restored the authority of those great instincts of our nature which his predecessor [Arcesilaus] appears to have discarded.

At *Tusc.* 1.24 and elsewhere, it is clear that Cicero appreciates that short dialectical exchanges are most appropriate for getting at assured truth but that the larger picture which can be brought out by continuous discourse

is useful for presenting the "truths" one might live by. For a discussion of pre-Ciceronic Stoic approaches to a coherence theory of truth, see Annas (1983: especially 86–100).
116. Above, 104-05, nn. 38 and 40.
117. Above, 100.
118. *Fin.* 4. 68–69; *Leg.* 3. 14.
119. *De Or.* 1.12, 43; 2.158–59; 3.65–66; *Amic.* 18; *Fin.* 4.5–7, 22, 55, 65; *Mur.* 6, 60–61, 63–64. See these Stoic characteristics exemplified: *Ac.* 2.137; *Tusc.* 5.103–05; *Parad., passim*; Long and Sedley, (1987: vol. 1: 253, 248). The context around Cicero's discussion of the widespread appeal of Epicureanism (*Pro Caelio*, 40–41) suggests that the Stoic alternative may offer a too high and, therefore inhuman, standard for humans. Griffin (1989: 8–10), Englert (1990), and Vander Waerdt (1994b: 4862–64) comments on Cicero's view of the rhetorical handicap of the Stoics and believes that the Stoics have more resources in this respect than Cicero allows. See Stem (2006) for an argument that the *Pro Murena* reflects not simply a rhetorical opportunity but rather Cicero's overall stance on the political liabilities of Stoicism.
120. At least partly contrary to Cicero's perception of the old Stoics, Erskine (1990) has argued that the Stoic tradition from Zeno was ever interested in politics, sought to influence political affairs, and had some successes. See also Vander Waerdt's review essay (1991), where he questions the degree of political activism Erskine attributes to the Stoics and brings out the variety within Stoic political philosophy. Annas (2013: 302 ff., 311) stresses the pull of Stoicism away from politics. See Schofield (1991: 125) on a Stoic approach to political activity. Caspar, specifically with respect to *Leg.* but somewhat in general, discusses Cicero's relationship to Stoicism, (2010: 8 ff. and *passim*.)
121. Chrysippus is alleged to have said that he never met in real life a Wiseman according to the Stoic expectation.
122. *Ac.* 2.107 and *Fin.* 4.23, 78–79 are places where Cicero favorably distinguishes Panaetius from the Stoics. His own emendation of Panaetius at *Off.* 1.10 can be seen as further pulling the Stoics down to earth. See also *Rep.* 1.34; Lévy (1992: 525–28), Long (1967) and Kidd (1971: 152–59) arguing persuasively against the dominant view, doubt that Panaetius altered the orthodox Stoic view on the supreme good. One can say that Cicero certainly resisted such an alteration. On Panaetius's acceptance, more than orthodox Stoics, of the irrational or emotional part of the soul, see Remer (2004: 150–51). On the critical influence of Polybius on *Rep.*, see How (1990: 28–29, 33); also on Polybius, Hahm (1995); on Cicero's differences from Polybius, see especially J. Atkins (2013: Chap. 3) and Kidd (1989: 38–50).
123. See the index for several earlier discussions here of the "Scipionic Circle."

124. In Thomas Pangle's words (1998: 261=62), Cicero is refashioning "out of Stoicism a teaching that gives full weight or due to the dimensions of political existence neglected by Stoicism."
125. *Off.* 3.20; *Fin.* 2. 45, 52; 5.64, 73–74; *Tusc.* 5.29–31, 37 ff. Cicero regards the Stoic teaching as lending itself to the rhetorical mode of philosophy, specifically to moral exhortation. Overall, Cicero hesitates between the Stoic teaching that virtue is the sole good and sufficient for supreme happiness and a Peripatetic approach that would acknowledge other goods besides virtue and thus be reluctant to conclude simply and definitively that virtue alone constitutes supreme happiness (*Ac.* 2.134). McConnell (2014: 184–85, *passim*) points to instances where Cicero prefers an "Academic" approach to moral/political dilemmas as more flexible than that of the Stoics. Cicero's preference for the Stoic formulation appears to be grounded in the attractiveness (i.e. potential effectiveness) of this teaching for the needed moral exhortation. Consider how Cicero uses the way of *honestas* in *Sest.* 23: see also Gorman (2005: 170–72). Book 5 of the *Tusculans* shows Cicero working out a defense of the Stoic view, yet he holds back from claiming that it represents the truth about supreme happiness, emphasizes the need to build up the attractiveness of virtue, and sees the Stoic view as compelling in that respect above all. Considering the nemesis of pain (*Tusc.* 5. 76–78), Cicero can be seen to be arguing that even if Stoicism is not true, it uplifts and serves the public good, just as Epicureanism, even if true, degrades and undermines the public interest. *Tusc.* 5.33; *Fin.* 5.79, 83; yet at *Tusc.* 5.82 (also, 4.53), he is saying that the Stoic view seems the "truest" (*verissime*) at this point. The "courageous" of that view and how it serves to build up virtue may give it the edge in seeming truest. For Cicero, this Stoic view is essentially correct even if his endorsement is a troubled one. Griffin (1995: 335–36) notes that two Stoic paradoxes which Cicero does not mock in his letters: the only good is virtue and virtue is sufficient for happiness.

Douglas is inclined to see more of a resolution of the issue in *Tusc.* 5 than I am. He observes (1995: 213), with some noteworthy qualifications, "[T]he doubts of *De Finibus* are almost resolved in the *Tusculans*. The status of the *sapiens*...and of Virtue as the only requisite for the happy life are, so far as may be, assured." Lévy (1992: 491) reminds us of all the indications in *Tusc.* 5 that the virtuous and supremely happy life defended here is the philosophical life, when he writes that we have here "neither confusion nor facile syncretism" but a serene affirmation of philosophy in the Platonic vein—that is the work of men of thought devoted to the ideal.
126. *Parad.* 4, 23; *Tusc.* 5.34, 48; *Ac.* 2.136. Cicero even has Piso, the Peripatetic spokesman, concede this at *Fin.* 5.84. In another sense of course, the New Academy is the Socratic school, yet Cicero also writes (*Tusc.* 4.6) of his own time being one in which the Socratic tradition has

settled in the Peripatetic school, meaning, it seems, the Old Academy. This tradition may seem to Cicero more positive, in having some affirmations, than the New Academy, and at the same time less rigid and totalistic in its claims than the Stoics.

127. Michel (1992: 84) reflects on this lack of realism which Cicero finds in the Stoics. *Fin.* 3.29 shows Cato pointedly presenting what for Cicero were both the attractive and unattractive aspects of the Stoic understanding of happiness; see also *Fin.* 4.20 ff.; *Leg.* 1.53 ff. The latter two books of *Fin.* and *Tusc.* 5 reveal Cicero's own struggle with the positive and negative features of the Stoic handling of happiness. See Algra's discussion (1997: 122 ff.), largely with Lévy, of Cicero's use of his sources for this dimension of *Fin.* and Cicero's struggle (130 ff.) with his skeptical restraints on an embrace of Stoicism. Also, Long (1967). The fullest discussion beyond the texts of Cicero on the issue he struggles with is found in Annas (1993: Chaps. 19–20); note 432–33, where she explicitly credits Cicero with seeing the difficulties on each side of the divide between the Stoics and Peripatetics on virtue and happiness. See also 180 ff. for her reflections on *Fin.* 5.

Cicero's struggle anticipates tensions that appear later in the history of moral philosophy between moral formalists and teleologists, the latter seemingly or made to appear to slide into utilitarianism. On distinguishing classical teleology, as found in Cicero and Aristotle, from modern utilitarianism, see an initial effort in Nicgorski (1984: 573–75). Cicero clings to the Stoic formulation because of an apparent fear that the Peripatetic position, as exemplified by Theophrastus, could slide into a utilitarian calculus or weighing of various goods. *Fin.* 5.12 (Piso speaking), 74 ff.; *Off.* 2.56. From such a calculated approach or weighing, Cicero appears to fear a weakening or undermining of the inherent appeal of the right. See also, S. White (1995: 236).

128. One can fairly say that the Peripatetic tradition has the resources for a distinction between the greatest single good—virtue or doing the right—and supreme happiness which would be virtue plus other "goods." The formulation of the Peripatetic understanding of happiness or the supreme good as "chiefly virtue" (*maxime honestas*) accurately reflects Cicero's overall understanding of the Peripatetic teaching. See also *Off.* 3.33, *Leg.* 1.54–55, *Fin.* 2.19, 68. There are clearly differences of emphasis within the Peripatetic school inclusive of Antiochus and the Old Academy (*Fin.* 5.12, 71 ff.; *Ac.* 2.132–34). It is the position of Antiochus that Piso is expounding and that Cicero is testing and partly criticizing in the fifth book of *Fin.*

129. Also, *Tusc.* 2.46.

130. Even when duty is shaped in the light of ordinary utilities, might it not be unpleasant and, therefore, not evidently productive of happiness or complete happiness? Cicero appears to be groping to say something like this:

Doing the right, doing one's duty, is always the highest good and at least the core of supreme happiness. He seems to require the distinction between the greatest good and supreme happiness so he might then say that by doing the right we do not attain every conceivable part of a happiness to which our nature points but the greatest happiness that our circumstances and context will allow.

131. A point that emerges and is developed in this book, especially in Chap. 2.
132. *Nat. D.* 3.66 ff.; *Div.* 1.6–7; 2.1; *Tusc.* 1.78; *Off.* 1.18.
133. *Fin.* 5.76. Recall the earlier discussion of Cicero's distress with and lack of interest in the Stoic assurance on perception and knowing.
134. *Div.* 1.23; 2.150.
135. *Div.* 2.37, 39; *Ac.* 2.128. At *Nat. D.* 3.60, Cotta argues that fables should be exposed so that religion may be saved.
136. *Off.* 1.2 (*non multum a Peripateticis dissidentia, quoniam utrique Socratici et Platonici volumus esse...*). Also 2.8, where Cicero does not use the term "Peripatetics," as he often does, but rather writes of the school of Cratippus, his son's Peripatetic teacher in Athens; the philosophy or school of Cratippus is called *antiquissima nobilissimaque*. Consider *Brut.* 250, where Cicero associates his own thinking with that of Cratippus. Nonetheless, How (1930: 27) hit the mark when he observed, "[I]t remains clear that Cicero, though he makes good use of the Peripatetics, is no slavish disciple of the School."
137. *Tusc.* 3.69, where Cicero indicates that he finds the understanding of philosophy in Aristotle and Theophrastus to be one of expecting philosophy to progress to complete explanation of all things. Also, *Ac.* 1.17 ff., Cicero has Varro speaking at this point.
138. *Fin.* 5.77, 80–81, 84. As noted earlier, Cicero, here, is specifically probing Piso's Antiochean and very Stoic-like version of the Peripatetic teaching on the ultimate end; it speaks of other goods than virtue but treats them as irrelevant, or largely so, to happiness. See Vlastos (1991: 216 n. 63) on the Antiochean position distinguished from the Stoic. Long (1988: 165–70, esp. n. 68) explicates the Stoic view and discusses differences with Vlastos. Cicero appears to prefer a more Theophrastean version of the Peripatetic position, one that more honestly confronts the relevance of goods of fortune and body to happiness; see *Fin.* 5.75, 77, 85–86, yet at *Ac.* 2.134, he levels against Theophrastus essentially the same critique made against Antiochus in *Fin.* 5. A different line of criticism of Theophrastus on happiness, a line coming more from a Stoic perspective, is found at *Fin.* 5.12 and *Tusc.* 5.23 ff., 47–48, 85. Though Cicero was clearly drawn in a certain respect to a Stoic position, and found the difference between the Stoics and Peripatetics on this matter a very vexing one, in which he admittedly went back and forth. *Ac.* 2.134, *Off.* 3.33, *Fin.* 5.12 (Piso speaking) and the *Tusculan's* passages above cannot readily and without additional argu-

ment be taken as Cicero's view. Yet Cicero himself is concerned with a Theophrastean type of slide to an ethics of calculation. See Glucker's thoughtful reflection (1995: 137) on Cicero's apparent inconsistency on this point. Glucker, here, may be stepping back somewhat from his earlier suggestion of Cicero being an easy-going, day-to-day changeable eclectic; see (1988: 64–66). Irwin (1986: 205–44) analytically explores the conflict between Aristotle's position and that of the Stoics on the nature of happiness, drawing heavily—but not exclusively—on *Fin.*

139. *De Or.* 1.43; 2.152, 160, 162; 3.67, 141; *Div.* 2.4; *Ac.* 2.119; *Fin.* 4.5–7; *Tusc.* 4.9; 5.85. Recall the earlier treatment of Cicero following Aristotle in joining practical wisdom to eloquence, and of his following the Aristotelian mode in his dialogues. Yet Cicero notes a hesitancy or reluctance that marked Aristotle's, apparently in contrast with his own, turn to rhetoric, Aristotle doing so under the spur of competition with Isocrates for students, *Off.* 1.4; *Tusc.* 1.7; *De Or.* 3.141. At *De Or.* 2.160 in the voice of Antonius, Aristotle is seen to have "despised" the technical aspects of the art of rhetoric.

140. Within the Peripatetic tradition, Cicero inclines to Dicaearchus's elevation of the active political life in opposition to Theophrastus's more traditional Peripatetic defense of the superiority of the philosophical life and of the goodness of knowledge in itself. For a fuller discussion of Dicaearchus's position and Cicero's attraction to it, see Nicgorski, (2013). There is much evidence throughout McConnell (2014) of Cicero's tendency on this issue. Cicero's letter to Atticus of May 59 (*Att.* 36), coupled with his handling of this issue in *Rep.* and *Off.*, his last philosophical work, indicate a profound and continuous struggle with this issue throughout his life.

141. *Off.* 3.33; *Leg.* 1.53; *Fin.* 2.38; *Ac.* 2.134.

142. *Fin.* 2.76.

143. *Off.* 1.6.

144. *Tusc.* 5.120, 87; 4.6; *Leg.* 1.38, 54–55; *Ac.* 2.15; *Off.* 1.6; 3.11,35. This is possible, as we have seen, because Peripatetics, like Antiochus, can be found emphasizing that doing the right secures supreme happiness, and Stoics can be seen saying that certain indifferent things are "advantages" and are to be "preferred." Irwin (1986: 240) properly denies that between Aristotle and the Stoics there is a mere verbal difference on this matter. Kidd (1971) provides a particularly lucid explanation of the Stoic "intermediates" and controversies related to that doctrine. Also see Douglas (1990: 153–54 n.47). Long (1967) explores Stoic efforts on the matter of "goods" to adapt in the light of dialectical probes of their position by Carneades.

145. *Fin.* 2.68; *Ac.* 2.132–34.

146. *Tusc.* 4.82: here, immediately after the *Fin.*, Cicero speaks of handling the foundational question as far as reason allows.

CHAPTER 4

Political Philosophy and the Roman Republic

> In order that these holidays may be chiefly employed in conversations most useful to the political community (*utilissimos rei publicae*), let us ask Scipio that he recount what he thinks to be the best type of polity (*optimum statum civitatis*). (Laelius in Cicero, *Rep.* 1.33)
>
> But neither am I satisfied with the writings on this question left to us by the greatest and wisest men of Greece nor am I so bold to rank my views superior to theirs. (Scipio in Cicero, *Rep.* 1.36)
>
> ...[O]ur political community (*res publica*) is not the work of a single genius but of many, nor was it formed in the life of one person but over a number of generations and centuries. (Scipio reporting Cato the Elder's view in Cicero, *Rep.* 2.2)

The question of the best political order is commonly and properly thought to be at the very center of the inquiry known as political philosophy. Its presence is revealed both in efforts at utopian construction and in searches for incontrovertible, if not a priori, principles of justice. That same question of the best regime can be found close to the surface and, thus, capable of arising in ordinary political disputes and discourse among thoughtful citizens. Such disputes and discourse, rising from the ordinary citizen's horizon to the question of the best regime, have been seen as "determining the orientation and scope" of the tradition of classical political philosophy, in which Cicero stood.[1] The political deliberation of thoughtful citizens is usually cast in terms of the useful and the just, concepts central to

Cicero's writings. As the fundamental question in political deliberation, the question of the best regime circumscribes an inquiry into a comprehensive politically just or right. Thus, in relationship to politics, a conception of the best political order stands as the overall right and virtuous (*honestas*) does with respect to all action or moral decisions. For Cicero, the question is a compelling and ineluctable one for any participant in political life, and it is especially necessary and useful for political leaders or statesmen to seek clarity and understanding of the politically right—that best of political orders.

When Cicero turns, in his *De Re Publica*, to this question of the best regime, he does so explicitly in the light of Plato's great and influential work on the question, *The Republic*. Though various and conflicting interpretations of Plato's intent in *The Republic* seem to have been around from the very beginning, the "city in speech," the "model" regime he presents there, had apparently already claimed during the ancient period a central and magisterial role for political philosophy. Evidence for this is found in the important and formative role that Plato's city has not only in Cicero's *Re Publica*, his major political work, but also, and much earlier, in *The Politics* of Aristotle.[2] Neither of these legendary students of Plato are entirely deferential—to understate the matter—to his best regime or, more precisely, to their understandings of that best regime. Cicero, in fact, appears to set aside a search for and statement of the best regime according to nature in favor of a depiction of what is taken as the best of actually realized regimes, the Roman Republic. This appearance has given rise to a tendency to see Cicero as more a patriot than a philosopher, or at the least to regard him as a somewhat diminished philosopher for so collapsing the ideal and normative into the real and descriptive. Such an interpretation readily lends itself to seeing Cicero's alleged philosophical timidity as a function of his self-interest or of class interests smugly satisfied with the essential state of affairs under the Republic.

However Cicero may differ from Plato, he seems also to follow him in the inquiry of political philosophy, in seeking a standard not only for political and legal reform but also for intelligent conservation of ancestral ways. There is considerable evidence, much of it in the *Re Publica* and *Legibus* written with Plato's comparable works in mind, that Cicero is acutely and sometimes painfully aware that the state of the Roman regime and its actions through the years of development do not simply represent the right and the best way.[3] He is not, however, insensitive—nor would one expect him to be as a political leader or author—to Roman attachment to their own political tradition and a Roman disposition in favor of the actual as opposed to abstract theorizing.[4] That Cicero stands in some way between Plato and the Roman ways is evident throughout the text of the *Re Publica*, as he works out his position on the question of the best regime. That position seems consistent with his genuinely philosophical attraction to Socrates and the Academic school, and with his explicit interest in the rhetorical mode of philosophy. In fact, his philosophical ground in the practical perspective seems to provide a way of allowing him to approach political wisdom by learning both from Plato and from the pragmatic tendencies of his Roman heritage.[5] The *Re Publica* should be seen not as a collapse of the philosophical into Roman patriotism but as representing Cicero's own practically informed but philosophical response to the question of the best political order.

The *Re Publica* is mostly in the dialogue form, and Cicero clearly employs its dramatic setting and *personae* to draw attention to the practical horizon in which he wants to approach the question of the best regime. The recognition of the high utility and responsibility of statesmanship is assumed in that horizon. The *personae* of the dialogue are leading statesmen from the second century, including Scipio Africanus Minor and Gaius Laelius, whom Cicero places in the dominant roles here and admires throughout his works.[6] Scipio and his circle, including Laelius, are seen by Cicero as not only marking the first opening of Roman leaders to Greek philosophy but also specifically welcoming philosophy in its Socratic form.[7] The dialogue takes place during a holiday from apparently pressing political responsibilities, but it will not turn out to be a holiday devoid of appropriate civic duty.

Before the dialogue actually commences, Cicero provides a preface to the first book, and in a sense to the entire *Re Publica*,[8] and, here, what is but suggested in the dramatic detail about this work's relationship to Cicero's practical perspective is stated very directly. This preface features a strong defense of statesmanship as the greatest necessity and highest calling among humankind, a defense already summarized in the previous chapter. Cicero explains this defense as an effort at "removing all hesitations of engaging in politics" (*dubitationem ad rem publicam adeundi*).[9] This effort is made so that the discussion of the political community (*de re publica disputatio*) which is to follow would not seem pointless or in vain (*frustra*). Philosophy is both defended and limited by Cicero's argument here that inquiry into politics, including the question of the best regime, is a useful and, thus, fitting activity for those responding to that necessary and high calling to statesmanship.[10] Cicero at once assures "those who might be moved by the authority of philosophers" that those philosophers, held in the greatest esteem by the most learned men (all evidence indicates he has in mind at least Plato and Aristotle), have examined politics and written about it and thereby performed a certain political function. Philosophers, in other words, are justified insofar as they contribute to the work of political leadership by illuminating the nature of politics.

As the dialogue begins and the arrival of its various participants is described, the assembling public leaders are seen struggling, some over what their topic should be for this leisurely, holiday conversation. By the time they settle, at the suggestion of Laelius, on asking Scipio to speak on the question of the best regime (*optimi status civitatis*),[11] it has been made clear that even their leisurely activities are to be responsible, that is, they must be related to their work as statesmen and that they must be, in a sense, useful. Trifling and amusing inquiries should take none of their time, and speculative inquiries, which might prove ultimately useful in some way in political or military leadership, are clearly to be subordinated to such directly relevant political inquiries as the question of the best regime. Thus, when Laelius comes to make his suggestion and the dialogue takes its specific initial focus, he is portrayed as saying what one might expect, given Cicero's own introduction, that this topic of the best regime calls forth, above all, conversation of the highest utility (*ad utilissimos rei publicae sermones potissimum*). The knowledge that is sought has the power to make those present better and happier.[12] This is, we recall, a type of inquiry into the right.

The Loving Quarrel with Plato

The first direct indication that Scipio's treatment of the best regime involves a quarrel with its inspiring source, namely Plato, occurs at the very beginning of his discourse in the first book. Claiming that this topic always gets his concentrated, careful attention and that its pursuit is clearly useful to the conduct of his political responsibilities, Scipio confesses that he is not satisfied with "the writings on this question left by the greatest and wisest men of Greece."[13] He at once, however, shows his great respect for those Greeks by indicating that he hesitates "to rank his views superior to theirs," and then concludes this segment of his discourse with the following observation:

So I ask you to hear me in the following light, as one not altogether unknowledgeable of Greek perspectives and not prepared, especially in this matter, to give precedence to their views over ours, but as one Roman citizen liberally educated through the care of his father and afire for learning from boyhood, yet having learned much more from experience (*usu*) and the lessons of the home than from books.[14]

Any doubt that the Greek writing, which Scipio has in mind, is, above all, Plato's *Republic* can be laid to rest as the second book begins and Scipio undertakes, claiming to follow Cato the Elder, his account of the Roman regime as the best of actual regimes:

The pursuit of the proposed topic will, however, be easier (*facilius*) if I will have set our polity (*rem publicam*) before you, first in its origins, then in growth and then in maturity and finally in its strong and robust state, than if I will have imagined (*mihi...finxero*) some polity as does Socrates in Plato's work.[15]

What could Scipio mean by "easier"? Is his, and apparently Cicero's, discontent with Plato, explained by the fact that Plato's city is simply too intangible, especially for Romans, to provide an effective response to the question what is the best regime? Perhaps this is part of the reason for not being satisfied with this writing of one of the "wisest" of the Greeks. It hardly seems to be the entire reason for the discontent with Plato's city in speech.

There are indications, in one of the more fragmented segments of the text, that certain specific practices and rules concerning sexual relations and common property in Plato's city disturbed Scipio and Cicero, just as some specific provisions had provoked Aristotle's dissent at an earlier time.[16] At this point in Scipio's discourse, as he appears to be favorably contrasting Roman ways of upbringing and training young men and potential leaders with those of the Greeks, Laelius is made to notice that Scipio chooses not to contend with "your dear Plato," not even mentioning him in a context in which it seems he too should be a target.[17] Again, the dialogue has drawn attention to the great respect with which Plato is being treated even while an apparently different and unPlatonic approach is taken in discussing the best regime. Thus, whatever be the full nature of the quarrel with Plato, it seems to be a loving quarrel. Scipio, perhaps like Cicero and his young interlocutor in the *Tusculans*, may be more inclined to go wrong with Plato than be right with his adversaries.[18] Playful though that remark of Cicero was, Plato's preeminence as a philosopher and a teacher of Cicero is in evidence throughout Cicero's writings.[19] Cumming aptly described him as "*homo platonicus.*"[20]

There is, however, more direct evidence of deference to Plato, and even of essential agreement with him, right in the *Re Publica* itself. Not only does Scipio, in the first book, directly and approvingly quote a lengthy passage from Plato's *Republic*, to describe how extreme democracy corrupts into tyranny, but also, and more importantly, he later confesses his essential agreement with Plato's political teaching in *The Republic*.[21] This latter passage (2.52) is important—indeed critical—because of its explicitness on Scipio's agreement with Plato and its revelation of Scipio's and no doubt Cicero's understanding of what Plato intended with his city in speech.[22] Scipio is found here observing that Plato sought and created a city "more to be wished for than to be hoped for," a city, as such, "not possible" but one "in which the very rationale [meaning] of political life can be perceived" (*in qua ratio rerum civilium perspici posset*).[23] Contrasting his effort here with Plato's, Scipio, then, immediately adds,

> I, however, if only I can find the right words, will so strive, with that very same understanding (*rationibus eisdem*) which he possessed, not in a semblance and imitation of a state (*in umbra et imagine*) but in a large and great polity (*amplissima re publica*), that I might appear to be pointing out, as if with a rod, the cause of every public good and evil.

Plato is thus taken, above all, to teach an understanding of the nature or rationale of political life (*rationem rerum civilium*), and it is this same understanding that accounts for the critical standards (*rationes easdem*) which Scipio and Cicero employ in *Re Publica*.

Shortly after this very important observation by Scipio, and in the course of his relating the rise of the Roman state, he observes, "[T]he very nature of political reality often overcomes reason" (*vincit ipsa rerum publicarum natura saepe rationem*).[24] It appears, then, that a paradox is reached, but by no means an intolerable or unreasonable one, for it seems that part of the very rationale or understanding of political life (*ratio rerum civilium*) is that political life *often* does not follow the way of reason (*ratio*). In this perspective, a rational understanding of politics encompasses that essential dimension of it which is not rational. It will be necessary to return to this perspective in the course of following Scipio's discourse on the best regime.

At this point, it is sufficient to notice that since Scipio and Cicero seem to regard this view of rationality's limits as an important truth about politics, and since they revere Plato and claim that he has taught the most important things about politics, Plato himself, in the absence of any disclaimer in the text, is likely a teacher of this truth. One way to teach it would be to sketch or imagine a perfectly rational city—the city in speech—and then to let appear the incredible gap between such a city and the way human beings are and conduct themselves. This leads to seeing Plato's city as not intended by him to be a practicable model for humans as they are known but rather as a city "more to be wished for than hoped for." This aspect of Cicero's text supports, then, an understanding of Plato's intent in *The Republic* that can be defended, as it was above, from the text of *De Re Publica* 2.52 itself. In this light, it is not surprising to find Scipio and Cicero disinclined to challenge or quarrel with Plato over specific institutions and practices of his city in speech. These specifics either are not very important set against the debt to Plato for his illuminating political fundamentals (*rationes*) or, and more likely in the light of what has preceded, are not intended by Plato as a practicable model to be followed or imitated.

If Plato is so understood by Scipio and Cicero, the problematic posed by the quarrel with him seems to intensify. Why should they be dissatisfied (*Rep.* 1.33) with Plato's approach to the best regime if it is meant to teach, among other principles, the very limits of rationality in politics, a perspective that they share with Plato, if they have not learned it and other of the most important political truths from him? In what way, then, could Scipio's treatment of the best regime be "easier" (*Rep.* 2.3) than Plato's? In what way would it be more effective, as implied (*Rep.* 2.52), for pointing out "the cause of every public good and evil"? Would it really be easier to accomplish what Plato had done with a concrete historical example of a regime? Again, is it simply the Roman preference for the concrete and tangible that is at issue here? Before a direct effort is made to answer these questions, by following Scipio's treatment of the best regime, two other relevant aspects of Cicero's writings need to be noted: Cicero's own sensitivity to the Roman hostility to philosophy and his awareness of the use of the perfect model or type as a way to advance understanding.

Cicero's respect for Plato and his specific debt to *The Republic* make it wholly inappropriate to see him as one who, according to Voegelin, "with a sneer dismissed the best polities of the Hellenic philosophers as fancies of no importance by the side of the best polity that was created on the battlefields by the *imperatores* of Rome."[25] There is, however, evidence that such opinions or similar ones about Greek philosophy were around, if not prevalent, among those Romans who knew anything at all of philosophy and Plato. Cicero is never forgetful of the Roman antipathy to philosophy, which went so far as a formal prohibition of philosophers in the previous century, little more than a generation before his Scipio and Laelius are portrayed as seeking to open doors and minds to Lady Philosophy. Given this resistance to philosophy, Plato's "fictitious" city in speech, probably, would have played into the hands of those who were inclined to deride philosophy as silly, irrelevant, and even, at times, dangerous. In his *De Oratore*, written in close conjunction with the *Re Publica*, Cicero portrayed Antonius as warning against the influence of philosophical books on the work of the active orator.[26] If such active leaders strictly confine philosophy to a restful holiday, they are, contends Antonius, less apt to find themselves drawing on Plato when their work brings them to speak "on justice and loyalty" (*de justitia et fide*).[27] What's wrong with Plato is that when he wrote on these themes, he "created on his pages a certain novel state (*novam quamdam finxit in libris civitatem*), insofar as what he thought to be the requisites of justice (*usque eo illa, quae dicenda de justitia putabat*) was incompatible with everyday life and the customs of states." Antonius, then, goes on to suggest that if peoples and states actually implemented Plato's ideas, there would be no free assemblies where oratory might flourish. Clearly, in this perspective Plato is held responsible for "far out" ideas and the specifics of his city in speech are taken as proposals meant for implementation. To some, perhaps most Romans—as in fact to so many thereafter in Western history—Plato's city seems to function nearly as a shorthand or symbol for the irrelevance and, the sometimes seductive and thus dangerous, irrelevance of the philosophic mind.[28]

Scipio and Cicero, as we have seen, also turn away from Plato's approach to the best regime, but they do so with a different understanding of his intent from what Antonius reveals and with much appreciation for what Plato has taught. Why they do this may become even more puzzling when another passage in the *De Oratore*, and through it another theme in Cicero's writings, is considered. Cicero utilizes a model or complete (*perfectus*) orator while appearing to eschew this approach with regard to the polity or regime. Crassus, the character in *De Oratore* who seems most clearly to represent the voice of Cicero, and whose major discourses dominate the dialogue, defends the great demands he is making on the orator that he sketches there by saying that it is proper to delineate the greatest orator (*summus orator*), for whenever one seeks to understand something, one looks to the "pure and perfect" (*absolutam et perfectam*) model.[29] Only, he adds, if one sets before oneself the perfect model will one be able to understand "the essence and nature of a thing" (*vim et naturam rei*).

In a later rhetorical writing, simply titled *Orator*, Cicero returns to the theme of the perfect orator (*summus orator*), and speaking directly in his own name and explicitly calling to mind Plato and his "ideas," he claims that by creating (*fingendo*) this orator, who likely never was and never is to be in the ordinary sense of becoming, he makes with his mind (*cogitatione et mente*) the perfect type (*perfectum genus*).[30] In a reference directly suggesting the opening of the sixth book of Plato's *Republic*, where Socrates relates how guardian-rulers, like painters who look to a model in mind of the best and truest, make practical decisions in the light of that true model of justice, Cicero compares the idea of the perfect orator to those ideas which Phidias, a great sculptor, and painters hold in mind when they create their imperfect approximations.

So Cicero, dissatisfied with Plato's approach to the best regime, seems to turn to that very approach, of constructing the perfect model, the model in speech, in considering the orator. This orator is the public leader or statesman.[31] In following Scipio's treatment of the best regime in search of understanding his discontent with Plato's approach, we will find ourselves be encountering this perfect orator/statesman within the very *Re Publica*. Though obscured by the fragmented condition of this work, a "shift of focus" from a Platonic best regime to a Platonic best orator can be seen to occur within this dialogue.[32]

Though Laelius initially called on Scipio to discourse on the best polity as one who is known to look to Rome's ancestral regime for his answer, Scipio does not appear to turn directly to Rome.[33] Rather, he proceeds systematically, as if he were a Greek, writing a treatise: He begins by defining a polity in the well-known segment on the meaning of *res publica*, reflects on the origins of political community in terms of the inclinations and needs of human nature, and turns, with an argument that suggests Aristotle's thought and clarity, to say that where there is to be community, there must be governance in the form of a deliberative or legislative power. As that power is placed in the hands of one or a few or all of the citizens, the essential simple regimes are generated, and each of these can be decent and good if the ruling element is just. Despite this possibility, there is a regime better than all of these—the best regime—that Scipio points to and that will turn out to be a judicious mixture of the three simple forms.

As Scipio proceeds to show the characteristic strength and weakness of each of the simple regimes, and thus indicates why no one of them can be the best, he reveals more about his discontent with Plato's city in speech. Elsewhere in his writings Cicero has acknowledged that it is from Plato and philosophy that he has learned that certain changes or revolutions in polities are to be expected in the ordinary course of things (*naturales esse quasdam conversiones rerum publicarum*).[34] Here in the *Re Publica* Scipio illustrates this truth, showing that the simple regimes, even if good and just, experience corruption, change, and revolution because of their respective defects and because there is at hand no "great citizen and nearly divine man" (*magnus quidam civis et divinus paene vir*) whose knowledge, foresight, and power would allow him to regulate and to keep such changes in his control.[35] Immediately after this observation, Scipio states that he "therefore" turns to the mixed regime as the best regime. Kingship and aristocracy are among the simple regimes, and what Scipio has apparently concluded is that philosopher-kings (that is, either such distinct excellence or politically empowered excellence) are not available to human communities as commonly experienced. There is, in other words, no political version of that wholly virtuous Stoic Wiseman available to humankind.[36] Thus, there can be no saving of the simple regimes through divine-like leaders, and precisely at this point in the discussion of various regimes, Scipio, in fact, turns away from the Platonic city in speech as the best regime, for he rules out the actuality of the superlatively virtuous individual who is also empowered. In turning to the mixed regime, Scipio turns to a possible model, a practicable model. One might reasonably say that Plato's intention, and so understood by Scipio and Cicero, with the city in speech is to turn the reader in search of just such a practicable model. This is the direction, we recall, that Aristotle takes and defends as legitimate for political science in his *Politics*. One might also say that here is a point where reason encompasses the lack of reason in political life by its compensation for that lack.[37]

Scipio has, then, spoken to the question of the best regime, but it should be no surprise, given the emphasis on the life of the statesman and on judging all activities in relationship to that life found in Cicero's preface and the early part of the dialogue, that his best regime is a realizable or practical one.[38] Scipio's quarrel with Plato's city in speech has primarily to do with the utility of that approach. In a dialogue where the emphasis, from the beginning, is on justifying all things in terms of their relationship to the active life of political leadership, it is the practicable best regime that merits attention.

Furthermore, to notice how Scipio has, here, spoken to the question of the best regime allows the correction of a common misunderstanding of the *De Re Publica*, namely that Cicero, through Scipio, simply offers Rome as his response to the question of the best regime. That best of achievable regimes, the mixed regime, which Scipio explains in Book I, is, we must emphasize, a properly philosophical response, and hence, in "universal terms."[39] One cannot, however, read on in the *Re Publica* through the second book without a sense of assurance that the experience of Rome, above all, has been instructive in Scipio's discovery of the mixed regime as the best.[40] Nor should it surprise us, in light of Cicero's skepticism and his way of finding duty and assessing philosophical positions, that experience would loom large in the determination of the politically right. As we know ourselves more fully only in practice, so too we know our political selves, our proper communal life. Thus Rome, specifically in her manifest political virtues, is reflected in the best regime even before the dialogue's turn in the second book to exemplify this best regime in Rome and its development. And it should also be noted that the mixed regime's being able to be so substantially instantiated in Rome makes more persuasive its alleged practicability.[41] Rome, however, is never presented as simply the best regime or as the best practicable regime; rather, it is utilized as the best exemplification among actual political communities of the best practicable regime.[42] Cicero has replaced Plato's fictive and unreal depiction of the best regime with a specific historical example of the best practicable regime. Insofar as Rome is, for Cicero, only the best exemplification of the best practicable regime, and Roman development to the mixed regime is as troubled as any human history, Rome too has its defects, and it is wholly consistent with Cicero's overall intent that these would be passed over or noted, but not stressed, in the course of his use of the Roman experience. The utility of what Cicero has done in this step goes well beyond some kind of nod to a Roman preference for the tangible and concrete, for Scipio's Roman exemplification of the best allows him to direct the attention of his fellow statesmen (and Cicero the attention of his readers) at the constitutional form and tradition in which they do their work and at the same time to try to protect, insofar as Rome is but an exemplification, the realm of prudence, thus avoiding the kind of controversies that arose from the very beginning around the specific institutions and customs of Plato's city in speech. That Cicero was not wholly, or even very, successful at avoiding such controversies is evident in the frequency that his use of Rome in the *Re Publica* is taken as a comprehensive idolization of Roman customs and institutions, that he is, in other words, taken as more the patriot than the philosopher.[43]

The interpretation above of Cicero and Scipio's decisive turn from Plato's city in speech (*Rep.* 1.45) because of the absence, in the good simple regimes, of an unassailable virtue of a "great citizen and nearly divine man," is supported by Scipio's later contrast of the first Roman tyrant, Tarquinius, with the model statesman (*rectori et gubernatori civitatis*).[44] Explicitly conscious, at this point, of how the Roman experience of tyranny's origin from monarchy differs from Plato's description of its genesis, Scipio chooses to set in contrast to the tyrant not the philosopher-king, as is done so predominantly throughout Plato's *Republic*, but a type of man whom he characterizes as "good and wise and experienced in matters of public utility and honor." This man is rightly said to be "a guardian and steward of the polity" (*tutor et procurator rei publicae*), as long as he functions as a "leader and pilot of the state" (*rector et gubernator civitatis*). This is the first instance in the *Re Publica* where there is a direct mention and a somewhat extensive discussion of that man whom we will be calling Cicero's model statesman. He is introduced here in direct contrast to the tyrant, as if to say that we are not to set over against tyranny, the worst of regimes, the rule of the one or few best or virtuous but rather the practicable ideal, which is the rule by and for the people conducted by statesmen. Since those kind of superior individuals, who can save the simple regimes from degradation, are not to be found, Scipio and Cicero are apparently interested in another more realizable kind of superiority (consider the examples of Roman history), which can work toward and, in fact, is critical to the success of the mixed regime.[45] The model statesman is that level of human achievement, critical to the effectual striving for and maintaining of the mixed regime.

In this same passage (*Rep.* 2.51), Scipio draws emphatic attention to this *rector* whom, he enjoins his listeners, one must seek to recognize and "who is able to protect the state by his counsel and deeds." This type of man, he adds, must be given much more attention in the remainder of his discourse, and there are indications that this does, indeed, happen, though substantial portions on this model statesman seem to be among the lost parts of the original dialogue.[46]

This best of actual regimes, Rome, is, then, the mediator in the movement of the *Re Publica* from a consideration of the best regime in principle to a consideration of the model statesman. The development of this practicable model of Rome exposes the dependence of the model on time and experience. Scipio and Cicero reveal that their primary interest is with the change in regime dynamics that constitute the substratum of time and political experience. Their concern with the fundamental political change is not limited to the largely progressive development illustrated by Rome and considered in some detail in Book 2.[47] What comes to light before that, and turns out to dominate the *Re Publica*, is a concern with degeneration and its patterns, and, in turn, a concern with stabilization and the balancing and mixing of regimes in the name of that stabilization. The potential change, whatever its form may be, that time allows and that experience illustrates draws attention to the frequent agent of such change, the possible moderator of it, the hoped for controller of it, namely, the leader or statesman (*rector* or *moderator*). The primary quality of this statesman, as of the orator considered above, is said to be prudence. And it is, as we recall, the very mind of the prudent person (*mens ratioque prudentis*) to which Cicero looks for an articulation of nature's way—of the duties binding on humankind. It is to the statesman and his civil prudence—political science as a practical science—that the *Re Publica* directs the reader.[48]

Cicero has taken up the central question of classical political philosophy, that of the best regime, and answered it in a way that makes the detailed provisions of a best regime less important and more simply speculative than the necessary qualities of statesmanship. His quarrel with Plato, if it be much of a quarrel, has to do with the utility of a detailed depiction of the city in speech. Much might be said to the effect that Cicero's turn to the practicable best regime and to its central figure, the statesman, is invited and, in fact, begun by both Plato and Aristotle.[49] Even the necessary and moral disciplining of the philosophical eros by political duty is not unknown to Plato and Aristotle. Overall, however, Cicero appears to be more decisive in asserting the primacy of statesmanship among the responsibilities of this human life, and this tendency makes him all the more inclined to focus on the nature and requisites of statesmanship.

The Imagery of Contract and the Importance of Consent

However much Cicero wishes to shift the focus of political philosophy and political amelioration from the best regime to the model statesman, that is, to the necessary qualities of statesmanship, the essential features of his best regime merit attention. These features must at least allow, and very likely encourage, the emphasis on statesmanship in Cicero's political thought. They provide, in other words, the context for his teaching on statesmanship. Up to this point, they have been approached in a broad and sketchy manner at best and chiefly as some model, called the practicable best regime or the mixed regime, drawn forth in reaction to Plato's city in speech. They have been seen as exemplified in the Roman Republic in its best moments, indicating a powerful and understandable role for the Roman experience in Cicero's determination of the best regime with its central role for statesmanship. In this study of Cicero as a philosopher, a fuller understanding of these features, which constitute his political principles, allows a closer look on how they relate to his philosophical foundations and approach to moral philosophy, considered in previous chapters.

Closer inquiry into Cicero's political principles takes on added significance when one recalls a tradition of commentary that portrays Cicero as the first "modern" political thinker, one whose writings mark a clear break from the prior Greek classical tradition. Over a hundred years ago, in their influential volumes on medieval political theory, the Carlyles argued that "the dividing-line between the ancient and the modern political theory" occurs in the period between Aristotle and Cicero and is signaled by the "change...startling in its completeness" between Aristotle's "view of the natural inequality of human nature" and Cicero's opposing view. In Cicero's and the later Roman thought they see "the beginnings of a theory of human nature and society of which the 'Liberty, Equality, and Fraternity' of the French Revolution is only the present-day expression."[50] Even the more moderate and plausible views of Cumming and Wood tend to provoke interest in the specific character of Cicero's political thought. The former finds Cicero shaping the classical tradition into "the guise in which it will exercise the most influence on the development of modern liberal political thought."[51] Neal Wood writes of Cicero's work as representing a "transition to modern political thought."[52] Has Cicero been incorrectly understood by such interpreters? On the surface there is evidence of a modern cast to Cicero's political thought, for concepts like "consent," "equality," and "progress" appear prominently. On the other hand, there is Cicero's own deep sense of continuity with the classical tradition: his fundamental Socratic allegiance, his deference to Plato with respect to his essential understanding of political life, and his explicit standing in the tradition of political inquiry marked by Plato and Aristotle. Cicero's political thought might, then, hold considerable potential for mediating between the political theory of classical Greece and the apparently more democratic ways of the present. Where does Cicero stand? Is such mediation possible? Or is this a case of confusion in Cicero's thinking?

There are three passages in Cicero's voluminous writings that especially might suggest that he is a social contract thinker in the prevalent modern sense. One or more of these passages are usually cited or are clearly in mind when a modern turn is found in Cicero. What follows immediately is an explication and commentary of the first of these passages, *De Re Publica* 1.39, the *classicus locus* for discussions of popular consent in Cicero. This exploration will naturally lead to examining Cicero's comments, especially those at *De Inventione* 1.2–3, on a bestial and solitary primitive state of humankind that seemingly preceded their coming into political community in any form. Finally, the discussion will turn to Cicero's most direct affirmation of equality among humans, given in his own voice, in *De Legibus* 1.29–30.

De Re Publica 1.39 directly evokes social contract imagery while serving as the foundation for the dialogue that constitutes Cicero's major work of political theory. The imagery and the notion of consent appear in the normative definition of a polity or political community, *res publica*, given by Cicero's apparent spokesman, Scipio, early in the dialogue.[53]

The definition is offered as a foundation for the discussion to follow on the proposed topic of the best regime (*optimi status civitatis*).[54] *Res publica* is said to be a property or thing of the people, *res populi*. This people is not, however, any and every assemblage of humans but specifically "a conjoining of a large number united by agreement in right and by common advantage" (*sed coetus multitudinis juris consensu et utilitatis communione sociatus*). A political community, then, is a people joined by agreement in right and by mutual advantage.

The first cause of this bonding, adds Scipio, is not so much human weakness as a certain natural gregariousness of humankind (*non tam inbecillitas quam naturalis quaedam hominum quasi congregatio*). In what immediately follows, there are indications that Scipio insisted on the naturalness and importance of human sociality through a thought experiment, a hypothesis on whether a person, with all material needs provided for, could ever be satisfied alone. Though the text of *De Re Publica* breaks off at this point due to a lost portion, the same thought experiment is performed by Cicero in his own voice at the end of Book I of *De Officiis*.[55] Cicero finds that a wise person (*sapiens*), one marked by an excellent mind (*optimo ingenio*), could not be so satisfied but rather is drawn to other human beings in mutual interaction in deed and thought. There are other indications in *Officiis* that such social rather than solitary activity is what nature calls the human being to. We are not born for ourselves, says Cicero, but for activities that ever have the potential to solidify human community: activities of giving and receiving, one form of which is speaking and listening.[56]

Late in the *Re Publica*, there is what one might call a filtered echo of the initial definition of *res publica*. In the legendary Dream of Scipio, Scipio reports the words of his great namesake and grandfather telling how the great god of the universe smiles upon assemblages and conjoinings of the people united in right, which are called polities (*concilia coetusque hominum jure sociati, quae civitates appellantur*).[57] At this climactic moment in the work, Cicero is apparently content to allow political communities (not Rome alone, for Scipio is here taking a universal perspective) be described simply as assemblages united in right.[58] The reduction or filtering of the formal definition given earlier directs our attention to what is left out in this later version, namely *consensu*, or the reference to agreement, and *utilitate communione*, the reference to common advantage. Have these been lost along the way because they are unessential? Or is Cicero being philosophically careless—an explanation once all too readily embraced when such apparent inconsistencies are found in Cicero? Or is the later formulation a more succinct one that, when we more fully understand the thought of Cicero through other passages in *Re Publica* and elsewhere in his writings, can be seen to incorporate what is not explicitly mentioned in this instance?

The last alternative seems compelling. Pursuing this matter opens to view the normative dimension of the initial definition and certain essential principles of Cicero's political philosophy. Since attention has already been given to Cicero's consideration of utility, it is easier to begin with the apparent disappearance of a "common advantage" (*utilitate communione*). Arguing, as we have seen, that right and advantage cannot, when properly understood, be distinguished, Cicero incorporates ordinary considerations of utility into the very notion of the right. Thus, to be united in right (*sociati jure*) would necessarily be to be joined in common interest or advantage. Advantage or *utilitas* enters into the very formulation of what is right, and, thus, it may be helpful at times, as in a first definition or in reflecting on the initial formation of political communities for reasons of security and protection, to make explicit mention that concrete common needs or utilities are part of the very *raison d'être* of political community.[59] It is also appropriate to note that this reconciliation of right and advantage entails expanding the concepts of needs and utility to cover the satisfaction of highest inclinations of human nature.

What, however, could be the explanation for the reduction of Cicero's initial definition to eliminate the word, *consensu*? Here one finds that just as other passages and texts of Cicero establish without question that right, properly understood, is inclusive of utility or advantage, so too can right (*jus*) as a basis of public unity be found to imply consent. *Consensus* then is the only way people can be joined in right (*sociati jure*); thus, there is no other way of being a political community. A statement in the third book of *De Re Publica*, apparently made by the dialogue's other major figure, Laelius, brings into sharp focus the essential voluntariness of life under right (*jus*).[60] Laelius, here, recounts how Tiberius Gracchus at one point, in contrast with his treatment of Roman citizens, failed to respect the agreed rights (*jura neglexit ac foedera*) of the allies and Latin nations and thus transformed Roman rule from one of right to one of force (*ad vim a jure traduxerit*), so that those who previously accepted this rule by choice (*voluntate*) were now to be held in line by fear (*terrore*).[61] Earlier in the second book, Scipio, having described the tyrant Tarquinius Superbus as from the beginning of his reign fearful and wanting (*volebat*) to be feared, concludes the segment by wondering if such a man can rightly be called human who does not seek (*velit*) a community of right (*juris communionem*) with fellow citizens.[62] Again, the underlying position seems to be that the fundamental political alternatives are force (*vis*) or right (*jus*) and, thus, that consent is implicit in *jus* or, in some sense, coincident with it.[63] This interpretation derives additional support from another observation in the section on Tarquinius, namely that his assassin, Lucius Brutus, acted for the protection of the liberty of the citizenry (*in conservanda civium libertate*).[64] So it seems that Cicero's view of what was at stake in tyranny was much more than individual acts of injustice, however outrageous, committed by Tarquinius: What was at stake was the essential and historic freedom of the Romans to act politically from choice rather than fear.[65]

Cicero makes frequent references to consent of the people to their government. The topic seems to be more than an incidental part of his political philosophy. While treating the line of kings from the first, Romulus, to the tragedy of the institution in Tarquinius, Cicero draws attention to the role of popular approval, and then, with the kingship of Numa Pompilius, to the custom of the king-elect seeking, as it were a second vote, to confirm that he is the choice of the people.[66] Roman monarchy being an elective one, the selection of each new occupant of the throne is much more an act of regime-choice—of fundamental popular sovereignty—than would be the selection of office-holders under a democratic or partially democratic constitution. Constitutional changes in the direction of oligarchy and aristocracy are also regularly related to popular choice and seen as dependent on it.[67]

Cicero's descriptions of the origins of political community support the importance of consent in a rightful founding. The initial coming together of people into a political community is always presented by him, either directly or implicitly, as a process of choice by humans as they constitute themselves as a people, a movement under law or right and away from the force of violence (*ad jus...sine vi*).[68] It is a process in which the only force applicable is the force (*vis*) of speech and reason, operative as humankind are persuaded, by those naturally gifted for such leadership, that their happiness is to be found in and through a political community.[69] These discussions of origins can be understood only as a description of an idealized process, which is as a representation of what normatively constitutes a true political community. Cicero knows, of course, that there are aggregations of human beings drawn together in other ways, and he knows those instances where people, though living in proximity, have lost the *res publica* that might once have characterized their being as a people.[70]

To argue, as just done above, that Cicero's treatment of origins can be understood as a representation—a poetic or mythic portrayal—of the essential elements in a genuine political community, namely consent in the right and the common utility, is not necessarily to surrender any claim to historical truth in Cicero's and other ancient descriptions of a primitive and even savage state of solitary individuals.[71] Cicero seems to have felt no inhibitions at embracing, in one or another form, speculation about a presocial and prepolitical state for humankind. Some, however, would argue that Cicero ought to have these inhibitions for the sake of consistency.[72] Cicero, after all, repeatedly affirms, as seen in Scipio's denial of man's self-sufficiency above, the inherent sociality of the human being.[73] Since the inquiry here has concluded that Cicero gives a critical role to consent in the forming and sustaining of political communities, it would seem close to affirming Cicero as a modern social contract thinker if the pre-consent state of man is one of individuality and essential equality in that fearful isolation. Cicero, however, may not see the primitive state as the fully human state for which all persons have potential, and that indeed seems to be the case.

Let us look to the key passage in *Inventione,* but let us approach it by some consideration of observations by Cicero in his preface to the third book of *De Re Publica.* Cicero is, here, discussing the human mental capacity to develop all the arts, from that of language to that of governance. He appears to be putting in narrative form the result of an analysis respecting human capacities and human differences. He writes of a bonding of previously solitary (*dissociatos*—estranged to one another) human beings by the pleasing force of speech.[74] Cicero appears, then, either to push beneath even the ties of family and kinship, which he had Scipio note as societal *elementa* earlier in the work, or to be assuming that the estrangement from which humankind is to be delivered by speech (and the reason that developed speech) is between families and kinship groups rather than between individual humans.[75] St. Augustine, looking at the same text of Cicero, with the apparent advantage over us of having it in an unfragmented form, and employing an often conventional view of a stepmother, sees Cicero holding that original nature is "less like a mother than a stepmother." In body, these first humans are "naked, frail, and weak. In soul, they are troubled, beset with fears, incapable of enduring toil, and inclined toward lust. In the very same soul, however, there lies hidden a divine spark of intelligence and reason."[76]

The overall picture that Augustine gives fits with what Cicero says unambiguously in the *Inventione* passage about the origins of political community. Here, Cicero writes of some ancestral wise and great man who is aware of human potential, especially that of the human mind. This leader, using reason and eloquence, brings together humankind initially bestial in behavior and dispersed (*dispersos*) in fields and hovering in forest huts. The new way of life to which humankind is led is a city life, wherein some persuade others of what they had themselves discovered through reason (*ratione*). What they had discovered was the importance of keeping trust (*colere fidem*), of maintaining justice (*retinere justitiam*), of voluntarily obeying others, and of expending efforts for the common welfare even to the point of giving one's own life. Humans are, thus, brought to see that their true interest and deepest satisfaction is found in principled cooperation with one another. It seems that humans can be drawn to a notion of the common good. What appears especially remarkable to Cicero, within this remarkable passage, is that speech was able to be both sufficiently substantial (*gravis*) and attractive (*suavis*) to bring a person with dominant physical power to the rule of right or justice without compulsion (*ad jus.....sine vi*), to lead such a person to surrender voluntarily that most pleasant customary dominance which had through age-old practice acquired the force of nature (*naturae vim*).[77] What is remarkable to the reader of Cicero in the context of this inquiry is that here Cicero makes absolutely clear that the primal state that he is describing is one of dispersal and self-centered existence, for humans in this pre-social state know not ratified marriages, their own children, or the value of fair laws. In sum, humans in this condition did nothing with reason (*ratione animi*).

Solitary and bestial beginnings for humankind do not, then, for Cicero, serve as the norm of nature. Nor does human insecurity or other material needs, in that initial condition, suffice to explain the coming together of humans in various communities. Nonetheless, immediate needs, like that of physical security, appear to be decisively operative as the reason and the felt need for forming and sustaining first communities. Cicero understands origins in essential agreement with Aristotle's teaching in the *Politics* that the "polis" begins for the sake of life but continues for the sake of the good life and that those men who first lead humankind into communities and toward justice are to be particularly praised.[78]

Cicero considers the role of leadership in the development of human communities of the utmost importance. From the very first elemental communities to a political community like the Roman state, reason and speech are critical to encouraging and directing human social inclinations, and these instruments of being human are differentially possessed by human beings.[79] This may account for it appearing that the very sociality or gregariousness of humans is differentially possessed. At the most primitive time, for example, certain individuals are seen as inclined to draw solitary humans together. At least some persons are envisioned as exercising leadership for reasons other than personal dominance or immediate personal gain. Some humans, apparently, realize earlier or more clearly than others human nature's full needs, and hence, full potential. No doubt such leaders are brought to higher levels of competence by the communities in which they participate, and, thus, some do indeed stand on the shoulders of others.[80] These leaders appear the mediators in a process in which reason and speech can reveal ever more of the fullness of nature's intent in human sociality, and human communities in turn allow and facilitate the development of reason and speech. Perhaps, one could say that inequality plays a role in the service of equality. It is this idea of equality in Cicero to which we now turn.

The Assertion and Implication of Equality

Popular consent is a requisite of a wholly just political community, of a true *res publica*: this important strain in Cicero's fundamental political thinking seems defensible only if human liberty and equality are taken as important principles or norms. There is ample evidence in his writings that Cicero does just that. The pivotal role of consent in his thought turns out to be an indicator that there is a basis deeper than often believed for his specific attachment to the traditional liberties of Roman citizens, as they were recurrently threatened by the widespread corruption of the late Republic and by the likes of Catiline and Caesar. Cicero's attraction to a Socratic doubt and mode of inquiry and his related association with the Academic school of philosophy reveal him holding up the importance of freedom of the individual judgment, at the least for the philosophically inclined. This importance is enhanced when his skeptical scrutiny is turned on dogmatic comprehensive explanations of the whole that so readily lend themselves to support the exercise of political authority on grounds other than consent. Furthermore, voluntariness is an essential characteristic of virtue for Cicero,[81] and he has argued that nature supports the desire for individual autonomy (*appetitio quaedam principatus*) that yields only to that person acting rightly and justly for genuine utility.[82] For Cicero, to be fully human is to be free, and to be free is to be a consenting partner in the political community.

It is, of course, not liberty alone but equality in liberty that supports and ultimately renders coherent the idea of popular consent as a requisite of fully just government. The ground of Cicero's commitment to equality indicates that it is more than a functional requisite of stability and effective procedures for consent. "There is nothing," writes Cicero, "so like another thing, so equal to it, as all of us humans are to one another."[83]

The very definition of the human person (*hominis definitio*), as Cicero continues, expresses the essential sameness of all who bear the name *homo*. All humans have received reason and therefore have access to right (*jus*), to what has been called the way of nature.[84] All, then, are capable of participating in an agreement based on *jus*. Essential human equality would be much more manifest, believes Cicero, were it not for the corruption of human potential through defective customs and opinions.[85] In this way, Cicero apparently explains the fact of significant inequalities among humans. Cicero always regards such inequalities as politically relevant, and this consideration and its merits need to be factored into any closer examination of whether Cicero's political practice is a responsible expression of his affirmation of equal liberty as the rule of nature. What is clear and beyond dispute is that in his finding liberty and equality as right according to nature, Cicero has in place a moral rationale or justification for his theory of consent, and accordingly there is no need to view the theory as a "mere" concession either to political necessity or traditional Roman beliefs about the *populus*. If, as has been argued earlier, a rightful binding of a people—a binding in *jus*—implies consent or agreement, then Cicero is clearly seeing the requisite of consent as part of that same universal moral bond in *jus* which all humans are capable of knowing and to which they are subject. While there seems to be in this understanding more than a "rhetorical genuflexion" to tradition or a concept without democratic implications, it is no exact and explicit mechanism for gaining consent nor a tangible instantiation of such a compact as the Mayflower Compact. Very likely, this lacuna is what the Carlyles and others have in mind when they do not find more than a germ of a theory of contract or compact in Cicero.[86]

Perhaps Cicero's failure to provide an exact and explicit mechanism for consent is neither his inadvertence nor any blindness or hostility to the implications of the fundamental norm of equal liberty. A couple of interrelated reasons merit consideration as an explanation of the absence in Cicero of a formulaic or mechanical expression of the authority or political sovereignty of the people. First, Cicero, whose life was schooled in political experience and whose eye was always turned to practice, might have thought such a formula often dangerous in its practical results to decent political achievements, including an environment of consent-gaining, which would always and everywhere take place under differing specific circumstances. He likely thought that, however much equality makes a moral claim, consent, in actuality, cannot be effectively turned into a simple tallying up of the superior number of equal units, and that consent, however garnered, is not the equivalent of right or in itself a good political achievement. This latter consideration leads to the second or what might properly be called the underlying reason for Cicero's apparent eschewing of a formula for popular consent, namely, that even a theoretic formula or mechanism would be very difficult for Cicero to craft precisely, because both in terms of the result of consent—the *jus* agreed upon—and the process of reaching that result, Cicero wants to provide for and to integrate the claims of both human equality and inequality. From the perspective of a simple and unqualified egalitarianism, a merely theoretic formula or mechanism for determining consent, and presumably the politically right, is a simple matter of addition.

One way to bring forward the side of Cicero's thought to which we have now been led, and to understand better his theoretical accommodation of the fact of inequality, is to recall the earlier argument that *jus* for him implies consent and to ask if the terms can be turned around and if one can say that consent implies the right (*jus*). Cicero's answer is primarily, but not entirely, in the negative. Consent is not, for him, simply the equivalent of the right. This position, evident throughout Cicero's writings, is present in some very revealing passages in *Re Publica* itself, where, as we recall, the dialogue begins with the formal definition of *res publica*. In the third book of *Re Publica*, Cicero presents Philus, in the Academic skeptical tradition of Carneades, making the argument that justice or right is simply conventional, namely the will of the most powerful or the result of agreement or consent between the people and the powerful.[87] Through presenting this position, Cicero acknowledges the claim that political communities, in their full range of types and with their various "justices," often seek to gain and generally seem to rest on consent or agreement (*pactio* is his term for the most explicit instance), but it is a consent achieved by deception or attained through fear and the calculation of the need for power to overcome fear. The kinship of at least some of these agreements to violence and compulsion is evident. They are agreements that have the form of consent, though they are clearly presented by Cicero as agreements in injustice which take to themselves the name of justice. They do not, then, exemplify the *consensus jure*, which defined the political community in the original definition of Scipio, for this *jus* is that which is grounded in nature and not in the will of the most powerful—whether it be of the one, few, or many or be generated by agreement among such elements.

That the *jus* which defines the *res publica* cannot simply be posited but must be found in nature is more directly stated by Cicero later in the third book, and near the very middle of the *Re Publica*, where Cicero has Scipio explicitly return to his initial definition and highlight the normative dimension of the definition.[88] His observations at this point make clear, however, not only that it is natural justice which must inform the *jus* that defines a people but also the necessity of actual consent. The norm for being a genuine *res publica* is, therefore, twofold. The passage in question, fragmented at the beginning, resumes with Scipio describing a cruel tyranny, where all are oppressed by one. This seems the extreme and clear case with which to make his point. He asks rhetorically whether such a political arrangement could possibly be a *res publica*, for it is marked by no singular bond of right nor agreement on unity (*neque esset unum vinculum juris nec consensus ac societas coetus*). Scipio then adds that though in the first two books they have spoken of tyranny as a diseased or defective (*vitiosam*) political community, reason now compels that it be seen as no *res publica* at all (*dicendum est plane nullam esse rem publicam*).[89] Laelius heartily agrees with Scipio and says that now he really understands the point of his entire presentation on the political community. Scipio then takes the lead, in an exchange with Laelius, and first applies what he has said of tyranny to the factious rule of a few, asking whether one could possibly call such an arrangement a *res publica* and using a couple of examples including that which he calls the most unjust (*injustissime*) rule of the Thirty in Athens after the Peloponnesian War. In the cases of both tyranny and faction, the evidence of lack of consent is clear and the emphasis of the presentation seems to be on that deficiency, but oppression and injustice are also mentioned respectively in the treatment of these two defective political arrangements. Their deficiency, then, lies not only in lack of consent but also in the false right or law with which they rule.

In turning to democracy, Scipio confesses that he is turning to the hard case for his claim that a bad or deficient political community is really no *res populi, res publica*—no political community at all. After all, what could belong more to the people, what could be more their property than an arrangement where all things are at their disposal? There, Scipio reports, the many (*multitudo*) punish, compel, seize, hold, and waste whatever they so will. Laelius then steps in and, with the apparent concurrence of Scipio, says that to let such a mob assume the name of a people is wrong, for a people, and Laelius here recalls Scipio's original definition, is to be characterized by agreement in right (*consensu juris*). Where the many rule, the deficiency cannot primarily be lack of consent for the many do what they will. Nor could Cicero mean here to introduce unanimity as effective consent and thus must imply the majority principle as the ordinary means of consent. The deficiency must, then, be found in the will of the many being not at all, or only on a hit-and-miss basis, an expression of the right (*jus*) as rooted in nature.[90]

THE NATURE OF GENUINE PROGRESS

Other parts of *Re Publica* and other writings of Cicero make clear his pointing to the leader, the statesman, and through the education of the statesman to the work of philosophy, as the means of keeping a popularly embraced *jus* based, and progressively ever more so, on its proper natural foundations. Thus leaders, with their instruments of speech and reason, are envisioned by Cicero as critical in his idealized descriptions of the forming of the first political communities. In other words, the very process of consenting, and specifically consenting to a rightful arrangement, will involve those disposed and prepared to use the instruments of speech and reason well. Consent itself seems to be a process whose proper outcome is dependent on an appropriate mixing of the inequalities and equalities of a primitive or prepolitical time. With respect to the day-to-day governance, namely the choice of a practicable best regime, Cicero seems, with his endorsement of the mixed constitution, to do what he can to institutionalize that same leadership and to make the bond of the political community a right (*jus*) that accommodates both fundamental equalities and inequalities. These are the objectives that Cicero seeks to attain by the specific institutional arrangements of the mixed constitution which come to light in the portrayal of the development of the Republic (*Rep.* 2), and in the details of Cicero's proposed fundamental laws (*Leg.*).[91] Both liberty and equality are to be given their dues. These features, as well as stability, appear to be viewed, at least in part, as conditions for the education of statesmen and, in turn, for the education of people and citizens in the right. The mixed constitution is, then, for Cicero the constitutional form that follows from and that perpetuates, as best as can be done under the usual conditions of humankind, the essential attributes of a true *res publica*. It represents the proximate political good as well as the practicable political model. It is both a realizable goal in itself and an instrument for moving toward a true *res publica* in the ever changing world. Among all political forms, it provides best for a progressive political course toward the realization of such a *res publica*, which would be a state of collective virtue, of philosophy fulfilled (*perfecta*) in a communal way of life.

The suggestions above that Cicero's description of political origins is intended by him as an idealized process and the suggestion immediately above that leadership is entrusted with a task of "progressively" grounding the *jus* of a political community in nature may bring one to wonder if there ever has been or will be a political community (*res publica*) that can, according to Scipio and Cicero, properly be called one. In other words, is there ever an actualization of a *res publica* that meets the twofold standard of being a community formed by consent, and by consent not to any current will of the group or prevailing standard but to true *jus*? While Cicero reveals and utilizes in *Re Publica* this philosophically precise understanding of *res publica*, Scipio's statement that a defective community like a tyranny "should in no way be called a political community" (*dicendum est plane nullam esse rem publicam*) can be taken to imply that tyranny is an extreme on a spectrum and that *res publica* has, overall for Cicero, a much looser popular usage. That the *Re Publica* as a whole reflects this looser common usage should not be surprising in the light of Cicero's rhetorical training and sensitivity. A number of times in other writings, Cicero criticized the Stoics for disabling themselves before general audiences by their insistence on using a specialized and peculiar understanding of terms. In accepting the looser usage of *res publica* overall, Cicero turns away from a disabling Stoic perfectionism that insists that where there is not agreement in complete justice there is no community at all.[92] In insisting, however, that not mere agreement or consent but what is agreed upon is also critical, Cicero turns away from a relativizing positivism that in effect would make the popular sovereignty moral sovereignty too.

Short of consent in perfect justice, how do consent and what is consented to, the *jus* of the community, work in Cicero's view amid the range of political communities that humans may ordinarily achieve? It appears that the beginning of an answer lies in recognizing that an understanding of the conditions of genuine consent in the true *jus*, namely an understanding of a true *res publica*, is to guide the decisions and actions of those operating in contexts where either or both consent and other aspects of *jus* are present in attenuated and incomplete forms. Overall, Cicero's insistence on consent in all political situations does not vary (though the form and clarity of that consent would seem to), while he seems more tolerant of imperfect realizations of that which is consented to—of those aspects other than consent in the just and right (*jus*).[93] One might say that *for political community (res publica) as ordinarily understood*, Cicero holds that consent is a necessary if not a sufficient condition. While full justice would be a condition of the perfection of the political community, consent seems a condition of the very being of a community or of its credibility as a community. The priority of consent among the elements of *jus* may well be explained by more than the fairly common notion that one must have a community before one can make it a better community. It may also be the case that consent is a requisite that works overall in favor of justice: At the very least, outrageous violations of justice will not long be accepted; at the most—and this means that a consent illuminated by reason and self-understanding—consent can work to draw the community toward the fullness of justice. How to make consent work in tandem with the right in varying circumstances is for Cicero a form of the question of how to pursue the best regime. This is clearly not a matter for disposition by a universal and mechanical formula, but a matter of judgment for the leader gifted with prudence. This leader is a requisite not only in the process of reaching for the mixed constitution but also in the very functioning of that constitution, for this constitution, with its institutionalization of consent and provisions for leadership, does not offer an assured or mechanical means for either maintaining a political direction that is based on consent and the right or for the continual adjusting necessary to maintain the regime itself.

In Cicero's normative definition of *res publica* we have found a way of describing what appears to be the goal of his practicable best regime, what in fact makes it a "best" political order. Working from the definition as we have done, one might call this goal "a consented to rightful ordering." That rightful order is seen by Cicero to arise from certain human inclinations and needs, and the political community and political leadership are seen as necessary utilities in the seeking of the fully human life.[94] Not surprisingly, then, on some occasions Cicero writes of the end of political life as living happily and virtuously (*beate et honeste*).[95] Such expressions of the end of political life, and thus of the government and its leadership, appear to be other ways of describing a state of general consent to a properly grounded *jus* or complete justice. This end and measure seems to be a fully virtuous society, a collective Stoic Wiseman. Such expressions of the goal as living *beate et honeste* remind us not only that the political community is to be serving the proper end (*honestas*) or happiness of its individual members but also that the political community in Cicero can be seen as the moral actor writ large: It seeks happiness defined as the right or overall good *(honestas)*; it can only achieve it with the best understanding available in the ordinary horizon; it above all wants to proceed with voluntary (consented to) acts, and what is to be chosen is the right as grounded in nature, inclusive of such utilities as security and property.

In concluding this phase of our inquiry, we have found that Cicero is a kind of social contract thinker, for he does give prominence to the act of popular consent in the formation of political communities and he provides at least hypothetical images of a precontractual state of the existence of apparently isolated individuals. Consent as a norm in rightly constituting community seems to imply a fundamental equality in a political sense, and Cicero seems to affirm directly the ontological and experiential grounds for a species-defining equality. However, the rule of unequal strength, primarily physical strength, operates in the images given of a precontractual state. Furthermore, whether or not there ever was such a state, it is inequalities in the powers of speech and reason that play critical roles in the developing (e.g. through winning consent) and maintaining of political communities.

Cicero is not, however, a modern social contract thinker in the way that is often understood. He denies that consent or will, whether individual or collective, in itself constitutes the right and hence the simply legitimate. He holds that true political community is grounded in justice that is based in the natural order of the whole. The precontractual state is in no way natural or normative; rather, in being integrated into community, man moves to realize his best potential, the fullness of his humanity, the end provided by nature. Perhaps Cicero's affirmation of human equality is the part of his thinking that is most in harmony with modernity. It is likely, however, that Cicero insists on no more than the equal opportunity to be part of a natural aristocracy and on a consent requirement that represents both the truth of that equality and a practical check on tendencies to forget or to obliterate for some the common humanity that all share. Politics, on the other hand, ever is for Cicero coming to terms with and utilizing inequalities.

What distinguishes Cicero, then, from the paradigm of modern social contract thinking can be seen as his effort to articulate, if not develop, important themes of the classical tradition of political philosophy. Beyond the obvious sharing of a teleological perspective on the naturalness of political community and the end of the human person, Cicero's stress on consent and equality can be understood as working out the implications of the role of autonomy in full virtue and of the preference for natural aristocracy in the work of his Greek teachers. Most often, those who set off Cicero against the earlier classical tradition on the grounds of the emphatic role of inequality in the latter misinterpret the teaching on slavery in Aristotle and/or fail to appreciate the egalitarian implications of the doctrine of natural aristocracy. These are, however, topics for another context and occasion.

Property: End or Means?

A topic that cannot be deferred because it is integral to Cicero's as well as almost every political philosophy is the role of property. Cicero is a strong defender of the decided Roman practice in favor of private property. In Cicero's understanding, concern for property on the part of the individual as well as the political community follows from a simple down-to-earth recognition that it is a primary utility in living in accord with nature. One might expect, then, that if Cicero is something more than an agent of his class or crude advocate of self-interest, his defense of private property is grounded in his effort to approach utilities in the light of nature's standard enriched by the guidance of experience or history. Overall, despite his spirited opposition in *Officiis* to dictatorially driven legislative approaches to the redistribution of wealth,[96] Cicero does not defend private property as something constituting the very end or goal of political community but as a critical element discerned through reason in living *beate et honeste*. That the end of a political or communal life is a happy and virtuous life does not mean for Cicero that positive law and governmental-sponsored activity are invariably the appropriate means. Cicero invokes custom and private activity, including charitable service and giving,[97] as instruments in pursuing this primary end of political community.[98]

Strong as was Cicero's defense of private property and his insistence on the political community's responsibility to secure property rather than threaten it, Neal Wood's claim that Cicero is the "first major social and political thinker of antiquity to stress private property, its crucial role in society and the importance of the state for its protection" seems initially, and at the least, too casual in bypassing Aristotle.[99] Wood's further claim that "[f]or Cicero the state exists primarily to safeguard private property and the accumulation of property, not to shape human souls according to some ethical ideal of the virtuous" is clearly at variance with the interpretation of Cicero in this book.[100] At *Officiis* 2.73, likely the critical passage in the interpretive difference being highlighted here, Cicero writes that political communities and cities were especially established (*ob causam maxime*) to protect possessions.[101] This single passage could well be interpreted, given what follows immediately in the text, to be pointing out that the initial consideration bringing humans together is security for what is their own. Such a position accords with Aristotle's observation that the polis or political community initially arises for the sake of life.[102]

There is in Cicero's writings no claim for a moral or nature-based absolute right to private property. Though Cicero's fears of specific forms of government-taking of a property may have kept him from developing further a potential role for the political community in economic reform and regulation, his work reveals the resources for, in concrete cases, making the common good of the political community the ultimate standard in such matters and drawing on a moral horizon in which respecting settled property rights is but one important consideration in living *honeste*.[103] One need not, of course, support Cicero's every policy choice or his personal choices with respect to purchases and ownership in order to see in his writings an overall coherent and largely Aristotelian approach to the economic dimension of public and private life.

Beyond the Roman Community

Just as Rome, having attained its mixed or balanced constitution at a certain point, served for Cicero as a useful exemplification of the practicable best regime—of a true *res publica* being made—so too did the Roman development to that point and Roman history in general provide much by way of illustration of the process of making consent work in tandem with right—of attaining a way of virtue as best as can be understood at any point in time. In Rome's experience, above all, Cicero finds the path of progress toward the best regime and the kind of leaders who can most ably steer the ship of state through the manifold dangers of time. Although Roman examples inform and influence Cicero's political philosophy, his philosophical writings show patriotism and nationalism under rational control. Cicero is, as we recall, a firm friend of Plato as well as of Rome. His use of Roman *exempla* is more than understandable, given his goal in writing and the rhetorical context. The indications of this rational control in the following paragraphs not only bring to light some of his reflection on the subject of the community of primary political allegiance, such as Rome is for him, but also work to support the argument presented earlier in this chapter that Cicero speaks to the question of the best regime in properly philosophic and universal terms. In the light of his moral philosophy, explored in the previous chapter, it is not surprising that he thinks his and all political attachments require support and constraint by reason—by a properly grounded sense of political duty. All specific political communities and their forms are judged against the very need in the nature of things that gives rise to them. Furthermore, Cicero, quite explicitly, thinks beyond Rome to a wider human community, if a politically unformed one.[104] The universalism and cosmopolitanism, so often associated with the ancient Stoic tradition, surface in Cicero,[105] and the basis for such a community can be found in his appeals to a common nature for moral standards and in his affirmation of an essential human equality.

In perhaps the most personal, touching, and memorable passage in his philosophical writings, Cicero portrays himself confessing to his brother Quintus and dear friend Atticus his deep attachment to his ancestral home of Arpinum and then responding to the query whether he regards this home or the city Rome as his fatherland.[106] Recalling Cato's attachment to Tusculum, the place of his birth, and to Rome, the place of his citizenship, Cicero acknowledges that he, Cato major, and the other offspring of Italian towns have, in a sense, two fatherlands, (*patriae*). Then, almost as a matter of discipline (*necesse est*), Cicero insists that the adoptive, more universal community which provides Roman citizenship must stand first in our love and ought to be the center of all of our efforts, even to the point of giving our life. This fatherland of citizenship comprehends that of birth and of natural and easy affection. Though Cicero, being an Arpinian and not being of the customary Roman ruling class, had ample reason for guarded and selective Roman loyalties at best, the conclusion he draws in *Legibus* accords with his consistent view of Rome as his—and most, if not all, Italians'—rightful political sovereign.[107] For him, Rome ever is the *patria* and "common parent of us all" (*communis parens nostrum omnium*), which he held up in the first Catilinarian address.[108]

In *Officiis*, Cicero provides a more directly philosophical and less personal and specific treatment of the place of the primary political community, *patria*, in human affairs. After surveying the various communities to which the human being is drawn—from the universal community among humankind sharing reason and speech to the intimate ties of family life and those best and strongest of ties in friendship—he concludes that reason's reflection on these various social inclinations leads to the view that no attachment is more significant (*gravior*), none more dear (*carior*) than that which joins each of us with the political community (*res publica*).[109] Duty is to be directed first to *patria* and *parentes*, and it is *patria* which embraces all those proximate attachments to parents, children, relatives, and friends.[110] Cicero sees, then, the political community, Rome in his case, as that association, not necessarily the strongest in initial or natural affection, which reason commends as the sovereign community, the rightful center of personal loyalties. What reason, apparently, discovers is that a certain kind of community, the equivalent of a "true polis," has the material as well as the qualitative aspects to provide for a virtuous and happy human life (*beata et honesta*). Neal Wood puts the matter aptly and keeps in mind a larger horizon when he writes of Cicero's *patria* or *res publica* that it "exists to forward and safeguard the distinctly human values of the members of universal society."[111] The application of reason's discovery, that is, the defense of a specific choice of a sovereign political community—for instance, the choice of Rome over Arpinum or Tusculum—would necessarily be context dependent and, again, a judgment of prudence.

The rational justification for Cicero's Roman particularism is, thus, based on his very universalism. This would account for the fact that Cicero's is not an enclosed particularism—an absolute patriotism. The practical sovereignty of the Roman *patria* overlaps with but is not coextensive with the moral sovereignty of reason and the community among humankind which it implies.[112] This understanding illuminates the framework that allows Cicero the Roman patriot to draw attention to the moral defects of his political community. And so he is found noting the deceptive and unjust treatment of foreigners, the mistreatment of allies, the interrelationship between unjust treatment of foreigners and the breakdown of justice and trust within Rome, Roman laws that deserve not the name, Roman military excesses, and wrongful infidelity to oaths given to enemies. Cicero is concerned that the Roman political community do its work and achieve its end within the ligatures of the universal human community.[113] Twice Cicero gives an approving voice to words used by Terence, "no human concern is alien to him" (*humani nihil a se alienum putat*).[114]

Cicero's ability to see Rome's demands and achievements in a much larger horizon than that of the Roman nationalist is never better expressed than in the justly treasured Dream of Scipio. Here, at the close of *Re Publica*, Scipio is portrayed being enjoined by his deceased grandfather and father to take up the role of leadership of the *patria*, for always and everywhere the serving leaders of political communities (not just the leaders of Rome) are to be rewarded in eternity.[115] *Patriae* are presented as the commanding centers of justice in a universe of political communities. The duty of political leadership enjoined upon Scipio is not, however, to be allowed to draw him to fix his thoughts on earthly concerns, on the usual glory that captivates political leaders.[116] The Rome that Scipio is called to serve is seen as miniscule in the larger universe and the glories her people give as insignificant to the person marked by true reason and virtue.[117] The tension between the patriot and the philosopher, between Rome and Plato, so embedded in Cicero himself, is thus poetically restated at the end of his great and very Roman political classic.

That tension has, as we have seen, been present both in the manner and substance of Cicero's response to political philosophy's central question: what is the best regime? The best regime, which Rome once so much exemplified, is to be a practicable framework for maintaining consent and achieving justice. Its ability to perdure and attain success turns on the presence of appropriately gifted statesmen. The qualities of the best or model statesman and how they might be achieved comes, in this way, to the center of Cicero's attention, both as a philosopher and as a lover of Rome, her future as well as her past.

Notes

1. That Cicero sees himself as standing in this tradition when he writes *Rep.* and *Leg.* is evident in *Div.* 2.3 and *Leg.* 3.14. The statement on "the orientation and scope" of classical political philosophy is by Strauss. Strauss explains that "the primary questions of classical political philosophy" and "the terms in which it stated them" were "not specifically philosophic or scientific"; rather, "they were questions that are raised in assemblies, councils, clubs and cabinets, and they were stated in terms intelligible and familiar at least to all sane adults, from everyday experience and everyday usage." Examples of such questions are "what group should rule, or what compromise would be the best solution—that is to say, what political order would be the best order." Strauss concedes that though the "immediate concern" of actual controversies is "the best political order for the given political community…every answer to that immediate question implies an answer to the universal question of the best political order as such." Thus Strauss speaks of "the natural tendency" of political controversy "to express itself in universal terms." Then Strauss clarifies this tendency by acknowledging

that though the classical philosopher understood the best political order as that "which is best always and everywhere," this is not to be taken to mean that he regards that order "as necessarily good for every community, as 'a perfect solution for all times and for every place': a given community may be so rude or so depraved that only a very inferior type of order can 'keep it going'" (1973: 79–87).
2. Erskine's treatment of the political thought of the Hellenistic Stoa shows *The Republic* as inspiration and foil in this tradition (1990: 30, 61, 71). Vander Waerdt (1994a: 281 ff., 302 ff.) explores the Stoic Zeno's "republic" or polity of Wiseman as a response to Plato's city in speech.
3. Such instances in Cicero are *Off*. 1.33, 35; 2.28–29; 3.28, 41,46–47, 49, 80 ff., 109, 113–15; *Rep*. 1.5–6; 3.41; *Leg*. 2.13–14, 23; 3.37; *Att*. 19–21; 92.
4. Ernest Fortin (1994: xvi) observes that Cicero "deftly conceals [Rome's] defects (but not without letting the informed reader know that he is fully aware of them)...." Mansfield (1996: 135) characterizes Book 2 of *Rep*. as a place "where Cicero, with fine irony and careful responsibility, blends an account of the origin of his own republic with the developments of the features of the best regime. This kind of history is both theoretical and practical because it supposes that nature and virtue are not so much in contest as in cooperation." Rawson remarks (1985: 216) that save, perhaps, for some political pamphlets "as far as we can see, there was nothing on political theory apart from Cicero's" *Rep*. and *Leg*. in the Roman tradition of the late Republic. In the preceding sentence, she notes that "an aversion to such abstract works seems to have made the Romans particularly dependent on historiography."
5. J. Atkins (2013) and J. Zarecki (2014) are two recent treatments of Cicero's political philosophy that, each in their own ways, have emphasized his attention to both the Greek philosophical tradition and Roman traditions and practices.
6. Scipio and Laelius are also utilized as *personae* in Cicero's *Sen*. and *Amic*. They say very little in *Sen*., being present only to introduce a discourse by Cato the Elder. The dramatic setting of *Amic*. occurs just after the death of Scipio, yet his words and thoughts are presented, explicitly at times, within the discourses of Laelius. For a fuller discussion of the relation between *Rep*. and *Amic*., see Nicgorski (2008).
7. *Rep*. 3.5–6; also 1.15 and *Amic*. 6–7. These men appear to function for Cicero as exemplar consular philosophers. In the light of their explicit tie to Socratic learning, the general practice of taking Scipio, their apparent intellectual and moral leader, as Cicero's spokesman makes sense. There are, however, good reasons for caution in concluding that Scipio is the exclusive voice of Cicero. One such reason is that Philus, who reluctantly

and against his convictions argues in the dialogue *contra* to the notion that justice is grounded in nature, is associated, in this role, with the Academic school to which Cicero gives his allegiance. Nor is it persuasive to argue that the major statement on natural law at 3.33 does not, given that it is spoken by Laelius, represent the view of Cicero. See Nicgorski (2012: 271–72).
8. Cicero follows here the general practice in his other dialogues, of opening most books with a preface or introduction (*prooemium*) wherein he speaks directly to the reader in his own name. The prefaces in this work are only partially extant, though we have what appears to be a substantial portion of that written for the first book, seemingly setting the direction and tone for the work as a whole. On the function of his *prooemia*, as well as overall reflections on his use of the dialogue form, see above, Chap. 2.
9. *Rep.* 1.12.
10. In his preface to *Ac.* 2 (5–6), Cicero defends philosophical conversations by public leaders as long as they are consistent with their public responsibilities; appropriately, given the nature of *Ac.*, his defense is less clearly restricted to political philosophy.
11. *Rep.* 1.33.
12. *Rep.* 1.32.
13. *Rep.* 1.35–36.
14. *Rep.* 1.36.
15. *Rep.* 2.3.
16. *Rep.* 4.4–5; Aristotle, *Politics* $1261^a2–1264^b25$.
17. Differences between Cicero and Plato on political/legal matters are suggested in a comment that Quintus, Cicero's brother, is portrayed as making in *Leg.* 2.17. Cicero does not speak directly to this suggestion, save to affirm that he tries to imitate Plato's mode of discourse and does not merely translate Plato's views, for he wishes to be himself.
18. *Tusc.* 1.39–40; also *Div.* 1.30, 62; *Orat.* 42.
19. Cicero describes himself as "a follower of Socrates and Plato" (*De Or.* 1.2). He takes Plato as clearly preeminent as a philosopher; see especially *Leg.* 2.14, 39; 3.1; *Rep.* 2.21 (Laelius speaking); *Nat.D.* 2.32 (Balbus speaking). At *Tusc.* 1.22, Aristotle is held first among thinkers, except for Plato, in brilliance (*ingenio*) and thoroughness (*diligentia*). In *Orat.* 10, Plato is called *gravissimus auctor et magister* with respect to both thought and speech. At *De Or.* 3.21 Plato is presented as a teacher of the unity of knowledge and at *Tusc.* 5.36 as a teacher of virtue as the chief good, both of these being functions very important to Cicero. References to Plato in Cicero's speeches and letters show him consistent in his high praise. In his *Pro Scauro* (4), Cicero refers to Plato as the greatest (*summus*) philosopher whose written work was done *graviter et ornate*. In *Pro Murena* (63), Plato

is presented by Cicero as his teacher along with Aristotle, who is said to be free of the immoderate aspects of the philosophical life manifested in certain Stoics. See also *Pro Rabirio Postumo* 23, *Att.* 89, and *QFr.* 1.29. As to the comparative standing of Socrates and Plato, Plato is consistently "the philosopher" (*princeps philosophorum*), and Socrates is the source or founder of philosophy in the form it takes in Cicero's time (*princeps* or *parens philosophiae*). A fuller discussion of these descriptions and the Socrates/Plato relationship in Cicero's eyes is found in Nicgorski (1992).
20. Cumming (1969: I, 190). Whether one agrees or not with his sense of the limitations of Cicero, Hösle (2008) explored fruitfully the dependencies and differences with respect to Cicero and Plato.
21. *Rep.* 1.67–68; 2.52.
22. This passage was often cited by Strauss as an apparent key to his interpretation of *The Republic*: (1953: 122, 1963: 41, 1964: 138, 1975: 1, 1989: 162).
23. Cicero here uses *optare* for "wishing for the impossible" and *sperare* for "hoping for the possible." Evidence for this being a habitual distinction in Cicero's work and its impact on Thomas More is found in Wegemer (1996: 110–11, 227 n.6). Here, it is proper to mention the interesting suggestion of Parens (1995: xx): "[B]ecause Plato's *Laws* as opposed to his *Republic*, presents his best politically possible city, one could say that both Cicero's *Republic* and *Laws* are commentaries of a sort on Plato's *Laws*."
24. *Rep.* 2.57. The limits of reason with respect to politics is an important theme for J. Atkins (2013).
25. Voegelin (1974: 128).
26. Cicero's letters and other evidence make clear that *Rep.* was written sometime between 55 and 51 B.C. and that the *De Or.* was completed by 54 or shortly thereafter. These two works stand together in time and apart from the great body of Cicero's other rhetorical and philosophical writings, which were done in the last years of his life, 46–43. Antonius in the *De Or.* seems to represent a "no nonsense" technical approach to oratory that might only slowly and cautiously open to the relevance of philosophical studies.
27. *De Or.* 1.224–25. Antonius seems to be implying that philosophy read and considered on a holiday for men bearing public responsibility will be a philosophy resistant to Plato's approach.
28. Cicero's comment to Atticus (*Att.* 21) that Cato, his contemporary, with his lofty and pure views would be more in place in Plato's republic than among the dregs of Romulus seems to be an indication of this popular shorthand.
29. *De Or.* 3.84–85.

30. *Orat.* 7–10. See Tarrant (1985: 118–19, 124–25) on Cicero's use of Plato in this passage and on Cicero's understanding that the "Ideas" exist only "within minds."
31. Cicero's *De Or.* uses *personae* who, like those of the *Rep.*, are active public leaders, and his chief rhetorical writings turn out to be defenses of the life of the statesman as providing the greatest service and, hence, the most fitting utilization of rhetorical ability and art. In the *prooemium* to the first book of *De Or.* Cicero describes true eloquence as derivative from "the arts of the most prudent persons" (*prudentissimorum hominum artibus, De Or.* 1.5, see also *Orat.* 44); we will see, in this and the following chapter, prudence emerge as the most necessary and chief characteristic of Cicero's model statesman. Crassus opens the dialogue in *De Or.* by describing the glory and power of speech as follows: "Nothing at all...seems to be more outstanding than the power of holding an assembly of men by speech, of drawing the support of the mind of men and of directing their wills where one wishes and diverting them from what one wishes" (*De Or.* 1.30). In the rhetorical writing of his youth, *Inv.* 1.2, Cicero shows the public leadership function of the art from its very beginnings. See Cumming (1969: I, 265–67), Davies (1971: 111) and Mitchell (1991: 29).
32. Cumming is, I believe, the originator of the phrase "shift of focus" (1969: I, 286) to describe Cicero's break with Plato and emphasis on "the ideal statesman." Such a "shift" is central to the interpretation of *Rep.* elaborated here but was first presented in my 1991 essay. This "shift" plays a key role in Ferrary's compelling interpretation of *Rep.* (1995: 49 ff.).
33. *Rep.* 1.34, 39 ff.
34. *Div.* 2.6–7.
35. *Rep.* 1.45.
36. Ferrary (1995: 70).
37. There is, then, no simple congruency between reason and political order, which is to say that there is no perfect and, hence, stable solution to the problem of politics. Ferrary's interpretation of the key passage, *Rep.* 2.57 (1995: 57 n. 21), emphasizes that the reason that is overcome by political developments is that of the prudence of the statesman. At *Leg.* 3.23, Cicero shows that institutions, which in general he and the Romans favor (e.g. tribunate and consulship) and which he gives roles to in the model mixed regime that Rome exemplifies, cannot be wholly freed from their potential for evil.
38. It is noteworthy that Polybius, who is generally thought to have influenced Cicero toward the mixed regime and who is presented in *Rep.* as having talked with Scipio (1.34), bans Plato's city in speech from a competition for the best constitution because Plato's city, not having been tested, is not a proven practicable model (vi. 47, 7–10). See Cumming (1969: I, 279, n.

71). Cumming also makes the interesting suggestion (I, 89–90) that Plato himself, in the *Timaeus*, is the source for Polybius banning Plato's city from competition. The suggestion is interesting partly because the *Timaeus*, having been translated by Cicero, apparently was carefully tended to by him. Aristotle's *Politics* (Book 2) or some other Peripatetic text might well be the basis for Cicero's critique of the practicalness of Plato's city. Lintott stresses the Aristotelian character of Cicero's mixed constitution over the Polybian influence on it (1997: 80–85). Lintott also highlights his understanding of how Cicero's and Polybius's approaches to the mixed constitution differ. On the Aristotelian and Platonic dimensions of this part of Cicero's thought distinguished from those of Polybius, see Ferrary (1984: 87–98 and 1995: 54 f.). On Polybius and Cicero on the mixed constitution, also see Millar (2002: 23 ff. and *passim*). J. Atkins (2013: Chap. 3) strongly differentiates Cicero's conception of the mixed regime from that of Polybius.

39. Scipio claims that he can define the best regime without a specific exemplification (*Rep.* 2.66); see also Polybius, vi. 3, 6–10 and Cicero's *Off.* 2.74, where Cicero is explicit about his universal intent.
40. This is not to claim, as the reader of Plato's *Laws* and Aristotle's *Politics* will know, that the concept of combining the simple forms of government toward a goal of a more stable and better regime is a Roman discovery. Marquez (2011), while focusing on the text of Cicero, explores the understanding of the ideal or theory of mixed government in classical antiquity and the role of leaders and a primary class in providing balance, justice, and a source of direction in mixed government.

    Lintott (1997: 80, 85) does not do justice to either Aristotle or Cicero by suggesting that they understand the mixed constitution as "static" rather than "dynamic" and that a dynamic mixed constitution based on a natural process like the one discerned by Polybius "cannot ensure its own ultimate survival." The latter suggestion introduces the implausible notion that such assurance is attainable.
41. T. White writes that Cicero uses the "historical exemplum" for "explanatory efficacy" and for the legitimization of the concept at issue by testifying to its "workability" (1981: 6).
42. Wood writes that for Cicero "Rome is not only the best practicable state, but, with only slight modification, the ideally best state" (1988: 66). My argument above is that the ideally best state is the best practicable state and that Rome is the best actualized exemplification of such a state. It is the best exemplification among actual communities, perhaps in part, because it is the most available and the most useful exemplum under the circumstances. J. Atkins (2013: 232) concurs with my understanding of Cicero's use of Rome.

43. Hathaway (1968: 3–4, 12) probes this subsequent difficulty for Cicero's thought well, arguing that Cicero is a Socratic political philosopher first and a Roman patriot second and that he strives to use Rome and her history to point to "eternal principles," but "precisely because his rhetoric is successful, he blurs the issue of the mortality of all earthly cities; he makes us believe that history culminates in some sense in Rome,...." See Cumming's thoughtful struggle with the question of whether Cicero's model is Rome (1969: I, 239, 279, n. 72, 303, 336, n. 57.
44. *Rep.* 2.51; also *Off.* 1.85. The model seems an exemplar of the consular philosophers.
45. At *Rep.* 1.69, Scipio states that significant moral failings (*vitia*) among the leaders (*principes*) will destabilize even the mixed regime. See Cumming (1969: I, 244–48, 267) for an effort to understand how Cicero's model statesman and mixed regime relate to one another. At 278, n. 61, he properly points to *Leg.* for "a precise institutional illustration of how psychologically indispensable is the leader's role."
46. Internal evidence in *Rep.* and *Leg.* and indications in his letters on the centrality of this model statesman to Cicero's political thought are discussed in Nicgorski (1991: 242–43, 250 n. 43). Also see *Att.* 126 and How (1930: 39–42). Powell (1994: 19–29) and Ferrary (1995: 49–55) have both highlighted this emphasis of Cicero, and recently there is Zarecki's important book-length study around this theme (2014).
47. That many leaders over a long time contribute to this development (*Rep.* 2.2) does not mean that some, as Romulus (*Rep.* 2.21), do not contribute significantly more than others. Ferrary writes of Cicero being influenced by the latter "alternative view" (1995: 55). Hösle (2005: 32, n. 12) sees the emphasis on individual contributions found in Cicero's Scipio to be a tacit correction of the elder Cato's view.
48. That the model statesman was intended by Cicero as his dominant theme in *Rep.*, or at least a co-theme with the issue of the best regime, is supported by two comments of Cicero in his letters. In a letter to his brother Quintus, in 54 B.C. (*QFr.* 25.1), a time when he seems to have been working on *Rep.*, Cicero is found discussing his first version of the dialogue and speaking of it as being concerned with "the best regime and the best citizen" (*de optimo statu civitatis et de optimo cive*). Five years later, in a letter to Atticus (*Att.* 161), Cicero recalls the *Rep.* as a place where he had treated "that man," that leader and guide (*moderatorem*) of the polity, "by whom we sought to judge all things" (*quo referre velimus omnia*). Cicero also refers the reader of *Leg.* (3.32) to the *Rep.* for a more exhaustive treatment of the role of the statesman and leading citizens and their influence on the moral character of a society. However, earlier (2.23; 3.4, 13), he thrice speaks of the topic of *Rep.* being the best state.

49. A comment by Cicero in a letter of 60 B.C. to his brother Quintus (*QFr.* 25.1) reveals what Cicero seems to regard as the essential teaching (*easdem rationes*) of *The Republic* and that this teaching can be seen as directing Cicero toward an emphasis on the statesman, his qualities, and his education. The passage begins with great praise for Plato and then speaks of his teaching that states will only be happy when either the wise and learned rule or those who rule devote themselves to learning and wisdom. In Cicero's words, what is needed in rulers is the pursuit of *doctrinam, virtutem et humanitatem*. See also *Fam.* 20.12.
50. Carlyle and Carlyle (1903: I, 8–9). The authors already had made a significant statement of Cicero's "modernity" when they chose to give to Cicero's political thought the first chapter of the first volume of their six-volume work. McIlwain (1932) follows closely the Carlyles in this respect; McIlwain observes that "Locke's theory of the rights of man as man antecedent to and independent of the state has been implicit in political thought ever since the Stoics and as a result of Rome's transmission of Stoic conceptions of equality" (114–15). Later (1947), he continues in this vein, citing, with evident approval, Lord Acton observing, "[I]t is the stoics who emancipated mankind from its subjection to despotic rule, and whose enlightened and elevated views of life bridged the chasm that separated the ancient from the Christian state, and led the way to freedom" (43 and 155–56, n. 3). Sabine, in his once widely used text (1937), also accepts the point of "divide" set by the Carlyles, remarking at one point on "the astonishing fact…that Chrysippus and Cicero are closer to Kant than they are to Aristotle" (141 ff., 165). Compared to the Carlyles and McIlwain, Sabine does not focus as exclusively on the differences over equality as on defining the new Roman and Ciceronian age. Sabine, instead, emphasizes the movement away from the polis-centered world that is thought to have informed and constrained Aristotle's understanding. What he sees emerging in Cicero is "the idea of the individual, a distinct item of humanity with his purely personal and private life, and the idea of universality, a worldwide humanity in which all are endowed with a common human nature." Like Sabine, Cumming (1969) and McCoy (1950 and 1963) locate a modern turn in terms of a clearer and enhanced role of the individual in Cicero's moral and political thought. McCoy ties this "bold contrast" between Aristotle and Cicero to the natural law doctrine in the latter, and Cumming actually specifically rejects an understanding of Cicero's modernity in terms of the idea of equality. For Cumming, see I, 135–36, 154, n. 2, and *passim*. For McCoy, see (1950: 678–88), especially 683, and (1963: 78 ff). Recently, J. Atkins (2013: 152) has offered a richly grounded and persuasive claim that Cicero incorporates "a conception of rights into his theory of political society."

51. Cumming (1969: I, 174).
52. Wood (1988: 10). MacKendrick (1989: 146) seems also to think of Cicero as "transitional," for despite the appearance of modern political concepts in Cicero, he claims that Cicero does not appreciate the social contract solution to the question of political authority.
53. On Scipio as spokesman for Cicero along with appropriate cautions, see n. 6 above and Nicgorski (1991: 232, 247 nn. 6–7).
54. The topic is proposed and this phrase used at *Rep.* 1.33. Readers of the Latin text will notice at once that the announced topic concerning *civitas* leads with no apparent apology or clarification to a discussion of *res publica*. There appears to be no overall pattern regarding when Cicero uses *civitas* and when he uses *res publica* to speak of the state or commonwealth ("State" or "Commonwealth" are the standard translations for *res publica*; my rendering will almost invariably be "polity" or "political community"). Thus *res publica* is not, as one might expect, restricted to the Roman polity after the fall of the monarchy and during the period conventionally known by historians as the Republican period. See Schofield (1995: esp. p. 66 ff). For an explanation of his preference to render the term as "commonwealth" and background on this traditional rendering, see Brunt (1986: 15 n. 4).
55. *Off.* 1.153, 157–58; also see 1.12; 2.73.
56. *Off.* 1.22; 3.25; *Fin.* 2.45–46. In a similar fashion, Cicero understands genuine friendship as not driven by weakness or need in a narrow sense; see the discussion of friendship in the following chapter.
57. *Rep.* 6.13.
58. J. Atkins (2013: Chap. 2) has properly taken the approach of treating the Dream of Scipio as integral to Cicero's political philosophy.
59. *Rep.* 1.39–41; *Inv.* 1.2–3; *Off.* 1.22; *Leg.* 2.11.
60. "Apparently" is introduced to acknowledge the difficulties posed for interpretation by the fragmentary character of the text of *Rep.* at this point; however, there is a strong basis in this case for the inference that Laelius is the speaker.
61. *Rep.* 3.41; there is a remarkable suggestion in this fragmented passage, which is made even more explicit in a similar passage at *Off.* 2.28–29, namely, that the neglect of *jus* in relation to non-citizens, as in foreign policy, comes to undermine the bond of *jus* that defines the political community among citizens. The result is that though the walls of a city may yet stand, its inhabitants will come to live in fear, and the *res publica* will be lost. The reverse also seems to hold in Cicero's eyes. Courageous and just action within the citizen-body against conspirators of all kinds is significant to others standing outside citizenship, to, in effect, all peoples. *Sest.* 38.
62. *Rep.* 2.45, 48.

63. Force should be also distinguished from legal compulsion, which Cicero acknowledges (*Rep.* 1.3) as an instrument of political leadership; however, even laws, reports Cicero when he explains his prefaces to the various parts of his model legal code (*Leg.* 2.14), should win compliance by persuasion and not simply by force.
64. *Rep.* 2.46.
65. At the very start of *Sest.*, Cicero links the condition of republic with the state of general or common liberty. Arena (2012) explores this and the other forms of liberty that mark the Roman Republic.
66. *Rep.* 1.52, 58; 2.4, 24 ff. especially 31. Also, How (1930: 31).
67. *Rep.* 1.51; 2.56, 61; *Leg.* 3.25. Schofield (1995: 77, 76, 79) writes of "a fundamental recognition of popular sovereignty" in Cicero. This seems so as long as we remain mindful, as will be clear later in this chapter in the consideration of rightful consent in Cicero, that such sovereignty is not moral sovereignty.
68. *Inv.* 1.2–3; *Sest.* 91–92. At *Off.* 2.40–42, Cicero indicates how the force of justice (*vis justitiae*) would animate a *res publica*, and how the desire for *jus* and specifically a fair or equitable *jus*, which is true *jus*, brought people to select the monarchs of the Roman past (see also *Off.* 2.73, *Leg.* 2.11, 3.4). All of these passages indicate, either explicitly or implicitly, that political authority is established by choice of the people—choice at least in the form of consent, choice that could and in most cases would, of course, be aided by persuasion. Nederman's work on the Ciceronian dimension of medieval and renaissance political thought involves him in looking particularly closely at *Inv.* and *Off.*, and the endeavor leads him to affirm a clear theory of consent in Cicero. He writes, "Cicero held that social and political arrangements were the product of explicit common agreement among primitive men arrived at through non-coercive means...." He adds that while not "a social 'compact' in the sense of a formal contract amongst a people," Cicero's consensual view entailed the compatibility of "a naturalistic explanation of the early development of social and political institutions" with the "doctrine that individual choice alone determined the existence of legitimate authority" (1988: 9–10); also (2000: 22). I think, on the basis of the texts considered in this section of this paper, that Nederman's overall sound view falls short in attributing to Cicero a position that "individual choice alone" determines legitimate authority. Rather, it seems that Cicero finds that choice is a necessary but not a sufficient condition of a well-founded or wholly just government. The claim for "individual choice alone" plus the terminology of "legitimacy," if warranted in the case of Cicero, would place him clearly on the side of the moderns.
69. *Off.* 1.12; *Rep.* 3.3.

70. *Rep.* 1.39, 3.43 ff.; *Off.* 2.28–29.
71. Strauss (1953: 96, n.22) cites various texts of Cicero and other ancient authors, indicating that "the assumption of savage beginnings" can be combined with "the acceptance of natural right." According to Strauss (97), what is being indicated by such assumptions is that "man's beginnings were necessarily imperfect." Bellarmine, though an Aristotelian who need not as such resist imperfect beginnings, attacks "Cicero and other pagans" in his *De Laicis* for portraying man's beginnings in such a savage and asocial way. His concern with Cicero's account may, above all, be motivated by a desire to protect the literal truth of the Bible with respect to the state of the first created humans. Glenn brought this surprising critique of Cicero, along with possible explanations, to my attention in a 2004 paper that appeared in 2009 (note specifically, 73–74). Carlyle and Carlyle (1903: III, 4, 107) point to a tradition of considering primitive and even bestial beginnings to human community in the thought of Stoics and Christian fathers.
72. How plausible is it to think of humans as ever outside family structures of some sort? Yet Cicero's expressions at *Inv.* 1.2. and *Tusc.* 5.5 suggest that the first stage of primitive human life was sexually promiscuous without stable married life and, accordingly, without the ability to know one's own children. Schofield (1995: 71) claims that *Inv.* 1.2–3 and *Sest.* 91–92 are contrary to other statements (such as *Rep.* 1.39) of Cicero that humans are naturally gregarious. Tuck (1979: 33, 44) seems inclined to agree. I disagree. The need for leadership and rhetoric in bringing humans into stable and just political communities does not constitute a denial of human sociality. My argument is elaborated in what immediately follows.
73. This theme in Cicero is not limited to his *Rep.* as Tuck suggests (33). It is notably present in *Off.*, which was very influential in the Renaissance.
74. *Rep.* 3.3.
75. The estrangement does seem to be between individuals in reports on the pre-societal state in *Inv.* and *Tusc.*
76. Augustine, *Contra Julianum*, IV. xii.60.
77. There appears to be no time, in Cicero's view, when all humans are equalized by having essentially the same drives or passions, as is the case in writings of Thomas Hobbes. See the very probing and insightful reflection on the similarities and differences between Cicero and Hobbes in the appendix (E. Atkins 1990: 285–89).
78. 1252b27–30, 1253a29–31.
79. E. Atkins (1990: 287–88).
80. In the light of origins and then maintenance and development of political communities, Cicero indicates that the right attitude, at least in the case of Rome, is one of gratitude to leaders and institutions. *Sest.* 136–37; *Rep.* 5.1–2.

81. *Off.* 1.28; *Ac.* 2.38–39.
82. *Off.* 1.13; Cicero appears, here, to be writing of a peak or completeness of human development in describing the sense of self-determination of that mind that desires the truth and is well-formed in it by nature (*animus bene informatus a natura*): a person whose mind is so formed will subject himself to no counselor, teacher, or ruler except one acting rightly and justly (*juste et legitime*) for true benefit (*utilitatis causa*). Such a self-understanding is for Cicero the basis for magnanimity (*magnitudo animi...humanarumque rerum contemptio*). Also, see Fetter and Nicgorski (2008) on magnanimity, as well as Schofield (2009).
83. *Leg.* 1.29 ff. (*Nihil est enim unum uni tam simile, tam par, quam omnes inter nosmet ipsos sumus*). However wanting one or another commentator has found Cicero's practical commitment to equality in the form of political applications, his theoretical embrace of the principle has been widely noted. Wood finds Cicero "a sincere and dedicated egalitarian in moral principle" but "unquestionably an inegalitarian in social and political theory and practice," and the latter is so "despite rhetorical genuflections to *populus Romanus*" (1988: 90–91, 96, 169). Earlier, Colish, in interpreting *Leg.*, notes that though Cicero argues in Book I "that all men are equal by nature through the common possession of reason, he makes no attempt to apply this principle to politics" (1985: I, 102). In a similar vein, Sabine (1937:167) finds that Cicero's theoretical "derivation of political authority from the people does not of itself imply any of the democratic consequences which in modern times have been deduced from the consent of the governed." Cumming too resists the democratic implications of Cicero's affirmation of equality, writing that this concept "was of no importance" to his treatment of political problems, for he sees no "egalitarian or revolutionary" implications in Cicero's work on politics; he acknowledges the theory of consent as a "merely formal concession to the democratic demand for equality" and Cicero's provision of liberty for the people as a grant only in a "formal, legalistic sense" (1969: I, 234, n. 74, 251). Strauss (1953: 135) hesitates to attach much importance to indications in Cicero "of a slight bias in favor of egalitarian conceptions," noting that his "writings abound with statements which reaffirm the classical view that men are unequal in the decisive respect and which reaffirm the political implications of that view." It seems that appreciating whatever "democratic implications" may impact on Cicero from his principles requires working out how his affirmations of equality and consent work within his larger understanding of the nature of humans and their communities. What follows is an attempt at this.
84. *Leg.* 1.33; also 1.16 and *Off.* 1.11–13. Another indication that Cicero regards the idea of human equality as generating the theory of consent is

found in how he describes democrats arguing for a constitutional arrangement of rights and offices that makes equality the exclusive or nearly exclusive consideration. This argument, at *Rep.* 1.48–49, *appears to assume equality as the condition among persons* in the process of constituting the *res publica* and to use that as an agreed upon basis for arguing that only the choice of democracy as form of government produces a true *res publica*, *res populi*, by maintaining equality in *jus*.
85. *Leg.* 1.29–30.
86. Carlyle and Carlyle (1903: 64, also 15–16); note here and in the immediately preceding pages that the Carlyles' highlighting of "modern" elements in Cicero did not blind them to Cicero's Aristotelian dimension in maintaining the natural sociality of humans and the necessary role of inequality in political practice in the light of "human diversity and corruption" (13). In noting both Aristotelian elements and an affirmation of natural equality in Cicero, they repair to an older denigrating view of Cicero's eclecticism (12), finding Cicero on this matter incoherent and "holding together opinions hardly capable of reconciliation."
87. *Rep.* 3.23 and 18 on role of fear. See *Leg.* 1.42, also 19 and 2.9,11 for indications of Cicero's view on this position.
88. *Rep.* 3.43–47.
89. This passage makes clear the normative dimension that Cicero intends with his use of *res publica*. There is already in Cicero's time a tradition of speaking of the true political community as opposed to those associations simply claiming its name in common usage. Recall that Haemon, in that heated exchange with his father Creon in Sophocles's *Antigone* (737), proclaims that "It's no city (*polis*) at all when possessed by one man." See Plato's *Laws* (713 ff.) for the observation that there is no true law or true polity unless they exist for the common good. Aristotle writes of the political community (polis) not as every aggregation of individuals but as that which is self-sufficient for the just and good life for its members (*Politics*, 1252^{b}28–1253^{a}39). Neither this tradition nor Cicero, as will be clear later, scorn the common and looser usage of the term for political community though a proper, normative usage has been introduced,

My earlier observation (n. 54 above) concerning the absence of a pattern in Cicero's use of *res publica* and *civitas* can now be recalled, and Wood's different conclusion on this matter can be addressed. Wood concludes (1988: 126) that there is a pattern, namely that Cicero uses *civitas* in viewing the polity "institutionally and constitutionally" and *res publica* when thinking of it "in terms of common interest and right." He does not cite any of the alternate uses of *civitas* and *res publica* in the *Rep.* in support of his conclusion. He points, rather, to *Leg.* 2.12 and *Paradoxa Stoicorum* 27, both being instances where Cicero argues, as he does at *Rep.* 3.43 ff.

regarding *res publica,* that a *civitas* cannot be a *civitas* if it is not characterized by law—not any rules or orders, but just laws. Carlyle and Carlyle (1903: 5, 14–15) bring the ingredient of justice to the fore in their discussion of the meaning of *res publica* for Cicero.

90. Schofield, (1995: 72 ff). On the independence of the right from the public opinion in Cicero's thought, see the previous chapter and also *Tusc.* 3.3; 5.104–05. The distinction between the right and the prevalent public opinion seems necessary to Cicero's view that the true interest of the people or democrats is to be found in the best or mixed constitution (*Phil.* 7.4).

91. Mitchell makes the discerning observation that the feature of the mixed constitution that chiefly interested Cicero was the idea that stable government depended on a carefully balanced distribution of rights and powers between different elements of society. He saw these elements as two, however, corresponding to what he considered the two great natural divisions in every body politic: the mass of the people, and the few whose abilities and standing set them apart and entitled them to a position of leadership.

    In terms of the political structures of the republic, this meant not so much some literal mixing of monarchy, aristocracy, and democracy as a combination of *libertas* for the people, and *auctoritas* for the *principes* or Senate (1991: 53, 52, n. 134, 55–56).

92. See Vander Waerdt on Zeno's "imaginary community" of sages, one not intended to be applicable to ordinary humans, and on the different intent of Cicero (1991: 187 ff., 196, 206 ff.; 1994a: 285 ff., 294–95).

93. Lacey (1978: vi) has properly observed, "Cicero was, and has always been, the most eloquent spokesman for those who believe that politics is the business of persuasion and the ballot-box, and not of coercion."

94. Insofar as the normative definition of *res publica* incorporates the notion of the fully human life, it has implicitly contained all along the notion of self-sufficiency, which is central to Aristotle's true polis.

95. *Rep.* 4.3, 5.6–8; *Leg.* 2.11. Also see *Leg.* 1.58 ff. and *Tusc.* 5.5, where law is seen as an instrument in developing and encouraging virtue. It is clear from several of the preceding passages that Cicero does not regard law as a preventing and punishing device (in other words, as an instrument of negative liberty) to be the appropriate means in all cases for pursuing the end of political community.

    Clearly, there is a difference of emphasis, at the least, between my interpretation of Cicero on the end of political life and Nederman's (2000: 26–27), who argues that Cicero "diminished the standards of public virtue in line with his belief in the primary social good of peace. Nederman does acknowledge Cicero's concern with the character of the leadership class rather than citizens at large. Though this chapter has emphasized the role of consent and equality in Cicero's thinking, such texts as *Sest.* 96–101, *Mur.* 15 ff., and *Off.* support a natural aristocracy toward which the artificial aristocracy, that is regnant in many situations, is to be bent.

96. See Dyck (1996: 360) on the circumstances that appear to have moved Cicero so vehemently about redistribution in this particular work.
97. Forms of *beneficentia* or *liberalitas*, which are primarily treated in *Off.* (see especially 1.92).
98. *Off.* 1.148; 3.67–69; *Rep.* 4.3.
99. Wood (1988: 11); later at 105 and 130 he acknowledges that Aristotle gives some significance to private property and seeks to differentiate, in his view, Cicero's greater emphasis on property.
100. Wood (1988: 11, 120, 132). A close and thorough examination of Wood's treatment of the property dimension in Cicero's political theory is found in Barlow (2012). Wood does acknowledge (11) that Cicero has "reservations" about his alleged view that the political community exists to secure and enlarge private property. Wood's Chap. 6 on "Private Property and Its Accumulation" tries to capture some of the complexities of Cicero's teaching on property by portraying Cicero as holding to an "enlightened" version of "economic individualism." Wood's interpretation of Cicero's thought seems colored by his suggestion of a kind of determinism or personal interest driving Cicero (105–06, 129). He writes, "Cicero's concern with private property is by no means confined to the realm of theory. A child of his time, he displays a pronounced desire for the acquisition of possessions and his own economic advancement. His preoccupation with property in public and private life and in his writings places him squarely in the social context of the late Roman Republic."
101. There is a similar passage at 2.78, where the protection of private property is said to be the appropriate (*proprium*) function of the political realm.
102. *Politics*, 1252b29; cf. *Inv.* 1.2–3, *Sest.* 91–92, *Rep.* 1.39.
103. Not only does Cicero deny that nature directly provides for private property (*Off.* 1.21) and offer an understanding of the political community as a common property (*res publica, res populi* as treated above) but he also highlights moral duties that require avoiding passivity in the face of injustice and positively contributing to the well-being of others through benevolent or charitable acts. Thus Book 1 of *Off.* (notably 23, 29, 31, 92) shows the resources for privileging the good of the community in specific choices over the simple protection and extension of private possessions. Book 2's treatment of taxation and the usual corrupt motives, in Cicero's view, for government-taking of property (74–79) as well as its use of the story of Aratus (81–84), Book 3's invocation of private property (53) in the disputation between Antipater and Diogenes, the response to Hecaton (63) Cicero invokes, and Cicero's portrayal (*Fin.* 3.67–68) of Cato's the-

ater-seat metaphor about the right-but-limited right of private property further show his rich resources for protecting property but not doing so in an unreasonable or absolutist way. What nature does appear to teach is that property belongs to the person endowed with the practical wisdom to use it well (*Rep.* 1.27; *Leg.* 1.25–26).

Neither Annas nor Long appear to see Cicero's view on property and property rights as I do. Annas (1989: 167 ff.), in the course of exploring the Stoic tradition of defending private property rights as consistent with the equality of all, shows how Cicero's statement of this tradition might be taken to claim a value higher than private property, but she concludes that Cicero is explicating, as an Academic, the Stoic tradition, and likely for himself he holds private property as the key human value. Long (1995a: 234 ff.) does not see or find significant resources in Cicero that can be and are at times employed to assert the community good or interest over property rights. He observes, "On Cicero's interpretation of justice, any intervention by government in the sphere of private ownership, whether by taxation or appropriation, is as flagrantly wrong as an individual's theft of another individual's property" (235–36). However, a few pages later (240), he is, perhaps, acknowledging the presence of such resources in Cicero's thought when he notes "the intellectual achievement" in *Off.* and that Cicero's theoretical emphasis on property rights can be separated from Cicero's politics.

104. For example, *Leg.* 1.32; *Amic.* 19–20.
105. The classic statement by Zeno, the Stoic founder, on this matter is preserved in Plutarch; see Watson (1971: 220). Pangle (1998: 238–39) describes this dimension of Cicero's writings as "the most searching, and at the same time most profoundly sympathetic and constructive, critique of Stoic cosmopolitanism that has ever been executed...." His analysis of Cicero's "sensible middle ground" (262) between Stoic idealism and anti-Stoic realism subsequently appears in the context of his book with Peter J. Ahrensdorf on political philosophy and international relations (1999). The Stoic background on the notion of universal citizenship and the idea that one at best develops toward such citizenship is illuminated in Schofield (1991: esp. Chap. 3). On the coincidence of utility and altruism, with respect to humanity at large, see Wright (1995: 190).
106. *Leg.* 2.3–5.
107. As How (1930: 30) writes, for Cicero "Rome is Italy and Italy Rome."
108. *Cat.* 1.17; see also, *Sest.* 29–30.
109. *Off.* 1.50–57.
110. *Off.* 1.57–58; *Rep.* 6.16.
111. Wood (1988: 140).

112. This practical sovereignty makes understandable and even useful the tendency, remarked on in *Rep.* 3.34, for citizens to see their polity as the whole world and thus not to be allowed to suffer destruction.
113. E. Atkins (1990: 247 ff.) explores the tension in Cicero's writing between his Roman patriotism and his affirmation of the universal human community. Her "suspicion" is "that Cicero never faced the question of the limits of patriotic duty...squarely...."
114. *Off.* 1.30; *Leg.* 1.33.
115. *Rep.* 6.13–29.
116. Barlow (1987: 371).
117. Also, *Leg.* 1.61–62.

CHAPTER 5

The Socratic Statesman

> For there is no other endeavor in which human virtue more nearly approaches the very nature (*numen*) of the gods than either in the founding of new polities or in the preservation of those already in being. (Cicero, *De Re Publica* 3. 12)
>
> Therefore we need magistrates, without whose prudence and care (*prudentia ac diligentia*) there can be no political community.... (Cicero, *De Legibus* 3. 5)
>
> For even if there is nothing in glory that should be sought, yet it follows virtue like a shadow. (Cicero, *Tusculanae Disputationes* 1. 109–10)

Cicero's model statesman is at the center of his political philosophy and is properly seen as the culmination of his philosophical work. That statesman and his necessary and, thus, defining qualities, which form the basis for an educational program, provide the primary locus for Cicero's merging of his Roman and Greek attachments: his love of Roman ways and his attraction to Greek philosophy. The model statesman serves as such a locus not only, and surely not primarily, because Cicero employs an explicitly Platonic approach, enriched by Roman experience, in turning to the *perfectum exemplum* to understand and teach. More significant as a point of integration is the Socratic character of the statesman Cicero comes to sketch and commend. Cicero's statesman is a philosophical statesman, who attends with care to experience and tradition.

That this statesman is appropriately called a Socratic statesman should not surprise us in the light of his openly acknowledged Socratic inspiration and direction to his philosophical work. Cicero regards his Academic skepticism, with its method of testing the opinions and claims of the other schools and its mixture of self-denying doubt and practical affirmation, as the authentic Socratic way. Further, the approach to philosophy that makes philosophy attractive and even compelling to Cicero is the Socratic orientation that focused upon and gave priority to the problems of human life—to the moral and political sphere. Socrates exemplifies for Cicero what grounds of assurance a practical orientation could provide to all of philosophical inquiry. He was a model of virtue even as he sought to understand virtue. He, thus, was able to show the path not only of critical philosophy, with its rigorous dialectical inquiry, but also of a philosophical approach that appreciated the need for appropriate rhetoric to defend and sustain the way of virtue, which at the very least meant the way of philosophy. For Cicero, the priority of statesmanship among duties and, hence, among possible ways of life is an unavoidable and ready conclusion from the Socratic practical perspective, as he seeks to read the message of nature in the light of commonly evident utilities. The need for statesmanship itself implies the requisites of the kind of statesmen who could provide for that need. These requisites show the statesman's Socratic character.

The conclusion Cicero draws from a practical Socratic orientation to philosophy concerning the priority of the life of statesmanship does not, however, appear to be faithful to Socrates. Though it is readily arguable that Socratic philosophy points to and culminates in the political life, Socrates specifically eschewed political leadership in the form of seeking and holding office.[1] Socrates thought that his call to inquire and to teach in Athens took priority to the chancy endeavors of practical politics. Cicero, as we have seen in the previous chapter, is aware of this difference between himself and Socrates as well as other outstanding thinkers and only reluctantly excuses them. In Cicero's eyes, Socrates seems to have insufficiently tended not only to the responsibility for political leadership but also to such practical requisites of it as the art of rhetoric. There are, then, differences between Socrates and Cicero, or, at the least perceived differences in the eyes of Cicero, along with his admiration for and emulation of Socrates. As he does with the Stoics, Cicero endeavors to bring Socrates, his primary Greek teacher and inspiration, and one whom he followed specifically in bringing philosophy into everyday life, yet more down to earth by elevating the importance of a Roman sense of requisite utilities. We are left with an important question for continuing consideration: Is Cicero's argument in these matters, an argument from the Socratic practical perspective, sound, or perhaps even superior to that which Socrates can be said to make? This much is certain: Cicero's Socratic statesman cannot be Socrates who turned from that way of life; the model, however, is approximated and exemplified in the consular philosophers—in Romans like Scipio or Crassus, and in fact in Cicero himself.[2]

That Cicero's thought comes around to center on a model statesman who bears a noticeable likeness to Cicero himself can readily be taken to support the view that Cicero's philosophical work is hardly serious, if not simply politically self-serving. Such an interpretation of this concept and its centrality to his thought is, however, much too facile and has probably been possible only because of the powerful predisposition against Cicero the philosopher in the last century and a half and because of the related failure to appreciate his explicitly Socratic orientation. The model statesman is, for Cicero, a matter of aspiration rather than one of actual and complete personal achievement. His letters show that Cicero is not without open self-doubt and self-criticism. He no more sees in himself the unqualifiedly best statesman than he sees in Rome the best regime. Yet he is on the path of this statesmanship. This way of life is both the focus of his confessed ambition and the resultant focus of his inquiry into duty. It is from his own experiences, no doubt, that he draws much in his understanding of the functions and requisites of this statesman. That the impetus to philosophy and its first fruit be self-direction is a deeply Socratic notion, which seems ever on the mind of Cicero. That he should measure himself against the noblest conception of statesmanship is a form of the very idea that Cicero holds up for guidance and attributes to Socrates in *De Officiis*: "Strive to be as you wish to be thought to be."[3]

THE REQUISITES OF STATESMANSHIP

What does it mean to be a statesman of the Socratic sort? What are the specific qualities that distinguish a Scipio and a Crassus? Underlying such qualities and, hence, even more important is the rationale or justification that leads Cicero to choose Scipio, Crassus, and even the elder Cato as *exempla*, to use and even bend history so as to be able to teach more effectively about, and to attract people to, his idea of a model statesman.[4] It is from the work or function of the statesman and orator that Cicero derives the necessary qualities of the statesman. In turn, these are markers that are critical in the determination of how one is to strive to be a statesman or how one is to educate others for political leadership. Elemental as it may seem, it is important to note that such determinations of an educational and developmental course for statesmanship can be seen as determinations of duty for Cicero. They are logically continuous in a process of finding the nature's way—of the derivation of moral duty, based on human nature's need for political community. Just as utility and necessity entered the process of elevating the duty of statesmanship over other ways of life, so do they function in setting some order of priority for the requisites of successful statesmanship. This specification of the requisites provides not only a sharper and fuller picture of the model statesman but also the basis for an ordered educational and developmental course, a curriculum, for statesmanship.

The previous chapter's detailing of Cicero's "shift in focus," from a model best polity to a model statesman, has already gone far in revealing essential requisites of that statesman. That statesman, after all, emerged as central in the light of the needs perceived for an effort to establish and maintain a mixed constitution in the ordinary course and flux of politics. Recall that Scipio introduced, as a contrast to the tyrant, not a philosopher-king but a type of man described as "guardian," "steward," "leader," and "pilot" of the political community, one able to protect the community "by his counsel and deeds," and one described as "good and wise and experienced in matters of public utility and honor" *(bonus et sapiens et peritus utilitatis dignitatisque civilis)*.[5] Scipio, there, called on his listeners to be on the lookout for this man and promised much more attention to him in the remainder of his discourse. The missing and badly fragmented portions of *De Re Publica* seem to have contained the substance of Scipio's and Cicero's detailed discourse on the model statesman, including attention to the education of this statesman.[6] There is, however, significant available material both in *De Re Publica* and in Cicero's other writings, especially *De Oratore*, to allow a more detailed view of this statesman and the course of education and development for such a person.

In fact, later, in the extant *De Re Publica* 2, we are able to see Scipio beginning to deliver on his promise to give much more attention to that "steward" and "guardian." At this point, he brings forward the man whom he has "long been seeking," portraying him as the apparent critical force in the founding and preservation of polities and specifically of that practicable best regime—the mixed constitution.[7] It is here that this type of man is explicitly called, at the suggestion of Laelius, the man of prudence *(prudens)*.[8] This prudence of the political leader clearly includes what Scipio, earlier in Book 2, called the object of his entire discourse and the basis of all political prudence *(caput civilis prudentiae)*, namely an understanding of "the course and changes of polities so that when one knows the tendencies of each polity one might be able beforehand to prevent *(retinere)* such developments or meet *(occurrere)* them in some way."[9]

This seems to be essentially the same civil prudence that Cicero finds present in a crucial if rudimentary way in the founding of regimes. In his description of political origins, he writes of a leader who utilizes reason and speech, and whom he describes, in one instance, as a wise *(sapiens)* and great man.[10] This leader, foreseeing the goods of communal life, finds the degree to which this teaching of reason, the fruit of his foresight, and consent can be brought together in the forming of a political community; drawing people by persuasion away from a dispersed and bestial way of life, he brings them together around their best interests, around, that is, an agreement in right *(jus)*. The idealized foundings that Cicero describes are portrayed as improvements in the human condition. The same prudence and skill required in such instances marks those leaders who over the years have made critical contributions to Rome's progressive development as an exemplary constitutional experience and who will be important to the progressive possibilities of the future. The point, here, in drawing out the reforming potential of the civil prudence of the model statesman is to make clear that however much Cicero seems to emphasize a prudence that protects against regime-degeneration and that works for stability, the statesman's prudence is richer in its potential fruit than such conservatism would suggest.[11]

That statesman, then, who is highlighted in *De Re Publica*, is predominantly characterized by civil prudence, which seems to be a quality of being able to discern political good and evil and choose the one and, thus, avoid the other. This inference to a definition is based on what Cicero appears to expect of civil prudence: preventing certain political changes, meeting other changes in some appropriate way, knowing the true advantages of political community and being able to draw people into such a community, and reforming and improving in a timely manner the existing political community. The definition inferred is supported by the specific definition Cicero gives of prudence in general as excellence "in the choice of goods and evils," in knowing what is to be sought and what is to be avoided.[12]

Cicero also specifically associates prudence with a type of foresight, and on one occasion he actually illustrates foresight by a number of examples, one of which is the prudent Solon's capacity to discern the rise of tyranny well in advance.[13] Civil prudence seems, then, to be a specific form of the virtue of prudence and, thus, requires this virtue and yet something more. That something more has to do with the specific domain of civil prudence, namely, that of politics. The specific knowledge of this domain would presumably be that of history, political forms, and law. Experience in this domain, so clearly elevated by Cicero again and again, is another important part of civil prudence. Experience *(usus)* is not only a mode of learning in the domain of politics but also a form of practice, hence making civil prudence as truly a virtue as its name suggests. Thus, ingredients of civil prudence are a specific kind of knowledge and practice, as well as the underlying general virtue of prudence.

That general virtue of prudence appears in Cicero's thought as the key virtue for the perfect or model orator of the rhetorical writings, as well as for the model statesman of *De Re Publica*. This is hardly surprising in the light of the evidence indicated earlier, that this orator is but another way to speak of—another approach to—the model statesman. To note how this general prudence emerges as the key among the requisites of oratorical success will provide, then, another approach to—another statement of—the requisites of statesmanship.

What is found of these requisites in the rhetorical writings is more directly, systematically, and fully stated and more explicitly turned into an educational curriculum for the statesman-orator than what can be found among the extant portions of *De Re Publica*. What I have inferred above about the requisites and educational needs of the statesman, from explicit descriptions of him and his work in the fragmented *Re Publica*, is in every respect reinforced and amplified by the treatise on his education, which emerges from the rhetorical writings. The difference between the two approaches is chiefly and understandably related to their different points of departure, in accord with the primary topic of each work. The *Re Publica*, being Cicero's principal political work, proceeds through a "shift in focus," from the best regime to the model statesman, for a quite direct discussion of the statesman's function and requisites and presumably his education. Both in what is said directly about the work of the statesman and in the examples of statesmanship in Roman development and the functioning of the mixed constitution, the statesman's need for rhetorical ability and art is evident: He is to counsel, tutor, and persuade in a system where achieving consent and respect for liberty are central and persisting features. *De Oratore* and Cicero's other major rhetorical writings (i.e. *Orator* and *Brutus*)[14] focus on and proceed from the generally conceded view of the work of the orator whose objective is effective persuasion and, accordingly, whose chief art is the commonly recognized art of rhetoric. Since the primary arena for oratory is the forum and the court, and since the art of rhetoric, if not common sense, teaches the need to know the subject matter on which one is to speak, the orator must, in fact, possess the knowledge and experience proper to the statesman.

Though, even if from different points of departure, Cicero's political and rhetorical writings come, in effect, to treat the model statesman in a mutually supportive and reinforcing way, the rhetorical writings, specifically *De Oratore*, bring to light the apparent difference with Socrates over the art of rhetoric already noted, and clearly reveal Cicero, following Plato, as a defender of the unity and utility of all knowledge. Both of these points contribute to understanding aspects of Cicero's thought that are not as directly broached in other writings and that further expose some of the tension in the very concept of the Socratic statesman.

What, then, according to Cicero, are the requisites for being the complete or perfect orator, and how does it happen that prudence comes to have the key position among them? However broad and demanding Cicero's concept of this orator is, at its core, as already indicated, is the common understanding of the art of rhetoric and practice in it. In *De Oratore*, he proceeds from the common understanding or ordinary horizon, as he does in other matters, to build up the full panoply of requisites of a true orator.[15] Cicero respects and teaches the technical details of the art of rhetoric as it had come down to him.[16] Yet, Cicero does not let the art of rhetoric, as generally known, be taken as the simple key to oratorical success. He elevates the relative importance of natural talent, effort, and experience or practice in relationship to knowledge of the formal art.[17] Furthermore, the art cannot be well used without the potential orator understanding the emotions and characters of men, knowing himself, and knowing that on which he will be called to discourse, that is, potentially all things but especially those most important matters which are likely to arise in the court and the forum.[18] Those especially important matters concern the just and the useful. Thus, the potential orator's learning is to emphasize what seemed earlier to be implied in civil prudence, namely, law, history, political constitutions, and human customs; however, his learning should be broad and he should aspire to understanding all things.[19] If he is an orator, says Cicero of himself, the credit belongs not to the workshops of the rhetoricians *(rhetorum officinis)* but to the open spaces of the Academy *(Academiae spatiis)*.[20] Philosophy is a requisite of oratorical excellence.

From work within or, one might say, with the very art of rhetoric, Cicero finds that each part of the art is in need of the same quality if it is to be well utilized, and therefore he holds that the art of rhetoric can be summed in a single principle: follow what is befitting or appropriate *(aptitudinem or decorem)*.[21] So in the finding of arguments, the division of the art known as invention *(inventio)*, one should select the appropriate arguments, from those possible on the matter at hand, for this audience with this speaker on this occasion; likewise, the speech should be ordered appropriately, and the style adopted should befit the thoughts and arguments as well as the other considerations.[22] One can obviously break the rule of appropriateness in many different ways: for example, speaking in a style unbefitting one's age or subject matter, or drawing out an argument for an audience that can grasp it at once and easily. That the art of speaking is, above all, to speak appropriately appears to be analogous to and a specific example of the general teaching of Cicero on the art of right living, which is also, as we recall, to act appropriately.[23] It is in judgment—a judgment that is willing to use the generalizations of the art of rhetoric but is not simply servile to them—that success is to be found. The judgment of appropriateness, which is critical to success in every department of oratory, is the judgment in which the prudent person excels. This pivotal role for prudence explains statements of Cicero such as his claim that true eloquence derives from "the arts of most prudent persons" *(prudentissimorum hominum artibus)*.[24] Prudence then is the defining quality of the true and complete orator.

Speech-making or any form of the use of rhetoric, like political leadership, is a specific form of human action. Thus, as there is a civil prudence, which is a species of general prudence, so there is a prudence especially tutored in the art and practice of rhetoric. Though Cicero does not put it in such terms, he seems to draw attention to what might be called rhetorical or oratorical prudence as the crucial quality in oratorical success and a species of general prudence. If there is a reason for Cicero not actually naming the rhetorical analogue for civil prudence, it could be because of his collapse of the orator into the statesman or, to state it another way, because the statesman's civil prudence and rhetorical prudence in the forum and the court are mutually inclusive. Though that would appear to be Cicero's understanding of the relationship of these two "prudences," a more likely explanation for his failure to specifically name a rhetorical prudence is his assumption that it is common knowledge that each art, and each realm of action, has its peculiar prudence. Each art is brought to perfection with prudence, he writes;[25] at another occasion, he reminds his readers that there is no human activity that can do without prudence.[26] Even in these statements, however, Cicero appears to be speaking more about the general quality of prudence as it bears on specific spheres of activity than about a variety of "prudences." In fact, Cicero's intent seems to be to emphasize general prudence as that which justifies, guides, and perfects all arts and activities. While respecting the evident need for specific knowledge and experience relevant to specific arts, Cicero's emphasis is on what unifies all human activities, and he resists, in accord with Plato, any notion of good or excellence as conceivably separable from the human good—the way of nature. Political skill and power without right is not statesmanship for him. Fine speaking without wisdom is not true eloquence. This unified learning, centered in prudence, is for Cicero the mark of a person educated in the arts appropriate to humanity, one who exemplifies broad learning, including the turn to philosophy in the Socratic manner, one like Scipio whom Cicero calls *humanissimus*.[27]

The fact that Cicero's model statesman, his proximate goal for political amelioration and well-being, and his model orator are chiefly to be characterized by general prudence is an indication of the importance of prudence in his thinking, in his entire approach to philosophy. Prudence, after all, could be described as excellence in thinking from the practical perspective and thus as the mark of the Socratic approach to philosophy. Often present in a prephilosophical form, it is the basis of reasonable assurance in knowing and in choice, even between the competing understandings of the good offered by different philosophical schools. It is through prudence in the philosopher-statesman that natural law—the way of nature—is articulated. Thus prudence is at the basis of all the virtues; it is the determiner of what constitutes virtue and arbitrates between virtues; it is, as such, prudence that elevates justice over the pursuit of knowledge. Prudence can properly be called the virtue of virtues.

The central role of prudence in Cicero's thought makes clear that for him it is through the good and the pursuit of it that all human activities can be found to be interrelated and ordered. It is prudence that can endorse and, thus, give moral significance to such useful activities as the life of political leadership and achievement in the art of rhetoric.[28] The conclusions Cicero draws from the practical perspective lead him, however great his Socratic inspiration may be, to criticize Socrates and to distinguish himself from his dominant mentor. Though he is indirect and very gentle, as we have seen, with Socrates and other great philosophers who withdraw from political leadership, he has his spokesman and special model Crassus directly and repeatedly criticize Socrates in *De Oratore* for his seeming diminishment of the art of rhetoric as reported in Plato's *Gorgias*.[29] What seems to concern Cicero is that Socrates has, perhaps inadvertently, fostered a kind of fragmentation in the world of learning and between and among its major forms; his seeming contempt for rhetoric, unjustifiable, in Cicero's eyes, in the light of the human condition, increases the likelihood that rhetoric will be taught separately from philosophy, that it will be thought that eloquence can be distinct from wisdom. Socrates, then, would work against his very overall mission, that which Cicero seeks to emulate in the Roman context, of putting philosophy in the service of virtue. Cicero seeks a statesmanship and eloquence that is marked by prudence, that is attached to and infused by the true human good *(honestate)*.[30] On such leadership depend the practicable best regime and whatever political well-being is possible. How to cultivate and develop that prudence—and primarily its link to true virtue—in those marked with the greatest talents for public leadership is clearly Cicero's dominant concern in his treatment of the education of the statesman/orator. What he provides in this respect is no less than an understanding of moral development, in which the just claims of the political community, the acclaim of others in the form of glory given, the role of friendship, and philosophy, all have important parts.

Developing the Prudent Statesman

Cicero's highlighting of prudence as the primary and defining quality of his model statesman and model orator constitutes, in effect, an emphasis on a state of soul or character as the key to what can be achieved politically. Above all, Cicero prizes and depends on the prudence of the leader for political well-being. Cicero appears to see this state of soul bearing its political fruit, shaping the entire way of life of the community, not simply through the acts and speeches of the leader, through, that is, the results of a proper civil and rhetorical prudence, but also through direct example of a well-ordered and just soul. Cicero states this directly, through Scipio, at the end of the second book of the *Re Publica*. Book 3, which could properly be called Cicero's book on justice and which appears to be concerned with the justice of political communities, is preceded and, in a sense, introduced by Scipio's insistence that the harmony which is justice in that prudent man's—the model statesman's—soul is to be source of it for the polity as a whole.[31] At this point, Scipio describes the single most important duty of the statesman *(rector)*, and one which encompasses all others, as being service as a moral exemplar. Given the use of exemplars in the form of actual historical figures, if somewhat idealized ones, in Cicero's own thought and writing, it is not surprising to find a theoretical statement, and an apparently strong one, on the leader's function as a moral exemplar.

Something that Scipio is made to say at this point, however, is especially significant in alerting the reader to the fact that the model statesman functions as a practicable goal and that *exempla* of the true statesman, in the form of actual historical figures, are, then, wholly appropriate and understandable. Cicero has not come to depend on that kind of a divine man whom Plato is thought to have utilized in his city in speech and from whom Cicero turned away earlier in *Re Publica*. Prudence as the soul's dominant quality is a check on unrealistic and, hence, foolish aspirations. What Scipio says is presented as a rule either equal in stature with the injunction to serve as an exemplar or as a primary instance of what it means to be such an exemplar. The statesman, says Scipio, is "never to cease from forming and examining himself" *(ut numquam a se ipso instituendo contemplandoque discedat)*. Thus, the model statesman's very virtue consists partly in his continual Socratic striving for self-understanding and moral improvement.[32]

This is no finished incorruptible philosopher-king, nor a Stoic perfect Wiseman, of whom Scipio speaks. It is a model on a more attainable, human plateau, yet the very incompleteness, the opening in this model to self-monitoring and self-improvement, reveals the usefulness of a concept of the model statesman/orator. The responsibility of self-improvement that rests on statesmen and potential statesmen entails the need for standards of excellence and virtue, for that concept of the perfect statesman who may have existed nowhere and to whom Cicero turned to express such standards.[33] As long as the perfect model includes the injunction to self-examination and self-improvement, and as long as the central and most important virtue of this model statesman is prudence, the model has a built-in protection against a corruptive and smug closure and against a dangerous stretching of the self toward an unrealistic and inappropriate personal standard.[34] In the ordinary human condition, it seems that prudence itself would acknowledge humankind's limitations with Socratic humility and would highlight the need and, where appropriate, the possibility for improvement. As the virtue of good choice, it leads to a developmental, and potentially progressive, context-sensitive approach to personal and political life. Cicero seeks to exemplify as well as to write about that leader, characterized above all by prudence.

Although in one sense the model statesman with his characteristic prudence is prior to the achievement of any instantiation of the best regime, the full story that Cicero tells reveals a mutual dependence of the statesman and the regime and the possibility of mutual interaction in what can be called a dialectic of development. The statesman's priority, which can make its strongest claim to truth in the case of origins or foundings and especially where he is seen as a direct divine instrument, has been accentuated hitherto in this analysis. The "shift in focus" to the statesman in Cicero's political thought was seen as motivated by a recognition that the model statesman is the proximate goal for political improvement—the primary means for attaining or maintaining the best practicable political order. In fact, any specific articulation of what constitutes the best practicable regime would seem to be a function of the prudence of a statesman. That model statesman cannot, however, finally be seen as independent of the surrounding social and political order. Assuming that this statesman is neither a god who descends among men nor a fabrication to be made regardless of the materials at hand, Cicero understandably sees him as one developed with the benefit of sound customs and laws. The innate sense of shame *(verecundia)*, the very seeds of virtue, will be nourished to development only under the sound institutions of good political communities.[35] In Scipio's words, "No one can live well except in a good polity...."[36]

Earlier in a passage, usually placed, on Augustine's authority, in Cicero's *prooemium* to the *Re Publica's* Book 5, Cicero makes a most succinct observation on the mutual interdependence of leaders and communities, noting that "...before our time, the ancestral tradition gave rise to outstanding men, and these in turn sought to preserve the traditions and practices of the past."[37] This summary view is, no doubt, an idealization of the Roman past that accordingly concentrates on preservation and that overlooks some of the shortcomings of men and practices in that past, which come to light elsewhere in the *Re Publica*, especially in the second book. If it were to be taken literally and comprehensively, the statement seems to envision a form of perfect moral-political circle, in which ancestral customs invariably give rise to model statesmen whose talents are solely devoted to preservation of those customs and never need to be turned to any task of modification or improvement of traditional ways. Such a picture is simply not consistent with the evidence that shows Cicero regarding self-understanding and the reading of nature in developmental terms, exhorting the statesman to continuing self-examination and improvement, and portraying the development of Rome's exemplary mixed constitution as a result of the contributions of many over a long period of time.

But one does not need to go beyond the one-page segment, in which this brief passage appears to see that Cicero cannot be taking such a moral-political circle as the simple picture of the past nor the one that can be simply entered in the present and future. The segment begins with a brief commentary on a line of Ennius proclaiming that the Roman political community *(res Romana)* stands on ancients customs and men *(viris)*. Cicero makes clear in what follows that the healthy Roman polity, which his generation inherited, could not have been founded or preserved for so long without good customs and laws as well as outstanding leaders. He regards it as fundamentally wrong to think that there can be a political achievement like Rome's with either traditions or men as the sole instrument. It is in this context that he observes, "...[B]efore our time, the ancestral tradition gave rise to outstanding men, and these in turn...." Throughout his lifetime, however, that Roman political community which was handed to him and his peers in a healthy state has not been renewed *(renovare)* nor its form and structure cared for and preserved. Not cared for and followed, the ancient ways, even it seems the structure and mode of operation of the *res publica*, drop from sight and are no longer understood. The great failure behind the lapse of the ancient constitution and ways is, for Cicero, the present scarcity of outstanding leaders *(virorum penuriam)*. It is not chance or destiny, adds Cicero, but our failings *(nostris vitiis)* that leave us "retaining the Roman polity in name, and having long since lost it in reality" *(rem publicam verbo retinemus, re ipsa vero iam pridem amisimus....)*.

If Cicero believed that the relationship between ancestral ways and outstanding men constituted some perfect moral-political circle, he would be hard pressed to explain how it came to unravel in his own lifetime. In other words, it would be hard for him to explain what we have seen is much on his mind, namely regime and institutional degeneration. Cicero is not, then, in his comments on ancestral ways and outstanding leaders simply holding out a view of a flawless, golden past to which current leaders must simply be devoted. His emphasis on recovery and preservation here, as we have seen elsewhere in his thought, reflects his judgment of what requires emphasis in his time—of a useful immediate political strategy. His larger theoretical intent is to draw attention to the interdependence of communal ways and statesman. The development of each, and the degeneration of each, is seen as a mutually interactive process: What has here been called the dialectic of development could as well be the dialectic of degeneration.

In Cicero's view, the mutual dependence of the community and the individual for their qualitative states is the core truth, underlying the teaching that the achievement of a good polity like Rome of the past is a collective achievement of many outstanding statesmen who build with the benefit of time and experience. Cato major, reports Cicero approvingly,

> taught that there never has existed so great a genius that at any point in time nothing would have eluded him, and that all of human ingenuity collected at a given time is not sufficient to provide that all things would be properly considered without the benefit of experience and the passage of time.[38]

For great political accomplishments, then, the statesman is dependent on the efforts of those who preceded and those who will follow him in contributing to the progressive realization of an attainable model.[39] This is clearly not an uncritical dependence on the past or tradition on Cicero's part, and it is probably more his qualified skepticism than his Roman ancestral piety which helps to explain his sensible deference toward cumulative experience interpreted by outstanding minds. The dependence on the past is specifically in relationship to the potential statesman's understanding and character, to, in other words, his prudence. For that critical dimension, his intellectual and moral development, he is dependent in significant ways on the polity that protects and educates him.

Friendship's Role in Statesmanship

An important theme for Cicero the political theorist concerns the mediation that friendship can, and likely needs to, provide if the political community is to be capable of having an effective role in developing and sustaining statesmanship. This is mediation between leaders and the political community on the one hand and potential leaders on the other. The space for friendship—the necessary liberties—would have to be secured by the political community for it to get, in turn, the benefits of friendship. Friendship, then, is the great communal or social requisite of statesmanship. Friendship, as such, entails not only excellent personal qualities such as the crown of prudence but also a form of human cooperation and interaction that is an apparent gift of the gods as much as is philosophy. What Cicero teaches about friendship seems to have been intended as a significant, if not decisive, step toward completing his political theory. He appears to have signaled its political importance by utilizing Scipio and Laelius as the major *personae* of his quasi-dialogue on friendship, which he titled *De Amicitia*.[40] Written some ten years after *De RePublica*, a period during which Cicero did most of his philosophical writing and many dialogues, he returned in *Amicitia* to give a central place to these two figures who had been so positioned in that earlier work.[41] Besides that tie, *De Re Publica* stands alone among Cicero's philosophical works in being explicitly invoked in *Amicitia;* Scipio's Dream at the end of *De Re Publica* and Laelius's defense of natural justice in the third book of *De Re Publica* provide the links between the works. *Amicitia* appeared shortly before Cicero's *De Officiis,* his last philosophical work, which contextualizes friendship within this moral treatise, specifically within justice, and directly refers readers back to *Amicitia* for the fuller treatment of friendship.[42]

Personal experience as well as Roman history and tradition seem to have contributed to Cicero's treating friendship explicitly and fitting it to his political theory at this late point in his life. Cicero dedicated *Amicitia* to his nearly life-long and dearest of friends, Atticus. Cicero has personally delighted in and benefitted from this deep relationship.[43] He has drawn on the tradition of the exemplary and close friendship between Scipio and Laelius. He utilized his contemporary Cato to expound in *De Finibus* the Stoic view that friendship, like justice, must be sought for itself. In *Amicitia,* genuine friendship is presented as giving rise to utility but not itself rising from utility. Where the useful or beneficial is the aim, "the sun" of true friendship cannot arise. Though it is the Epicurean calculus which takes the sun away that is chiefly on Cicero's mind, Atticus, his Epicurean friend, is among those who live better than their principles and thus has the capacity to be a true friend.

True friendship, for Cicero, is like the true statesmanship or the perfectly just political order, never realized completely; knowing its nature, however, is a critical need for the sake of action in the direction of living well or in accord with nature. Such a perfect friendship is defined by Laelius, in *Amicitia*, as "nothing other than an agreement (*consensio*) on all things human and divine, an agreement accompanied by good will (*benevolentia*) and affection (*caritate*)."[44] Recall from the *Re Publica* the definition of a republic or political community as a "joining of many people through an agreement on right and common interest" (*juris consensu et utilitate communione sociatus*).⁴⁵ Consent is seen to have a role in both of these social formations. Friendship, clearly, runs deeper and, thus, demands more in calling for agreement on the very nature of things.

That deep agreement would be, in the best of cases, about the true human end or genuine happiness. Fully comprehended and not something subject to majority opinion, that end is virtue with friendship, both as goods in themselves and as constituents of true happiness. As Cicero beautifully expresses this,

> Friendship was provided by nature as an aide to virtue, not an accomplice in wickedness; so it is that no solitary virtue but only one deeply allied with the other [friendship] can attain the greatest of goods. But if there be such a union, or if there ever was one or ever will be one, it must be regarded as the best and happiest of alliance toward the highest good of nature.⁴⁶

What is manifest in the ontological agreement expected in the best of friendships points to what must underlie the agreement in the right (*just*) that is a critical element in the basis of a genuine republic. Neither friendship nor the civil community can rest on arbitrary choices of any "sovereign" element, including that of majority public opinion.

Like the inclination to social and, thus, political community, the draw to friendship is not the result of a weakness or an immediate need but an inclination toward human fulfillment.⁴⁷ The germination of such a true friendship seems to stand in the tradition of Socrates's and Cicero's skeptical approach to philosophy and her claims. Knowing one's ignorance and knowing well, if anything, love—love of the beautiful and the good—which are the hallmarks of Socrates, appear to inspire the practical yet ennobled view of friendship in *Amicitia*. Uncharacteristic of Cicero's other work, *Amicitia* excludes overt mention of Greeks and Greek teachings and does not mention even Socrates by name. Yet it clearly refers to him three times under the title "the wisest of the Greeks."⁴⁸

Friendship among all citizens of a political community might be the tempting description of a perfect regime, but it is beyond reach and would, perhaps, simply have to be left as a mere "city in speech," a dangerous one at that. Aristotle and Cicero, both students of Plato, objected to this dimension of his alleged best regime. Yet friendship among individual citizens is more attainable than any uniting all citizens, even if this personal friendship, too, is never fully realized. It is this friendship that Cicero sees as able to contribute to the development and support of statesmen and, thus, to the progressive possibilities for the political community. It played a part in his life—most concretely and specifically through Atticus. It is necessary, however, for understanding the full impact of the operable concept of friendship for Cicero, to accept some attenuation of perfect friendship to see how such personal relations as that between a wider circle of close associates (for Cicero, Brutus, and Varro for example), correspondents, teachers, family rightly disposed, and students as exemplified in the young *personae* of many of Cicero's dialogues and the addressees of the *De Officiis,* can have some of the qualities of true friendship and can be parties in friendship. Cicero showed a clear understanding that friendship can be attenuated by physical separation or relatively few opportunities to live together or to have mutual exchanges in any way. The overall conditions for the highest form of friendship and for sustaining it are explored in *Amicitia*.[49] But above all, true friendship is rare because the attainment of virtue by persons and the meeting of the virtuous in circumstances that might generate friendship are themselves so rare.

True friendship or, in reality, an approximation to true friendship, is that relationship where mutual support is given in the ups and downs of pursuing the path of virtue in politics and where there is mutual encouragement in self-examination. It becomes an agent in not only sustaining the virtuous but also in passing virtue's ways, including the requisite knowledge for leadership, from generation to generation. In the epilogue to the long Scipio-inspired discourse by Laelius in *Amicitia,* the intergenerational dimension of the work of friendship is highlighted. Its placement here and its notable eloquence are indications of the likely great significance of this passage not only to Cicero's understanding of how the necessary virtue of the Republic or some future republic might be nourished and passed on but also to Cicero's self-understanding of what he was doing in these writings of his last years.[50] Laelius observes that the "law of our life and nature" is that one generation follows on another, that generations do not in their entirety drop away at once, and that they interpenetrate through friendships of the young with the old. Immediately after those observations, Scipio's absence through his sudden snatching by death is recalled, and Laelius insists that for him, Scipio yet "lives and will always live," for it is the "virtue of that man" that he loved and that remains alive and will be heralded into future generations.

While a good in itself and an aid to even greater things, friendship appears for Cicero to be the most important instrument in the micropolitics of Roman life, where constitutional development and leadership turn on political alliances and the give-and-take of personal interactions and relationships. Those alliances and interactions seem to have become terribly corrupted in the late Republic into forms of servile clientelism, bitter factionalism, and outright conspiracies for power and control. Perhaps that is not peculiar to Rome but is an ever-present possibility and, in fact, the reality, especially where political life is essentially free. The mutual support of friends in such a politics and their cross-generational enrichment and sustenance seems for Cicero truly the last and best hope.

However dependent Cicero's statesman is on the political community—for what he has become and what he can do in that community and for the rising generation—once the very personal role of friendship is seen as important, larger theses of cultural and social determinism become less credible. Cicero does not see the statesman as a mere captive and reflection—an epiphenomenon—of his polity's ways, nor does he see the statesman as a personally insignificant moment, instrument, or link in a larger historical process beyond human control. It is the "scarcity" of statesmen traced to "our failings" that Cicero has spoken of in describing the corruption of the ancient constitution in his time. The statesman to whom he looked has a freedom to be responsible and a capacity to choose well in the light of whatever circumstances he faces;[51] he is distinguished as a model statesman by various abilities of leadership and, above all, by his capacity for prudence and his will to pursue the political good by counsel and deeds. The virtues of both the true friend and the model statesman are constant even as circumstances and regimes vary; they are virtues known to a prephilosophic moral awareness, and it is this awareness that prevents a statesman from being simply the voice of a tradition and allows him to correct and improve it.

Cicero expects the model statesman to have the capacity to see beyond prevailing public views and to, in effect, be a leader of public opinion.[52] As a person distinguished by prudence, he is to be, after all, an interpreter of the nature's way. He cannot be simply and totally a child of his society and his time. Those gifted in genius by nature are seen by Cicero as best able to carry out such leadership as well as all the responsibilities of statesmanship. Perhaps with himself and clearly with Caesar very much in mind, Cicero elsewhere reports that those marked by natural genius are also especially moved by the love of glory—the praise of other human beings.[53] This is the Achilles' heel of the potentially model statesman, but it is also the instrument to which Cicero turns to develop genuine prudence in statesmen. Those with outstanding gifts, then, are capable of a crucial transcendence of their community and yet are drawn by their love of praise to the very standards and ways of the community around them. One might see in this the divergent pulls to philosophy and to political life experienced by some of the best-endowed people, like Cicero himself. Cicero's resolution of the tension in favor of a philosophically informed political life is not irrelevant to how he treats that love of glory which is so apt to lead the most talented astray. It seems that the most important thing a community could do for the development of statesmen is to turn that love of glory to a good end.

The Troubled Path of Glory

An interpretation that finds Cicero utilizing the love of glory as the chief instrument in the intellectual and moral development of the model statesman allows one to make sense out of his ambivalence and seemingly contradictory statements about this motive of the most talented. It also checks the tendency to see Cicero's approval of the love of glory as a simple concession to his own and Rome's oft-thought characteristic weakness. This is not to deny that Cicero's personal struggle with the love of glory is very much involved with his consideration of the topic. Plutarch had found Cicero's "passion for distinction" to be one of his chief character flaws.[54] In fact, Cicero's personal aspirations as a statesman, an orator, and a philosopher, as well as the struggles with his own weaknesses, seem to be much on his mind throughout his entire consideration of the model statesman; one could hardly expect otherwise from a Socratic, who insisted that philosophy was to be self-appropriated and fruitful in the direction of life rather than a mere intellectual or academic exercise. Cicero thought that the pursuit and love of glory had shaped his own life.[55] He wrote a work *De Gloria* which, save for some fragments, is lost to us. There are, however, substantial discussions of glory in the second book of *Officiis* and in the *Re Publica*, as well as less extensive reflections at other points in his works. Glory was clearly an important theme for him. His defense and use of the love of glory brought the censure of Augustine, and Petrarch consciously followed Cicero in his own ambivalence on the love of glory and personal struggle with it.

"The prospect of glory," writes Cicero, in arguing for public honors to encourage the arts, "moves all to efforts" *(omnesque incenduntur ad studia gloria)*, and those pursuits not generally esteemed will lie unattended.⁵⁶ Since the desire for glory is, according to Cicero, especially apt to arise "in the greatest souls and most brilliant minds" *(in maximis animis splendissimisque ingeniis)*,⁵⁷ one would expect that it could be instrumental to the greatest and most beneficial of human deeds. It is not, then, surprising to find Scipio in *Re Publica* viewing political accomplishments in this light. He claims that "many admirable and wonderful deeds were done by our ancestors moved by the desire for glory *(multa mira atque praeclara gloriae cupiditate fecisse)* and that "the statesman ought to be nourished on glory" *(principem civitatis gloria esse alendum)*.⁵⁸

Despite such achievements, actual and potential, through the instrumentality of the love of glory, Cicero kept ever before his readers the danger this desire poses. In those passages in the *Officiis* where he notes the frequent presence of the desire in the people most gifted by nature and seems to have especially Caesar in mind, he is found stressing the danger that justice will be pushed aside in the pursuit of glory and that the injustice from those so gifted is likely to be on a grand scale.⁵⁹ That most people lose sight of justice in pursuing glory was an axiom of Cicero's moral and political analysis. He found frequent examples of this: In his oration, *Pro Sestio*, he charges one Quintus Metellus with showing more concern for his own glory than for the evident public good, and later in the same speech he describes Publius Vatinius, one of his persistent enemies, as burning with the desire of glory *(flagrans cupiditate gloriae)* when he sought to act so as to win popular applause.⁶⁰ True and wise greatness of soul *(vera et sapiens animi magnitudo)* finds integrity and the right *(honestum illud)* not in glory, the applause of the ignorant multitude, but in actual deeds of virtue.⁶¹

The ambivalence in Cicero on glory can be seen in the statements of his Scipio throughout the *Re Publica*. He, who just above was seen remarking on how the desire for glory has wrought great achievements in the past and should be utilized to nourish the statesmen of the future, is made to observe that *cupiditas gloriae* is a disorder of the soul if it leads to rebellion against reason.⁶² More clearly at variance with those endorsements of glory above is Scipio's statement near the beginning of the dialogue that political and military offices—even the great ones—are not to be sought for rewards or glory but are to be submitted to out of duty.⁶³ This seemingly harsh or lofty view of the desire for glory reflects the understanding Scipio achieved with the aid of the shade of his grandfather as recounted in the Dream of Scipio at the end of the work.⁶⁴ There Africanus the grandfather, even as Scipio is reminded that his human duties—above all that of political leadership—are to be heeded as long as the soul yet lives in the body, leads him to a marvelous perspective on the universe of planets and stars, in which the earth is so very small. In the most important respects, this vision of the Dream is now literally accessible to us in the photography of the space age. The perspective is that of the true view of reality, and it is said by Africanus to await at least some souls after release from the body. While sharing the wonder-filled perspective of the universe with Scipio, Africanus rebukes him twice for keeping his attention too narrowly fixed upon the earth, and on the second occasion Africanus speaks directly to the passion for glory that this looking to earth represents in such a man as Scipio and other Roman leaders, as no doubt it once did for Africanus himself, the third-century Roman hero who brought down Hannibal. Amid the vastness of the cosmos—the very distances of the earth itself and the numberless generations that have preceded and will follow—Africanus sets the pursuit of glory among Roman leaders. In this perspective, that reveals the infinite and eternal dimensions embedding man, he shows the miniscule scope of the Roman Empire itself. Scipio is instructed to look always to the heavenly things and to despise those merely human. He is asked what glory there be that is really worth pursuing and is told that there is no glory worthy of the name in whatever transient fame one might attain among mere pockets of people on this vast earth.

These statements of Africanus prepare the way for introducing a concept of true glory, befitting humans in their very nature. This true glory is that which shines forth from one who is on the path of virtue *(ipsa virtus trahat ad verum decus)*. It seems to be the very splendor of virtue that Cicero highlighted elsewhere in his writings, in treating nature's inclinations and the attractiveness of the Stoic conception of happiness. Here, at the peak of the discourse of Africanus, there is a switch to the term *decus* in place of *gloria*, which had been used almost invariably to this point,[65] and *decus* is used again by Scipio in a brief response to Africanus that follows almost immediately and in which Scipio professes a life-long emulation of the glory *(decoris)* of Africanus. Continuing to use the cognate of *gloria* even after *decus* replaces *gloria* in the Latin text, as the two leading English translators do and as I have done here in paraphrasing,[66] appears to be useful if not necessary to make clear the evident continuity in the discourse from the glory of the world, which the leading Romans seek, to the attractive splendor or true distinction of virtue, which Africanus in the heavenly light of wisdom would have them seek. In fact, at places in other works where Cicero speaks in his own name of this apparent peak, he uses the literal phrase "true glory" *(vera gloria)*.[67] Here, in the Dream of Scipio, the movement signified by the introduction of *decus* is made even more emphatic by this term's initial use being preceded by *verum*.

Decus, in the light of other uses by Cicero, says much more than *gloria* about the nature of the peak or fulfillment suggested in the Dream. It seems to be a way of describing the beauty of the fullness of virtue such as is attainable among human beings—the beauty of the genuinely prudent person, that is, of the true statesman. In Cicero's work on the model orator, we found that *decus* stems from fidelity to the rule of rules of the rhetorical art, namely, to do what is appropriate and befitting, which was to include the moral dimension (i.e. speaking as befits distinctively human action). The appropriate truly decorates, or makes splendid, the speech and the orator.[68] The full moral significance of *decus*, which came to light, as one might expect, in the *Officiis*, was considered in Chap. 3. There, *decus* was found used in apposition to *honestas*, the right or overall virtue—the arch-rule and goal of human life—that which is wholly appropriate to and adorns a human being. At this point we are especially prepared to appreciate a dimension of the use of *decus* in *Officiis*. There, it appears in initial and provisional opposition to *gloria*: *Decus* is introduced with *honestas* in the first book, and *gloria* is presented and explored in the second as a major form of *utilitas*. The tension and ultimate reconcilability between the useful and the right appears to be represented in the relationship between *gloria* and *decus*. *Decus* is, then, a rich and key concept in the moral philosophy of Cicero, and it is introduced by Africanus at the peak of his discourse in the Dream to name the splendor of excellence—the shining of virtue—that is true and enduring glory.

Have we, however, come upon a contradiction in Cicero's *Re Publica*, as one commentator insists, between the negative judgment in the Dream on the desire for glory among humans and statements by Scipio earlier in the dialogue (but, of course, after the experience of the Dream), where this desire appears to be welcomed and even fed?[69] The partial and fragmented text we have of the *Re Publica* and the long independent textual histories of the Dream and the rest of the *Re Publica*,[70] not to speak of the convention of regarding Cicero's philosophical consistency with something less than respect, may make it easy to be content with this view that there is a fundamental contradiction at hand. But it is unnecessary to accept this view; it is possible to see Scipio's statements, and all of those in the dialogue relevant to glory, as plausibly consistent when seen in a framework that is shaped neither by an uncritical acceptance of the desire for the glory of humans nor by a simple contemptuous rejection of it. It is just such a framework of ambivalent appreciation for the desire for glory that has already been suggested as evident in the other statements of Cicero and in his own life. Attention to how the treatment of the love of glory can be seen as consistent in the *Re Publica* brings out how this love functions as an instrument in the development of the model statesman and opens to a fuller view of the deep unity of the *Re Publica* and the coherence of its major themes.

With the key passages in the *Re Publica* on the love of glory already before us, let us return to the beginning of the text as we have it. Cicero's preface to the first book, and plausibly to the entire *Re Publica*, shows him praising as exemplar statesmen certain famed Roman leaders of the past, including Scipio and Africanus, and the great deeds they performed for the safety of Rome. After specifically praising the legendary Cato and singling out his accepting the tempests and trials of public life throughout his years rather than escaping to the tranquil leisure readily available to him, Cicero remarks,

> I insist on this one point, nature has left humankind in such need of virtue *(necessitatem virtutis)* and has provided so strong an inclination for defending the common welfare *(amorem ad communem salutem defendendam)* that all the attractions of pleasure and leisure cannot overcome this force.[71]

This is likely the first conclusion, the first clear affirmation, in Cicero's opening preface; it is certainly that in the text, albeit fractured, as we have it.

If one were not led to ask at this point how does nature so provide or how does such an inclination arise, that question would be forced to the surface by the remainder of the *Re Publica* with its continual emphasis on the critical parts taken by Roman statesmen. Not only their heroic actions of great political significance, such as founding and revolution, but also their recurrent efforts in the development of the Rome's exemplary polity and in the necessary balancing and rebalancing of the mixed constitution in the face of changing circumstances brings the statesman to the center of attention. Those lost sections of the *Re Publica*, where the model statesman and his education were treated more extensively, must have considered the question "how does nature so provide?" so that nature's givens might be utilized in the development of statesmen for the present and future. It seems that in those *lacunae* there was even more of what we find in the fragments of Book 5, notably the observations of Scipio on the great deeds of ancestors wrought by *cupiditas gloriae* and the injunction to nourish the statesman on glory.

If there should not be, even in the *Re Publica's* missing portions, more detail on how nature provides for distinguished service to the polity, it would be because the answer was so evident to Cicero and other Romans. Their self-understanding was that desire for glory had accounted for Rome's collective achievements and for notable individual contributions to the leadership of the Roman polity. Cicero observes that like him Romans were greedy *(avidi)* for glory—greedy beyond the level that marked other nations. And Roman successes fed their desire for glory.[72] The Roman self-understanding seems also reflected in the observation of Cicero that the Roman people has already achieved the great glory that makes it stand out in the history of nations.[73]

If Cicero had thought the desire for glory simply bad, he or anyone seeking to be effective as leader or teacher in Rome would nonetheless have had to accept and build upon this trait. As we have seen, this desire for the glory that humans give is welcomed and utilized by Cicero through his Scipio in *Re Publica*. Elsewhere, Cicero makes clear that the quest for glory can draw men away from distractions and ordinary vices and draw them to public service.[74] Furthermore, the regard of other humans is presented as a useful asset that is not to be scorned in a happy and successful life.[75] The love of glory seems, then, to be an important instrument in the moral development of Cicero's model statesman.

Virtue as True Glory

Rarely, however, does Cicero mention the desire for glory, or employ it, without a direct or indirect cautionary note that presents success or popularity as not to be confused with true glory. Even when he praises Caesar, in the *Pro Marcello*, as one most greedy *(avidissimus)* for glory and one called to achieve a level of it well beyond the capacities of other men, he adds, as if to keep a doubt before the reader, "if indeed glory be that illustrious and widespread fame *(fama)* of great services either done for friends, for the nation or for humankind."[76] The positive side of this approach to glory is that Cicero is ever associating the way of true glory with the path of virtue. Even if glory were not to be sought, writes Cicero, "it follows virtue like a shadow."[77] Cicero endeavored to wed the desire for glory to the pursuit of virtue. Part of this effort of Cicero was to portray even the nation's glory as founded in virtue. Accordingly, Rome is said to stand out in history because of her virtuous ways.[78] Only through the joining of virtue and glory could the problematic nature—the evident ambivalence—of the desire for glory be overcome. Only in this joining could he himself be what he aspired to be. The factionalism and turmoil of his life, with so many talented leaders alternatively at each other's and the polity's throat, was but the latest and thus most vivid experience in a history of Rome, which reveals the truth that Rome needed not simply public leaders but virtuous leaders.

In Cicero's most explicit and extensive consideration of the desire for glory—a segment of the *Officiis* introduced by him as an apparent summary of important points of his now lost work *De Gloria*—he analyzes glory so as to reveal why the desire for it can be made, on its own terms and not simply because it is useful to the community's good, to transform itself into the pursuit of virtue. Every aspect of glory—namely the love, confidence, and genuine admiration of the people—depends ultimately, as to whom they are directed, on the fact that all of our souls are drawn to virtue. "And the love of the many," writes Cicero,

> is deeply stirred by any indication and reputation of generosity, kindness, justice, fidelity and of all those virtues that reveal a gentle and obliging character. Since that very quality which we call the right and befitting *(honestum decorumque)* is itself pleasing to us and attractive to the souls of all by its nature and beauty, and appears especially splendid in those virtues just noted, we are brought by nature itself to love those in whom we think such virtues reside.[79]

Cicero, thus, is found teaching that the enlightened path to glory, even as glory is ordinarily understood, is the road of virtue. It is interesting to notice, primarily to appreciate the stark difference from Machiavelli, that Cicero twice explicitly rejected fear as a mode of commanding public support in favor of the virtuous path to public affection and support, which he thought to be more reliable.[80]

Cicero's hardly surprising conclusion, concerning the public's high regard for those leaders who manifest virtue, has recurrently given rise in human experience to interest in the appearance of virtue rather than the substance of it. That elemental point has not been lost on Machiavelli or the run-of-the-mill politician. Nor was it an undetected possibility for Cicero, but he took the position, citing Socrates, that the best way to appear virtuous is to be virtuous.[81] And so an appeal to utility rightly understood continues to operate in his argument. The overall argument with which Cicero reached out to glory-seeking Romans cannot and does not, however, offer individuals surety of success in terms of worldly glory. There are at least two problems, both of which Cicero himself noted, regarding the course he commended as a fail-safe technique of achieving glory. He observes—and this necessarily brings his personal experience to mind—that being virtuous is often not sufficient for glory. One must also be skillful or fortunate—or even both—in the process of bringing one's qualities before the public,[82] and then too, circumstances and the disposition of the public are not always such that virtue will be rewarded even if it is perceived. Despite the long-term or general truth in his argument that the public wants and honors virtue, at given times and even through the entire lifetimes of individuals, the public, often because it is misled, will fail to honor those whom it truly wants and needs to hold up. This is why Cicero writes that it is the praise of the good and wise that must be sought if one is following the path of virtue: they provide a better measure that one is on the right path.[83]

Cicero's awareness of these problems, illustrative of the difficulty of an individual's reconciling the pursuit of earthly glory with the path of virtue, does not mean that his appeal to glory-seeking Romans is a kind of noble lie or simply an exoteric teaching. Cicero appears to have believed that the most probable means of securing glory, in most circumstances, is the way of virtue. That probability increases when glory is located in a public esteem that transcends the popular favor or disfavor of one's own limited lifetime—an esteem, then, that represents at least a partial realization of immortality. To be memorialized—to be remembered: this is the immortal glory that Rome's leading men ever sought through their own deeds and through the great city itself. Although virtue would likely be glorified more in the context of the long-term regard of the people and one's polity than in one where immediate applause is glory's measure, still a simple congruence of virtue and glory cannot be assured until glory is found in virtue itself.

Scipio, in *Re Publica* and specifically in the shift from *gloria* to *decus*, represents the process of coming to locate glory in virtue. Philosophy represented by the perspective on human affairs, which Scipio is led to take, provides the understanding and the confidence for affirming virtue as the true glory of man.[84] In this we see Cicero's own very rhetorically powerful statement on what he regards as the foundational question for all philosophy: that concerning the genuine happiness and the true end of human actions. The Dream, both the vision beheld and the admonitions and exhortations of Scipio's grandfather and father, provides a poetic statement of the most important fruit that Cicero sought from philosophy. It represents what philosophy can do for the potential statesman. Philosophy elevates rather than denigrates the duties of public leadership;[85] what it denigrates is a focus on human glory. The Dream is a statement of an enlarged or deepened self-understanding, as the self is seen in the larger context of the wholeness of nature.

De Re Publica presents the possibility of an ascent through several types of glory, which can motivate potential statesmen. All humans are moved by praise and acclaim, and this cannot be ignored in educating potential statesmen. One should, it seems, seek through what is praised, by the examples set before potential statesmen and by showing them the deep public yearning for virtue and hence the inclination to honor virtue, to transform that desire for glory—notably strong in the most talented—into the pursuit of virtue. A more complete and assured transformation, however, could be found in making virtue itself glorious. Perhaps the practice of virtue induced by the praise of the wise and the good can draw people to delight in virtue itself. It would not be surprising to find Cicero making this point, but what he does clearly say through Scipio and the Dream and what he also support throughout his writings is that philosophy is necessary for self-understanding and for attaining a true perspective on human affairs. His call is for a Socratic statesman, and his very emphasis on the role of the statesman emerges from a Socratic way of life and orientation to his inquiry. Through philosophy, virtue can be seen, to the degree humanly possible, as its own glory, as a satisfying goal in itself. Ascent to this conception of true glory is not only to attain the genuine object of individual desire but also to provide for the public need for virtue, for only in this way would virtue be protected from the ever dangerous propensities of mere glory-seekers. The ascent to a true conception of glory cannot be seen as easily accomplished or as entirely possible while humans are yet set on this earth. Scipio's ascent was aided by the gifted presence of Africanus, a divinized ancestor. To teach about the ascent, specifically for statesmen, and to strive for it personally, as Cicero himself did, are forms of endeavoring to achieve the goal Plato outlined, the joining of power and philosophy, and in this case, in the context of republican politics. The Socratic Scipio is for Cicero more the practicable human model than any divine philosopher-king in the manner of a perfect Stoic Wiseman.

The Dream provides a perspective not only on the individual—on a Scipio and Cicero—but also, as we have already seen, on Rome and her aspirations. Although Scipio is called several times for a renewed commitment to the Roman *patria* and to his duties there, this is done from a horizon that transcends Rome—a horizon not so clearly in evidence throughout the preceding books of the *Re Publica*. The perspective of philosophy in the Dream provides a basis for checking the recurrent slide to a blinding and self-destructive pride in individuals and nations. Furthermore, virtues seen in the horizon of philosophy can no longer be centered in the survival and well-being of particular polities, unless those communities, in some way, embody or serve what nature requires for humankind. Cicero's shaping of the virtues appears to carry the tradition of classical philosophy yet further from a heroic ideal and from being instruments of narrow patriotism. This dimension of the virtues comes especially to the fore in his exposing "the gentle and obliging character" to *honestas*. It is Cicero, also, who could praise compassion (*misericordia*) as a virtue and way to glory and who could also be attracted by the example of Regulus who accepted death rather than break a promise given to an enemy.[86] One sees, in this drawing of the classical virtues away from the heroic ideal and in a number of Cicero's other ideas like that of a transcendent perspective on one's particular polity and that of a universal human community, some important reasons why notable early Christian thinkers welcomed his thought and worked from it.

One final point about the perspective of the Dream concerns the suggestion of personal immortality, which is implied in the very fabric of this part of the dialogue. The "living" Africanus, and the attribution of that quality to others who have died, seems for Cicero to be more than useful literary license. At certain other times, when he wrote of the quest for immortal glory, he half-playfully and half-seriously entertained the thought that such glory would be worthwhile only if its seeker continues to be conscious to enjoy it, and he delights in that possibility.[87] In the end, Cicero's Academic skepticism appears to apply to this matter: There is no certain way of knowing this immortality. Yet after his model Socrates, Cicero hopes for such immortality and thought it a likely truth.[88] Having been led to see true glory in *decus* and *honestas*, Scipio introduces his recounting of this experience, his Dream, observing that "[T]though awareness of one's own splendid deeds is sufficient reward for the wise, yet- such god-like virtue seeks not statues cast in lead or triumphal processions of fading laurels, but some more stable and enduring type of reward."[89] Here, the very passage, in which Cicero's Scipio affirms that "awareness of one's own splendid deeds is sufficient reward for the wise," appears to raise a doubt about the claim. It is not, of course, the traditional

Roman "statues cast in lead or triumphal processions" that are sought. What Scipio, the advocate of Socratic learning, seems to confess is that the possessor of a "god-like virtue" yearns to share in a god-like existence.

NOTES

1. Plato, *Apology of Socrates*, 31^d–32^a.
2. Crassus, compared with Scipio, appears to be Cicero's yet more practical and, hence, even more Roman Socrates; see *De Or.* 1. 204, 3.15–16, where he is treated as a model of his type and explicitly compared with Socrates even as he is differentiated. See DiLorenzo's treatment of Crassus (1978: 247 ff.) as a Ciceronian model in contrast with Socrates. Crassus, then, is not only called upon to describe the perfect orator in *De Or.*, but also, appropriately for Cicero who always prefers the voice of experience and achievement in such discussions, is seen to best approximate this orator. Mitchell (1991: 46) argues that Crassus, even more than Scipio, is the model that Cicero holds up for himself and other Roman leaders. At one point (*Off.* 2. 47) Cicero compares Crassus favorably with Demosthenes, whom he regards as the closest approximation ever (*Orat.* 6, 23; *Brut.* 35) to the perfect orator. Demosthenes, though a Greek, is seen by Cicero as a philosophical statesman; his oratory was informed and enriched by his having sat at the feet of Plato (*Orat.*15; *Brut.*121). On the other hand, Cicero prefers Demosthenes over Isocrates and Lysias, the other prominent Greek orators, chiefly, it seems, because he utilized his rhetorical abilities for direct participation in the contentions of public life, in contrast with their exclusive devotion to the writing of speeches (*De Optimo Genere Oratorum* 17; *Brut.* 32–35).
3. *Off.* 2. 43.
4. In dialogues, especially the *Rep.* and *De Or.*, where the model statesman comes to have a central role, Cicero can be seen, in his choice of *personae* and of what they are portrayed doing and saying, to exemplify certain qualities before he specifies them directly. The analysis that draws him to exemplify use certain *exempla* must always interest us more than the *exempla* themselves in endeavoring to understand Cicero's thought. T. White's observation, noted in the previous chapter, that Cicero uses "historical exemplum" for "explanatory efficacy" and for the legitimization of the concept at issue by testifying to its "workability" is applicable to the concept of model statesman, as well as that of model regime. Whatever liberties Cicero may take with history in accord with his rhetorical purpose—such as overlooking flaws of character or the much commented upon harmonizing of relationships between the Cato major and Scipio and his friends—

would seem limited by the same rhetorical purpose. Manifestly incredible claims for historical figures may threaten explanatory efficacy and would clearly undermine *exempla* serving as evidence of the workability of a concept like that of the model statesman.

5. *Rep.* 2. 51.
6. *Rep.* See the indications of this in the extant fragments of Book 5 and at 2. 51, 66–67.
7. *Rep.* 2. 65 ff.
8. *Rep.* 2. 67.
9. *Rep.* 2. 45. That Scipio all along has been most interested in the possession by leaders of such political prudence sheds new light on his great interest in Plato as manifested in the first book, in a long direct quotation concerning the degeneration of democracy from *The Republic*. A Plato describing the courses and changes of regimes is more relevant to the useful political knowledge Scipio and Cicero seek than a Plato detailing the provisions of the city in speech. Scipio has wanted, from the start of the *Re Publica*'s dialogue, to bring the discussion around to the political leader whose prudence, above all other qualities, is the critical quality in good political practice understood as moving, as best as one can, to attain or preserve the practicable best regime. Again, the reason of the prudent man encompasses the less than reasonable tendencies of political life, in this case, those ever-recurring tendencies to regime-instability.
10. *Inv.* 1. 2.
11. Barlow (1987: 367) has aptly portrayed Cicero as seeing a need "for a virtually continuous process of refounding." Regime maintenance ever takes new forms with the continual changes that time brings. Recalling that Cicero (*Leg.* 1. 18–19) sets the standard of justice as "the mind and reasoning of the prudent man," that man "who combines the art of ruling with knowledge of nature," Barlow observes (369) that in practice, "the unchanging standard gives rise to manifestly changeable results." In a similar vein, Wood (1988) notes that the long-term goal of Cicero's statesman is the preservation of the "moderation and balance" of the mixed constitution (193), and that the leading men charged with this responsibility are not a law unto themselves but servants of "a supreme law" (189). The "continuous refounding," which Cicero's statesman engages in, should not be seen as merely reactionary or checking evil tendencies, as Cumming suggests (1969: I, 274, n. 28). Also, see Ferrary (1995: 55–56, 62–63).That Cicero is most open and emphatic about the statesman's protective, preservative function can readily be taken to support the long-standing charge that his own political practice was flawed by a blindness to the Republic's incapacities to deal adequately with the problems of the time. There is no definitive way to deny this charge and the possibility that Cicero's political

thought was itself infected with his weakness. There is, however, another way to think about his emphasis on the preservative function of the statesman's prudence. The dramatic date for the *De Re Publica* is 129 B.C., a time which Cicero and others before and after him regarded as politically healthy and largely, though not entirely, prior to the political troubles that came ever increasingly to unsettle Roman politics and eventually to undo the Republic. It is, then, dramatically consistent with Cicero's view of the Roman Republic as an exemplary achievement that the perspective of 129 would emphasize regime maintenance in the face of various incipient threats. This is not, however, to forego the possibility and likelihood that Cicero was comfortable emphasizing regime maintenance to his readers of the 50s. This could very well be an important prudential act of Cicero himself, for while he clearly holds to an understanding of philosophy and virtue that admits of progressive possibilities, the requisite setting for such developments is a stable regime where liberties are protected; thus, the fundamental stance of Cicero is one of holding to the Republic as the best available basis for the kind of personal developments critical to Rome's political health. One might say that preservation of a certain kind of regime, the mixed traditional constitution, implies progressive possibilities.

12. *Off.* 3. 71, 1.153; *Fin.* 5. 17–18, 67–68. A reader may be puzzled by Cicero's seemingly interchangeable use of *prudentia* and *sapientia*, which is in evidence in the previous paragraph's alternate descriptions of the political leader as *prudens* and *sapiens* and which is present throughout his writings. The virtually synonymous use of these terms (Mitchell, 16) is especially evident at *Off.* 1. 15–16, where Cicero uses both terms in discussing the customary virtue concerned with the investigation and discovery of truth *(indagatio atque inventio veri)*, that which is generally rendered as the virtue of wisdom. The basic virtue is exclusively called *prudentia* and understood with respect to good and evil at *Inv.* 2. 160, this being the very work in which Cicero has characterized the political founder as *sapiens*. When he has occasion to define these terms separately, a distinct understanding of each is clear: *Prudentia* is defined as here in the text; *sapientia* (as at *Tusc.* 5. 7) as "the knowledge of things divine and human as well as the beginnings and causes of all things." At *Off.* 1.153, Cicero has occasion to directly distinguish and define *sapientia* and *prudentia*, citing as he does it the Greek distinction between *sophia* and *phronesis*.

Citing *Off.* 1.153 but seeking to explain the Stoic usage rather than Cicero's, Striker claims that the Stoics consistently understood *phronesis* "as knowledge of things to be done and not done, or knowledge of goods and evils, rather than knowledge of truth and falsehood and of the order of the universe" and that they "must have held that *sophia* includes *phronesis*"

(1991): 42–43, n. 25; also Long and Sedley (1987: vol. 1: 379–80, Stobaeus, 61G). The true Wiseman in the Stoic tradition would of course possess prudence as well as all the other virtues, and this connection between *sapientia* and *prudentia* may well account for some of the interchangeable usage of these terms in Cicero's texts. At *Leg.* 2. 8, *sapientia* is used to describe both understanding of the law of the universe and understanding of what is to be sought and what is to be avoided.

There is a suggestion, in the phrasing of *Off.* 1.153, that Cicero regards the distinction as more Greek than Roman. That Cicero knows the distinction between these terms and can employ it but does not consistently do so (for instance in *Inv.* and *Off.*, the first and last of his philosophical writings) may well reflect the elevation of prudence in his thought, which reflects the role of the practical perspective, his Socratic way into all philosophy. For Cicero, prudence is wisdom in its most useful mode (philosophy must teach duties), and it is to be the basis for judgements about the truth of the ultimate and divine things. Yet Cicero does seem to understand knowledge of self, on which prudence rests, as capable of development insofar as one comes to understand the whole of which the self is a part (*Leg.* 1. 60). For Cicero, prudence is not merely derivative from some more comprehensive wisdom; rather, there is mutual dependence and dialectical relationship between prudence and wisdom, and if one may speak of a core or foundation to wisdom, it is, as Socrates exemplified, prudence.

Insofar as there is a distinction in Cicero between *sapientia* and *prudentia*, it bears a close correspondence between the two tasks of philosophy evident in his work and treated above at the beginning of the second chapter. That wisdom not only begins in prudence but also ends in it seems to be entailed in his teaching on *perfecta philosophia*. Recall that the elder Cato, without formal philosophy, was called *sapiens Cato* and was spoken of both as unexcelled in prudence *(nemo prudentior)* and one marked by complete or mature wisdom *(perfecta sapientia)*.

13. *Div.* 1.111; also *Leg.*1. 60 and the fragment from Nonius placed at *Rep.* 6.1. Since prudence does not result from comprehensive and assured knowledge, it seems inappropriate to describe the providence of the divine mind as prudence: *Nat. D.* 2.58; 3.38.
14. Internal evidence in these three works as well as Cicero's direct statement support the conclusion that these are his major rhetorical writings; Cicero's statement occurs at *Div.* 2. 4, where, as he is listing his philosophical works, he remarks that, following Aristotle and Theophrastus, he believes his "oratorical books" should be included and enumerates them as "the three books of the *De Oratore*, a fourth, the *Brutus*, and a fifth, the *Orator.*" *Div.* was written when, it appears, all of the seven works traditionally known as the rhetorical works had already been completed. Evidence internal to the

texts of these three major works suggests that Cicero sought to link them together so that the three taken as a whole represent a five-book statement by him on the art of rhetoric and the perfect orator.

15. The main conversation in the *De Or.* seems to be one in which young potential statesmen learn from old accomplished statesmen that more is necessary for true eloquence than what the teachers of rhetoric say, and for that matter, what most people believe. Philosophy comes to be defended in a conversation among public leaders with no philosophers present. In the discussion of the art of rhetoric by the more Roman and practical speaker of the major participants in the dialogue, namely, Antonius, recommendations emerge that point beyond the common art of rhetoric as such: The orator who is virtuous, who knows human nature so as to know his audience better, who knows well the material he is likely to be called to discuss, and who possesses sense enough to judge rightly what is befitting a given context is one most able to use successfully art of rhetoric. Crassus, the other major speaker, in his treatment of the art emphasizes the importance of knowing the material to which one is applying the art of rhetoric and being able to follow the befitting or appropriate in all matters. Crassus explicitly draws the conclusion to which the analysis of Antonius appears to point, that is, that the orator will be best equipped with both knowledge and prudence when he has studied the most important questions about all things, when he becomes, in other words, the philosopher.

The *Brutus*, a history of orators revealing more failures than successes, supports the thesis of *De Or.*, namely that it is a difficult and great accomplishment to be a perfect or true orator. This work, dedicated to that potential statesman, the prominent Brutus of Cicero's own lifetime, concludes (330-33) with Cicero admonishing him to set himself off from common pleaders and to seek the distinction in oratory that so very few in the entire history of Greece and Rome have achieved. The *Orator* begins with Cicero indicating that he is responding to a request of Brutus for a portrayal of the perfect orator.

16. Books 2 and 3 of *De Or.* are said, by Cicero himself (*Att.* 89), to be a technical discussion; technical aspects are clearly present especially in the second book where Antonius treats three of the five traditional parts of the art of rhetoric: invention, arrangement, and memory; Crassus in the third book is called upon to discuss ornamentation and delivery. *Inv.* 1. 9 and 2. 178 indicate that this work of Cicero's early years was to be part of a larger treatise on rhetoric. See also *Part. Or., Top.* and parts of *Orator* for Cicero's involvement with the technical aspects of the art.

17. *De Or.* 1.113-34, 137, 146; 2. 30, 84-87, 147, 150; 3. 209; *Brut.* 320.

18. *De Or.* 1.48, 60, 63; 2. 37, 337; 3. 54; *Orat.*15, 118; *Brut.*143-44; *Part. Or.*140; *Inv.* 2. 25.

19. *De Or.*1.159, 165 ff. 201; 2.1–9, 60, 66–68, 333–37, 342–49, 363; 3. 54, 75–76, 122, 125, 145; *Orat.* 47, 70, 118–20, 141; *Brut.*150, 155, 161, 167, 322; *Part. Or.* 62–67, 71–100, 129–31, 140.
20. *Orat.*12.
21. This is the quality, Crassus is made to say (*De Or.* 3. 91), that brings a speech to the peak of excellence. See also *De Or.* 1.132; *Orat.* 71, 73–74, 123; *Off.* 1.128–29.
22. *De Or.* 2. 86, 333; 3. 204, 210–12, 221; *Orat.* 24–32, 47, 71–74, 100, 119, 123, 226; *Brut.* 202 (The orator may even distort to speak overall in an appropriate fashion, 42, 62); *Part. Or.* 30, 129.
23. As the speaker determines appropriateness by attention, above all, to his objective, that being persuasion in most instances, so does the human being determine appropriateness in all actions by attention to the ultimate end, that being the proper understanding of happiness.
24. *De Or.* 1. 5 in Cicero's *prooemium*; see also *De Or.* 1.132; 2.131, 307; 3. 95, 212; *Orat.* 44, 70, 101; *Brut.* 93.
25. *Fin.* 4. 76.
26. *Orat.* 44; also *Brut.* 23 where Brutus is portrayed as recognizing that prudence is necessary for the orator just as it is for the general.
27. *Verr.* 2. 4. 98; *Rep.* 1. 27–28; 2. 36; *De Or.* 3. 21; Gwynn (1926: 5); Marrou (1956: 98–99) on *humanitas* as the fullness of culture and its pursuit being a continuing lifetime task; also. Nicgorski, (2013a: 18 ff).
28. We have reached a point at which it is possible to understand better the nature of my disagreement with those who claim that rhetoric provides the unifying perspective in Cicero's thought. Both rhetoric and philosophy are for Cicero justified and unified within the need for statesmanship; one might say that, rather than a "rhetorical culture," it is a "political culture" that informs all of Cicero's thinking including that on the art of rhetoric.
29. *De Or.* 1. 47, 63; 3. 60, 72, 122, 129; Crassus is the spokesman in all the preceding passages, save the last in which a minor figure in the dialogue makes the point in the form of recapitulating what Crassus has said. Though Cicero seems to implicate Plato as part of the object of his criticism (*Orat.* 12–13), his statement at this point is a mixed one that also acknowledges that Plato has done much for the enrichment of rhetoric. Overall, on the relationship of rhetoric and philosophy, and specifically in *De Or.*, Crassus seems to look primarily to Plato for direction. In this respect, the central teaching of the *Phaedrus* seems to be a model for Cicero, for the art of rhetoric in the service of the good and the true is also what Cicero ultimately commends. *De Or.* is explicitly given a dramatic setting like that of the *Phaedrus* (*De Or.* 1. 28). Appreciative acknowledgements of Plato also mark the beginnings of the *Brutus* (24) and the *Orator* (3–10). Cicero is, then, quite aware of a fuller and more positive teaching

of Plato about rhetoric than that which he and many have seen in the *Gorgias*. Perhaps the excessive criticism of the art of rhetoric and the contemptuous tone toward it that Crassus finds in the *Gorgias* reflect a then prevalent way of reading Plato's teaching in that work—an interpretation which Cicero wants to check in a fashion similar to his apparent concern to correct a general view of what Plato is teaching in *The Republic*. This is not to say that he does not hold Socrates/Plato somewhat responsible for the way their teaching is being understood.

Though the fragmentation of knowledge and excessive specialization is seen as the primary harmful effect of the criticism of rhetoric in the *Gorgias*, Crassus himself holds Plato up (*De Or.* 3. 20–22, also 1.193–94) as a teacher of the unity and interrelatedness of all knowledge; Socrates's practice as a teacher (*De Or.* 1. 139) also tends to hold learning and eloquence together. One might say that Plato develops the best elements in Socrates: At *Ac.* 1. 7–19, Varro—the student of Antiochus, a professed restorer of the Old Academy, and the learned friend of Cicero to whom this work is dedicated—speaks of Plato as developing philosophy in its wholeness and taking a part in the development of a system, characteristics that are said to differentiate him from Socrates.

30. *Inv.* 1. 1; *De Or.* 1. 31–34.
31. *Rep.* 2. 69; also *Leg.* 3. 21–32; *Tusc.* 5. 47.
32. Benardete (1987: 308) sees self-knowledge as the hallmark of the Socratic philosopher to whom Cicero is attracted.
33. Cumming (1969: 263, 279 n.72, 285) sees Cicero as identifying the ideal statesman with certain real statesmen of Roman history. Cicero's more practicable model is not, however, wholly captured by any specific historical instantiation (*Orat.* 7–10), though it is best exemplified by Roman historical examples. My argument in this section seems, then, to provide a plausible resolution to the difficulty encountered by How (1930), when he finds (41) Cicero, at times, writing of the statesman as "a purely ideal figure" and at other times treating his concept with "plain references" to specific historical personages. At this same point, How makes the interesting observation that

> Cicero's *princeps* is an unofficial leader, swaying the state by his wisdom and the prestige of his past services, as did Scipio in his last years, or Cicero himself in the struggle with Antony, not a magistrate however exalted. It is, I think, significant that there is not a word of any such magistracy in the constitution laid down in the *Laws*. Cicero's statesman need not, it seems, be a magistrate, that is an actual holder of political office, but it would be going too far and in the face of other textual evidence to conclude that he cannot, by definition, be a magistrate.

34. The *perfecta philosophia* or *perfecta sapientia* of a Cato or a Scipio or a Crassus would presumably be characterized by prudence, by a "perfection" befitting human—not simply divine—excellence.
35. *Off.* 2. 15; *Rep.* 5. 6; *Leg.* 3. 4–5. Without such support, the seeds or sparks of virtue have been known to be extinguished; see *Leg.* 1. 28 ff. and *Tusc.* 3.1 ff. Also, Ferrary (1995: 64).
36. *Rep.* 5. 7.
37. *Rep.* 5. 1–2.
38. *Rep.* 2. 2.
39. Barlow (1987: 367).
40. Called here a "quasi-dialogue" because so much of it consists in two long discourses by Laelius, the content of which came largely from what he recollected Scipio had said about friendship before his very recent death. Scipio is present only through his ideas and some of his actual words now being remembered. A close analysis of the entire *Amic.* is found in Nicgorski (2008), to which certain parts of this section of the book are indebted.
41. The only other use of the *personae* of Scipio and Laelius by Cicero is in *De Senectute*, where they have a minor role as facilitators of the opening of a discourse by Cato Major.
42. *Off.* 1. 55–56; 2. 30–31.
43. The depth of this attachment and how it parallels features of friendship in *Amic.* can be sampled in *Att.* 18, 164; at times Cicero and Atticus exchanged letters on a daily basis.
44. *Amic.* 20.
45. *Rep.* 1. 39.
46. *Amic.* 83.
47. *Amic.* 22, 26–27, 31, 47, 87–88.
48. *Amic.* 7, 10, 13.
49. A much fuller exploration of these conditions is found in Nicgorski (2008).
50. *Amic.* 100 ff.
51. Note how Cicero himself, so deeply respectful of past thinkers and leaders and of the Roman tradition, regards his own independence from such precedents. See *Orat.* 169–70 where Cicero, after professing his deference to the authority of age and antiquity's precedents, says that he does not demand of antiquity what it lacks but praises what it has *(Nec ego id quod deest antiquitati flagito potius quam laudo quod est....)* and seeks to be free to criticize antiquity. Note *Arch.* 15–16, where Scipio is among those natural geniuses who are capable of a certain critical independence from the learning and formative power of their communities.
52. *Fin.* 2. 49–50; *Orat.* 237–38; *Tusc.* 3. 3; 5. 104–05.
53. *Off.* 1. 26, 65.

54. Plutarch (1960: 118 [3]).
55. *Att.* 17.
56. *Tusc.* 1. 4. In *Arch.* 26, Cicero emphasizes how desire of praise extends to all by wondering why philosophers write their names on the very books in which they condemn the love of glory (also see, *Tusc.* 1. 34–35).
57. *Off.* 1. 26.
58. *Rep.* 5. 9.
59. *Off.* 1. 64–65; 26.
60. *Sest.* 37, 134.
61. *Off.* 1. 65.
62. *Rep.* 1. 60; *Tusc.* 4. 37–48.
63. *Rep.* 1. 27.
64. *Rep.* 6. 13–29.
65. *Rep.* 6. 25–26. Regarding the prior use of *gloria* in the text, the only exception appears to be at 3. 6–7, where derivatives of *laus* (praise) and *ornare* (to honor) are used; Laelius is the speaker at this point in the dialogue. Leeman (1949: 186), writing about the concept of glory in Roman society, spoke of aspects of it being designated

> by various terms *(fama, laus, honor, claritas)* as in Greek. Glory and its aspects are only parts of a wide range of notions characteristic of the relations between citizen and society in Rome, like *gratia, potentia, potestas, auctoritas, dignitas, honor.* In this group the specific importance of *gloria* is that of designating the (subjective) splendour and the (objective) acknowledgement as a consequence and a reward of extraordinary virtue…

Shortly prior to this, Leeman noted, "[T]he transition from 'splendour' to 'fame' is essentially a change of subject and object, a well-known phenomenon in language." Leeman did not note *decus* as a possible substitute for or aspect of *gloria*. He has suggested in the comments above that there is a residual notion of *gloria* in Roman usage that distinguished it from *fama* and associated it with *virtus*. In the face of a looser popular usage of *gloria*, it seems that Cicero may have sought to bring this residual notion to the forefront with the term *decus* and with the phrase *vera gloria*.

66. Sabine and Smith (1929) and Keyes (1959). The recent translations by Powell (1990) and by Rudd (1998) follow this convention in its rendering of *verum decus* in the first of the two usages of *decus* in *Rep.* 6. 25–26, while those of Zetzel (1999) and Fott (2014) translate the phrase as "true honor."
67. See, for example, *Off.* 2. 43; *Sest.* 139. Cicero does not invariably do this. Sometimes he makes the same point in another way, as in *Tusc.* 3. 3 (also

to a degree at 5. 104–05) where he distinguishes *popularis gloria* and *solida gloria*. At *Fin.* 3. 56–57, Cicero has Cato expounding Stoic views and claiming that *bona fama* is a better Latin rendering of the Stoic school's *eudoxia* than *gloria*.
68. *De Or.* 1. 132, 3. 212.
69. Leeman (1949:185, also 188) observes, "Moreover contradictions exist between the attitude towards glory in the *Somnium* and the rest of the *De Republica*, where it is judged of in a positive sense." It appears that Leeman did not notice certain statements of Scipio (*Rep.* 1. 27, 60) considered above, which indicate the same or a very similar attitudes toward glory in the Dream and early in the *Rep.*
70. Our major source for the extant *Rep.*, the Vatican manuscript discovered in 1820, does not contain the Dream, which comes through a separate manuscript tradition; see Powell (1990: 119, 133).
71. *Rep.* 1. 1.
72. *Leg. Man.* 7.
73. *Leg. Man.* 6; *Sest.* 143.
74. *Sest.* 138; *Rep.* 4. 6–7; *Fin.* 5. 69.
75. *Off.* 2. 31 ff.
76. *Marcell.* 25–26.
77. *Tusc.* 1. 109–110; also *Arch.* 14–15; *Sest.* 143.
78. *Verr.* 2. 4. 81.
79. *Off.* 2. 32 ff.; see also *Amic.* 28–29.
80. *Off.* 2. 24–26; *Phil.* 1. 33.
81. *Off.* 2. 43.
82. *Off.* 2. 44 ff.; *Leg. Man.* 47.
83. *Tusc.* 3. 3 ff.; *Att.* 17; *Sest.* 137–39. In *Ac.* 2. 4–7, the goodness and glory of philosophical discussions is noted in contrast with a public opinion that is generally hostile to them.
84. See *Tusc.* 5. 70–71 for a similar perspective on virtue and as evidence that the Dream of Scipio is essentially a metaphor for philosophy's discernment of virtue as the true good, out of a process of knowing the self in the context of the whole. The passage that follows at *Tusc.* 5. 105, where the troubles that come from any kind of involvement with the people and public opinion are contrasted with the sweet joy of scholarly leisure (*otium litteratum*) that entails contemplation of infinity and the heavens, should not be read as a Stoic-like rejection of political responsibility but rather as an effort to guard against the allure of false glory and to draw to thinking that contributes to virtuous ways and true glory. At *Brut.* 59, Cicero observes that a human being's glory (*homini decus*) is said to be in her mind or intellect (*ingenium*). This is wholly consistent with finding human

glory in virtue, for reason is the human key to following nature and thus to the life of virtue.
85. The Dream affirms humankind's social and political nature and the consequent human responsibilities. Particularly at *Rep.* 6. 13, Africanus indicates that it is the will of the supreme deity for humans to be joined together according to right *(jure)* in polities and that the leaders of these communities are to have the special protection and encouragement of that god.
86. *Lig.* 37. On Regulus, see *Off.* 1. 39; 3. 99 ff.
87. For example, *Sest.* 47, 131; *Arch.* 30; *Rab. Perd.* 29–30; *Tusc.* 1. 32–36.
88. See Powell (1990: 163–65) for a summary of the case for Cicero's dependence on Plato on the topic of immortality. *Sen.* 78; *Tusc.* 1. 35; 5. 70; *Hortensius* (Grilli 1962 frs. 110, 112, 114–15, pp. 51–54). "Consular philosophers" have come to be defined by some, largely on the basis of *Hortensius*, fr. 114, as those inclined to accept the prospect of personal immortality (Hagendahl, 1967: II, 584). Rawson (1975: 237, 240) notes Cicero's argument and hope regarding immortality yet observes earlier (227), when discussing his reaction to his daughter Tullia's death, that he "was not even a firm believer in a future life, and certainly he never mentions its possibility in the letters of this time." At *Tusc.* 1. 79–81, it is reported that Panaetius made arguments against immortality, which Cicero seems to think could be refuted. Given the range of positions represented in Cicero, Gibbon (1900–01: Chap. 15, 55, n. 51) remarks, "[T]he writings of Cicero represent in the most lively colours the ignorance, the errors, and the uncertainty of the ancient philosophers with regard to the immortality of the soul." To this he properly adds, in a note, that in *Tusc.* 1, *Sen.* and the Dream of Scipio, Cicero provided "in the most beautiful language, everything that Grecian philosophy or Roman good sense could possibly suggest on this dark but important subject."
89. *Rep.* 6. 8.

Epilogue

Cicero is a Socratic in a Roman toga, who loved philosophy from his earliest days and was immersed in Roman history and experience. His practical perspective, so congenial to Rome, undergirds and informs all his thinking and unfolds in a way of life. That perspective depended on a natural or prephilosophic attunement to virtue, entailed an expectation of real fruit from philosophic inquiry, and elevated to moral status matters useful to an aspiration for a virtuous political community. Yet he knew that there could be too narrow an embrace of "the Socratic turn." He took on the grave civic responsibilities of a Roman citizen and took them all the way to the very peak of leadership, holding out for himself and others, largely through a literary legacy, the model of a Socratic statesman.

That Cicero approaches in the manner of Socrates those deepest human concerns such as personal immortality, the existence and nature of the gods, and the nature of the whole is but one indication of the many we have seen of his self-confessed Socratic inspiration and allegiance. When Cicero's thought culminates in a focus on the model statesman, who is, above all, to be a philosophical statesman who finds glory and happiness in virtue itself, he is not commending any philosophy, such as the Stoic philosophy, which appropriates to itself the name of philosophy. He is, rather, turning the statesman to a Socratic approach to philosophy. Socrates's practical or moral orientation seems to hold a special attraction to Romans and those inclined to statesmanship, and for these, including Cicero himself, it could be seen as a notably congenial way into philosophical inquiry. Socrates and his approach to philosophy functions as Cicero's standard in his finding his own way among the philosophical schools of his lifetime. His fundamental allegiance to the Academic school and its mode of inquiry and qualified skepticism are seen by him as acts of fidelity to Socrates. In the Socratic manner, then, and with the evident prephilosophical practical reliances that allowed Socrates an attractive way of life even as he questioned and inquired, Cicero tests the teachings of the schools and focuses philosophical inquiry on the various teachings concerning the highest good or ultimate end of human actions.

Appreciating the nature of Socrates's practical or moral orientation to philosophy and Cicero's appropriation of it is critical to seeing the coherence of Cicero's thought. Furthermore, Cicero can be understood as taking this approach in his own distinctive direction and thus bringing his thought on some matters into tension, if not outright conflict, with the apparent Socratic positions. Cicero incarnates the practical or moral orientation in Socrates's bringing of philosophy down from the heavens and into the homes and everyday lives of humankind. For Cicero, this means that philosophy is worthless and certainly unworthy of its very name if it does not point out moral duties, thus giving direction to life and bearing fruit in lives informed by virtue. Further, it means that the foundational question, on which rests both the determination of duties and all reasonable assurance in inquiry, is the one concerning the highest good and ultimate end. We are, thinks Cicero in accord with his Socratic model, naturally attuned to happiness in ways that allow reasonable assurance on this matter. Insofar as the response to this key question is taken as foundational for all philosophy, it appears that a form of prudence and its reliances is prior even to philosophy. In that context, philosophy seems to itself become a form of moral virtue. To become philosophical in the light of "the Socratic turn"—the direction to which Cicero exhorts Rome's leaders and potential leaders—is to be interested in clarifying and deepening what is understood from the practical perspective, that residual prephilosophical prudence. From the seeds inherent to that perspective—human inclinations, reason, and experience—philosophical inquiry can flower out to a fuller and more detailed moral and political wisdom and even beyond, to a greater understanding of all things. Much in Cicero's philosophical works is evidence of just such a flowering. That those philosophical works reveal not only the critical, inquiring spirit generally associated with

Socrates and philosophy but also a rhetorical dimension makes sense in the light of the role of the prephilosophical in the practical approach to philosophy, in the light, in other words, of the fact that philosophy itself must be chosen, and of the expectation that philosophy is to culminate in virtuous action.

Cicero's approach to philosophy out of the practical perspective need not and ought not be understood as confining philosophy to moral and political inquiry. This point is made in a positive way in the phrase just above, indicating that the approach can flower out to a "greater understanding of all things." Cicero's claim that Socrates first called philosophy down from the heavens is best understood not as a claim that he was the first in human history to seek and to exemplify practical wisdom, or that he thought the more traditional topics of natural philosophy worthless, but that he was the first—once philosophy was established as a way of life having the object of understanding the nature of things—to give philosophy a different primary object and initial focus.[1] The practical perspective is marked out by that initial focus (what constitutes happiness or the good?) and that primary object (the actual achievement of happiness), and in these Cicero follows Socrates. These provide the basis for the priorities and order in action and inquiry, which are expressed through a fundamental sense of utility. That Cicero finds much learning and inquiry which is not strictly moral or political to be useful to human happiness accords with his own respect and love of learning of all kinds as well as with his great attraction to Plato, whom he regards as first among philosophers, one who proceeds from Socrates but goes beyond him. Cicero, even in his apparently practical *Re Publica* and *Legibus*, reveals himself to be concerned with a too narrow, too confining, too practical, and too Roman understanding of "the Socratic turn."

Though he does not ever implicate Socrates himself in such a narrow understanding, Cicero does have differences with Socrates. Overall, these differences can be characterized as an effort to bring Socratic philosophy yet further down from the heavens and into the lives of human beings as they are commonly known. They can also be characterized as efforts to moderate a purity and severity in the thought and life of Socrates, which later gives rise to a rigorous Stoicism. The explicit and notable differences involve (1) Cicero's effort to open the concept of happiness as consisting solely in virtue to accommodate the ordinary sense of utilities, (2) Cicero's concern that Socrates has not been sufficiently appreciative of the importance of rhetoric and hence the value of the art of rhetoric, and

(3) Socrates's failure to recognize the priority of statesmanship even over philosophy. In these respects, Cicero seems to be deflecting the relatively practical Socratic orientation of the Greeks yet more in the direction of common experience and Roman practicality. Socrates's apparent philosophical radicalism is tempered in Cicero's hands by common sense and Roman ancestral virtue.

The key concept and primary moral and political objective in which Cicero synthesizes his attraction to Greek inquiry and the sensibility of Roman practicality is the model statesman—the philosophical statesman. Cicero's thought begins, above all, from the concerns of statesmanship—concerns that not only never leave him but, in fact, also direct in important ways his broad inquiry into the philosophical teachings of his time. His thinking culminates in a rich understanding of the vital function of the statesman in moral and political amelioration and in an emphasis on the Socratic statesman as model. Early in life, Cicero was on a course of becoming an orator/statesman; later in life, he appears intent to influence by his thinking and writing the formation of a new generation of potential statesmen to salvage what could be saved of Rome's best political traditions and to renew the Republic. It is artificial and wrong—and simply unSocratic—to sever Cicero's life as a struggling statesman in the late Republic from his thought. His life is very much bound up with his philosophical work but not, it seems, in any way that would discredit him as a philosopher, as some have suggested . He can be rightly seen as a Socratic in a Roman toga and with the grave responsibilities of a Roman citizen who seeks and rises to leadership. We know a fair amount about Cicero's own difficulties as he sought to be a Socratic statesman, including his struggle with what he regarded as the false glory of political acclaim. His imperfections, as he strove to be what he wished to be and thought to be, ought never obscure the nobleness of his aspiration and the coherence and attractiveness of his Socratic approach to political life.

There is, as we have found, basis in the thought of Cicero for certain long-standing views about him. He has been seen as standing with one foot in the Greek world and one in the Roman, as bridging between pagan and Christian thought, and as marking an important turn in ancient philosophy's development toward modern political thought. If, then, as this book contends, he is not mindlessly eclectic and simply confused as a thinker, he would seem to be quite central to and among the most interesting thinkers in the Western tradition. Though the renaissance in the

Cicero studies of the last two generations has prepared those so inclined, we have yet to comprehend him well. A first step is to appreciate how his practical perspective on philosophy might be seen to undergird and inform all his thinking and to unfold into a way of life enriched and directed by philosophy.

Notes

1. A fuller discussion of Cicero's understanding of Socrates, and his taking his orientation from Socrates, can be found in Nicgorski (1992: 224, *passim*).

REFERENCES

1. John Adams. 1851. A Defence of the Constitutions of Government of the United States of America. In *The Works of John Adams*. Boston: Charles C. Little and James Brown.
2. Allen, J. 1997. Carneadean Argument in Cicero's Academic Books. In *Assent and Argument*, eds. Brad Inwood and Jaap Mansfeld, 217–56. Leiden: Brill.
3. Algra, K.A. 1997. Chrysippus, Carneades, Cicero. In *Assent and Argument*, eds. B. Inwood and J. Mansfeld, 107–39. Leiden: Brill.
4. Annas, Julia, and Jonathan Barnes. 1985. *The Modes of Scepticism: Ancient Texts and Modern Interpretations*. Cambridge: Cambridge University Press.
5. Annas, Julia. 1980. Truth and Knowledge. In *Doubt and Dogmatism*, eds. Malcolm Schofield, Myles Burnyeat and Jonathan Barnes, 84–104. Oxford: Clarendon Press.
6. ———. 1986. Doing Without Objective Values: Ancient and Modern Strategies. In *The Norms of Nature*, eds. Malcolm Schofield and Gisela Striker, 3–30. Cambridge: Cambridge University Press.
7. ———. 1988. The Heirs of Socrates. *Phronesis* 33(1): 100–12.
8. ———. 1989. Cicero on Stoic Moral Philosophy and Private Property. In *Philosophia Togata*, eds. Miriam Griffin and Jonathan Barnes, 151–73. Oxford: Clarendon Press.
9. ———. 1993. *The Morality of Happiness*. Oxford: Oxford University Press.
10. ———. 1994. Plato the Skeptic. In *The Socratic Movement*, ed. Paul A. Vander Waerdt, 309–40. Ithaca: Cornell University Press.
11. Arena, Valentina. 2012. *Libertas and the Practice of Politics in the Late Roman Republic*. Cambridge: Cambridge University Press.

12. Arkes, Hadley. 1992. That 'Nature Herself Has Placed in our Ears a Power of Judging': Some Reflections on the 'Naturalism' of Cicero. In *Natural Law Theory*, ed. Robert P. George, 245–77. Oxford: Clarendon Press.
13. Atkins, E.M. 1990. Domina et Regina: Justice and Societas in De Officiis. *Phronesis* 35(3): 258–89.
14. Atkins, Jed W. 2013. *Cicero on Politics and the Limits of Reason*. Cambridge: Cambridge University Press.
15. Baraz, Y. 2012. A Written Republic: *Cicero's Philosophical Politics*. Princeton: Princeton University Press.
16. Barlow, J. 1987. The Education of Statesmen in Cicero's *De Republica*. *Polity* 19(3): 353–74.
17. ———. 1999. The Fox and the Lion: Machiavelli replies to Cicero. *History of Political Thought* 20(4): 627–45.
18. ———. 2012. Cicero on Property and the State. In *Cicero's Practical Philosophy*, ed. Walter Nicgorski, 212–41. Notre Dame: University of Notre Dame Press.
19. Barnes, Jonathan. 1989. Antiochus of Ascalon. In *Philosophia Togata*, eds. M. Griffin and J. Barnes, 51–96. Oxford: Clarendon Press
20. ———. 1997. Logic in *Academica* I and the *Lucullus*. In *Assent and Argument*, eds. B. Inwood and J. Mansfeld, 140–60. Leiden: Brill.
21. Basore, John W., trans. 1935. De Otio. In *Seneca: Moral Essays, Volume II*, Loeb Classical Library. Cambridge: Harvard University Press.
22. Beard, Mary. 1986. Cicero and Divination: The Formation of a Latin Discourse. *The Journal of Roman Studies* 76: 33–46.
23. Beiner, Ronald. 1989. Do We Need a Philosophical Ethics? *Philosophical Forum* 20(3): 230–43.
24. Benardete, Seth. 1987. Cicero's *de legibus* I: Its Plan and Intention. *American Journal of Philology* 108(2): 295–309.
25. Bentley, Richard. 1743. *Remarks upon a Late Discourse of Free Thinking in a Letter to F.H.D.D. By Phileleutherus Lipsiensis*. Cambridge: J. Bentham.
26. Bett, Richard. 1989. Carneades' *Pithanon*: A Reappraisal of Its Role and Status. In *Oxford Studies in Ancient Philosophy*, vol. VII, ed. Julia Annas, 59–94. Oxford: Oxford University Press.
27. Bloom, Allan. 1991. Interpretive Essay. In *The Republic of Plato*, 305–46. New York: Basic Books.
28. Brittain, Charles, trans. 2006. *On Academic Scepticism*. Indianapolis, IN: Hackett Publishing.
29. Brochard, Victor. 1923. *Les Sceptiques Grecs*. Paris: Librarie Philosophique J. Vrin.
30. Brunschwig, Jacques. 1986. The Cradle Argument in Epicureanism and Stoicism. In *The Norms of Nature*, eds. M. Schofield and G. Striker, 113–44. Cambridge: Cambridge University Press.
31. Brunt, P.A. 1986. Cicero's *Officium* in the Civil War. *The Journal of Roman Studies* 76: 12–32.

32. Burnyeat, Miles. 1982. Idealism and Greek Philosophy: What Descartes Saw and Berkeley Missed. *The Philosophical Review* 91(1): 3–40.
33. ———. 1983. Can the Skeptic Live His Skepticism? In *The Skeptical Tradition*, ed. Miles Burnyeat, 117–48. Berkeley: University of California Press.
34. ———. 1984. The Sceptic in His Place and Time. In *Philosophy in History*, eds. Richard Rorty, J.B. Schneewind, and Quentin Skinner, 225–54. Cambridge: Cambridge University Press.
35. ———. 1986. Carneades Was No Probabilist. Paper kindly shared with author.
36. ———. 1997. Antipater and Self-Refutation. In *Assent and Argument*, eds. B. Inwood and J. Mansfeld, 277–310. Leiden: Brill.
37. Buckley, Michael. 1970. Philosophic Method in Cicero. *Journal of the History of Philosophy* 8(April): 143–54.
38. Carcopino, Jerome. 1951. *Cicero: The Secrets of His Correspondence*. New Haven, CT: Yale University Press.
39. Carlyle, R.W., and A.J. Carlyle. 1903. *A History of Mediaeval Political Theory in the West*. London: Blackwood & Sons.
40. Caspar, Timothy W. 2010. *Recovering the Ancient View of Founding: A Commentary on Cicero's De Legibus*. Lanham, MD: Lexington Books.
41. Colish, Marcia. 1978. Cicero's *De Officiis* and Machiavelli's *Prince*. The *Sixteenth Century Journal, Central Rennaissance Conference* 9(4): 80–93.
42. ———. 1985. *The Stoic Tradition from Antiquity to the Early Middle Ages*. Leiden: E. J. Brill.
43. Couissin, Pierre. 1983. The Stoicism of the New Academy. Reprinted in *The Skeptical Tradition*, trans. and ed. Miles Burnyeat, 31–63. Berkeley: University of California Press.
44. Crosson, Frederick. 1988. Religion and Natural Law. *The American Journal of Jurisprudence* 33: 1–18.
45. Cumming, R.D. 1969. *Human Nature and History: A Study of the Development of Liberal Political Thought*, vol. 2. Chicago, IL: University of Chicago Press.
46. Davies, J.C. 1971. The Originality of Cicero's Philosophical Works. *Latomus* 30: 105–19.
47. Dillon, John. 1988. 'Orthodoxy' and 'Eclecticism': Middle Platonism and Neo-Pythagoreans. In *The Question of "Eclecticism,"* eds. John M. Dillon and A.A. Long. Berkeley, 103–25: University of California Press.
48. DiLorenzo, Raymond. 1978. The Critique of Socrates in Cicero's "De Oratore": Ornatus and the Nature of Wisdom. *Philosophy & Rhetoric* 11(4): 247–61.
49. ———. 1982. Ciceronianism and Augustine's Conception of Philosophy. *Augustinian Studies* 13: 171–76.
50. Donini, Pierluigi. 1988. The History of the Concept of Eclecticism. In *The Question of "Eclecticism,"* eds. J.M. Dillon and A.A. Long, 15–33. Berkeley: University of California Press.
51. Douglas, A.E. 1962. Platonis Aemulus. *Greece & Rome* 9(1): 41–51.

52. ———. 1965. Cicero the Philosopher. In *Cicero*, ed. Thomas Dorey, 135–170. London: Routledge.
53. ———, ed., trans. 1985. *Tusculan Disputations I*. Warminster: Aris & Phillips.
54. ———. 1990. Commentary: Tusculan Disputations V. In *Tusculan Disputations II & V*. Warminster: Aris & Phillips.
55. ———. 1995. Form and Content in the *Tusculan Disputations*. In *Cicero the Philosopher*, ed. J.G.F. Powell, 197–218. Oxford: Clarendon Press.
56. Dyck, Andrew R. 1996. *A Commentary on Cicero, De Officiis*. Ann Arbor, MI: University of Michigan Press.
57. Engberg-Pedersen, Troels. 1986. Discovering the Good: *Oikeiōsis* and *Kathēkonta* in Stoic Ethics. In *The Norms of Nature*, eds. M. Schofield and G. Striker, 145–84. Cambridge: Cambridge University Press.
58. ———. 1990. *The Stoic Theory of Oikeiosis*, Studies in Hellenistic Civilization, 2. Aarhus: University Press.
59. Englert, Walter. 1990. Bringing Philosophy to the Light: Cicero's *Paradoxa Stoicorum*. In *The Politics of Therapy: Hellenistic Ethics in Its Rhetorical and Literary Context*, ed. M. Nussbaum. *Apeiron* 23(4): 119–42.
60. Erskine, Andrew. 1990. *The Hellenistic Stoa*. Ithaca, NY: Cornell University Press.
61. Ferrary, Jean-Louis. 1974. Le Discours de Laelius dans le Troisième Livre du De Re Publica de Cicèron. *Mélanges de l'École Française de Rome. Antiquité* 86(2): 745–71.
62. ———. 1977. Le discours de Philus (Cicéron, 'De Re Publica', III, 8, 31) et la philosophie de Carnéade. *Revue des Études Latines* 55: 128–56.
63. ———. 1984. L'Archéologie du *De Re Publica* (2, 2, 4-37, 63): Cicéron entre Polybe et Platon. *The Journal of Roman Studies* 74: 87–98.
64. ———. 1995. The Statesman and the Law in the Political Philosophy of Cicero. In *Justice and Generosity*, eds. André Laks and Malcolm Schofield, 48–73. Cambridge: Cambridge University Press.
65. Fetter, James, and Walter Nicgorski. 2008. Magnanimity and Statesmanship: The Ciceronian Difference. In *Magnanimity and Statesmanship*, ed. Carson Holloway, 29–48. Lanham, MD: Lexington Books.
66. Fortin, Ernest L. 1978. Augustine, Thomas Aquinas, and the Problem of Natural Law. *Mediaevalia* IV: 179–208. Reprinted 1996. *Classical Christianity and the Political Order*, ed. Brian Benestad, 199–222. Lanham, MD: Rowman and Littlefield.
67. ———. 1994. Introduction. In Augustine, *Political Writings*, eds. Ernest L. Fortin and Douglas Kries, vii–xxix. Indianapolis: Hackett Publishing Company.
68. ———. 1996a. Augustine and the Problem of Modernity. *Benestad*: 137–50.
69. ———. 1996b. Politics and Philosophy in the Middle Ages: The Aristotelian Revolution. *Benestad*: 177–98.

70. ———. 1996c. The Political Implications of St. Augustine's Theory of Conscience. *Benestad*: 65–84.
71. Fott, David, trans. 2002. Montesquieu's "Discourse on Cicero". *Political Theory* 30(5): 733–37.
72. ———. 2008. How Machiavellian is Cicero? In *The Arts of Rule: Essays in Honor of Harvey Mansfield*, eds. Harvey Claflin Mansfield, Sharon R. Krause and Mary Ann McGrail. Lanham, MD: Lexington Books.
73. ———. 2012. The Politico-Philosophical Character of Cicero's Verdict in *De Natura Deorum*. In *Cicero's Practical Philosophy*, ed. Walter Nicgorski, 152–80. Notre Dame: University of Notre Dame Press.
74. ———, trans. 2014. *Marcus Tullius Cicero, on the Republic and on the Laws*. Ithaca: Cornell University Press.
75. Fowler, D.N. 1989. Lucretius and Politics. In *Philosophia Togata*, eds. M. Griffin and J. Barnes, 120–50. Oxford: Clarendon Press.
76. Frede, Michael. 1987a. Stoics and Skeptics on Clear and Distinct Impressions. In *Essays in Ancient Philosophy*, 151–78. Minneapolis: University of Minnesota Press.
77. ———. 1987b. The Skeptic's Beliefs. In *Essays in Ancient Philosophy*, 179–200. Minneapolis: University of Minnesota Press.
78. ———. 1987c. The Skeptic's Two Kinds of Assent and the Question of the Possibility of Knowledge. In *Essays in Ancient Philosophy*, 201–222. Minneapolis: University of Minnesota Press.
79. ———. 1999. Stoic Epistemology. In *The Cambridge History of Hellenistic Philosophy*, eds. K. Algra, J. Barnes, J. Mansfield, and M. Schofield, 295–322. Cambridge: Cambridge University Press.
80. Garsten, Bryan. 2009. *Saving Persuasion: A Defense of Rhetoric and Judgment*. Cambridge: Harvard University Press.
81. Gibbon, Edward. 1900–1901. *The History of the Decline and Fall of the Roman Empire*, vol. 2, ed. J.B. Bury. London: Methuen.
82. Gildenhard, Ingo. 2007. *Paideia Romana. Cicero's Tusculan Disputations*. Cambridge: The Cambridge Philological Society.
83. Gill, Christopher. 1988. Person and Personality: The Four-*Personae* Theory in Cicero, *De Officiis* I. *Oxford Studies in Ancient Philosophy* 6: 169–99.
84. Glenn, Gary. 2009. Natural Rights and Social Contract in Burke and Bellarmine. In *Rethinking Rights: Historical, Philosophical and Theological Perspectives,* eds. Kenneth Grasso and Bruce Frohnen, 58–79. University of Missouri Press.
85. Glucker, John. 1965. Consulares Philosophi Again. *Revue des Études Augustiniennes* 11: 229–34.
86. ———. 1978. *Antiochus and the Late Academy*. Göttingen: Vandenhoeck & Ruprecht.

87. ———. 1988. Cicero's Philosophical Affiliations. In *The Question of "Eclecticism,"* eds. J.M. Dillon and A.A. Long. Berkeley, 34–69: University of California Press.
88. ———. 1992. Cicero's Philosophical Affiliations Again. *Liverpool Classical Monthly,* 17 (November) 9: 134–38.
89. ———. 1995. *Probabile, Veri Simile,* and Related Terms. In *Cicero the Philosopher,* ed. J.G.F. Powell, 115–44. Oxford: Clarendon Press.
90. ———. 1997. Socrates in the Academic Books. In *Assent and Argument,* eds. B. Inwood and J. Mansfeld, 58–88. Leiden: Brill.
91. Görler, Woldemar. 1995. Silencing the Troublemaker: *De Legibus* I. 39 and the Continuity of Cicero's Skepticism. In *Cicero the Philosopher,* ed. J.G.F. Powell, 85–113. Oxford: Clarendon Press.
92. ———. 1997. Cicero's Philosophical Stance in the *Lucullus.* In *Assent and Argument,* eds. B. Inwood and J. Mansfeld, 36–57. Leiden: Brill.
93. Gorman, Robert. 2005. *The Socratic Method in the Dialogues of Plato.* Stuttgart: Franz Steiner.
94. Griffin, Miriam. 1989. Philosophy, Politics and Politicians at Rome. In *Philosophia Togata,* eds. M. Griffin and J. Barnes, 1–37. Oxford: Clarendon Press.
95. ———. 1991. Introduction. In *Cicero, On Duties,* eds. M.T. Griffin and E.M. Atkins, xix–xxi. Cambridge: Cambridge University Press.
96. ———. 1995. Philosophical Badinage in Cicero's Letters to his Friends. In *Cicero the Philosopher,* ed. J.G.F. Powell, 325–46. Oxford: Clarendon Press.
97. ———. 1997. The Composition of the *Academica.* In *Assent and Argument,* eds. B. Inwood and J. Mansfeld, 1–35. Leiden: Brill.
98. ———. 1997. From Aristotle to Atticus: Cicero and Matius on Friendship. In *Philosophia Togata, vol. 2: Plato and Aristotle At Rome,* eds. M. Griffin and J. Barnes, 86–109. Oxford: Clarendon Press.
99. Grilli, Albertus, ed. 1962. *Hortensius.* Milano: Instituto Editoriale Cisalpino.
100. Gwynn, Aubrey. 1926. *Roman Education from Cicero to Quintilian.* Oxford: Clarendon Press.
101. Habicht, Christian. 1990. *Cicero the Politician.* Baltimore, MD: The Johns Hopkins University Press.
102. Habinek, Thomas. 1990. The Politics of Candor in Cicero's *De Amicitia.* In *The Politics of Therapy: Hellenistic Ethics in Its Rhetorical and* Literary *Context,* ed. M. Nussbaum. *Apeiron* 23(4): 165–85.
103. Hagendahl, H. 1967. *Augustine and the Latin Classics.* Göteborg: Universitatis Gothoburgenses.
104. Hahm, D.E. 1995. Polybius' Applied Political Theory. In *Justice and Generosity,* eds. André Laks and Malcolm Schofield, 7–47. Cambridge: Cambridge University Press.
105. Hankinson, R.J. 1997. Natural Criteria and the Transparency of Judgement. In *Assent and Argument,* eds. B. Inwood and J. Mansfeld, 161–216. Leiden: Brill.

106. Harris, Bruce. 1961. *Cicero as an Academic: A Study of De Natura Deorum*. Auckland: University of Auckland Bulletin.
107. Hathaway, R.F. 1968. Cicero, *De Re Publica* II, and His Socratic View of History. *Journal of the History of Ideas* 29(January–March): 3–12.
108. Holton, James. 1972. Marcus Tullius Cicero. In *History of Political Philosophy*, eds. Leo Strauss and Joseph Cropsey, 130–150. Chicago: Rand McNally.
109. Hookway, Christopher. 1990. *Scepticism*. London: Routledge.
110. Horowitz, Maryanne Cline. 1998. *Seeds of Virtue and Knowledge*. Princeton, NJ: Princeton University Press.
111. Horsley, R.A. 1978. The Law of Nature in Philo and Cicero. *Harvard Theological Review* 71(January–April): 35–59.
112. Hösle, Vittorio. 2005. A Form of Self-Transcendence of Philosophical Dialogues in Cicero and Plato and its Significance for Philology. *Graduate Faculty Philosophy Journal* 26(1): 29–46.
113. ———. 2008. Cicero's Plato. *Wiener Studien* 121: 145–70.
114. Hossenfelder, Malte. 1986. Epicurus—Hedonist Malgré Lui. In *The Norms of Nature*, eds. M. Schofield and G. Striker, 245–64. Cambridge: Cambridge University Press.
115. How, W.W. 1930. Cicero's Ideal in His *De Republica*. *Journal of Roman Studies* 20: 24–42.
116. Hume, David. 1927. Dialogues Concerning Natural Religion. In *Hume Selections*, ed. C.W. Hendel Jr.. New York: Charles Scribner's Sons.
117. ———. 1939. *An Enquiry Concerning Human Understanding*. In *The English Philosophers from Bacon to Mill*, ed. Edwin A. Burtt, 585–689. New York: Random House.
118. ———. 1962. *A Treatise of Human Nature*. Cleveland: The World Publishing.
119. Hunt, H.A.K. 1954. *The Humanism of Cicero*. Melbourne: Melbourne University Press.
120. Hyneman, Charles. 1959. *The Study of Politics*. Urbana: University of Illinois Press.
121. Inwood, Brant. 1987. Commentary on Striker. *Proceedings of the Boston Area Colloquium in Ancient Philosophy* 2: 95–101.
122. ———. 1990. Rhetorica Disputatio: The strategy of de Finibus II. In *The Politics of Therapy: Hellenistic Ethics in Its Rhetorical and Literary Context*, ed. M. Nussbaum. Apeiron 23(4): 143-64.
123. Irwin, T.H. 1986. Stoic and Aristotelian Conceptions of Happiness. In *The Norms of Nature*, eds. M. Schofield and G. Striker, 205–44. Cambridge: Cambridge University Press.
124. Jaeger, Werner. 1934. *Aristotle: Fundamentals of His Development*, trans. Richard Robinson. New York: Oxford University Press.
125. Jardine, Lisa. 1983. Lorenzo Valla: Academic Skepticism and the New Humanist Dialectic. In *The Skeptical Tradition*, trans. and ed. Miles Burnyeat, 253–89. Berkeley: University of California Press.

126. Jones, Peter. 1984. *Hume's Sentiments: Their Ciceronian and French Context*. Edinburgh: Edinburgh University Press.
127. Kerford, G.B. 1978. What Does the Wise Man Know? In *The Stoics*, ed. John Rist, 125–36. Berkeley: University of California Press.
128. Kesler, Charles. 1985. *Cicero and the Natural Law*. Ph.D. Dissertation. Cambridge: Harvard University.
129. Keyes, C.W, trans. 1928. *Cicero, De Re Public, De Legibus, Loeb Classical Library*. Cambridge: Harvard University Press.
130. Kidd, I.G. 1971. Stoic Intermediates and the End for Man. In *Problems in Stoicism*, ed. A.A. Long, 150–72. London: The Athlone Press.
131. ———. 1989. Posidonius as Philosopher-Historian. In *Philosophia Togata*, eds. M. Griffin and J. Barnes, 38–50. Oxford: Clarendon Press.
132. Koester, Helmut. 1968. NOMOS PHYSESIS: The Concept of Natural Law in Greek Thought. In *Religions in Antiquity*, ed. Jacob Neusner, 521–41. Leiden: E.J.Brill.
133. Kries, Douglas. 2003. On the Intention of Cicero's *De Officiis*. *The Review of Politics* 65(4): 375–93.
134. Lacey, W.K. 1978. *Cicero and the End of the Roman Republic*. London: Hodder and Stoughton.
135. Laursen, J.C. 1992. *The Politics of Skepticism in the Ancients, Montaigne, Hume, and Kant*. Leiden: Brill.
136. Leach, Colin. 1981. Review of Thomas N. Mitchell's Cicero: The Ascending Years. *Notes and Queries New Series* 28 (August, 4).
137. Lee, R.W. 1954. *Elements of Roman Law*. London: Sweet & Maxwell.
138. Leeman, Anton. 1949. *Gloria*. Rotterdam: N. V. Drukkerij M. WYT and Zonen.
139. Levine, Phillip. 1957. The Original Design and the Publication of the *De Natura Deorum*. *Harvard Studies in Classical Philology* 62: 7–36.
140. Lévy, Carlos. 1984. La Dialectique de Cicéron dans les Livres II et IV du *De Finibus*. *Revue Des Études Latines* 62: 111–27.
141. ———. 1992a. *Cicero Academicus*. Rome: École Française De Rome, Palais Farnèse.
142. ———. 1992b. Cicéron Créateur de Vocabulaire Latin de la Connaissance: Essai de Synthèse. In *La Langue Latine Langue De La Philosophie*, 91–106. Rome: École Française De Rome, Palais Farnèse.
143. ———. 2012. Philosophical Life versus Political Life: An Impossible Choice for Cicero? In *Cicero's Practical Philosophy*, ed. Walter Nicgorski, 58–78. Notre Dame: University of Notre Dame Press.
144. Lintott, Andrew. 1997. The Theory of the Mixed Constitution. In *Philosophia Togata, vol. 2: Plato and Aristotle At Rome*, eds. M. Griffin and J. Barnes, 70–85. Oxford: Clarendon Press.
145. Lom, Petr. 2001. *The Limits of Doubt: The Moral and Political Implications of Skepticism*. Albany, NY: State University of New York Press.

146. Londey, David. 1984. An Open Question Argument in Cicero. *Apeiron* 18(2): 144–47.
147. Long, A.A. 1967. Carneades and the Stoic Telos. *Phronesis* 12: 59–90.
148. ———. 1980. Stoa and Sceptical Academy: Origins and Growth of a Tradition. *Liverpool Classical Monthly* 5 (October) 8: 161–74.
149. ———. 1986. *Hellenistic Philosophy: Stoics, Epicureans, Sceptics*. Berkeley: University of California Press.
150. ———. 1988a. Ptolemy *on the Criterion*: An Epistemology for the Practicing Scientist. In *The Question of "Eclecticism,"* eds. J.M. Dillon and A.A. Long, 176–207. Berkeley: University of California Press.
151. ———. 1988b. Socrates in Hellenistic Philosophy. *Classical Quarterly* 38(1): 150–71.
152. ———. 1995a. Cicero's Plato and Aristotle. In *Cicero the Philosopher*, ed. J.G.F. Powell, 37–61. Oxford: Clarendon Press.
153. ———. 1995b. Cicero's Politics in *De Officiis*. In *Justice and Generosity*, eds. André Laks and Malcolm Schofield, 213–40. Cambridge: Cambridge University Press.
154. Long, A.A., and D.N. Sedley. 1987. *The Hellenistic Philosophers*, vol. 2. Cambridge: Cambridge University Press.
155. Mackendrick, Paul. 1989. *The Philosophical Books of Cicero*. New York: St. Martin's Press.
156. Mackenzie, Mary Margaret. 1988. The Virtues of Socratic Ignorance. *Classical Quarterly* 38(2): 331–50.
157. Mansfield, Harvey C. 1996. *Machiavelli's Virtue*. Chicago: University of Chicago Press.
158. Marquez, Xavier. 2011. Cicero and the Stability of States. *History of Political Thought* 32(3): 397–423.
159. Marques, Xavier, and Nicgorski, Walter. 2008. La Loi de la Nature et la Nature de la Loi dans la Pensée Politique de Cicéron. In *Droit Naturel: Relancer L'Histoire?*, eds. Louis-Léon Christians, François Coppens, Xavier Dijon, Paul Favraux, Gaelle Fiasse, Jean-Michel Longneaux et Muriel Ruol, trans. Xavier Dijon, 157–91. Bruxelles: Bruylant.
160. Marrou, H.I. 1956. *A History of Education in Antiquity*, trans. George Lamb. New York: Sheed and Ward.
161. McConnell, Sean. 2014. *Philosophical Life in Cicero's Letters*. Cambridge: Cambridge University Press.
162. McCoy, Charles N.R. 1950. The Turning Point in Political Philosophy. *American Political Science Review* 44(September): 678–88.
163. ———. 1963. *The Structure of Political Thought*. New York: McGraw Hill.
164. McIlwain, Charles. 1932. *The Growth of Political Thought in the West*. New York: Macmillan.
165. ———. 1947. *Constitutionalism: Ancient and Modern*. Ithaca: Cornell University Press.

166. Michel, Alain. 1992. Cicéron et la Langue Philosophique: Problèmes d'Éthique et d'Esthétique. In *La Langue Latine,* 77–89. Rome: École Française De Rome, Palais Farnèse.
167. Micken, Ralph. 1970. Introduction. In *Cicero on Oratory and Orators,* trans. and ed. J.S. Watson. Carbondale, IL: Southern Illinois University Press.
168. Millar, Fergus. 2002. *The Roman Republic in Political Thought.* Hanover, NH: University Press of New England.
169. Mitchell, Thomas N. 1991. *Cicero: Senior Statesman.* New Haven, CT: Yale University Press.
170. Mitsis, Phillip. 1988. *Epicurus' Ethical Theory: The Pleasures of Invulnerability.* Ithaca, NY: Cornell University Press.
171. ———. 1994. Natural Law and Natural Right in Post-Aristotelian Philosophy. The Stoics and Their Critics. *Aufstieg und Niedergang der römischem Welt* II.36.7: 4812–50.
172. Nederman, Carey. 1988. Nature, Sin and the Origins of Society: The Ciceronian Tradition in Medieval Political Thought. *Journal of the History of Ideas* 49(January–March): 3–26.
173. ———, trans. 1990. *John of Salisbury's Policraticus.* Cambridge: Cambridge University Press.
174. ———. 1990. Nature, Justice, and Duty in the *Defensor Pacis*: Marsiglio of Padua's Ciceronian Impulse. *Political Theory* 18(November): 615–37.
175. ———. 2000. War, Peace, and Republican Virtue: Patriotism and the Neglected Legacy of Cicero. In *Instilling Ethics,* ed. Norma Thompson, 17–29. Lanham, MD: Rowman and Littlefield.
176. Newman, John Henry. 1873. Marcus Tullius Cicero. In *Historical Sketches.* London: Basil Montagu Pickering.
177. Nicgorski, Walter. 1984. Cicero's Paradoxes and His Idea of Utility. *Political Theory* 12(November): 557–78.
178. ———. 1992. Cicero's Socrates: Assessment of 'the Socratic Turn.' In *Law and Philosophy: The Practice of Theory,* eds. J. Murley, R. Stone and W. Braithwaite, 213–33. Athens, OH: Ohio University Press.
179. ———. 1993. Nationalism and Transnationalism in Cicero. *History of European Ideas* XVI(January): 785–91.
180. ———. 2002. Cicero, Citizenship and the Epicurean Temptation. In *Cultivating Citizens,* eds. Dwight Allman and Michael Beatty, 3–28. Lanham, MD: Lexington Books.
181. ———. 2008. Cicero's Distinctive Voice on Friendship: *De Amicitia* and *De Re Publica.* In *Friendship and Politics: Essays in Political Thought,* eds. John von Heyking and Richard Avramenko, 84–111. Notre Dame: University of Notre Dame Press.
182. ———. 2012. Cicero and the Rebirth of Political Philosophy. Reprinted in *Cicero's Practical Philosophy,* ed. Walter Nicgorski, 242–82. Notre Dame: University of Notre Dame Press.

183. ——. 2013a. Cicero on Aristotle and the Aristotelians. *Hungarian Philosophical Review* 57(4): 34–56.
184. ——. 2013b. Cicero on Education: the Humanizing Arts. *Arts of Liberty: A Journal on Liberal Arts and Liberal Education* 1(1): 1–22.
185. Nussbaum, Martha. 1994. *The Therapy of Desire*. Princeton, NJ: Princeton University Press.
186. O'Connor, David K. 1989. The Invulnerable Pleasures of Epicurean Friendship. *Greek-Roman-and Byzantine Studies* 30(Summer): 165–86.
187. Ochs, Donovan J. 1993. *Consolatory Rhetoric: Grief, Symbol and Ritual in the Greco-Roman Era*. Columbia: University of South Carolina Press.
188. Olshewsky, Thomas M. 1991. The Classic Roots of Hume's Skepticism. *Journal of the History of Ideas* 52(April/June): 269–87.
189. Pajewski, Allesandro. 2012. *The Face of Nature: Hume and Darwin on Analogy and Emotion*. Chicago: University of Chicago Press.
190. Pangle, Thomas. 1998. Socratic Cosmopolitanism: Cicero's Critique and Transformation of the Stoic Idea. *Canadian Political Science Association* 31(2): 235–62.
191. Pangle, Thomas, and Peter J. Ahrensdorf. 1999. *Justice Among Nations*. Lawrence, KS: University of Kansas Press.
192. Parens, Joshua. 1995. *Metaphysics as Rhetoric*. Albany, NY: State University of New York Press.
193. Peterssen, T. 1920. *Cicero: A Biography*. Berkeley: University of California Press. Reprinted 1963. New York: Biblio and Tannen.
194. Plutarch. 1960. Cicero. In *Plutarch, Eight Great Lives*, trans. Dryden revised by A.H. Clough. New York: Holt, Rinehart & Winston.
195. Popkin, Richard H. 1979. *The History of Scepticism from Erasmus to Spinoza*. Berkeley: University of California Press.
196. Powell, J.G.F. ed., trans. 1990. *Cicero: On Friendship and the Dream of Scipio (Laelius de Amicitia and Somnium Scipionis). Edited with an Introduction, Translation and Commentary*. Warminster: Aris & Phillips.
197. ——. 1994. The *rector rei publicae* of Cicero's *De Republica*. *Scripta Classica Israelica* 13: 19–29.
198. ——, ed. 1995. *Cicero the Philosopher*. Oxford: Clarendon Press.
199. ——, ed., trans. 2006. *M. Tulli Ciceronis De re publica, De legibus, Cato Maior De senectute, Laelius De amicitia*. Oxford: Oxford University Press.
200. Rahe, Paul. 1994. Cicero and Republicanism in America. *Ciceroniana* 8: 63–78.
201. Rawson, Elizabeth. 1974. *Cicero*. London: Allen Lane. Reprinted 1983. Bristol: Bristol Classical Press.
202. ——. 1985. *Intellectual Life in the Late Roman Republic*. London: Duckworth.
203. Reesor, Margaret E. 1951. The 'Indifferents' in the Old and Middle Stoa. *Transactions and Proceedings of the American Philological Association* 82: 102–10.

204. Reid, James S., ed. 1885. *The Academica of Cicero*. London: Macmillan.
205. Remer, Gary. 1999. Political Oratory and Conversation: Cicero versus Deliberative Democracy. *Political Theory* 27(1): 39–64.
206. ——. 2004. Cicero and the Ethics of Deliberative Rhetoric. In *Talking Democracy: Historical Perspectives on Rhetoric and Democracy*, ed. Benedetto Fontana, Cary J. Nederman and Gary Remer, 135–62. University Park, PA: Pennsylvania State University Press.
207. ——. 2009. Rhetoric as a Balancing of Ends: Cicero and Machiavelli. *Philosophy and Rhetoric* 42: 1–26.
208. Richard, Carl. 1994. *The Founders and the Classics*. Cambridge: Harvard University Press.
209. Rist, John. 1969. *Stoic Philosophy*. Cambridge: Cambridge University Press.
210. Rolfe, John C., trans. 1966. Cornelius Nepos. In *Lucius Annaeus Florus, Cornelius Nepos*. Cambridge: Harvard University Press.
211. Rouse, W.H.D. 1956. The Phaedo. In *Great Dialogues of Plato*. New York: Mentor Books.
212. Ruch, Michel. 1958. *L'Hortensius de Cicéron: Histoire et Reconstruction*. Paris: Les Belles Lettres.
213. ——. 1959. *Consulares Philosophi* chez Cicéron et chez Saint Augustin. *Revue des Études Augustiniennes* 5: 99–102.
214. Rudd, Niall, trans. 1998. *Cicero, The Republic and The Laws*. Oxford: Oxford University Press.
215. Sabine, George, and Smith, Stanley, trans. 1929. *Cicero, On the Commonwealth*. Columbus: Ohio State University Press.
216. Sabine, George. 1937. *A History of Political Theory*. New York: Holt.
217. Schmitt, C.B. 1972. *Cicero Scepticus: A Study of the Influence of the Academica in the Renaissance*, vol. 52 of the International Archives of the History of Ideas. The Hague: Springer.
218. ——. 1983. The Rediscovery of Ancient Skepticism. In *The Skeptical Tradition*, trans. and ed., Miles Burnyeat, 225–51. Berkeley: University of California Press.
219. Schofield, Malcolm. 1986. Cicero For and Against Divination. *The Journal of Roman Studies* 76: 47–65.
220. ——. 1991. *The Stoic Idea of the City*. Cambridge: Cambridge University Press.
221. ——. 1995a. Cicero's Definition of *Res Publica*. In *Cicero the Philosopher*, ed. J.G.F. Powell, 63–81. Oxford: Clarendon Press.
222. ——. 1995b. Two Stoic Approaches to Justice. In *Justice and Generosity*, eds. André Laks and Malcolm Schofield, 191–212. Cambridge: Cambridge University Press.
223. ——. 2009. Republican Virtues. In *A Companion to Greek and Roman Political Thought*, ed. Ryan Balot, 199–213. Chichester: Wiley-Blackwell.

224. ———. 2012. The Fourth Virtue. In *Cicero's Practical Philosophy*, ed. Walter Nicgorski, 43–57. Notre Dame: University of Notre Dame Press.
225. Sedley, David. 1983. The Motivation of Greek Skepticism. In *The Skeptical Tradition*, ed. Myles Burnyeat, 9–29. Berkeley: University of California Press.
226. ———. 1989. Philosophical Allegiance in the Greco-Roman World. In *Philosophia Togata*, eds. M. Griffin and J. Barnes, 97–119. Oxford: Clarendon Press.
227. ———. 1994. The Cure of Souls. *Times Literary Supplement* 4670(June): 9–10.
228. ———. 1997. Plato's *Auctoritas* and the Rebirth of the Commentary Tradition. In *Philosophia Togata, vol. 2: Plato and Aristotle At Rome*, eds. M. Griffin and J. Barnes, 110–29. Oxford: Clarendon Press.
229. ———. 1998. *Lucretius and the Transformation of Greek Wisdom*. Cambridge: Cambridge University Press.
230. Sextus Empiricus. 1967a. Against the Logicians. In *Sextus Empiricus II*, trans. R.G. Bury. Harvard University Press: Cambridge.
231. ———. 1967b. Outlines of Pyrrhonism. In *Sextus Empiricus I*, trans. R.G. Bury. Cambridge: Harvard University Press.
232. Shields, Christopher J. 1994. Socrates Among the Skeptics. In *The Socratic Movement*, ed. Paul A. Vander Waerdt, 341–66. Ithaca, NY: Cornell University Press.
233. Smith, Philippa. 1995. A Self-indulgent Misuse of Leisure and Writing? How Not to Write Philosophy: Did Cicero Get It Right. In *Cicero the Philosopher*, ed. J.G.F. Powell, 301–23. Oxford: Clarendon Press.
234. Sparshott, F.E. 1978. Zeno on Art: Anatomy of a Definition. In *The Stoics*, ed. John Rist, 273–90. Berkeley: University of California Press.
235. Stahl, William H. 1962. *Roman Science*. Madison, WI: University of Wisconsin Press.
236. Steinmetz, Peter. 1989. Beobachtungen zu Ciceros philosophischen Standpunkt. In *Cicero's Knowledge of the Peripatos*, eds. William W. Fortenbaugh and Peter Steinmetz, 1–21. New Brunswick, NJ: Transaction Publishers.
237. Stem, Rex. 2006. Cicero as Orator and Philosopher: The Value of the *Pro Murena* for Ciceronian Political Thought. *The Review of Politics* 68(2): 206–31.
238. Stokes, Michael C. 1995. Cicero on Epicurean Pleasures. In *Cicero the Philosopher*, ed. J.G.F. Powell. Oxford: Clarendon Press.
239. Stough, Charlotte L. 1969. *Greek Skepticism*. Berkeley: University of California Press.
240. Strauss, Leo. 1953. *Natural Right and History*. Chicago: University of Chicago Press.

241. ——. 1963. Plato. In *History of Political Philosophy*, eds. Leo Strauss and Joseph Cropsey, 7–63. Chicago: Rand McNally.
242. ——. 1964. *The City and Man*. Chicago: Rand McNally.
243. ——. 1973a. Restatement on Xenophon's *Hiero*. In *What Is Political Philosophy?* 95–133. Westport, CT: Greenwood Press.
244. ——. 1973b. On Classical Political Philosophy. In *What Is Political Philosophy?* 79–94. Westport, CT: Greenwood Press.
245. ——. 1975. *The Argument and the Action of Plato's Laws*. Chicago: University of Chicago Press.
246. ——. 1989. *The Rebirth of Classical Political Rationalism*, ed. Thomas Pangle. Chicago: University of Chicago Press.
247. Striker, Gisela. 1980. Skeptical Strategies. In *Doubt and Dogmatism*, eds. M. Schofield, M. Burnyeat and J. Barnes, 54–83. Oxford: Clarendon Press.
248. ——. 1986. Antipater or the Art of Living. In *The Norms of Nature*, eds. M. Schofield and G. Striker, 185–204. Cambridge: Cambridge University Press.
249. ——. 1987. Origins of the Concept of Natural Law. In *Proceedings of the Boston Area Colloquium in Ancient Philosophy* 1, ed. John J. Cleary. Lanham, MD: University Press of America.
250. ——. 1988. Greek Ethics and Moral Theory. In *The Tanner Lectures on Human Values*, ed. Grethe B. Peterson. Cambridge: Cambridge University Press.
251. ——. 1991. Following Nature: A Study in Stoic Ethics. *Oxford Studies in Ancient Philosophy* 9: 1–73.
252. ——. 1996. Epicurean Hedonism. In *Essays on Hellenistic Epistemology and Ethics*. Cambridge: Cambridge University Press.
253. ——. 1997. Academics Fighting Academics. In *Assent and Argument*, eds. B, Inwood and J. Mansfeld, 257–76. Leiden: Brill.
254. Tanner, R.G. 1972. Cicero on Conscience and Morality. In *Cicero and Virgil*, ed. John R.C. Martyn, 87–112. Amsterdam: Hakkert.
255. Tarrant, Harold. 1985. *Skepticism or Platonism?* Cambridge: Cambridge University Press.
256. Tarver, Thomas. 1997. Varro and the Antiquarianism of Philosophy. In *Philosophia Togata, vol. 2: Plato and Aristotle At Rome*, eds. M. Griffin and J. Barnes, 130–64. Oxford: Clarendon Press.
257. Thorsrud, Harald. 2012. Radical and Mitigated Skepticism in Cicero's *Academica*. In *Cicero's Practical Philosophy*, ed. Walter Nicgorski, 133–51. Notre Dame: University of Notre Dame Press.
258. Tuck, Richard. 1979. *Natural Rights Theories*. Cambridge: Cambridge University Press.
259. Vander Waerdt, Paul A. 1987. The Justice of the Epicurean Wise Man. *Classical Quarterly* 37: 402–22.
260. ——. 1988. Hermarchus and the Epircurean Genealogy of Morals. *Transactions of the American Philological Association* 118: 87–106.

261. ——. 1991. Politics and Philosophy in Stoicism. *Oxford Studies in Ancient Philosophy* 9:185–211.
262. ——. 1994. Introduction. In *The Socratic Movement*, ed. Paul A. Vander Waerdt, 1–22. Ithaca: Cornell University Press.
263. ——. 1994a. Zeno's *Republic* and the Origins of Natural Law. In *The Socratic Movement*, ed. Paul A. Vander Waerdt, 272–308. Ithaca: Cornell University Press.
264. ——. 1994b. Philosophical Influence on Roman Jurisprudence? The Case of Stoicism and Natural Law. In *Aufstieg und Niedergang der römischem Welt*, II.36.7: 4851–4900.
265. Vlastos, Gregory. 1982. The Socratic Elenchus. *Journal of Philosophy* 79(11): 711–14.
266. ——. 1985. Socrates' Disavowal of Knowledge. *The Philosophical Quarterly* 35(138): 1–31.
267. ——. 1991. *Socrates: Ironist and Moral Philosopher*. Ithaca: Cornell University Press.
268. Voegelin, Eric. 1974. *The Ecumenic Age*. Baton Rouge, LA: Louisiana State University Press.
269. Walsh, P.G., trans. 2001. Cicero's *On Obligations*. Oxford: Oxford University Press.
270. Watson, Gerard. 1971. The Natural Law and Stoicism. In *Problems in Stoicism*, ed. A.A. Long, 216–38. London: The Athlone Press.
271. Wegemer, Gerard. 1996. *Thomas More on Statesmanship*. Washington, DC: The Catholic University of America Press.
272. ——. 2014. *Young Thomas More and the Arts of Liberty*. Cambridge: Cambridge University Press.
273. West, Thomas G. 1981. Cicero's Teaching on Natural Law. *The St. John's Review* 32(Summer): 74–81.
274. West, Thomas G., Grace Starry, trans. 1998. The Apology. In *Four Texts on Socrates*, 63–98. Ithaca, NY: Cornell University Press.
275. White, S.A. 1995. Cicero and the Therapists. In *Cicero the Philosopher*, ed. J.G.F. Powell, 219–46. Oxford: Clarendon Press.
276. White, Thomas. 1981. A Philosophical Examination of Cicero's Utopianism. A paper for the annual meeting of the American Political Science Association.
277. Williams, Michael. 1988. Scepticism Without Theory. *Review of Metaphysics* 41(March): 547–88.
278. Wiseman, T.P. 1990. The Necessary Lesson. *Times Literary Supplement* (June 15–21): 647–48.
279. Wood, Neal. 1988. *Cicero's Social and Political Thought*. Berkeley: University of California Press.
280. Woolf, Raphael. 2015. *Cicero: The Philosophy of a Roman Sceptic*. London: Routledge.

281. Wright, M.R., trans, ed. 1991. *On Stoic Good and Evil*. Warminster: Aris & Phillips.
282. ———. 1995. Cicero on Self-Love and Love of Humanity in *De Finibus* 3. In *Cicero the Philosopher*, ed. J.G.F. Powell, 171–95. Oxford: Clarendon Press.
283. Zarecki, Jonathan. 2014. *Cicero's Ideal Statesman in Theory and Practice*. London: Bloomsbury Academic.
284. Zerba, Michelle. 2012. *Doubt and Skepticism in Antiquity and the Renaissance*. Cambridge: Cambridge University Press.
285. Zetzel, J.E.G. 1972. Cicero and the Scipionic Circle. *Harvard Studies in Classical Philology* 76: 173–79.
286. ———, trans. 1999. *Cicero, on the Commonwealth and on the Laws*. Cambridge: Cambridge University Press.
287. Zoll, Gallus. 1962. *Cicero Platonis Aemulus: Untersuchung über die Form von Ciceros Dialogen besonders von De oratore*. Zurich: Juris-Verlag.
288. Zuckert, Michael. 1989. 'Bringing Philosophy Down from the Heavens': Natural Right in the Roman Law. *The Review of Politics* 51(Winter): 70–85.

Index of Citations of Cicero

A
Ac. (Academica)
1.3	84
1.5	54,138
1.7-19	49,51,87,89,152,239
1.37	129-30,143
1.41	45
1.43	39,49,85
1.44-45	38,46,86-87
2.4-9	39,43,46,82,85,146, 189,242
2.10	51-52
2.11	39
2.12	43
2.14-15	85
2.17-18	45
2.29	38
2.31	45
2.32	40,43,46,88
2.33	46
2.37-39	133,198
2.59-60	52
2.61-62	46,52
2.63	15,41,51
2.64	51
2.65	53,89
2.66-68	45,52,54,137
2.73	38
2.74	85
2.76-77	86
2.78	43
2.79 ff.	45
2.99 ff.	43,45
2.104	52
2.107	149
2.108-09	44,82
2.113	52
2.114-15	58,153
2.119-20	58,153
2.123-24	56
2.127-28	43,54,56,146,152
2.129	38,53
2.130	40
2.132-34	39,53,150-53
2.136	150
2.137	52,149
2.143	52
2.144-45	45
2.147	53
2.148	51

268 INDEX OF CITATIONS OF CICERO

fr.19	43	420	129
		425	144

Amic. (De Amicitia)
4-5	91-92
6-7	92,188,240
10	240
13	240
18-20	134,142,146,149,202,240
22	240
26-27	240
28-29	142,242
31	240
37-38	143
47	240
82	143
83	240
85	141
87-88	240
100 ff.	240

Arch. (Pro Archia)
14-16	83,240,242
18-19	147
26	241
30	243

Att. (Epistulae ad Atticum)
13.16	51
13.19	51
13.21	47
13.22	51
17	147,241-42
18	240
19-21	188,190
23	84
36	153
89	94,190,237
92	188
126	193
161	193
164	240
294.3	11
326	53,93
363	89
417	129

B

Brut. (Brutus)
23	238
24	238
31	54
32-35	233
42	238
59	242
62	238
93	238
121	233
131	48
143-44	237
150	238
155	238
161	238
167	238
202	238
250	152
292	85
304-24	12
315	52
320	237
322	238
330-33	237

C

Caecin. (Pro Caecina)
65	140
70 ff.	145

Cael. (Pro Caelio)
40-41	149

Cat. (In Catilinam)
1.17	202

D

Div. (De Divinatione)
1.4-7	147,152

1.23	152
1.30	189
1.62	189
1.111	236
2.1-4	11,15,36,38-39,48,50, 53,58,91,128,147, 152-53,187
2.4-5	133,236
2.6-7	83,133,191
2.37	152
2.39	152
2.150	84,152

F
Fam. (Epistulae ad Familiares)

20.12	11,194
20.23	94
63.2	138
110.16	91
177.5	133,147
216.2-3	137-38,143
362.4	147

Fat. (De Fato)

1	84-85
2	85
3	95-96
4	85

Fin. (De Finibus)

1.1-2	82,137
1.3	59
1.11	53,134
1.13	54,82
1.15	82
1.23	147
1.25	137
1.26	138
1.27	54
1.45-46	137
1.71	147
2.1-3	61,84-85
2.4-5	38,89
2.15	89
2.17	90
2.19	151
2.23-24	91
2.28	133,143
2.35	40,133
2.36-37	132,138,142
2.38	153
2.42	53
2.43	40
2.44-55	11,39,54,97,133,137-38, 144,146,150,195,240
2.68	151,153
2.73	137,147
2.74	48
2.76	153
2.78-79	144
2.80-81	133,138
2.85	147
2.86	53,89
2.90	89
2.117-18	137,147
3.1-3	54
3.4	83
3.6	39
3.8-9	51
3.19	82
3.20-25	130,138
3.26	38
3.29	151
3.37	143
3.40	147
3.56-57	242
3.58	130,143
3.67-68	201
3.70	144
4.5-7	149,153
4.12	146
4.14	39
4.15	129
4.18	143,146
4.20 ff.	151

4.22	149
4.23	128,149
4.24-27	130,143,146
4.47	138
4.49	40
4.55	149
4.60	40
4.65	149
4.68-69	149
4.76	238
4.78-79	149
5.6	89,95
5.11-12	129,139,146,151-52
5.14-16	39,53,128
5.16-22	55,131,134,140,235
5.23	40
5.38	91
5.40	134
5.41-44	95,134,139
5.46	134
5.53-54	83
5.58	134
5.61-63	143
5.64	150
5.67-68	56,143,235
5.69	130,143,242
5.71-74 ff.	137,150-51
5.75	152
5.76-77	19,43-44,53,152
5.79	150
5.80-81	146,152
5.83	150
5.84	90,150,152
5.85-86	53,152
5.93	137

H
Har. Resp. (De Haruspicum Responso)
32	141

I
Inv. (De Inventione)
1.1	48,239
1.2-3	96,169,191,195-97, 201,234
1.9	237
1.52-53	85
1.57	45
1.90	89
2.5	58
2.9-10	39
2.25	237
2.53-55	134
2.65 ff.	135,140
2.156 ff.	134
2.159	142
2.160-61	135,140,146,235
2.173-75	139,144,146
2.178	237

L
Leg. (De Legibus)
1.4	50
1.14	141
1.16	140,198
1.17-19	135,140-42,199,234
1.21-23	48,139
1.25-26	142,202
1.28-30	141,169,198-99,240
1.32	48,96,143,147,202
1.33-34	89,97,146,198,203
1.36	50
1.37	48
1.38-39	48,50,121,123,153
1.42-43 ff.	144,146,199
1.44-45	131,143
1.53-55	52,133,151,153
1.57	131
1.58-62	48,91,134,142,146,200, 203,236
2.3-5	202

2.8-10	139,141-42,199,236	1.60	57,93,147
2.11	140,195-96,199,200	2.32	189
2.12	199	2.58	236
2.13-14	142,188-89,196	2.168	93
2.17	189	3.1	93
2.23	188,193	3.38	236
2.39	189	3.60	152
3.1	189	3.66 ff.	152
3.4-5	193,196,205,240		
3.13	193		
3.14	55,149,187		
3.21-32	191,193,196,239		
3.37	188		

Leg. Man. (Pro Lege Manilia)
6	242
7	242
47	242

Lig. (Pro Ligario)
37	243

M

Marcell. (Pro Marcello)
25-26	242

Mur. (Pro Murena)
6	149
15 ff.	201
60-61	149
63-64	149,189

N

Nat. D. (De Natura Deorum)
1.2	57
1.4	82
1.6	39
1.10	82
1.11	39,84-85
1.12	43,45,57
1.16	133
1.36	141
1.57	93,147

O

Off. (De Officiis)
1.2-4	84,90,96,134,145,152
1.4-7	11,39,53,128-29,131,153
1.8	129,131
1.9	128,133-34
1.10	134,149
1.11-14	106,134,139,143,195-96,198
1.15-16	235
1.18	152
1.19	11,39,53,146
1.20	145
1.21	201
1.22	12,145,195
1.23	201
1.26	240-41
1.28	146-47,198
1.29	201
1.30	203
1.31-32	131,201
1.33	188
1.35	188
1.39-40	131,243
1.50-58	144,146,202,240
1.64-65	240-41
1.66	146
1.69-73	146-47
1.85	193
1.90	89
1.92	146,201

1.93-94	96,143	3.46-47	188
1.95	146	3.49	188
1.100	143	3.50 ff.	131
1.108	85	3.53	201
1.110	147	3.63	201
1.128-29	238	3.67-69	140-41,201
1.148	89,143,201	3.71-72	56,140,235
1.153-60	144,146-47,195,235	3.76	142
2.1	143	3.77	146
2.7-8	39-41,44,82,128, 140,152	3.80 ff.	188
		3.91-92 ff.	131
2.9	133,146	3.99	144,243
2.15	240	3.100 ff.	131
2.18	143	3.109	188
2.24-26	242	3.113-15	188
2.28-29	188,195,197	3.118	137
2.30-32	240,242	*De Optimo Genere Oratorum*	
2.35	128,143	17	233
2.40-42	144,196	*De Or. (De Oratore)*	
2.43	89,233,241-42	1.1-4	146,189
2.44 ff.	242	1.5	191,238
2.47	233	1.12	149
2.51	84	1.28	89,238
2.56	151	1.30	191
2.73	184,195-96	1.31-34	239,242
2.74-79	192-201	1.43	149,153
2.81-84	201	1.47	95,238
3.4	146	1.48	237
3.11	89,133,146,153	1.60	153,237
3.13-16	129,134,138,142,146	1.63	237-38
3.17	138	1.83	143
3.18-19	128,131	1.113-34	96,237-38
3.20	150	1.137-39	237,239
3.23	140-41	1.146	237
3.25	195	1.159	238
3.27	141	1.165 ff.	238
3.28	188	1.193-94	239
3.29 ff.	131	1.197	146
3.33	53,131,151-53	1.201	238
3.34	131,133	1.204	89,233
3.35	143,153	1.224-25	190
3.41	188	2.1-9	238

INDEX OF CITATIONS OF CICERO 273

2.17-18	53	3.210-12	96,238,242
2.30	237	3.221	238
2.35	91	3.226	147
2.37	237	\multicolumn{2}{l}{Orat. (Orator ad Brutum)}
2.60	238	3-10	189,191,233,238-39
2.62	96	12-13	238
2.64-70	96,238	14-15	89,233,237
2.84-87	237-38	23	233
2.131	238	24-32	238
2.147	237	42	189
2.150	237	44-47	191,238
2.152	153	62-64	90
2.158-59	149	70	238
2.160	153	71-74	238
2.162	153	100	238
2.269-70	85	101	238
2.307	238	118-20	237-38
2.333-40	134,237-38	123	238
2.342-49	238	141	238
2.363	238	169-70	240
3.15-16	233	226	238
3.20-22	189,238-39	237-38	46,88,240
3.54	237-38		
3.55	96		

P

Parad. (Paradoxa Stoicorum)

3.60	84,92,95,238
3.62	40
3.63-64	48,146-48
3.65-66	149
3.67	85,153
3.71-73	91,238
3.75-76	238
3.77-80	146
3.84-85	190
3.91	238
3.95	238
3.122	238
3.129	95,238
3.137	146
3.141	153
3.145	238
3.204	238
3.209	237

4	150
23	148,150
27	199

Part. Or. (Partitiones Oratoriae)

30	238
62-67	238
71-100	134,238
129-31	238
140	237-38

Phil. (Orationes Philippicae)

1.33	242
7.4	55,200

Q Fr. (Epistulae ad Quintum Fratrem)

1.29	11,190
25.1	193-94

R

Rab. Perd. (Pro Rabirio
  Perduellionis Re)
29-30   243
Rab. Post. (Pro Rabirio Postumo)
23   190
Rep. (De Re Publica)
1.1-13   55,75,92,141-42,145-47,
          188-89,196,242
1.15   188
1.19-20   146
1.27-28   141,202,238,241-42
1.31-37   55,145,147,149,155,
          161,189,191,195
1.39-41   144,146,148,169,191,
          195,197,201,240
1.45   166,191
1.48-49   199
1.51   196
1.52   196
1.58   196
1.60   241-42
1.67-68   190
1.69   193
2.1   13
2.2   155,193,240
2.3   161,189
2.4   196
2.21   189,193
2.24 ff. 196
2.31   196
2.36   238
2.45   195,234
2.46   196
2.48   195
2.51   166,193,234
2.52   160-61,190
2.56   196
2.57   190-91
2.61   196
2.65-67   192,234
2.69   239

3.3   138-40,196-97
3.4-7   92,145-46,188,241
3.8   48,93
3.12   205
3.13   141
3.18   199
3.19-23   144,199
3.32   48
3.33   189
3.34   203
3.41   188,195
3.43-47   197,199
4.3   200-01
4.4-5   189
4.6-7   242
5.1-2   197,240
5.6-8   143,145,200,240
5.9   241
5.11   96
6.1-20   146,195,202,236,243
6.13-29   145,203,241,243
Q Rosc. (Pro Roscio Comoedo)
143   141

S

Scaur. (Pro Scauro)
4   189
Sen. (De Senectute)
2   83
4   92
5   92
11   146
78   243
85   55,138
Sest. (Pro Sestio)
23   131,150
29-30   202
37   241
38   195
47   243
91-92   196-97,201

INDEX OF CITATIONS OF CICERO 275

96-101	201	2.58	142
131	243	3.1-2	82,240
134	241	3.2-3 ff.	138-39,142,200,240-42
136-39	197,241-42	3.6	38,82
143	242	3.8	89
		3.13	82
		3.31	89
T		3.34	83
Tusc. (Tusculanae Disputationes)		3.36-38	48,56,142
1.1-6	48,84,96,146,241	3.41 ff.	132
1.7-8	84-85,88,91,153	3.44 ff.	138
1.16-17	43,56,84,87	3.48-51	48,137,147
1.22	189	3.55-56	82-83
1.24	48,148	3.68-70	82,152
1.30	141	4.5-7	54,58,83-84,138,146,
1.32-36	241,243		150,153
1.39-40	189	4.8	84
1.44-45	146	4.9-10	96,153
1.47	46	4.33	96
1.48	56	4.37-48	241
1.55	55,132	4.53	150
1.64	48,142	4.60-61	96
1.71	89	4.80	89
1.74-76	146	4.82	39,58,153
1.78	56,152	5.5	59,83,197,200
1.79-81	243	5.7	235
1.89 ff.	146	5.10	54
1.97-100	87,89	5.11	84,92
1.109-10	205,242	5.18-19	96
1.112	89	5.23 ff.	152
1.119	59	5.26-31	89,138,150
2.1	82	5.33-34	58,150
2.4-5	58,82	5.36	189
2.7	54	5.37 ff.	150
2.9	96	5.47-48	89,150,152,239
2.10-11	82,89,142	5.50	134
2.13	48,59,96	5.66	146
2.16	142	5.68	89
2.27-28	48,147	5.70-72	142,146,243
2.32-33	143	5.73	138
2.46	151	5.76-78	150,242
2.47	91	5.82	148,150

5.85	152-53	5.111	146
5.87 ff.	133,153	5.115	146
5.91	89	5.119-20	131,133,153
5.93 ff.	137		
5.95	137		
5.97	89	**V**	
5.103-05	96,139,146,149,200, 240,242	*Verr. (In Verrem)*	
		2.4.81	242
5.108	54	2.4.98	238

INDEX

A
Academic (school) Chap. 1 & Notes
  passim, 67, 77 ff, 104, 125–26,
  131, 142–44, 150, 175, 177, 206
  Fourth, 41–42, 49
  Middle, 39
  New, 16–18 ff, 22, 24, 48, 50,
    60–61, 64, 72
  Old, 16, 49, 52, 134, 151, 239
Adams, J., 7, 12
Aenesidemus, 17, 39–40, 42
Aetius, 144
Ahrensdorf, P., 203
Algra, K., 45, 54
Allen, J., 41
Annas, J., 9, 10, 38, 40, 42–43,
  46–47, 82, 92, 131, 133–34,
  149, 151, 202
Antiochus, 10, 15–18, 25–26, 28–29,
  39–41, 48–52, 55, 85, 89, 95,
  134–37, 151–53, 239
Antipater, 201
Antonius, 96, 153, 162, 190, 236–37
Aratus, 201
Arcesilaus, 16–17, 21, 23, 29, 38–41,
  43–44, 46–49, 52, 61, 64, 66–67,
  77, 84–86, 148
Arena, V., 196
Aristotle, 2–3, 7, 11–12, 22, 42, 55,
  73, 91–95, 99, 102, 104,
  116–17, 126, 137, 147, 151–53,
  156, 158, 164, 167–69, 183,
  189–90, 192, 194, 199, 201,
  220, 236
Arkes, H., 131, 133, 143
Atkins, E., 4, 9, 143, 197, 203
Atkins, J., 2, 9, 140–41, 149, 188,
  190, 192, 194–95
Augustine, 2, 7, 12–13, 39, 173,
  197, 223

B
Balbus, 93, 189
Baraz, Y., 11
Barlow, J., 201, 203, 234, 240
Barnes, J., 10, 38–43, 45–48, 52, 58
Basore, J., 146

Beard, M., 93
Beiner, R., 57–58
Bellarmine, R., 197
Benardete, S., 89, 91, 140, 239
Bentley, R., 58, 85, 87, 93
Bett, R., 41, 43–44, 46, 53, 55, 130
Bloom, A., 82
Blossius, 143
Brittain, C., 49, 57
Brochard, V., 40
Brunschwig, J., 132
Brunt, P., 128, 143, 195
Brutus, L., 171
Brutus, M., 221, 237–38
Buckley, M., 10, 90–92
Burnyeat, M., 38, 41, 43–44, 46–47, 51, 55, 58, 86

C

Caesar, 175, 222, 224, 228
Carcopino, J., 12
Carlyles, 168, 176, 194, 197, 199, 200
Carneades, 7, 16–19, 23, 26–28, 35, 39, 41, 43–44, 46–49, 51–53, 55–56, 58, 66, 84, 91–94, 125–26, 141, 148, 153, 177
Caspar, T., 140, 147, 149
Catiline, 13, 15, 25, 175, 185
Cato the Elder, 13, 72, 74–75, 92, 155, 159, 185, 188, 207, 218, 227, 233, 236, 240
Cato Minor, 85, 90–91, 144, 151, 190, 219, 242
Catulus, 15, 25–29, 36–37, 51–52
Charmades, 93
Chrysippus, 135, 149, 194
Cicero, Quintus, 185, 189, 193–94
Colish, M., 144, 198
conscience, 6, 99, 109, 111, 142

correspondence (Cicero's letters), 12, 51, 53, 93–94, 128, 150, 189–90, 193, 207, 240, 243
Cotta, 57, 77, 93, 147, 152
Couissin, P., 41
Crassus, 85, 92, 95, 123, 146, 163, 191, 207, 214, 233, 237–40
Cratippus, 152
criterion of truth, 15–16, 18–19, 29, 35, 38, 56
  effective criterion, 32–33, 36–37, 55, 81, 89, 101, 118, 120, 123, 126–27
Critolaus, 92
Creon, 199
Crosson, F., 135
Cumming, R., 160, 168, 190–95, 198, 234, 239

D

Davies, J., 11, 191
decus, 110–11, 119, 225–26, 232, 241–42
Democritus, 21, 38, 46
Demosthenes, 233
Descartes, 7, 20, 38, 46
dialectical strategy, 41, 47
dialogue form, 62–63, 77, 90, 94, 157, 189
Dicaearchus, 153
Diderot, 53
Dillon, J., 4, 10, 39
DiLorenzo, R., 91, 233
Diogenes, 92, 201
Diogenes Laertius, 131, 142
Donini, P., 10
Douglas, A., 46, 77, 84–85, 91, 93–94, 150, 153
Dream of Scipio, 146, 170, 186, 195, 224, 226, 242–43
Dyck, A., 129, 144, 201

E

eclecticism, 2, 4–5, 10–11, 22, 36, 42, 58, 153, 199, 248
education, 3–5, 15, 95, 117, 119, 144, 179, 194, 205, 208, 210, 214, 227
elenchus, 84–85
Engberg–Pedersen, T., 130–31, 135, 148
Englert, W., 50, 149
Ennius, 217
Epicureanism, 3, 12, 19, 23–24, 32, 47–48, 54–56, 61, 71, 85, 90, 100, 105, 112, 114–18, 121–23, 126, 132–35, 137–38, 143–45, 147, 149–50, 219
Erasmus, 95
Erskine, A., 137, 139, 149, 188
exempla (models), 10, 45, 67, 109–10, 116, 142, 184, 188, 193, 207, 209, 215, 217, 219, 227, 233–35

F

Ferrary, J–L., 10, 49, 57, 137, 140, 191–93, 234, 240
Fetter, J., 142, 198
Fortin, E., 135, 139, 141–42, 188
Fott, D., 57, 91, 139, 141, 146, 241
Fowler, D., 145–46
Frede, M., 39–43, 45–47, 52, 56–57, 130

G

Garsten, B., 9, 43, 84, 89, 95, 137, 147
Gibbon, E., 243
Gildenhard, I., 147
Gill, C., 128
Glenn, G., 196
gloria (glory), 223–26, 230, 241–42

Glucker, J., 5, 11, 39–40, 42–44, 49–51, 53–56, 87, 153
Gorgias, 63, 74, 84
Görler, W., 11, 17, 41, 45, 48, 50–54, 56, 58
Gorman, R., 83–86, 90–91, 96, 143, 150
Gracchus, T., 171
Griffin, M., 9–10, 13, 50–53, 128, 133, 149–50
Grilli, A., 11, 46, 50, 53, 57, 89, 91, 95, 143–44, 146, 243
Grotius, 140
Gwynn, A., 142, 238

H

Habicht, C., 12, 146
Habinek, T., 5, 10
Haemon, 199
Hagendahl, H., 243
Hahm, D., 149
Hankinson, R., 41, 45, 55
Harris, B., 58, 132
Hathaway, R., 135, 193
Hecaton, 201
Hegel, G., 119
Hellenistic philosophy, 3, 5, 16, 43, 56, 82, 86
Heraclides, 94
Hobbes, T., 197
Holton, J., 42
honestas (right/honorable), 55, 97, 100, 101–02, 105–07, 109–12, 124, 131, 139, 143, 150–51, 156, 182, 214, 226, 232
Hookway, C., 38, 42, 56
Horowitz, M., 83, 142
Horsley, R., 10, 52, 136, 139
Hortensius, 26–27, 29–30, 46, 50–51
Hösle, V., 190–93
Hossenfelder, M., 132

How, W., 239
humanitas, 4, 9, 11, 75, 213, 238
Hume, D., 18–19, 40, 42–45
Hunt, H., 18, 42, 133
Hyneman, C., 2, 9

I
Inwood, B., 54., 90, 132–33, 139
Irwin, T., 130, 153
Isocrates, 153, 233

J
Jaeger, W., 94
Jardine, L., 95
Jefferson, T., 7, 12, 132
Jerome, 8
John of Salisbury, 49
Jones, P., 45
Jowett, B., 134
Justinian, 140

K
Kant, I., 67, 194
Kerford, G., 130
Kesler, C., 52, 54–55
Keyes, C., 141, 241
Kidd, I., 129, 135, 149, 153
Koester, H., 135–36
Kries, D., 133–34, 144

L
Lacey, W., 200
Lactantius, 95, 140
Laelius, 11, 48, 72, 75, 92, 108, 141–42, 146, 155, 157–59, 162–63, 171, 178–79, 188–89, 195, 209, 219, 221, 240–41
Laurand, L., 12
Laursen, J., 2, 9, 38, 40, 42–43, 45, 47

Leach, C., 12
Lee, R., 141
Leeman, A., 241–42
Levine, P., 93
Lévy, C., 5, 11, 13, 39, 41, 43–45, 47–48, 50–53, 55, 90, 129–30, 132, 137, 144, 146–47, 149–51
Lintott, A., 192
Locke, J., 2, 194
Lom, P., 9, 11, 38, 53
Londey, D., 131
Long, A., 5, 10, 39–42, 44–45, 47, 52, 54–56, 84, 86–87, 91, 128–36, 142–46, 149, 151–53, 202, 236
Lucretius, 40, 46, 145
Lucullus, 21, 25–30, 38, 40, 43, 45, 51–52, 64, 85
Lysias, 233

M
Machiavelli, N., 2, 229
MacIntyre, A., 57
MacKendrick, P., 49, 92–93, 128, 132, 195
Mackenzie, M., 87
Mansfield, H., 188
Marquez, X., 192
Marrou, H., 12, 144, 238
McConnell, S., 150, 153
McCoy, C., 194
McIlwain, C., 194
Metellus, Q., 224
Metrodorus, 15, 38, 64
Michel, A., 46, 151
Micken, R., 12
Millar, F., 192
Mitchell, T., 191, 200, 233, 235
Mitsis, P., 130–33, 135–37, 140
mixed constitution, 4, 164–66, 168, 179, 181, 184, 191–93, 200, 208, 210, 217, 227, 234–35

model or best regime/constitution 4, 117–18, 155–59, 161–65, 167–69, 179, 181, 184–85, 187–88, 191–93, 200, 207–08, 210, 214, 216–17, 220, 233–34
Moliere, 20
Mommsen, T., 119
Montesquieu, 2, 91
More, T., 190
Myth of Er, 96

N

Nederman, C., 50, 142, 146, 200
Nepos, 89, 96
Newman, J., 83, 148
Niebuhr, B., 12
Nonius, 236
Nussbaum, M., 11, 40, 43, 47, 53, 56, 82, 133, 145

O

Ochs, D., 83
O'Connor, D., 133, 145
Olshewsky, T., 42–45, 51–52

P

Pajewski, A., 45
Panaetius, 10, 92, 98, 101, 103, 124, 128, 130–31, 133, 142, 149, 243
Pangle, T., 150, 202
Parens, J., 190
perfecta philosophia., 73–76, 78–79, 81, 91, 98, 236, 240
perfect (model) orator, 75, 96, 143, 163, 210–11, 213, 215, 226, 233, 237
Peripatetics, 53, 87, 91, 118, 124–26, 131, 134, 146, 150–53, 192
Petersson, T., 12
Petrarch, 9, 223

Philo, 16, 18–19, 41, 43–44, 47, 49, 55, 57, 91, 95, 136, 139, 142
philosophy *passim*
  consular philosophy, 7, 33, 55, 75, 115, 124, 131, 188, 193, 207, 243
  foundations of, 6–7, 15–16, 30–31, 36, 38
  pre–philosophical, 6
  Socratic orientation, 6, 119, 206–07, 248
Philus, 77, 141, 144, 177, 188
Photius, 42
Piso, 16, 53, 55, 83, 91, 95, 102, 107, 131, 134, 138, 140, 143, 150–52
Plato, 2–3, 7, 12, 17, 22, 34, 39, 59–60, 67, 84–85, 87, 90, 94–95, 104, 116–17, 126, 137, 147, 152, 156–69, 184, 187–92, 194, 199, 205, 211, 213–15, 220, 231, 233–34, 238–39, 243, 247
Plutarch, 95, 135, 147, 202, 223, 241
Polybius, 92, 124, 149, 191–92
Popkin, R., 38
Posidonius, 4, 10, 124
Powell, J., 39, 129, 135, 193, 241–43
practical perspective, 5–6, 31–32, 34–36, 55, 97, 118–20, 157, 206–07, 213–14, 236, 246–47, 249
princeps/rector (statesman, *passim*), 11, 166–67, 190, 215, 239
probabile (probable, *passim*), 18–19, 43–44, 54, 58
Protagoras, 63
prudentia (prudence, *passim*), 73, 205, 235–36
Publius, 2
Publius Vatinius, 224
Pufendorf, 140
Pyrrho, 17, 39–40, 47
  Pyrrhonist, 17–18, 35, 39–40, 43, 47, 49, 52, 56, 58

R

Rahe, P., 11
Rawson, E., 12, 94, 129, 146, 188, 243
Reesor, M., 130
Regulus, 144, 232, 243
Reid, J., 89, 94
Remer, G., 144, 149
res publica (political community), 23, 121, 144, 155, 157–58, 160, 163, 166, 169–70, 172, 175, 177–81, 184, 186, 195–96, 199–201, 217
   civitas, 155, 158, 162, 166, 169, 193, 195, 199–200, 224
Richard, C., 11–12, 128
Rist, J., 130–31
Rolfe, J., 89, 96
Romulus, 172, 190, 193
Rouse, W., 88
Rousseau, J., 2
Ruch, M., 50, 55, 91
Rudd, N., 141, 241

S

Sabine, G., 141, 194, 198, 241
Sandbach, F., 130
sapientia (wisdom, *passim*), 74–75, 91, 235–36, 240
Schmitt, C., 41–42, 52, 95
Schofield, M., 48–49, 54, 135–36, 140, 143, 145, 149, 195–98, 200, 202
Scipio Africanus Minor, 11, 74, 92, 139, 146, 155, 157–67, 169–71, 173, 177–80, 186–88, 191–93, 195, 207 ff.
Scipionic Circle, 75, 92, 124, 149
Sedley, D., 4, 10, 38–42, 44–45, 47, 52, 54–56, 83–84, 130–31, 133–36, 142–45, 149, 236

Senate, 74, 92, 126, 200
Sextus Aelius, 141
Sextus Empiricus, 35, 39, 54, 56, 82
Shields, C., 45, 47
skepticism (radical), 20–21, 40, 86
Smith, P., 96
Smith, S., 141, 241
Socrates 7, 17, 21–22, 31, 37–39, 45, 48, 60–70, 73–75, 78, 80–82, 84–90, 92, 94–97, 102, 104, 107, 109, 126–27, 133, 137, 147, 157, 159, 163, 189–90, 206–07, 211, 214, 220, 229, 232–33, 236, 239, 245–47, 249
Sparshott, F., 45
Stahl, W., 92
Steinmetz, P., 49
Stem, R., 149
Stobaeus, 236
Stoicism, 3, 9, 24, 42, 45, 54, 85, 123–26, 130, 134, 136, 149–51, 247
Stokes, M., 56, 132
Stough, C., 41, 56, 148
Strauss, L., 13, 139, 187, 190, 197–98
Striker, G., 40–41, 44–45, 130, 132–35, 137, 139, 235

T

Tanner, R., 133
Tarquinius, 166, 171–72
Tarrant, H., 10, 39, 41–44, 46–49, 54, 87, 93, 191
Tarver, T., 95
Theophrastus, 151–53, 236
Thorsrud, H., 44, 50, 52
Torquatus, 61–62, 85, 90
Tuck, R., 197

U

universal community, 185
utilitas (the useful/beneficial *passim*), 97, 101–02, 107, 133, 144, 146, 169, 170–71, 198, 208, 220, 226

V

Valla, L., 95
Vander Waerdt, P., 48, 130, 132–33, 135–36, 145, 149, 188, 200
Varro, 29, 39, 49, 53, 66–67, 133, 152, 221, 239
Vatinius, P., 224
verecundia, 106, 111, 143, 216
virtue (*passim*)
  natural, 120, 125–26
Vlastos, G., 64, 85–89, 128, 152
Voegelin, E., 162, 190

W

Walsh, P., 129
Watson, G., 139, 202
Wegemer, G., 11, 190
West, T., 88, 135
White, S., 83, 151
White, T., 192
Williams, M., 43, 46–47
Wilson, J., 128
Wiseman (Stoic), 9, 45, 52, 102–03, 106, 109–10, 123–24, 129–30, 134, 140, 149, 164, 181, 188, 215, 231, 236
Wiseman, T., 9
Wood, N., 2, 9, 168, 186, 192, 195, 198–99, 201–02, 234
Woolf, R., 2, 9, 54
Wright, M., 135, 202

Z

Zarecki, J., 2, 9, 188
Zeller, E., 18
Zeno (Stoic founder), 20, 46, 56, 67, 123, 129, 135, 142, 146, 149, 202
Zerba, M., 144
Zetzel, J., 51, 92, 141, 241
Zoll, G., 94
Zuckert, M., 141

The manufacturer's authorised representative in the EU is Springer Nature Customer Service Centre GmbH, Europaplatz 3, 69115 Heidelberg, Germany. If you have any concerns regarding our products, please contact ProductSafety@springernature.com

Printed and bound by CPI Group (UK) Ltd, Croydon, CR0 4YY

23/03/2026

02076682-0007